W9-CDK-013

MEXICO

A COMPLETELY UP-TO-DATE GUIDE
TO AN EXTRAORDINARY COUNTRY

BY HILARY HYLTON

★

TexasMonthlyPress

Texas Monthly Press, Inc.
P.O. Box 1569
Austin, Texas 78767

A B C D E F G H

Library of Congress Cataloging in Publication Data

Hylton, Hilary.
    Mexico – the Texas monthly guidebook.

    Bibliography: p.
    Includes index.
    1. Mexico – Description and travel – 1981 –   – Guidebooks. I. Texas monthly (Austin, Tex.) II. Title.
    F1209.H94 1983   917.2′04833   83-483
    ISBN 0-932012-32-9

Text Design by Susan Ebert
Cover Design by Hixo, Inc.

For my brother, Christopher

CONTENTS

CONTENTS

ACKNOWLEDGMENTS

Assembling a guidebook is a difficult and complex task. I wish to thank several people who played vital roles in producing *Mexico*. They include, first and foremost, editor Barbara Rodriquez, whose guidance and good humor helped create not only this book but also a friendship; copy editor Anne Morris and proofreader Beth W. Allen, whose diligent work was much appreciated; and contributors Jean Williams Barac, Jane Bussey, George Coleman, Donna Deteau, Sallie Gonzales, Stephen Harrigan, Norma Roland, and Richard Zelade, whose observations about hotels, restaurants, and sights were helpful in assembling the city listings. Suzanne Winckler's inside information for bird-watchers traveling in Mexico and listings of prime birding locations are invaluable to bird enthusiasts of all levels.

In addition, I would like to thank Susan Ebert, who supervised the final production process, and typesetters Kathy Brown, Connie Kanetzky, Mike McLean, and Chris Raesz. The maps were designed by Terry Toler.

I must also thank the Mexican tourist authorities and the many hundreds of Mexican people I met during my travels south of the border. The people of Mexico are her greatest asset, and their graciousness toward inquiring visitors kindles lasting appreciation.

HOW TO USE THIS GUIDE

Mexico has always been one of the world's best travel bargains — a land of great beauty and contrasts, where visitors can avail themselves of the traditional hospitality at bargain prices. Although prices have risen in recent years, peso devaluations have made Mexico vacations popular once again among residents of the United States, Canada, and Europe, where currencies have held up against the falling peso. The tourist industry is a major force in the Mexican economy, and although the peso devaluations have taken their toll on the country's citizens, Mexico will benefit from the increased influx of tourists' dollars, francs, and deutsche marks.

Texas Monthly's *Mexico* is intended to help you enjoy Mexico's beauty and her bargains, to serve as both a handbook as you travel in Mexico and a vacation planner to be read at leisure before you go. Here at the beginning of the guide, you will find basic information that will help you plan your trip; in addition, the volume includes an essay on the history and politics of Mexico and a collection of vital statistics about the country and its people — in short, the kind of information informed travelers should have at their fingertips.

The subsequent chapters, each numbered and identified by a stylized Mayan symbol representing that number, focus on different facets of the country — the two largest cities, Mexico City and Guadalajara; the colonial towns; the extensive archaeological sites; and Mexico's unparalleled beaches. Each chapter is divided into two sections — one devoted to giving the reader an overview, a "feel" for the city or resort, and the second, a compilation of things to see and do. In these listings you will find detailed information concerning hotels, restaurants, tourist services, museums, and transportation in and around each city, beach resort, or archaeological site. Addresses are listed by Mexican custom — street name first and number second. There are several Spanish designations used in the listings — *apartado postal* means post office box, *pte.* or *poniente* means west, *nte.* or *norte* means north, *ote.* or *oriente* means east, *sur* means south, and *playa* means beach.

In addition to background information and listings, you will find essays on food and shopping along with a mix of vacation ideas and tips titled **The Unique and the Random.**

The book is designed to give would-be travelers an armchair tour of Mexico before they embark on a trip. After that introduction they can carefully plan a vacation itinerary to suit their preferences and then take along the guidebook as a companion. The lists at the back of the book giving addresses and phone numbers of Mexican and US embassies, tourist offices, and consulates along with a Spanish glossary make this volume a useful reference book as well. We welcome readers' comments and invite travelers to keep us informed about their favorite haunts in Mexico.

Owing to recent peso devaluations, some hotel room rates and restaurant prices have plummeted; others have been adjusted to reflect the peso's value vis-á-vis the dollar. Throughout this guidebook, we have used two rating systems — one for hotels, another for restaurants.

Constant changes in the tourist industry make drawing up city listings like the ones in this book more than challenging. In addition, Mexico's recent economic upheavals, while advantageous to US, Canadian, and European travelers, have left their mark on many Mexican businesses.

Listings were compiled as near to the publication date as possible; we do recommend, however, that you make your reservations in advance, and always check to be sure a restaurant is still in operation before taking a costly taxi ride across town for dinner.

HOTELS

Shortly before publication date, the Mexican government instituted a new mandatory rating system designed to help tourists determine hotel costs before arriving in Mexico. Recent peso devaluations had created some confusion. Under the new scale, hotels are assigned maximum rates for a double room (no minimums are set). The government divided the country into six zones and set room rates according to facilities and location. Prices must be posted at the hotel. Payment can be made in foreign currency at the prevailing exchange rate. Visitors paying with a credit card will receive a bill in pesos that will be processed at the current exchange rate. (Prior to the installation of this new system, some unscrupulous hotels were charging their dollar customers more.)

The rating scale will be updated by the government twice annually. If you have any questions about the scale, contact the nearest Mexican tourist office. Report any violations of the rate scale to the tourist authorities. The government has pledged to levy a large fine on first-time violators, and successive violations may result in the closing of the hotel.

The official government scale is complicated. In order to simplify the rate scale, we have rated hotels listed in this book with the letters A, B, C, and D. The official Mexican government scale is adapted in part below, keyed for easy reference to our A, B, C, and D scale:

> A: 5,000–11,000 pesos
> B: 3,500–5,000 pesos
> C: 1,500–3,000 pesos
> D: 1,000–1,500 pesos

Although border town listings may include Texas hotels bearing designations according to this scale, these hotels are not bound by the maximum rates set by the Mexican government and prices may be higher. At publication date, the US dollar–peso exchange rate was approximately 150 pesos to the dollar. Your bank or travel agent can provide you with the current rate. "Cr." indicates the hotel accepts major credit cards, "N." that it does not.

RESTAURANTS

Restaurants have been classified according to the following price scale, which indicates the cost of dinner for two with drinks or wine:

> Inexpensive: Under $15
> Moderate: $15–$30
> Expensive: $30–$50
> Very expensive: Over $50

Restaurants that accept most major credit cards are indicated by "Cr." Those accepting none carry the notation "N."

BOCADITOS

Scattered throughout the book are special tips called *Bocaditos* — these "litle morsels" or tidbits of information offer you special insight into a particular region or town, inside information on our favorite sights and customs, and give advice on specific places or events.

A MEXICO PRIMER
THE PROFILE OF A COUNTRY

Mexico is a sensual, addictive jigsaw puzzle of a land that draws the visitor back time and time again — a land where visitors can escape their daily grind and settle into their relaxed alter egos, a place where sensualists can feel at home. The land itself is a visual feast of constantly changing vistas, and the people, the majority of whom are a mixture of Old World and New, act out their lives before this backdrop of mountains and jungle, pyramids and booming cities with a dramatic intensity and artistic flair not evident in the colder lands to the north.

Beyond the Rio Grande, Mexico rises like a vast prayer — two thirds of the country is covered by mountains. The Sierra Madre Occidental and Oriental, aptly named for Mother Earth, dominate and protect the country. As the land narrows, the two ranges meet to form a great *cordillera*, a volcanic ring that surrounds the heart of the country, Mexico City. These are not Wordsworth's daffodil-bedecked hills or Byron's Alps, but New World mountains that occasionally shake with volcanic tremors, a reminder that the world is young. In the north they surround ascetic plains studded with Joshua trees; in the south they hide ritual cities where man-made pyramids of stone emulate the mountains.

Mexico is dominated by her geography. The north is barren, scarred with canyons and desolate plains. In central Mexico valleys are nour-

1

ished by the Lerma River and a series of mountain lakes that make the state of Michoacán Mexico's Garden of Eden. Farther south, the dark green mountains of Oaxaca are etched against an azure sky alive with small fast-moving white clouds. Each day clouds brush the mountaintops and rain falls on the milpas, ancient cornfields where timeless furrows erupt when the earth moves. Beyond lies Chiapas; softer and rounder, the mountains there are covered with jungle growth that becomes more dense as one approaches the Guatemalan border and that enfolds a multitude of secret places where men once worshiped merciless gods. To the southeast of the capital, on the Gulf Coast of the Mexican isthmus, lie the dark, petroleum-rich jungles of Tabasco. Beyond, to the northeast, is the Yucatán peninsula, a flat limestone shelf that juts out into a transparent ocean and draws barrier islands and coral reefs to its shores. And surrounding the country like a golden rim are its beaches. It is some 2,200 miles from El Paso del Norte to Mérida in the Yucatán, 2,200 miles through a land with only one geographical constancy — its beauty.

Mexico's population is extremely diverse. In remarkable contrast to the people of the United States, the majority of Mexico's indigenous people survived conquest. Today, approximately 75 to 85 percent (figures vary) of the population is mestizo, having a mixture of Spanish and Indian blood; however, that does not mean that the population is homogeneous. Each state, city, and town, even each village, has its own identity, and the variety of Mexico's indigenous groups and the regional differences among the mestizos have created a diverse population. Approximately 5 to 15 percent of the population remains pure Indian, although many more follow Indian customs and speak Indian dialects. Even in Mexico City, pockets of Aztec Indians survive. There are 56 identifiable Indian groups in Mexico, speaking two hundred dialects. In addition, there are several large ethnic groups within the country's 70 million people — Spanish, African, Asian, Korean, Chinese, French, British, Greek, Sephardic Jewish, and Italian. Outside Ciudad Juárez thrives a Mennonite community made up of Western European settlers; in the mountains of Guerrero, not far from Acapulco, descendants of African slaves follow African tradition in their architecture and clothing; and in Puebla, Italian restaurants reveal the city's heritage.

Mexico is a land of contrasts — remote villages, cities with populations of 15 million, farms where Mayan *campesinos* placidly grow and harvest corn using the same methods as their preconquest ancestors, and petroleum rigs manned by mestizos eager to play a part in the country's future. In the United States, the gringo is born into a homogeneous world, a world where Everytown, USA, has its hamburger stands and its local newspaper, where one language dominates, where superhighways link all four points of the compass, where regional differences are the subject of columnists' banter and football rivalries. But Mexico is a maze of exotic differences and contradictions.

If any one symbol could be said to represent modern Mexico, it is the so-called Aztec calendar, the Stone of the Sun, which hangs in the National Museum of Anthropology in Mexico City. It is a potent symbol that speaks of mystical rituals and blood sacrifices. Every 52 years, as decreed by the ancient astrologers and their calendar, the *tonalpohualli* ("wheels of time") locked, and the Aztecs prepared for the end of the world. Pots were broken, children and women were hidden from the sun lest they be turned into animals, and the Aztec world waited for the end. On the date prescribed by astrologers as the fated day, Hernán Cortés, wearing a fair beard, arrived from the east. Thought by the Aztecs to be the returning Quetzalcoatl, Cortés pulled down the Stone of the Sun, and sacrificial altars gave way to gilt-covered *retablos*, feathered crowns became sombreros, and the gods were toppled from the pyramids.

Traveling through Mexico, one still can easily imagine that the world, so alive, so intense, sits upon the edge of the cataclysm and yet at the brink of creation. Time is a cyclical quantity in Mexico. On the Pacific Coast Eden-like lagoons cry out for the brush of Rousseau while farmers, plowing their ancient mountainside fields, come upon little stone gods. In Mexico modern meets ancient in a confusion of beauty and reality.

This is Mexico: a country born of the dolorous blood of the Spanish and the mystic spirit of the Indians. Two peoples — one ruled by Quetzalcoatl and Tláloc, the other by Abraham and Allah, Jesus and St. Paul — now one people. Two peoples both looking heavenward for salvation, one to the star of the Nativity, the other to Quetzalcoatl, the plumed serpent that rises with the evening star.

Of course, attempting to understand Mexico's duality is essential only if you hold to the old adage that travel broadens the mind. Making the effort to understand is the difference between a tourist and a traveler. While is it not easy to understand Mexico, it is difficult to resist her attraction. Come south to adobe villages cradled in the arms of the Sierra Madre, where the only sound after sunset comes from the cantina. . . . Come south to Michoacán, where tall pines are wreathed in mist and green-eyed children bundled in serapes toss pine cones at the goats. . . . Come south to the land of coconut groves and lagoons fringed with chartreuse banana palms, the land of hammocks and warm breezes. . . . Come south to colonial towns with red-tiled roofs and white walls, vivid sunlight and cold, dark churches with golden altars that shimmer like treasure. . . . Come south to a land of pink geraniums and yellow gladiolus, cream-colored beeswax candles and bright red peppers, blue madonnas and mangoes cut like great orange flowers, black pots and brown clay whistles.

But for all its bountiful flowers, dazzling coastlines, and inviting colonial villages, Mexico is also a fast-growing Third World country that possesses unmeasured oil reserves, one of the world's fastest growing populations, and twentieth-century cities of commerce. Although

MEXICO

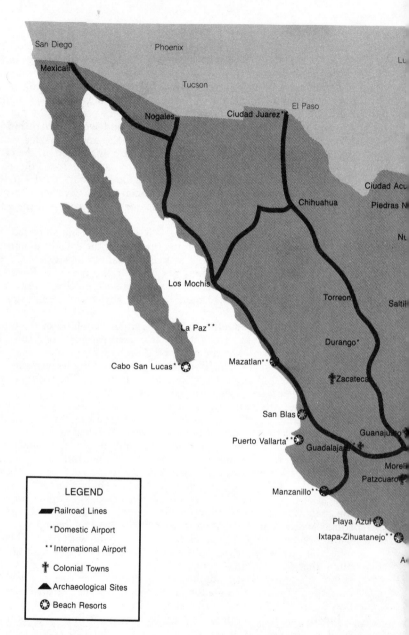

San Diego

Phoenix

Lu

Mexicali

Tucson

Nogales

El Paso

Ciudad Juarez**

Ciudad Acu

Chihuahua

Piedras N

N

Los Mochis

Torreon

Salti

La Paz**

Durango*

Cabo San Lucas*

Mazatlan**

†Zacateca

San Blas

Puerto Vallarta**

Guanaju o

Guadalaja

Morel

Patzcuaro

Manzanillo**

Playa Azul

Ixtapa-Zihuatanejo**

A

LEGEND

- Railroad Lines
- * Domestic Airport
- ** International Airport
- † Colonial Towns
- ▲ Archaeological Sites
- ✪ Beach Resorts

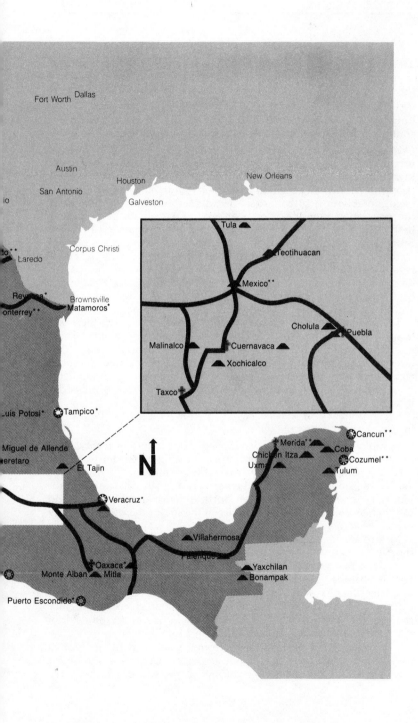

gathering statistical data about Mexico is hampered by geography and resources, we have collected below some basic information to satisfy the curious traveler. The facts and figures quoted here were assembled from sources that often varied among themselves.

Population: Estimated at 70 million in 1980. If the present birth rate continues, Mexico's population will double every 20 years.

Demographics: Approximately 65 percent of the population lives in urban areas. This figure is deceptive because many of Mexico's small towns and villages are essentially rural in character. The indigenous people of Mexico and the immigrant population have become assimilated, notably during the last six decades. About 75 to 80 percent of the population is mestizo, or people of mixed blood; 10 percent is descended from the Spanish Creoles; and approximately 10 percent is Indian. The majority of the population — 97 percent — is Roman Catholic, but religious observances and views differ across the country. More traditional services are held in the cities in which the Spanish imposed an order similar to that observed in Spain; in the rural areas, the Spanish priests incorporated local customs into religious practices, and many celebrations have direct links to the Mesoamerican past.

The vast majority of Mexico's people are poor, although there is a large middle class and the rich have accumulated great wealth. There is high unemployment in several areas of the country, notably the large cities and along the US-Mexico border. The last decade has been characterized by a flight from rural areas to the capital, an immigration the government has attempted to discourage by locating industries in other cities.

Life expectancy in Mexico has risen from 37 years in 1930 to 61 in 1970.

Geography and Climate: Mexico is shaped like a horn of plenty, with its widest point at the northern border, which is about thirteen hundred miles long. No major river crosses the country, but the Rio Bravo del Norte (Rio Grande) marks the northern border. The country provides a geographic bridge between North America and the tropics, and the climate is determined by altitude. In the south, the isthmus is only 125 miles across.

Mexico encompasses 760,000 square miles, much of it dominated by the Sierra Madre Oriental and Occidental and the ring of volcanic mountains that surrounds the capital. The highest mountain, at 18,700 feet, is Orizaba. The two nearby snowcapped peaks of Popocatépetl and Iztaccihuatl reach 17,883 feet and 17,338 feet, respectively. Agriculture in Mexico depends on the many mountain rivers that are dry much of the year and filled only during the hurricane season. Half of the country receives less than 24 inches of rain annually.

The geography of the land ranges from the savannah in the Yucatán to the coniferous forests high in the sierras, mangrove swamps on the coast, and cool pastureland on volcanic slopes east of Mexico City.

The capital, Mexico City, is on a lake bed surrounded by mountains. With a population of some 15 million people, it is the geographic heart of the country.

Government: The country is divided into 31 states and one federal district. Each state has a unicameral legislature, but the national government is made up of executive, judicial, and legislative branches. The national Congress has 64 senators, two from each state and the federal district, and 178 deputies, members of the lower house called the Chamber of Deputies. Free trials and due process are guaranteed under the constitution. The Napoleonic Code of justice, popularly known for its "guilty until proven innocent" concept, is a dominant factor in the judicial process. The president is elected every six years and may not succeed himself. (For a detailed look at Mexico's political system, see **Mexico Past and Present.**)

Mexico maintains a small army, estimated at 70,000 men, an even smaller navy with 7,600 sailors, an air force of some 6,000 men, and a marine force of 900. The army plays a minor role in the government.

Economy: During World War II, Mexico emerged as an industrial nation. Until that time, much of the population lived in rural areas, and the old colonial towns — Guanajuato, Zacatecas, Pachuca, and Taxco — were the major mining centers. These cities have since declined in population as the economic centers of the country grew up around Monterrey in the north, the capital, and Guadalajara.

Mexico now produces one fifth of the world's silver, petroleum, and hydroelectricity. Other exports include uranium, fluorite, iron, and coal. The country that had honey as a major product in Mayan times is now the world's largest exporter of that commodity. Mexico also produces half the world's supply of hormones. Two other products that generate substantial revenue are hardwoods and chicle, which is used in the manufacture of chewing gum.

Agricultural products exported include tobacco, sugar, henequen, cotton, and coffee. Large amounts of fruits and vegetables are exported to the US from Mexico.

Labor is cheap and plentiful. Half of the nonagricultural work force is unionized, and unions play a major role in the government. The minimum wage is adjusted every two years and varies from region to region.

Communications: The government owns and operates the telegraph and telephone services, as well as a national airline, and it influences the major newspaper and television operations. Most Mexicans are literate, because education is compulsory for a minimum of three years in rural areas. Both private and public schools flourish. There are 35 universities in Mexico; the largest is the University of Mexico, located in the capital. Many Mexicans speak English fluently.

The Arts: Spanish culture and pre-Columbian culture have combined in Mexico to produce a unique artistic heritage. Literature, art, music, and dance have flourished. Throughout this guide, there are numerous references to Mexican culture, and the bibliography at the back of the book lists works of interest to those readers who desire more knowledge of Mexico's cultural heritage.

Mexico boasts some of the best museums in the world, world-class symphony orchestras, outstanding art museums (notably those concerned with Mexico's great muralists), great libraries, and architectural wonders. Mexico's museums and galleries are public places that charge only minimal fees so that all citizens may enjoy their benefits.

2

MEXICO PAST AND PRESENT

HISTORY AND POLITICS THROUGH THE YEARS

Under the pink granite dome of the State Capitol in Austin, the great seals of six nations are set in mosaic in the rotunda floor. The lilies of France; the castles of Spain; the lone star of the Republic of Texas; George Washington astride the white charger of the Confederacy; the eagle of the United States; and the eagle, snake, and cactus of Mexico—these are the symbols of the nations whose flags have flown over Texas soil. Several times each day guides lead groups of tourists through the Capitol, elucidating tales and legends from Texas history. During one such tour, a young guide was overheard to say, "As you all know, Mexico used to be part of Texas." A slip of the tongue perhaps, and definitely not a part of the regular script. However, such a statement serves to illustrate that history, like its cousin rumor, is a subjective affair.

This account of Mexico's past doesn't pretend to be an in-depth, scholarly look at that nation's history; rather, this chapter is designed to help you distinguish your Carranzistas from your Zapatistas and to help you recognize this national hero or that historical monument. In short, it is hoped this history will prevent you from committing a faux pas, or even worse, an international incident at a national shrine. After all, consider the reaction if a tourist climbed onto Abe Lincoln's marble lap at the Lincoln Memorial or a foreign visitor turned to you at the

9

Jefferson Memorial and said, "Who is this guy with the ponytail, anyway?"

This is a layman's guide to Mexico, but it's not intended as a brief, quickie look at Mexican history. This chapter has been divided into several sections to simplify a complicated history. Mexico's history is no more difficult to understand than any other nation's, but it is filled with uprisings, revolutions, and changing alliances. And throughout Mexico you will see statues of national heroes, and monuments to independence and revolution stand in the plazas, parks, and boulevards, daily reminders of the country's tumultuous past.

The guide begins with the Spanish Conquest in 1519. Familiarity with preconquest history is, of course, vital to understanding and appreciating Mexico; this information is included in the chapter entitled **Mexico of the Ancients.**

Mexico Under Spain

It took two years for Hernán Cortés and his conquistadores to subdue Mexico. Taking advantage of Indian rivalries, religious beliefs, and popular legend, the Spanish conquerors brought down the powerful Indian empire in an amazingly short time. You won't find any monuments dedicated to the Spanish conquistador. While some historians defend him, Cortés and his fellow adventurers are currently in disfavor, although Cortés's Palace in Cuernavaca still retains his name. You are more likely to see monuments to Indian leaders, such as the large statue of Cuauhtémoc, the last of the Aztec kings, which stands at one of the major intersections on the Reforma in Mexico City. Cortés and his followers were men of adventure who chafed under the Spanish bureaucracy that quickly took root in Mexico. The Church had been represented among the original conquistadores, but then the Church and State combined to form an awesome, monolithic order that had little regard for men of action and independence. Cortés lingered in Mexico but was a disillusioned and embittered man. Others, like Bernal Díaz del Castillo, remained in Mexico but found themselves in conflict with the new government; the names of such men crop up frequently in the court records of the time. The reactions of the Spaniards to their newfound wealth and power varied. Beltrán Nuño de Guzmán, one of the most despised of the conquistadores, unleashed a reign of terror in western Mexico until he was curbed by the power of the Church.

To keep order, Spain instituted a viceregal system in its new territory, an extension of the mother country's absolute monarchy, with the viceroy representing the king and allowing little or no autonomy for the colony. At the local level, the viceroy was represented by the *alcalde* or *corregidor*, but even the most trivial matters were settled at the viceregal level. The viceroy was the representative of a kingdom that laid claim to much of the Western world, some of it settled, much uncharted. New Spain included Mexico south to Panama, north to California, east to Florida and Georgia, across the Pacific to the Philippines, and throughout the Caribbean, where the European powers played a chess game with the small lush islands that dotted the ocean. The throne of Spain was occupied by the House of Hapsburg, which ruled in an absolutist manner until the end of the seventeenth century. Cousins to the Austrian Hapsburgs, these Spanish kings also ruled part of the Netherlands. (This Hapsburg connection was one of the tenuous reasons given by Archduke Maximilian of Austria for his claim to the throne of Mexico in the nineteenth century.) The Church maintained a powerful relationship with the Spanish kings, who enjoyed special privileges granted by Pope Leo X, including the right to name bishops, usually a papal prerogative. The role of clergymen in the conquest, the importation of the Inquisition to Mexico, the struggles for power in the New World by the various religious orders — all illustrate the close relationship between the Church and the State in Mexico.

Perhaps because of the power of the priests in preconquest times, the Roman Catholic Church quickly and easily assumed a similar role in the lives of the Indians in Mexico. Ten years after the conquest, it was reported the brown-skinned Virgin of Guadalupe had appeared to an Indian on a hill outside Mexico City; the site of the vision happened to be near a temple dedicated to Tonantzín, the mother god of the Aztec pantheon. The Indian's cloak, bearing the image of the Virgin, now hangs in the revered shrine of Our Lady of Guadalupe in Mexico City. The violent, warring gods of the ancients were replaced by the humble, abject saints of the Catholic Church; and the veneration of the Virgin, perhaps out of a need for solace and protection, became a major characteristic of the Mexican Church. Under the protective cloak of the Catholic Church, the Indian "found a place in the cosmos," Mexican poet Octavio Paz writes. The Indian enjoyed a special protected status as a ward of the Crown and had the right of direct appeal to the viceroy. Also, the lands belonging to the Indian communal groups (*calpulli*) were left intact under the viceroys. (The *calpulli* lands were broken up in the mid-1800s.) Some historians, while recognizing the Spanish as conquerors and oppressors, have suggested these provisions helped the Indians survive in Spanish-dominated Mexico. They were not free men, and much of the wealth sent back to Spain was the result of Indian labors, but the relationship between conqueror and conquered was not without its benevolent aspects.

From 1519 to 1701 the Hapsburgs reigned and consolidated their empire. As the State grew, the Church flourished. In time, Spaniard and Indian, encouraged by the priests, began to intermarry and the *mestizo* (mixed-blood) population grew. In addition, there were the Creoles (*criollos*), Mexicans of Spanish descent, and the *gachupines*, an opprobrious term that referred to those Spaniards who came to Mexico to seek wealth or to govern and then returned to Spain.

11

At the top of the social scale was the viceroy, ensconced in Mexico City's Chapultepec Castle; he ruled at the king's pleasure. There were both good and bad viceroys, and a fortune could be made in this office. The king's mines in Mexico produced much of the world's silver, and the riches of the East came through the port of Acapulco. Still hanging in Chapultepec Castle are the viceregal portraits, a series of mannered paintings, which illustrate the evolution of sixteenth-century ruffs and pointed beards into the curls and powdered wigs of a later age.

At the bottom of the social scale was the peon, usually of Indian or mestizo blood, a peasant who was held at the hacienda under a burden of debts. Nominally free, the man and his family were kept in peonage because they depended on the bounty of the landowner and on credit available at the hacienda's store. To live, a peon had to eat; to eat, he had to borrow; to borrow, he had to pledge his labor.

Until the end of the last century, events in Mexico were tied to European politics. When a new ruling house came to the throne of Spain in 1701 and was upheld in the War of the Spanish Succession, the effects were subsequently felt in Mexico. The new rulers, the Bourbons, cousins to the French kings, ruled by divine right. They were autocrats, as were their Hapsburg predecessors; but, like their French cousins, these Bourbons toyed with the ideas of the Enlightenment. Spain was no longer a medieval nation. Mexico, to the Bourbons, was a vast bank, an unlimited resource of wealth. Industrial innovations, prompted by the scientific discoveries that flourished during the Enlightenment, swept Europe in the early eighteenth century. The king's mines produced even more silver than before, and the haciendas grew. But the Bourbons, particularly the French branch of the family, were soon to learn that you can't pick and choose an idea here, a scientific discovery there, brushing all other intellectual progress aside. Free-thinking gives way to freedom seeking, and as the natives grew richer, they became restless. The Creoles were impatient to run their own affairs. Transplanted European settlers have always been a threat to colonial empires. The Bourbons, in an attempt to placate the Creoles, created special privileges (*fueros*), which would become a bone of contention in later revolutionary times. In 1784 Charles III instituted a new bureaucratic system, still under viceregal authority, but one that allowed a small degree of independence; New Spain was divided into *intendencias*, regions that enjoyed limited autonomy.

But while Charles III was placating the Creoles, the specter of revolution and war loomed on the European horizon. Militarism was the order of the day in Britian and Russia, where the governments were alarmed at the instability of Europe. The American colonists were feeling their oats, and the French had told Charles's Bourbon cousin to hand in his badge. By the end of the eighteenth century, Europe was in chaos. Spain was occupied in 1808 by Napoleon Bonaparte, who placed his brother Joseph on the throne there. (In the Bonaparte family, Napoleon had all the political savvy; Joseph was a disaster.)

News from Europe was slow to arrive, but when word did come, many Mexicans were alarmed at the thought of the "godless" Corsican ruling Spain. By this time, Ferdinand VII was the king of Spain in exile. (Things start to get complicated here—pen and paper might help you keep score.) Joseph Bonaparte wasn't doing too well in his battle against the Spanish and British troops during the Peninsular War; the Duke of Wellington, soon to be Napoleon's nemesis at Waterloo, was winning. At this point, the Spanish liberals decided to take advantage of King Ferdinand's absence by convening the Cortes, the Spanish parliament, which hadn't met in eons. In 1812 they drafted a liberal constitution in the name of the absent Ferdinand. The conservative Creoles in Mexico, firm believers in a strong union between the Church and State, were worried that the liberal constitution in Spain would disrupt their government in Mexico. The viceroy was kept busy coping with uprisings from the Left and the Right. Out of this confusion in Europe sprang the seeds of Mexico's independence.

Independence

A Creole priest, Padre Miguel Hidalgo y Costilla, responded to the news of Bonaparte's takeover with a cry for independence. He called for the expulsion of the *gachupines* and rule by the Mexicans. "Mexicanos, viva México!" his famous *grito*, or cry, was issued on September 16, 1810, on the steps of his parish church in Dolores in the state of Guanajuato, now called Dolores Hidalgo in his honor. Marching on the *gachupín* stronghold, the mining town of Guanajuato, Hidalgo led his band of followers in an assault against the Alhóndiga, the fortified granary where the local population had sought refuge. The granary fell, and Indians, Creoles, and mestizos were massacred. In turn, Hidalgo was defeated in January 1811 at the Battle of Calderón, captured in March, and executed in July. His head hung on the ramparts of the Alhóndiga for ten years as a grim reminder to all insurgents. Hidalgo, usually shown in frock coat, his balding head covered only on the sides by long white hair, is revered as a great Mexican hero, the Father of Independence. Historical opinions of him vary, but one thing is sure: he was the first to lead the Mexican people in revolt but not the last. Revolution became a way of life in Mexico for the next 120 years.

Following Hidalgo's death, the cause of independence was taken up by another priest, José María Morelos, who operated with his guerrillas in the south. Morelos convened a national congress at Chilpancingo in 1813, and the congress issued a declaration of independence from Spain in 1814. (The date of the *grito*, September 16, is more widely celebrated as Independence Day in Mexico.)

Meanwhile, back in Spain, Ferdinand VII had returned to the throne. He promptly nullified the liberal Spanish Constitution of 1812. This action pleased many Mexican conservatives but dismayed the

Spanish liberals. Ferdinand faced problems on the home front. In 1815 Morelos was captured, defrocked as a priest, and shot. His guerrillas returned to the hills. A large statue of Morelos stands in the island village of Janitzio, near Pátzcuaro. Similar to our own Statue of Liberty, the monument houses a set of stairs and a lookout. The city of Morelia is also named in Morelos's honor.

Back to Spain—the liberals, chafing under the rule of Ferdinand (remember, much of Europe was "liberalized" by now), decided to force the king's hand, and in 1820 Ferdinand accepted the liberal constitution. In Mexico, conservative Creoles responded by turning to a military leader to establish an independent, conservative regime. Agustín de Iturbide was the son of a rich Creole, and it was to this handsome military figure that the conservatives looked for leadership. Iturbide had fought against Hidalgo and was charged with battling Morelos's guerrillas, now under the leadership of Vicente Guerrero (pencils out again). But Iturbide pulled a trick on the conservatives; he met secretly with Guerrero and the two formed a "Plan." (In Mexico, plans are always "Plans" or leaders issue *pronunciamientos*, or pronouncements.) The Plan of Iguala called for a dominant conservative Roman Catholic state church; a constitutional monarchy (they hoped Ferdinand VII would accept, but if not, they would settle for a lesser prince); and a congress, charged with drawing up plans for elections. Guerrero and Iturbide joined forces—the guerrillas and the Creole militias—to form the Army of the Three Guarantees to carry out the promises made in the Plan. Together, the two leaders controlled much of Mexico.

Just as Iturbide and Guerrero went public with the Plan of Iguala, the new Spanish captain general, head of Spain's armed forces in the New World, arrived in Mexico. Unfortunately, Juan O'Donojú arrived before his troops, under the mistaken impression that the Creole militias were loyal to Spain. On August 24, 1821, O'Donojú, whose position was what diplomats like to call "untenable," signed the Treaty of Córdoba, recognizing the independence of Mexico. Spain disavowed O'Donojú's actions, but it was a fait accompli and the treaty date is generally accepted as the anniversary of Mexico's break with Spain.

For two years, from 1821 to 1823, Iturbide headed the council of regents as the new Mexican Empire, as it was now called, struggled to establish a government. All the Central American *intendencias* were represented at the council, and each was given an opportunity to remain in the new empire or withdraw; several withdrew. The search for a constitutional monarch ended when Iturbide was proclaimed emperor on May 18, 1822. The monarchy was declared hereditary, and the United States recognized the new regime. However, this was to be a short-lived empire and events began to follow a soon-to-be familiar pattern. The army, led by General Antonio López de Santa Anna, revolted. (Iturbide had made the fatal mistake of insulting the general in public.) An enigmatic figure whose presence on the Mexican stage was to be felt for the next three decades, Santa Anna has been called the archetype of the South American dictator.

Santa Anna

Supported by the old guerrillas led by Guerrero, Santa Anna declared Mexico a republic on December 2, 1823. Iturbide abdicated and went into exile in Europe. In 1824, believing that the Mexican people desired his return, Iturbide came back and was promptly shot. (Later his son was taken into the family circle of Archduke Maximilian, who had no children of his own.) Iturbide's neoclassical profile can be seen on the old five-peso coins in Mexico; he is a slight Napoleonic figure with curling hair.

In 1824 a constitution was adopted and Mexico was divided into nineteen states, four territories, and a federal district encompassing the capital. The constitution abolished slavery, which, thanks to peonage, was never really an issue in Mexico. (Slavery was an issue in Texas, where Anglo settlers had brought their slaves with them.) Under the constitution, Indians lost their status as wards of the state. Essentially, power still lay in the hands of a few; and as the mines played out, guerrillas made travel hazardous, and politicians unleashed attacks on the *gachupines*. Many of the Spanish settlers returned to Europe, taking their capital and their expertise with them.

Mexico was plagued by rising foreign debts, corruption, and army unrest fueled by guerrilla leaders or malcontented generals. Taxes, particularly customs duties, were spent before they were raised in an effort to keep the army happy. Basically, the country was divided into two political factions, the centralists and the federalists. (Mexican federalism was not similar to US federalism.) The centralists were conservatives who wanted a strong central government, a state church under the auspices of the Roman Catholic Church, and a national army. The federalists wanted limited central government, local militias, power for the states, and abolition of the *fueros*, those special privileges assigned to the Creoles and the ecclesiastics. The presidency and power swung back and forth between these two factions for 20 years, and Santa Anna was always on hand, apparently immune to political conviction but entranced with power. Vicente Guerrero, the guerrilla leader, overthrew a centralist government in 1829, but was in turn overthrown by the same government. Betrayed by a friend, he was imprisoned in 1831 and then executed at the Dominican monastery known as the Convent of Cuilapán in Oaxaca. The ruined monastery still stands, and the wall where Guerrero faced a firing squad is marked with a monument. Out of this confusion, Santa Anna finally emerged as president in 1834.

Meanwhile, some 30,000 Anglos had settled in Texas and their close ties to the United States, whose policy of Manifest Destiny was perceived by Mexico as a threat, prompted the Mexicans to limit immigration and impose certain measures on the *tejanos*. Some have called those measures harsh restrictions; others say they were necessary. In 1836 Sam Houston's Texians declared their own republic. The rest is history, which is written in several shades of ink on both sides of the border. The bottom line is that Texas became a republic and Santa Anna went home to less than a standing ovation. In 1845 Texas joined the Union, confirming Mexico's worst fears. Santa Anna was overthrown, and Mariano Paredes y Arillaga, a centralist, took over as president of Mexico.

Gringos Go Home

Following Santa Anna's disgrace and exile, the United States declared that the agreement between the general and the Texans had called for the border to run along the Rio Grande. Paredes disagreed and said the Nueces River was the border agreed upon. The Nueces runs some one hundred miles north of the Rio Grande, and in the 1840s the land between the two rivers was, for the most part, unoccupied. In 1845 President James Polk tried to persuade Paredes to accept the Rio Grande border and agreed to throw in California for good measure. Paredes refused. Polk then ordered American troops to occupy "American" territory between the Nueces and the Rio Grande. Soon after the occupation he announced that American blood had been spilled on American soil, a double whammy in international politics. No one paid much attention to Congressman Abraham Lincoln, who kept insisting that the administration reveal the exact location of this infamy. War between the United States and Mexico was declared in April 1846. The Americans promptly captured California and New Mexico, and General Zachary Taylor crossed the Rio Grande and engaged in several sorties in northern Mexico.

In Mexico, Paredes was overthrown and Santa Anna returned. He marched north and almost beat Taylor in a bloody battle at Buena Vista, but instead he retreated to defend the capital. Back in Washington, General Winfield Scott had been ordered to land his marines at Veracruz and capture the capital. Scott defeated Santa Anna at Cerro Gordo in April 1847, one year after war had been declared, and Scott took the capital in September. (This exploit contributed the first line to the famous marine song that begins "From the Halls of Moctezuma. . . .") The siege of the capital had tragic repercussions. Chapultepec Castle was being used as a military school, and the young cadets, many of them not even in their teens, pledged to fight for their country and their honor by defending their school. Several threw themselves from the ramparts, rather than be captured by the marines. A huge colonnaded monument to *Los Niños* ("the children") *Héroes* stands at the entrance to Chapultepec Park, where it serves as a poignant reminder of past difficulties and misunderstandings between the United States and Mexico.

The war ended with the capture of Mexico City. Santa Anna went into exile, and the Treaty of Guadalupe Hidalgo, in 1848, established the Rio Grande and the Gila River as the border. In addition, Mexico was paid $15 million for California, and the United States government assumed $3.25 million in claims by US citizens against Mexico.

Santa Anna Returns

By 1853 Santa Anna was back and this time as "indefinite dictator." All should now address him as "His Serene Highness," the outrageous general proclaimed. To raise funds, he sold the Mesilla Valley to the United States for $10 million, called the Gadsden Purchase in US history books. But Santa Anna's days were numbered; he had been involved in or was responsible for the loss of over half of Mexico's territory to the United States. At the same time, two of the most influential conservative leaders died, and power slipped away from the old Creole party. The young were humiliated by Santa Anna's losses, and a new breed of politicians, the Reformers — Benito Juárez among them — was emerging. In New Orleans, Juárez plotted while waiting out his exile.

The Reform Movement

In 1854 Santa Anna was overthrown and the following year exiled to Colombia. He eventually came back to Mexico, but as an ineffectual leader; he died in 1867, unrecognized by his countrymen. With Santa Anna in exile and the conservative movement leaderless, the liberals took the reins of power. Juárez returned from exile and became minister of justice. Historians always use words like *stoic* and *taciturn* to describe Juárez and to point to his pure Zapotec Indian blood as the origin of his quiet, firm, inflexible character. He was born a poor Indian in Oaxaca. A local priest took him into his household and encouraged him to join the Church, but Juárez chose the law instead, a fateful decision for Mexico. His laws did more than any others to strip the Church of power. Dressed in black, his hair severely combed across a broad forehead, Juárez is depicted on statues and murals throughout Mexico; his portrait appears on the blue 20-peso note. Juárez is often called the "Lincoln of Mexico."

The Reform movement achieved its goals through three documents, the Ley Juárez (Juárez Law), the Ley Lerdo (named after Miguel Lerdo de Tejada, the minister of finance), and the Constitution of 1857. Essentially these laws abolished the *fueros,* the privileges of the Creoles and the Church to try cases in their own courts; disestablished the Catholic Church as a state religion by allowing secular education and civil marriages and burials; set up an agricultural economy with the emphasis on individual small plots; and broke up the large landholdings of the Church and forbade the Church or any civil corporation to own property. The new constitution was antislavery, increased the power of the central government, and guaranteed free speech and press. Under the Reformers, the communal Indian landholdings were broken up and sold to individuals. Some critics say this act and the emphasis on small landholdings were to prove fatal to the Indians and mestizo peasants; small plots became yet smaller with each generation as fathers subdivided their land among their heirs. However, this emphasis on land reform became a theme in Mexican politics that reached a roar during the revolution. This tenet remains a sacred commitment, at least on paper, in Mexican politics today.

The Constitution of 1858 remained in force until 1917; however, resistance to it was immediate. The Church and the military opposed the constitution, and the Church threatened to excommunicate anyone who supported it. Civil war erupted, and when the moderate President Ignacio Comonfort was forced into exile, Juárez succeeded him, setting up his government in Veracruz because the conservatives held Mexico City. The United States recognized Juárez's government, but most of the European powers supported the conservatives. In response, Juárez declared that all property owned by the Church, with the exception of actual church buildings, was to be confiscated without compensation. In addition, he proclaimed that only civil marriages were legal and that cemeteries were state property. The country was in a state of anarchy. In 1861 Juárez and the liberals, with US aid, managed to recapture the capital, but the conservatives had turned to Europe for help. Exiled conservatives persuaded Napoleon III, nephew of Bonaparte (Napoleon I) and now leader of France, to invade Mexico and place a second emperor on the throne. To the north, the United States was plunged in civil war and unable to prevent foreign intervention in Mexico.

Napoleon and his wife, Eugénie, persuaded Archduke Maximilian of Austria, a younger son of the ruling Hapsburg House, and his wife, Charlotte, known as Carlota, to assume the Mexican throne. Carlota was the daughter of King Leopold of Belgium, favorite uncle of Queen Victoria. European politics was still a family affair, and Napoleon persuaded the Spanish and British to join the French in a punitive expedition against the Mexicans, who owed some $80 million in foreign debt to the European powers. The exact amount was disputed among the three powers, and Great Britain and Spain withdrew from the expedition as soon as it landed at Veracruz.

The second empire in Mexico is a poignant episode in that country's history. Maximilian was, perhaps, more in tune with the ideas of the Reformers than the conservatives who backed him. Although not an innocent victim in the whole affair, Maximilian is a tragic, forsaken figure. Rumor persisted in Europe that he was really the grandson of Napoleon Bonaparte—his mother was very fond of Napoleon's only son by his second wife, Archduchess Marie-Louise of Austria; but whether that is true or not, he did suffer the fate that plagued most second sons of monarchs. His brother, Franz Joseph, claimed the spotlight and allowed his younger brother no part in government. The Hapsburg family forced Maximilian to renounce his claims to the Austrian throne before he left for Mexico, a wrenching experience for him. (There was no way Maximilian could know that Franz Joseph would lose his only heir, Rudolph, at Mayerling in a suicide-murder pact.)

Maximilian was a victim of Napoleon III's ambition, his desire to form a Latin league that would dominate and unite southern Europe and Central America. Napoleon sent 30,000 French troops to Mexico under the command of the high-handed General Achille François Bazaine who promptly offended the conservative officers of the Mexican army. The French were temporarily halted at Puebla on May 5, 1862 (now celebrated as Mexico's second day of independence), by a Texas-born general, Ignacio Zaragoza. But eventually, the French captured the capital.

Maximilian arrived in Mexico believing the people had called for his ascension to the throne, but his power base lay among the conservatives whom he alienated, even as Bazaine had. Maximilian refused to take the advice of a papal nuncio and declared freedom of religion in Mexico; he also backed up Juárez's proclamations ordering the sale of the Church's property. His support dwindled rapidly, but Maximilian, overwhelmed by his popularity with the ordinary people, decided to stay. He was convinced the Mexican people wanted peace under his rule. In a fateful move, he declared that all republicans were bandits and followed this with a second decree, issued when he thought Juárez had fled to the United States, that ordered all guerrillas to be court-martialed and shot. (Juárez had issued similar decrees against the royalists in 1862.)

Meanwhile, the American Civil War ended, and in Europe, Napoleon was under fire at home. The US government supported Juárez and made its feeling known to both the French and the Austrians, who were asked to discourage further Austrian volunteers. Napoleon squirmed out of the adventure by declaring his troops would be withdrawn because Maximilian hadn't fulfilled his part of the deal by bringing peace to Mexico. Perhaps because of his pride or the forced renunciation of his Hapsburg rights to the Austrian throne, Maximilian pledged to stay. He sent Carlota to Europe to plead with Napoleon and Eugénie for aid. She was denied and went on to Rome to plead their cause before Pope Pius IX. While in Rome she went insane. Carlota never saw Maximilian again; she lived in a Belgian castle until 1927, suffering from delusions that she was still in Mexico.

Maximilian took his small force of 9,000 loyalists and sought refuge in Querétaro, north of Mexico City. There the republicans fielded an army of 42,000, which besieged the archduke on a hill near the city. During the fight, Maximilian lost 4,000 men but refused to surrender. A follower betrayed him in exchange for a promise by the republicans to spare Maximilian's life; republican soldiers, disguised as loyalists led the way through Maximilian's lines. The archduke and his generals and followers were captured, and, under Juárez's decree of 1862, court-martialed and sentenced to die. Petitions asking Juárez to spare Maximilian's life poured in from all over the world. Despite a special plea by the United States, Juárez ordered Mexico's second ill-fated emperor to be shot on the Hill of the Bells outside Querétaro on June 19, 1867.

The presence of Maximilian and Carlota can be felt at Chapultepec Castle, even though there are no public monuments in this couple's honor. However, Mexico City owes much of its beauty to the planning by the ill-fated couple. The widening of the Paseo de Reforma was just one of their projects.

Maximilian's death mask and the guns that killed him lie in Chapultepec Castle.

Juárez Returns

Following the expulsion of the foreign interventionists, Juárez was returned to power and reelected president of the republic. The United States and Mexico patched up their relations and entered a phase of friendliness. In 1871 Juárez was again elected president in an election bid opposed by Porfirio Díaz, a name soon to become synonymous with power in Mexico. The next year Juárez died and was hailed as the Lincoln of Mexico. The transfer of power was relatively calm, and Sebastián Lerdo de Tejada, brother of the author of the Ley Lerdo, took over the presidency. Under Lerdo, the constitution was amended and the Church and State formally separated. But in 1876 Díaz stepped from behind the scenes to oppose Lerdo's bid for reelection.

Porfirio Díaz

For 36 years Porfirio Díaz dominated Mexican politics either as president or the power behind the office. It took a bloody revolution to unseat him. Like Juárez, Díaz was a full-blooded Indian from Oaxaca, but he was a Mixtec. Although his political beliefs were not substantially different from Juárez's, Díaz did not think the Mexican people were ready to rule themselves. His philosophy was to force the people into progress, to use *pan* or *palo* ("bread" or the "club"). Díaz supported the ideas of the *científicos*, intellectuals who saw industrial progress as a key to solving Mexico's woes. They encouraged economic development, foreign investment, and the growth of a government bureaucracy. To eliminate opposition, Díaz embraced the army and the Church, and employed local political bosses (*jefes políticos*) to maintain his support. During the Díaz reign, large petroleum concessions were granted to foreign companies and huge haciendas once again appeared in the rural areas. Díaz also formed the feared *rurales*, the federal police charged with stamping out pockets of bandits. And as in czarist Russia, French culture was encouraged. It was chic to speak French, to assume French customs, and to dress in the latest French fashions. As in the case of Santa Anna, there are few public acknowledgments of Díaz, except for the street bearing his name in his hometown of Oaxaca. Díaz is most often depicted as a decadent old man surrounded by the idle rich. He appears thus in the murals of Diego Rivera and other Mexican artists. Díaz seemed to be in complete control, but beneath the surface there simmered discontent.

The Revolution

To understand the Mexican Revolution, one must strive to remember that it was a peculiarly Mexican phenomenon. It was not directly influenced by the Russian Revolution or the French Revolution, although revolutionary writers of those periods may have inspired some of the early leaders. (One unsuccessful group of anarchists was influenced by the writings of Mikhail Bakunin.) The Mexican Revolution was a response to the status quo in Mexico. There were many factions and shifting alliances, but basically the chronology is this:

Around 1900, radicals opposed to Díaz and his *científicos* (many of whom had grown rich from their economic schemes) began to emerge in exile. In St. Louis, Missouri, the Regeneration movement, essentially anarchists, plotted under the leadership of Ricardo Flores Magón. They sought a one-term presidency, free education, land reform, anti-clerical measures, no foreign investment, and the confiscation of the wealth of *científicos*. The Regeneration group played a minor role in the revolution; however, their demands were embraced by others and were incorporated in the Constitution of 1917.

Díaz's troubles began when he put down strikes in Veracruz, drawing the attention of US journalists. In the United States, yellow journalism was at its height and attacks on big government (by big newspapers) were daily fare. Eager for a story, the US press turned south to examine the Díaz regime. One enterprising reporter got an interview with the aging dictator and had a scoop when Díaz announced in 1908 that he would not seek reelection in 1910, because the time had come for democracy in Mexico. The lights turned green. Anti-Díaz forces rallied, among them Francisco I. Madero, the scion of a wealthy family, who gave freely to the Regeneration group until he discovered their anarchistic purpose. Madero formed the Anti-reelectionists and campaigned in 1909 against Díaz. Apparently, Díaz didn't think anyone would take the newspaper story seriously; he had no intention of stepping down. Madero was arrested, and Díaz was proclaimed the new president. Madero escaped from prison and fled to San Antonio, Texas, where he announced the Plan of San Luis Potosí. This plan called for all Mexicans to take up arms against Díaz on November 20, 1910 (the official birthday of the Mexican Revolution).

There were no mass uprisings on November 20; however, the Madero family fortune fueled the guerrilla war chests and federal troops were besieged in their garrison in Ciudad Juárez, across from the US city of El Paso. Madero returned to Mexico, and the federal commander at Juárez surrendered. The revolution had begun, and the following May, Díaz retired into comfortable exile in Paris.

The country was now ablaze with uprisings. In the south, Emiliano Zapata (head of the Zapatistas, a land reform movement) refused to lay down his arms following Díaz's departure. In Mexico City, a congress proclaimed Madero president. The capital city was surrounded by counterrevolutionaries, eager to overthrow Madero. President William Taft had instructed Henry Lane Wilson, his ambassador to Mexico, to remain neutral during the struggle; however, Wilson either assisted or had previous knowledge about a betrayal by Madero's vice-president, Victoriano Huerta. Madero was shot on Huerta's orders. In the north, Venustiano Carranza and Pancho Villa joined to oppose Huerta and called for elections. The new US president, Woodrow Wilson, wanted Huerta out; using a flimsy excuse, US troops once again landed at Veracruz. Huerta was overthrown in 1914.

Now the alliances shifted. Zapata and Villa joined to fight Carranza and his lieutenant, General Alvaro Obregón. Villa was defeated at Celaya in 1915, but the war continued in the north.

In 1916, with Central and Southern Mexico calm, Carranza called a constitutional congress, which drafted the Constitution of 1917. Zapata was kept in line by the inclusion of his land reform demands. Under the new constitution, the office of vice-president was abolished and the political machine system (jefes políticos) was abandoned. Foreign investment was limited and the central government strengthened. Carranza was elected president in 1920 and the government recognized by the United States. Zapata had been betrayed and killed in 1919. Pancho Villa lived until 1923, when he died in an ambush. Carranza didn't institute social reforms fast enough to suit his old comrade General Obregón, so Obregón joined two powerful northern chieftains, Plutarco Elías Calles and Adolfo de la Huerta, in opposing him. Carranza was overthrown and killed as he fled the capital.

It has been estimated that one in eight Mexicans lost their lives during the Mexican Revolution; virtually every family was touched by death. It was a time of upheaval unmatched in Mexican history, and many sought escape by fleeing north to the United States.

When Obregón assumed the presidency in 1920, he bribed the old revolutionaries into contentment. He instituted land reform and placed more land in the community farms, called ejidos. He encouraged Mexico's great muralists to document the revolution. Although de la Huerta contemplated a coup in 1924, it failed, and Mexico finally achieved some measure of stability.

Obregón's other ally, Calles, became president in 1924. His term was marked by increased land redistribution and renewed, vigorous anti-clerical measures. Again, a US ambassador played a role in Mexican internal affairs, but this time, Ambassador Dwight Morrow helped mediate the Church-state battle that erupted in western Mexico with a rebellion by the Cristeros, Roman Catholic militants.

In 1928 the constitution was amended to allow a six-year term rather than a four-year term for the president, and the words no reelection were changed to read *no successive reelection,* allowing Obregón to run for another term. Before he could be inaugurated, however, he was assassinated by a religious fanatic. Calles, who could not succeed himself, formed the National Revolutionary Party, and a series of short-term presidents served while Calles actually ruled.

In 1934 the party supported General Lázaro Cárdenas, who, following his inauguration, challenged the power of Calles, forcing him into exile. On March 18, 1938, Cárdenas expropriated the foreign oil companies. President Franklin Roosevelt attempted to gain a bargaining chip by threatenting to suspend all purchases of Mexican silver, but Cárdenas was adamant. Once again, a US ambassador to Mexico stepped in. Josephus Daniels, who, as secretary of the navy during the revolution, had ordered the landing at Veracruz, settled the dispute on terms favorable to Mexico.

Two generals sought the presidency in 1940, General Manuel Avila Camacho (supported by Cárdenas) and General Juan Andreu Almazán, who secretly asked the United States for money to fund a coup. The United States turned him down, and Vice-President Henry Wallace was sent to represent the government at Camacho's inauguration.

This newfound mutual confidence between the United States and Mexico blossomed diplomatically in 1941, when many long-standing disputes were settled and the dollar was pledged to support the peso. World War II brought cooperation between Mexico and the United States; Mexico supplied many of the raw materials for the war effort.

After World War II, Miguel Alemán ascended to the presidency, and the ruling party's name was changed to the Institutional Revolutionary Party (PRI is its Spanish acronym). The mantle of power has passed peacefully from one president to another since then. The history of Mexico in the decades since World War II is the history of the PRI. Like any system, the Mexican government has its detractors; however, Mexico has been able to face its problems of unemployment, inflation, and poverty in an atmosphere of relative stability.

Politics

The workings of Mexico's political system are unfamiliar to most tourists, but then a town meeting in Vermont, question time in the British House of Commons, a Democratic Convention in Chicago, and this month's coup in Bolivia are all exercises in power that seem unfathomable to the uninitiated. Mexico's political system is no easier to understand than our own, and understanding the system is further complicated by the persistent duality, the confusion between appearance and reality that pervades Mexican culture. What appears to be and what is are seldom the same in Mexico.

On paper, the political system in Mexico is a democratic republic with a strong federal base; in reality, the country is ruled by an elite oligarchy under the auspices of the PRI. The PRI has ruled Mexico, under one name or another, through the office of president, since 1928. The PRI is a monolith of continuous power; a coalition of disparate groups born out of the confusion of the Mexican Revolution. Under the PRI banner, labor (*trabajadores*), peasants (*campesinos*), and the middle classes, many of them government bureaucrats (*populares*), join. The PRI is both the political party that dominates government and the bureaucrats who regulate it. The PRI *is* the Mexican government.

PRI leaders ascend to power through the bureaucracy which is dominated by the party. The president of Mexico, the head of the PRI, is all-powerful. Some suggest the stability of the Mexican system derives from this monolithic, pyramidal design and it remains stable because no Mexican president has ever wielded all of his power. Change and progress, even philosophical differences, are tolerated within the party as dictated by tradition. Some critics see irony in the name of the party — institutional revolution — and criticize the PRI for its failure to live up to the promise of the Revolution, notably land reform. However, in foreign policy, Mexico is a left-leaning leader of the Third World and her leaders have been active in attempting to generate communication between the poorer nations and the more prosperous West.

The Mexican president is limited to one six-year term; he may not succeed himself and he chooses his own successor — usually a low-profile, faithful party member who is named late in the president's term. This limitation on succession has constricted abuse of power at the top, but although no president has named a family member to succeed him, charges of nepotism are often heard in connection with top government jobs going to sons or sisters.

The president of Mexico is a powerful symbol. His face and the PRI green and red party letters appear everywhere: on walls and lamp posts, scrawled on boulders by the highway and on posters in every city plaza. In 1982, a relatively unknown cabinet minister, Miguel de la Madrid Hurtado, became a household word overnight when he was nominated by the party to succeed President José López Portillo. The initials MM appeared everywhere. Mexicans elevate their political leaders to hero status and presidents become cult figures during the six-year term. Nine opposition parties, embracing the political spectrum, are allowed to participate in state and federal elections; however, they never win a majority of seats in the national 400-member Chamber of Deputies or the 64-member Senate. Election results are canvassed and confirmed by the Chamber, where the PRI dominates. Occasionally, a city may elect a mayor from one of the opposition parties, but generally the PRI dominates the system. Those parties not receiving a certain percentage of the vote may not participate in the next election.

The Constitution of 1917 calls for separation of powers, free elections, a powerful central government, and the elimination of the office of vice-president — a move to ensure the system against coups. The Constitution also promises land reform for the peasants and guarantees the right to strike to labor unions. But since the PRI embraces labor and has made its leaders part of the ruling oligarchy, strikes are unusual. The PRI is also friendly to big business and follows a policy of low taxes, government price supports, and import controls. While there are some very rich men in Mexico, they maintain a low profile in politics. Unlike the military in other Latin American countries, the army in Mexico has not been a powerful force in the political system. The army is quite small and has spent much of the last decade fighting small bands of guerrillas in the remote mountains of southern Mexico and working with the U.S. Drug Enforcement Agency to fight drug trafficking.

According to Alan Riding, longtime Mexico City bureau chief for *The New York Times,* the political system in Mexico is all subtlety. Riding writes that Mexicans are at ease with the system because "after each major social convulsion, they have gradually returned to it. It existed under the Aztecs, it was retained by the Spanish empire, it brought stability under the 19th century dictatorship of General Porfirio Díaz, and it functions today. It operates like the Mexicans themselves. At the formal level, it offers the security of ritualistic role-playing, avoiding confrontations, or even frankness. But on a day-to-day basis, it is flexible and accommodating. It is formally idealistic, as are most Mexicans, yet it also reflects the cynicism and corruption that many people accept as a part of their lives. And the natural fatalism and extraordinary patience of the Mexicans guarantee its continuity: with the start of each administration comes a new chance of power, a chance that can be won only through silence and subservience."

However, there are Mexican critics of the system, both vocal and revolutionary. Little is heard or said in Mexico about the small pockets of guerrillas who operate in the remote mountains of Guerrero, but they do exist. In some areas of the country, particularly in the north and the extreme south, the hammer and sickle, the symbol of the communists, can be seen painted on signs; and in the conservative state of Guanajuato, the Sinarquistas, right-wing traditionalists who have been described as sharing the views of the Spanish fascists, have a strong foothold. Resistance to the political status quo has been isolated and infrequent, and so far, Mexico's foreign policy support of Cuba has appeared to stave off any threat from that Latin American neighbor. The PRI has walked the fine line of institutionalized revolution.

In spite of criticism and some isolated opposition, the Mexican political system appears to be stable, one of the most stable in a region of the world where instability is the norm. Occasionally, there are small uprisings by discontented landless peasants who seek land reform. There has been some breakup of the once huge haciendas, but Mexico's leaders face a dilemma in the area of land reform. Mexico has a food crisis. The country imports corn to feed a booming population, expected to reach 100 million people by the year 2000. It has been estimated that four million peasants are waiting for land; that 60 percent of the country's population is malnourished and 40 percent illiterate. The president is vested with tremendous power and can make sweeping changes. However, the problems are vast. Mechanized farming on a large scale is what many experts say Mexico needs, but the promise of land reform and a family plot is imbedded in the Mexican Revolution.

Another problem facing modern-day Mexico is the concentration of industry in three major cities—Mexico City, Guadalajara, and Monterrey. Mexico City is a city in crisis where overpopulation, pollution, and terrible traffic problems grow worse at an alarming rate—problems shared by other large cities in the world. The government has tried to encourage decentralization and industry relocation and has tried to stop rural residents emigrating to the major metropolitan areas. But still Mexico City's barrios grow.

Economic woes plague the country—a staggering inflation rate, estimated by some at over 500 percent in the years 1977–82, and a large foreign debt fueled by purchases of consumer goods from abroad by Mexico's growing middle class. Unemployment in some areas, notably along the US border reaches 35 percent (some experts estimate 50 percent), and a small percentage of the population earns most of the wealth. Mexico has been reluctant to allow foreign investment. This xenophobic attitude has some legitimate origins. Foreigners have exploited Mexico, and so far this insistence that solutions be Mexican, rather than foreign, has kept foreign ideologies like Castro's communism from taking hold.

Though plagued by social and economic problems, Mexico enjoys the advantage of oil. A few months after President López Portillo assumed office in 1976, the discovery of massive oil reserves was announced. (The presence of such large oil reserves had been known for some time, and the subsequent announcements of the size of the reserves invite debate.) Estimates have gone as high as 285 billion barrels. Mexico's natural tendency towards independence of action and neutrality was mirrored in the country's decision not to join OPEC, the world oil cartel. Gradual development of the oil reserves was the policy adopted by López Portillo. Mexico could look to her neighbor Venezuela to see what quick profits from oil could do to an economy—Venezuela has very little industry and her imports of foreign consumer goods are high, fueling a high inflation rate. The failure of US–Mexico negotiations to establish a market for Mexican natural gas and the world oil glut in 1981 had a negative effect on Mexico's economy. Whether the wealth from the oil will trickle down to the poor is a question constantly raised in the Mexican press. The primary oil and gas industries are government owned; however, secondary products such as plastics and fertilizers are produced by independent business. Critics have characterized Mexico's government monopoly, Petróleos Mexicanos (PEMEX) as labor-rich and management-poor.

Of course, Mexico's northern neighbors see themselves as a natural market for Mexican oil and gas. Negotiations have been marked by the frustrations and misunderstandings common between the United States and Mexico. Relations between the two governments are better than they were in the last century, but cultural misunderstandings on both sides of the border still surface readily. Many Mexican historians point to the reign of Porfirio Díaz when foreigners were allowed a free economic hand in Mexico and to the loss of Mexican territory under Santa Anna as reasons for Mexican sensitivity. The US–Mexico border is the only place in the world where a Third World country shares a common frontier with a prosperous world power. Tensions and differences in perception are to be expected. Illegal immigration of Mexicans into the United States has further aggravated the relationship, although some social scientists say the flow of Mexican aliens into the United States acts as a safety valve for the Mexican government. Mutual understanding of mutual problems has been difficult to achieve.

An understanding of some of the problems facing Mexico, and an understanding of her political system, her economy, and her history may help us as individuals to improve relations with our Mexican neighbors.

3

THERE AND BACK AGAIN

Vacation Planning and Survival

Thanks to Texas' Mexican-American heritage, Texans, whether native or self-appointed, enjoy an easy familiarity with many of the customs and rituals of the Mexican culture. Any Texan worth his lime and salt takes his jalapeños hotter than Muleshoe in summertime and his margaritas with more bite than a Highland Park Kaffeeklatsch. But because you know your *fajitas* from *flautas*, don't be lulled into thinking that Mexico City is just San Antonio with more Volkswagens. They may sell as many tortillas at the Safeway in Laredo as they do in the Durango market, but ask for a burrito in Chihuahua and you'll get a little donkey. There are cultural subtleties at work here.

Mexicans generally regard individual Texans as *simpático*, and they will help *tejanos* over the cultural hump that separates us. However, collectively, Texans are the spiritual heirs of Sam Houston and his Texians. One look at a wall map in a Mexican government office and you will discover that you have been skiing the slopes of northern Mexico on your annual trek to Steamboat Springs. Forget the Alamo. The first time you hear yourself saying, "Why, back home in Texas, we . . ." bite your tongue. Differences in historical perspectives, politics, and social customs are interesting to observe, but leave the arguments to the politicians and the professors. Abandon your pragmatic, Teutonic views for a week or so; develop a Gallic shrug; and practice saying, *momentito,* or even *mañana.* Assume a blasé, relaxed air — but remember, you will have more success keeping this mask of nonchalance in place if you plan your trip with all the cunning of a Pancho Villa.

If this is your first trip to Mexico, don't try to see too much of the country at once. Pick your destination, read as much as you can about the area, plan your itinerary, and keep in mind that this is a vacation, not a sight-seeing orgy.

Relax before you go. Don't catch the first plane out on a Friday night. Travel, particularly airline travel, can be exhausting. If you relax before you go, and arrive at the airport with time for a drink or a cup of coffee, you will be better able to adapt to unfamiliar surroundings, changes in altitude and climate, and sudden cultural differences.

If you are not fluent in Spanish, brush up on a few phrases. A simple *gracias* can help bridge those cultural gaps. Many Mexicans, unlike most Americans, are bilingual or multilingual, and they speak excellent English. Your attempt to speak Spanish is a courtesy that usually will be met with understanding if not comprehension.

WHEN TO GO

Generally, the climate in Mexico is ruled by altitude. The changes in seasons are subtle, and in most of the country, the winters are only slightly colder than the summers. With the exception of those cities on the Coastal Plains and the Yucatán Peninsula, most of the major cities are located in the mountains, where there are cool nights and afternoon showers during the rainy season (May through October). Pack a raincoat and use those brief afternoon showers for a siesta, a museum visit, or an hour of watching puddle hoppers, from the comfort of a sidewalk café on the town square.

Along the East Coast and in Yucatán, hurricane season (May through September) can bring several days of drizzle or downpour, depending on the storm's position. The Yucatán peninsula is hot and humid all year, cooler on the coast because of the balmy Caribbean trade winds. During the summer, the East Coast is humid while the Northern Plains around Monterrey are dry, dusty, and hot. The East Coast and northern Sierra Madre suffer from *nortes,* the northers familiar to residents of the Southwest in the United States. These cold fronts move down from Canada in the fall and winter, bringing sudden cold, strong winds and sometimes rain.

The Pacific Coast is hot year-round, sometimes humid with afternoon showers in the summer. Sunshine is the norm, and most days are glorious but hot in a lazy, tropical way. Watch out for sunburn; the Pacific breeze is deceptively cooling, so wear a hat if you are sensitive to the sun. Sunburn can also be a problem in the Southern Highlands of Oaxaca and the Chiapas, where temperatures range in the 70s and 80s during the day, cooling to the high 50s or 60s at night. The mountain air is cool, even in the daytime.

The Pacific Coast and the Southern Highlands experience occasional volcanic tremors as does the capital city.

Mexico City is a pleasant, temperate city with generally comfortable temperatures—in the 70s and 80s in summer, 50s and 60s in fall and winter. However, an occasional temperature inversion owing to unusually hot weather and pollution can cause uncomfortable temperatures in the 90s. The nights are cool, even chilly, year-round, and in the summertime there is usually an afternoon thundershower. Pollution from the city's factories and automobiles approaches dangerous levels on some days; the city is ringed by mountains that trap the air and compound the problem. (Monterrey also has a pollution problem.) Visitors with breathing difficulties are advised to leave the city if the pollution index climbs too high. Fortunately, there are several day trips from the capital that are easy to make on those days when the pollution is a problem.

The cities of the Central Plateau—Guadalajara, Guanajuato, Morelia, San Luis Potosí, and others—are cooler than Mexico City and enjoy temperatures in the 60s in summer and the 50s in winter. A sweater or jacket is advisable for sight-seeing in those areas.

Perhaps a more important consideration to keep in mind as you plan your trip is Mexico's penchant for celebration. Fiestas, both political and religious, play havoc with the calendar. The whole country often grinds to a halt during a national fiesta, which can be the best time to visit Mexico; but remember, reservations are absolutely essential on those days and sometimes must be made months in advance. Banks, most businesses, and government offices close on national holidays. Often these same offices will close during local fiestas also.

Major holidays include:

January 1, New Year's Day

February 5, Constitution Day

March 21, Birth date of President Benito Juárez

May 1, International Workers' Day

May 5, Cinco de Mayo, a celebration of Mexican independence from the French and Austrians, the anniversary of the defeat of Napoleon III's French troops at Puebla in 1862

September 1, Mexico's equivalent to our State of the Union address

September 16, Diez y Seis, a celebration of Mexican independence from Spain, marking the day Father Miguel Hidalgo issued the *grito*, the cry of "Mexico for the Mexicans"

October 12, Columbus Day, Día de la Raza

November 20, Anniversary of the Mexican Revolution

December 25, Christmas Day

In addition, both Easter and Christmas weeks are favorite vacation times for Mexican families.

CHOOSING A HOTEL

Mexico offers a wide range of accommodations, from beautiful colonial inns to modern American-style hotels. There are downright cheap hotels, terribly expensive (by Mexican standards) hotels; art deco dowagers; cold, converted convents; and family-style boardinghouses. But no matter where you stay, chances are the water pressure in the shower will be low.

Hotels in Mexico City, Guadalajara, and the other major cities are a pleasant mix of American and Mexican customs. In the resort areas, particularly Acapulco, if you close your eyes in most hotel lobbies, you will swear you are in Miami. However, even the popular resort areas offer a variety of hotels for the traveler with a taste for the authentic. If you really want to experience the best of Mexico, stay in one of the country's *posadas*, the old haciendas or religious buildings, which have been converted into country-style inns. These hotels are very popular with Mexico's middle and upper classes, and while they are a little more expensive, they are a joy to stay in. They are usually very quiet, tastefully decorated with antiques, and offer a graceful and relaxed way to experience Mexico.

When you make your reservations, keep in mind the hotel's location, especially in a place like Mexico City. Staying in the Zona Rosa, the capital's restaurant and gallery district, may cost a little more but will save you money in cab fares. Also, remember to ask for a back room or pick a hotel on a quiet street if you are a light sleeper. A room with a view is marvelous during the daytime, but traffic noises, especially in Mexico City, can continue throughout the night.

Reservations are not always necessary if you are an experienced traveler in Mexico; however, they are advisable for the first-time visitor and should always be made in the major cities, resort areas, and for fiesta days. Once you have chosen a hotel, the easiest way to make a reservation is to call or write well in advance of your trip. Telephone calls to Mexico from the United States are not expensive. Ask for the reservations desk; most major hotels are staffed by bilingual personnel. Send any letters by airmail. Arrange to send a cashier's check (some hotels require a one-night deposit), and ask for a confirmation letter in return. Take the letters and copies of your cashier's checks with you when you go on vacation.

Travel agents will make hotel reservations for you free of charge if you make your airline reservations through them; otherwise there is usually a small fee. (Be sure to ask your travel agent the price range at the hotel of your choice; some agents will assume you want the top of the line.) Even if you make your reservations through a travel agent, request a written confirmation or telex copy *from the hotel*.

Try to make all your reservations before you leave. Avoid making long-distance calls from your hotel within Mexico to confirm or change a reservation; these calls are extremely expensive. In many cases, hotels owned by chains maintain offices in the major cities. If you need to confirm or change a reservation, check the local Yellow Pages to see if your next hotel is part of a chain with an office where you are currently staying.

If you do arrive without a reservation, or your plans go awry, you can seek help from the Mexican tourist office or the local US consulate. Many consular officers know the best places in town for stranded gringos. In Mexico City, the tourist office maintains a 24-hour information line — 250-0123 — write that number on your cuff. You can call to get information, to seek help, to make a complaint, or to get legal assistance. All hotel rates must be registered with the government and posted in your room. If you think you are being ripped off, call the tourist office — your complaint will be taken seriously.

One important thing to remember when you make your hotel reservations is that most hotel rooms in Mexico have single beds. If such an accommodation is going to ruin your vacation, ask for a double bed *(cama matrimonial)*. Make sure your travel agent knows your preference. (Most of the new resort hotels in places like Cancún and Ixtapa look exactly like the rooms of chain hotels in St. Louis, Chicago, New York, and Cleveland.)

During the peak season in resort areas and in older hotels, particularly near the remote archaeological sites, the price of your room may include meals. The so-called American Plan (AP) now is standard in places like Acapulco during the winter season. Usually, the American Plan allows you to eat three meals a day in the hotel's restaurants but only during specified hours; if you show up after the designated breakfast hour, you will be charged. Some hotels offer a Modified American Plan (MAP), which includes either one or two meals a day. Room rates without meals are designated as European Plan (EP).

BUSINESS TRAVEL

Perhaps the operative phrase for US and Canadian businessmen heading south of the Rio Grande is "slow down." The pace of the Mexican business world is not quite as hectic and high pressured as it is in North American cities. That's not to say that big deals and important decisions are not made in Mexico. It's just that the style and the pace are different. Many of the top business executives in Mexico were educated in American universities and in Europe. Their cosmopolitan education means they can move comfortably from Mexico City to New York to Toronto and on to Paris. But when in Mexico City, to paraphrase the old saying about Rome, the pace and tone of business is decidedly *mexicano*.

Businessmen usually meet friends and associates for coffee and a snack in the morning; some don't arrive at the office before noon. Much of Mexico's business is conducted in cafés and favorite clubs.

Lunch is leisurely and can be a good time to get to know a client. Lunch hour isn't just one hour and is often from about 1 P.M. to 4 P.M. Afterwards, businessmen return to their offices and work until about 7 P.M.

Appointments are flexible. Don't expect your 4 P.M. meeting to start at 4 P.M., although government bureaucrats are usually more punctual. You may have to schedule numerous meetings with several levels of employees before you settle your business. Usually the man at the top makes the decisions, and definite answers from underlings can be hard to get.

Business in Mexico is still, generally, dominated by men. There are very few women in business, and female executives or representatives of US companies may find establishing a business relationship difficult. Introductions from mutual friends or acquaintances will help. Whether your Spanish is adequate or good, hiring a translator is considered good form. Of course, most Mexican businessmen speak excellent English. In addition to a handshake, you will be welcomed with an *abrazo*, a bear hug that denotes mutual respect and affection. Try to follow local custom as carefully as possible, and don't be reluctant to ask advice.

Mexicans themselves will tell you that the pace in Monterrey is a little more like that in US and Canadian cities. Monterrey is a powerful center of money and influence in industry, and Monterrey businessmen are considered frugal and not as passionate as their countrymen — sort of the New Englanders or Scotsmen of Mexico. The pace is a little faster in Monterrey.

The key to business success in Mexico is sensitivity to the country's social and cultural makeup. A wise businessman or businesswoman will read as much as possible about the country before embarking on a trip south.

TRAVEL FOR THE HANDICAPPED

For the handicapped, travel in the so-called developed countries can be difficult; travel in Third World countries like Mexico can be even more of a problem. Airlines are sensitized to the problems facing wheelchair-bound travelers, and ticket agents may be able to help in making plans. Generally, most of the new hotels are a little easier to navigate than others, and because Mexico is a labor-intensive country, there are always plenty of personnel on hand to assist a handicapped traveler if architectural barriers exist.

There are several organizations in the US that either organize trips for the handicapped or supply travel tips. They include Flying Wheels Travel, 143 W. Bridge St., P.O. Box 382, Owatonna, MN 55060; Rambling Tours, Inc., P.O. Box 1304, Hallandale, FL 33009; Catholic Travel Office, Suite 520, 1019 19th St. NW, Washington, DC 20036; Handy-Cap Horizons, 3250 E. Loretta Dr., Indianapolis, IN 46222;

and Evergreen Travel Service, Inc., Wings on Wheels, 19505 44th Ave. W, Lynnwood, WA 98036.

TRAVELING WITH CHILDREN

Traveling with children always poses special problems. Finicky eating, boredom, and baby-sitters are just a few of the difficulties parents must cope with on vacation.

Mexican food is not necessarily hot and spicy. Kids love refried beans—fun to play with and not so bad to eat. Mexican bread and pastries are delicious; add some fresh strawberry jam (*mermelada de frescas*) from Irapuato, and most children will gobble it up. Avoid dairy goods—milk is pasteurized in most places but has a different flavor. Juices and soft drinks are popular among Mexican children at mealtime—try Sidral, a good apple drink. Unfortunately, American junk food has invaded the Mexican scene, and you'll find everything from Tootsie (*Tuitsie*) Rolls to *Pan Bimbo*, the Mexican equivalent of our rubbery white bread.

Don't worry too much about table manners. Because so much Mexican food is finger food, small children won't have too much trouble adjusting their table manners. In many Mexican families, children are the center of attention, and they are allowed free rein in most restaurants, especially on Sunday afternoon when the family often gathers for a long, leisurely lunch.

Boredom doesn't have to be a problem. Although most children won't find a tour of the National Cathedral very interesting, they are sure to be entranced by the exhibits at the National Museum of Anthropology—life-sized Indian hunters, big stone snakes, and carvings of skulls provide all the gore and horror most 11-year-old boys find intriguing. Interest may peak after the family has climbed the first pyramid, but many of the archaeological sites are awe-inspiring even to the most jaded American youngster. And Mexico has some of the best children's parks in the world—the amusement park in Chapultepec Park, Mexico City, with its Russian Mountain roller coaster; Africam in Puebla; and the CICI seaquarium in Acapulco.

Baby-sitting can be a problem. When you make your reservations, ask about baby-sitting services. If none are available, ask the housekeeper if one of the maids will be available, at an extra cost, to baby-sit on certain evenings. You might also inquire about lifeguard facilities when you make your reservations. Under no circumstances allow your children to swim unobserved in Mexico's oceans. Those spectacular waves are dangerous, and the beautiful blue water often masks riptides and even sharks.

A Mexican vacation can be enjoyable for the whole family if everyone is involved in the planning—see who can learn the most Spanish, have family conferences about what to do and where to go, and discuss the many interesting aspects of Mexican culture.

GETTING THERE

BY AIR

Major international carriers fly from approximately 50 US cities to locations throughout Mexico, the usual points of entry being Mexico City, Monterrey, Guadalajara, Cancún, Ixtapa/Zihuatanejo, and Acapulco. Mexico has two airlines that also serve international and domestic routes—Aeromexico and Mexicana, both of which are government owned.

Deregulation has made the airline industry a buyer's market, particularly in Mexico, which enjoys fierce competition between US carriers and the cheaper Mexican airlines. Promotional fares by various airlines are constantly being offered through national advertising campaigns. Check out various fares before you choose a carrier or a destination. It may be cheaper to fly to a major city and then rent a car, take the train, or go by bus to your final destination; it may also make your trip more interesting. Cities served by US carriers include Mexico City, Guadalajara, Monterrey, Mérida, Cancún, Cozumel, Acapulco, Puerto Vallarta, Manzanillo, Mazatlán, and Ixtapa/Zihuatanejo.

Mexico's airlines do not offer first-class seats, although some routes have executive-class seating, which leaves the middle seat empty. You might consider flying an American carrier first-class on your flight home—a good way to relax for the final few, hectic hours of your vacation.

Remember to reconfirm all international reservations 72 hours before flight time and domestic reservations 24 hours before flight time. This is especially important in order to avoid a penalty charge by Mexican carriers. If you call to change your reservation to a later flight, but fail to cancel your original reservation, you will be charged a portion of the ticket price. If you cancel or change your reservation 24 hours before your flight, you won't be charged; however, if you change your reservation within 24 hours and fail to cancel previous reservations, you will have to pay a portion of the ticket price in addition to the price of your new ticket. The amount is determined by how close to flight time you cancel—the closer, the higher the penalty. Check with the airline to determine cancellation policy when you make your reservation.

If you plan to fly into Mexico on an American carrier and then switch to a Mexican carrier for a domestic flight, make all your reservations through the American carrier and you will be given a discount on your Mexican domestic travel. This makes Mexican airlines a great bargain for travelers—a round-trip ticket from Mexico City to Oaxaca, made through an American carrier for an international visitor, can cost as little as $50. Unfortunately, Mexican airlines don't always run on time; don't depend on making a tight connection between a domestic flight and an international one.

All travelers must pay a departure tax at Mexican airports — 450 pesos on international flights, 240 pesos on domestic flights. (Further rate hikes are expected. Be sure to ask an airline representative *before* you arrive in Mexico.) Baggage allowances vary with the price and class of your ticket; check with the airline before you go. Always check your baggage through to your final destination, and remember to take a small carry-on bag with essentials, especially medication. Never put money or valuables in your baggage.

There are customs entry points at the larger airports in Mexico; however, if you're going to a smaller city, you may have to go through customs before you reach your final destination. The airline agent should be able to tell you where your customs entry point will be when you check your baggage.

Ground transportation and porters are available at all the main airports in Mexico. Some hotels also offer limousine service from the airport; check when you make your reservations. Cab fares are established at a fixed rate in certain cities, and these rates are often posted outside the terminal. However, in Mexico City there is no set rate. The standard fare for two from Mexico City's International Airport to the downtown hotels is approximately 150-200 pesos. Always settle on the fare before you get into the cab.

In Mexico City, a fleet of minibuses shuttles visitors from the airport to downtown hotels. These red VW buses are run by SETTA, whose name appears on the back and sides of the buses. The minibuses are cheap — about 60-75 pesos for two with luggage. The fleet is located at the end of the international terminal; turn left as you leave customs, walk to the end of the concourse, and exit through the last door on the right. Go to the cashier's booth, tell the staff the name of your hotel, and buy your ticket. You can also make a return reservation by calling the SETTA number on your ticket stub.

The Metro, Mexico City's world-renowned subway, also serves the airport, but large bags are not allowed on board. If you have a small carry-on bag and it's after rush hour, you may be able to use the subway.

BY TRAIN

Next to driving, traveling by train is the most leisurely way to see Mexico. The three major railroad routes from the Texas-Mexico border south are from Nuevo Laredo, Ciudad Juárez, and Brownsville south to Mexico City. There are garages in El Paso and Laredo where you can store your car, or you can fly or take the bus to the border cities.

The Aztec Eagle leaves Nuevo Laredo at 6:55 P.M. daily and arrives in Mexico City at 8:40 P.M. the following day. There is no dining car service. The trip from Ciudad Juárez takes two days — the train leaves at 6:25 P.M. and arrives at 7:00 A.M. on the second day. Remember, Mexico does not observe daylight saving time; thus clocks vary on both sides of the border at certain times of the year. The main railroad station in Mexico City, Buenavista Station, is centrally located on Avenida Insurgentes and is just a few blocks from many of the major hotels on the Reforma.

Railway tickets to Mexico are incredibly cheap. A one-way, first-class ticket can be bought on the Aztec Eagle for less than a tank of gas; a Pullman costs approximately double a first-class ticket. The trip south is relaxing, the scenery magnificent, and at each stop vendors sell everything from tamales to blankets.

At this time no printed timetable for the Mexican railroad system is available. The easiest way to get information on train travel is to write to your nearest Mexican tourist office and request information on a specific route. (A list of Mexican tourist offices in the US and Canada appears at the back of the book.) In return you will receive either that route's timetable or the telephone number and address of the railroad company. Information is also available from the US office of the Ferro-carriles Nacionales de México, the Mexican national railroad. Write to Mexican National Railways, 489 Fifth Avenue, Suite 2601, New York, NY 10017, or call 212-682-1494. Some travel agents have information on Mexican trains.

Train travel within Mexico is also very inexpensive. There are several famous train journeys, such as the Copper Canyon ride; or you can travel by train between the major cities. You can also get information about train schedules and routes by visiting the nearest railroad station once you arrive in Mexico. Telephone calls can be confusing, especially if you don't speak Spanish, but most stations in the larger cities have bilingual reservations clerks. When you make your reservation, be sure to ask if there will be a dining car on the train; if not, take along a box lunch. Many hotels prepare them. Two popular domestic routes run from the capital to Guadalajara and to Oaxaca, both through beautiful mountain ranges. Other popular routes include Mexico City to Mérida, from the capital to Veracruz, and through the beautiful mountains of Michoacán with stops in the craft-rich towns of Uruapan, Pátzcuaro, and Morelia.

BY BUS

Most Mexicans travel by bus, and there are classes to accommodate everybody's pocketbook, from super-deluxe to third-class. Tourists should plan to travel by the super-deluxe, deluxe, and first-class buses; six hours in a third-class bus with chickens, diesel fumes, and a goat or two is for the hardiest of travelers.

Bus tickets, even in the top classes, are inexpensive—a one-way ticket to Acapulco from Mexico City can be purchased for much less than a tank of gas. Bus travel is efficient but can be nerve-racking if you are unfamiliar with Mexican driving habits.

If you travel from the US to Mexico by bus, Greyhound or Trailways will make your reservations, take you to the border, transfer you to a Mexican bus line, and make your return reservations. Greyhound has an office in Mexico City at Reforma 27 and serves as an agent for several Mexican bus lines.

Bus reservations are best made in person, and no round-trip tickets are available. If you interrupt your journey, remember to make connecting reservations as soon as possible. Seats on most first-class and deluxe buses are assigned, the buses are air-conditioned, and some even serve drinks and have hostesses. However, stops along the way for food and refreshment can be disappointing; take along a box lunch.

BY SHIP

Cruise ships operate out of Texas, California, New York, and Florida ports. The usual ports of call include Cozumel, Acapulco, Puerto Vallarta, and Mazatlán. Check with your travel agent for cruise information, as itineraries change frequently.

BY PRIVATE PLANE OR BOAT

Flying your own plane or sailing a boat into Mexico can be more trouble than it's worth. The red tape is incredible, and you may find yourself suspected of hauling marijuana, or in the middle of a tuna war. If you don't mind hassles, check with the nearest Mexican consulate for import regulations. A California business has a complete listing of airports in Mexico. For information write to Pilots Reservation Service, P.O. Box 80324, San Diego, CA 92138.

BY CAR

Traveling by car is the best and the bravest way to see Mexico, so we have devoted the next chapter to the subject.

GROUP TRAVEL

Many travel agencies, airlines, and resorts offer group packages that can be a bargain, especially for the first-time visitor, women traveling alone, or the less than adventurous. You can always break away from the established routine after you have enjoyed the complimentary cocktail. If you are considering a group tour, be sure to shop around and compare costs.

There are several standard tours offered in Mexico — the Mexico City–Cuernavaca/Taxco–Acapulco tour, the Guadalajara–Puerto Vallarta tour, the Cancún–Mérida tour, and the Guadalajaran–Mexico City tour through the colonial towns of Central Mexico. The Mexico City tours usually include visits to the pyramids, the National Museum of Anthropology, the Ballet Folklórico, and the Floating Gardens of Xochimilco.

The biggest drawback to an organized tour is that often too much is crammed into too few days — the "If it's *martes,* it must be Mérida" syndrome. For example, Taxco, often only an afternoon on the tour circuit, is worth a much longer stay, especially if you enjoy relaxing in beautiful colonial surroundings.

Several prestigious travel agencies offer special tours of Mexico for the visitor interested in a particular aspect of Mexican culture or history, such as archaeology, cuisine, and colonial towns. These tours are often staffed by specialists. Your travel agent should be able to help you find a tour suited to your interests.

CHOOSING A TRAVEL AGENT

Visit two or three travel agencies before you complete your plans. Some agents are more familiar with one area of Mexico than another; some specialize in package tours; others in individualized travel. Finding an agent who is knowledgeable about Mexico's trains, for example, can be difficult and may take several calls.

If you have a complaint when you return, you may report the agency to the American Society of Travel Agents, Consumer Affairs Dept., 711 Fifth Avenue, New York, NY 10022 (most agents are members of this professional organization), or call the Better Business Bureau.

GETTING AROUND IN MEXICO

We have already mentioned buses, trains, and domestic airlines. Rental cars cost about the same as they do in the United States, although devaluation may make the rates cheaper. And there is no substitute for taking on a Mexican city in an orange Volkswagen. You will need a credit card, your passport, and a valid United States driver's license to rent a car. Cash and a tourist card may suffice, but a passport and a credit card make the transaction easier. (Belonging to a rental car club, for example, Hertz Number One Club, can also help — all your paperwork will be filled out and waiting for you.) Reservations should be made well in advance by calling one of the toll-free numbers that rental agencies maintain in the United States. Remember, fiestas in small towns and national holidays can affect the number of cars available.

Taxis are the most common method of transportation for tourists, although the adventurous try the local public transportation. Ask your hotel desk clerk, the bell captain, or call the local tourist office for assistance with bus schedules. The ground rule here is *always* ask the price before you get in. If you want to visit an out-of-town ruin or market, bargain and establish a day or half-day rate. If your Spanish is meager (most Mexican cabbies have a working knowledge of English), ask your bell captain to bargain for you. Don't forget to tip the bell captain.

It is not customary to tip taxi drivers, but most customers give whatever small change is left. It is a universal law that no cabbie ever has the exact change.

Mexico City also has a system of small cabs called *peseros,* usually VW bugs, which operate on the theory that if enough people are going the same way, they can squeeze together and get there faster and cheaper. Hail one, ask if they're going your way, and squeeze in.

The capital's superb subway system operates from six in the morning to midnight and carries about two million passengers a day. For some reason, many tourists fail to use the excellent Metro despite the fact that it is the easiest and cheapest way to get around the city. During rush hour riding any subway can be an intimate experience.

However, even during rush hour the Mexican Metro is very efficient and a wait longer than a minute or two is rare. Take your first ride in the afternoon, not during rush hour when signs reading Women and Children Only–This Way are somewhat disconcerting to the uninitiated.

Mexico City also boasts a special squad of policemen who speak several languages and are posted in tourist areas to assist visitors. They wear various national flags on their shirt pockets and lapels and will approach you as you walk along the city's main boulevards and avenues to ask if you need assistance. These policemen can provide directions to museums, shops, markets, and restaurants or hail a cab for you. In other cities, don't hesitate to ask a policeman for help. The majority of Mexico's policemen are honest and helpful. However, never allow a policeman, or any stranger, to get into your car, particularly if he appears to admire it or has asked you to sell it; that's illegal. The US Embassy has issued this warning to US citizens in Mexico.

All over Mexico you will see signs in hotel lobbies and on the streets advertising sight-seeing tours. Before you sign on, ask other guests at your hotel if they have taken the tour, or call the local tourist office for advice about local tours. Most legitimate tour guides in Mexico are licensed by the government and must meet rigorous language and education requirements. If you take a tour and you're not satisfied, register a complaint with the tourist office.

HOW MUCH WILL MY TRIP COST?

Because Mexico's economy is linked to our own by geography and tradition, our economic woes affect Mexico. In addition, the Mexican economy has suffered in recent years from high inflation rates and a balance of trade problem. For many years the peso, the national currency of Mexico, was set at 12.5 pesos to the dollar. Under the Echeverría presidency, which ended in 1976, the peso was allowed to float and fell in value. The rate varied from 21 to 24 pesos to the US dollar. Daily variances were slight. Then, during the final year of President José López Portillo's six-year term, the peso was devalued twice; subsequently, it was devalued again by incoming President Miguel de la Madrid at the end of his first month in office, late December 1982. (At publication time, the peso stands at approximately 150 pesos to the dollar.)

Devaluation is a boon for US tourists, but it plays havoc with the

Mexican economy and is not regarded as a boon by many Mexican citizens, particularly those with narrow or fixed incomes. Mexico's vast oil reserves have contributed some stability to Mexico's economy; however, the 1981 world oil glut was one of the factors that led to the recent devaluation of the peso. Traveling in Mexico is a bargain for US visitors, but inflation, rising prices, and the luxury tax, the 10 percent IVA, similar to the European VAT (Value Added Tax), have taken their toll on those bargain rates. Still, it is possible to spend less and get more for your travel dollars in Mexico than in most vacation spots in this hemisphere.

You can know travel costs and room rates before you leave on vacation; it's the other costs — meals, cabs, and shopping sprees — that are hard to estimate. A good rule of thumb is to plan to spend as much as you would in the United States and then be pleasantly surprised when everything (almost everything) costs less. When you plan your budget, remember to include money for tips, shopping, taxis and buses, meals, entertainment, and sight-seeing.

Keep all your money in traveler's checks in US dollar amounts as a safeguard against sudden devaluation. In the past, the Mexican government has ordered prices to remain stable and fixed during a devaluation. If you suspect a merchant or hotel is trying to change the price of goods or services to reflect the devalued peso, complain and contact the nearest tourist office. (Local tourist offices are named in each city's listing.) Change a few dollars before you leave for small denominations of pesos for taxis and tips. Dollars are accepted in Mexico, particularly at the border, but in the interior there is often confusion over exchange rates.

Hotels will exchange traveler's checks, but they charge a small service fee and usually offer less than that day's official exchange rate. Banks offer better rates and are located in the main business districts of each community. They are open from 9:00 A.M. to 1:30 P.M., Monday through Friday. In smaller towns and villages, particularly the marketplaces, most merchants will accept only hard currency.

Personal checks are not accepted at most hotels, shops, and banks in Mexico unless you have prearranged for this privilege. Some stores along the border will accept personal checks if you have a valid Texas driver's license. Be warned — writing a hot check in Mexico is a serious offense.

American Express offices will cash personal checks if you are a card holder. (Some of the lesser known traveler's checks are sometimes difficult to cash.)

Major credit cards are accepted in Mexico, but be wary of businesses that try to assess a service charge on credit card purchases. Don't pay it. In an economy where the currency floats, the shopkeeper may be trying to hedge his bets. Charges are processed quickly and at the rate on the day they are received, not charged. Keep your receipts, particularly if your credit card company no longer returns to you the copies of your charges. A travel diary with a record of all your expenditures is useful when you return through US Customs and when you get home and try to figure out how much you really spent.

Mexican money is divided on the decimal system and, like Canadian currency, is color coded. The system is easy to understand and, because of the custom of portraying national heroes on the currency, is an easy way to take a history lesson. The only confusion may come over the five-peso piece — there are two. A new five-peso coin shows Quetzalcoatl, the plumed serpent, on one side. The older five-peso coin depicts the ill-starred Emperor Iturbide in a neoclassical pose. The Mexicans use the dollar sign to denote pesos, so don't be alarmed when you see a steak listed at $60. The notation *m.n.* — *moneda nacional* — is also used.

A word about tipping: Mexico is a labor-rich country, and tourism, a service-oriented industry, is vital to the national economy. Don't be a cheap gringo. Service is usually excellent; if it isn't, tip accordingly. The same tipping standards apply — 10–15 percent for waiters, 10 percent for barbers and hairdressers. A standard tip for porters and bellboys is the peso equivalent of 50 cents a bag.

NECESSARY TRAVEL DOCUMENTS

If you are a US citizen, a passport is not necessary for travel in Mexico. You will need a tourist card issued by the Mexican government. You can obtain this card (really a thin, not very sturdy, piece of paper) at the nearest Mexican consulate. You will need to prove you are a US citizen — birth certificate, voter's registration card, passport. Many of the airlines serving Mexico, some travel agencies, automobile clubs, and insurance agencies selling Mexican insurance also provide tourist cards to customers. You will need the same proof of citizenship. It is best to obtain your card several days or weeks before your trip. You can obtain a card at the border; however, it's simpler to do this before you leave.

If you are not a US citizen, or if you are a resident alien of the United States, check with the nearest Mexican consulate for information on entry requirements.

Tourist cards are valid for up to six months. You will be asked how long you intend to stay in Mexico and how you plan to go there — this information will be marked on your card. If you drive into Mexico or if you don't know how long you plan to stay, say six months; it's easier to get a six-month card initially than to try to renew a card once you are in Mexico.

When you enter Mexico, one copy of the card will be kept by Mexican immigration officials. *Do not lose your copy.* You will be required to surrender your copy as you leave Mexico, and you may be asked to produce it while you are there. If you lose your copy, you will need a letter from the police verifying your loss. If you lose your card, before you delve into the mysteries of Mexican bureaucracy, ask the nearest US consulate for help. (Mexican consulates and tourist offices in the US and Canada, and US and Canadian embassies and consulates in Mexico are listed in the back of the book. Each city's listings also include a section called "Tourist Services.")

MEXICAN CUSTOMS INSPECTION

If you fly into Mexico, the customs procedures are usually brief and perfunctory. If you drive, the search may be longer, especially if you look like what the Mexicans call a *jippie*.

There are several basic guidelines to follow:

Don't take luxury items into Mexico with the purpose of selling them. If you take along a new hair dryer or camera, take it out of the box so that it looks used.

Drugs, legal that is, should be left in their original containers and should be clearly labeled. Drugs illegal in the United States are just as illegal south of the border, and the penalties for sale or possession may be even higher in Mexico.

You are allowed to bring in one camera and 12 rolls of film per family member; however you may fudge on this a little.

You can bring in 200 cigarettes, 50 cigars, and up to nine ounces of tobacco. You may also bring in one bottle of wine and one quart of liquor. Champagne and Scotch are good choices, especially if you are visiting friends or celebrating an anniversary; French Champagne is terribly expensive in Mexico. American cigarettes are available in Mexico, and Mexico produces some excellent hand-rolled cigars. Cuban cigars are also available in Mexico, but don't try to bring any back into the United States.

Tools, artists' supplies, children's toys, books (expensive in Mexico —please, no pornography), camping equipment, sporting goods—all for personal use—may be brought into Mexico. There are special regulations covering firearms; check with the tourist bureau. In addition, you may bring six gifts totaling no more than $80 in value.

There is a standard approach to customs agents all over the world: smile, say hello, and do as you are told. It usually works.

WHAT SHOULD I PACK?

If you are heading for the beach, leave your ties and cocktail dresses at home; unless you are a disco freak, you won't need anything more formal than a caftan. Swim wear is expensive, so buy at home. But you will find bargains in cotton dresses, blouses, and men's *guayaberas* (cotton shirts) in the markets. There are few bargains in the coastal resorts, even in the markets, but check out the local market before you go boutique hopping.

In Mexico City and other large metropolitan cities, when you make your dinner reservation, ask if there is a dress requirement, or ask your hotel bell captain. Dresses or suits for women and coats and ties for men are more suitable at better restaurants, especially in Mexico City — even in the cafés of the Zona Rosa you will feel more comfortable in "office" clothes than in jeans.

American women dress more casually than their Mexican middle- and upper-class sisters (certain parts of Houston and North Dallas excluded). Mexican women dress fashionably, to the point of overdressing by most American tastes. Slacks are not worn often, but the tourist should keep in mind comfort as well as appearance — jeans or a skirt worn with a jacket at night is acceptable, unless you are dining out.

Women should not wear shorts in the cities or towns. Mexican women, particularly the Indian women, are modest in their dress. Shorts are okay for the beach, pyramid climbing, and camping, and you will probably need a hat at the archaeological zones. Mexican men rarely wear shorts.

Good walking shoes are essential. Wear comfortable clothes during the day as you sight-see or shop. Don't attempt to climb the ruins in heels or smooth-soled shoes; you can fall off and injure yourself seriously.

There is no excuse for looking wrinkled in Mexico. Most hotels offer one-day or two-day dry-cleaning and laundry services for minimal amounts. One-day service is usually 50 percent more, but even that amounts to a small charge. A small travel iron or steam wrinkle remover is a good investment. You won't need an electrical current converter in Mexico. The current is 110 volts, dipping to 55 in some remote areas.

Some other odds and ends to consider packing:

A small coffee maker or heating coil — good for that morning caffeine fix or late-night cup of tea.

A flashlight — perhaps a penlight model, handy at archaeological zones, also for reading menus in places like Oaxaca, where the electricity is turned off for an hour every night at 7:30.

Shampoo, deodorant, cologne, and other drugstore items — expensive in Mexico. Make sure the caps are screwed on tightly and transfer everything to plastic bottles. Pack an extra toothbrush. Some French perfumes are good buys in Mexico, especially at airport duty-free shops.

Epsom salts — just a small box, but a great relief for tired, aching feet.

A small plastic hip flask — when filled with water can be a godsend while climbing pyramids or wandering through endless museums.

Mosquito net or spray — this may sound as though you are preparing for a trip to darkest Africa, but one night in a screenless room in a quaint colonial hotel will make you wish you had thought of it. Mosquito net can be folded into a small package and hung over the bedposts or in the window. It can mean the difference between a good night's sleep and misery.

Swiss army knife — can opener, scissors, nail file, and all-purpose tool. Once you own one, you will never go anywhere without it.

First-aid kit — aspirin, Kaopectate, Pepto-Bismol, Band-Aids, first-aid cream. Grocery store samples are good to collect for your travel kit. Mexican pharmacies are well stocked with equivalent items, but go prepared.

Kleenex — those little packages are ideal to stuff in a purse or pocket, because some Mexican bathrooms do and others don't.

A raincoat, poncho, or umbrella — remember those afternoon showers.

Don't overpack. Take along small containers of necessary toiletries. And don't take too many clothes; try to minimize your load and keep in mind that you can always send clothes out to be laundered and that you will probably buy clothes in Mexico.

FOOD

We've devoted a whole chapter to food and drink in Mexico, but here are some general guidelines. Most hotels catering to the tourist trade are now serving breakfast buffet-style; you can eat heartily for what it costs for an Egg McMuffin and coffee in the United States. Lunch is a leisurely affair in Mexico and doesn't usually begin until 1:30 or later. Many restaurants serve a *comida corrida* (a sort of blue plate special, or several courses at a fixed price); you will need a siesta afterward. Dinner is often eaten late in the evening, around nine, but most restaurants are familiar with the strange eating habits of gringos, and you won't be turned away if you arrive at seven.

Overeating is a distinct temptation for tourists in Mexico — the food is good and there's so much of it. That brings us to . . .

MEDICAL PROBLEMS

Tourists, no matter if they travel to London or to Christmas Island, invariably get what is called by a variety of tasteless names throughout the world — in Mexico it's "Moctezuma's revenge," or *turista*. Climate, the water, cooking oils and methods, spices, and overindulgence — all contribute to *turista*. There are ways to minimize the risk. First, try not to make a fuss about the subject. Mexicans are understandably sensitive about it. Most drinking water in the larger cities and towns is potable; however, drinking water anywhere has its own set of bugs. You are used to the bugs in your water at home; it's the new ones that will get you. Of course, there are areas where the water is not potable. Thus there is danger, even in Mexico City, of contamination by typhoid or amoebic dysentery. The best way to avoid such a problem is to drink purified water *(agua purificada)*. Most hotels and restaurants serve only purified water and ice. If you are in doubt, ask, quietly and politely. Or you can order Mexico's equivalent of Perrier — mineral water *(agua mineral)*, either carbonated *(con gas)* or noncarbonated *(sin gas)*. Two favorite brands are Tehuacán and Penafiel.

A common pitfall for many gringos is gorging on all that fresh tropical fruit at breakfast; if you can't resist, make sure you have a couple of fresh rolls *(bolillos)*, too.

If you do get an upset stomach, take it easy and try some of those remedies you brought along from home — Pepto-Bismol, Kaopectate, or Donnagel. Or buy Lomotil (you won't need a prescription) from the nearest Mexican pharmacy. If your illness seems more serious, ask the hotel to call its house doctor; most hotels keep one on call. And keep your receipts, because your insurance company should cover you in Mexico. (Some recent research in the United States indicates that a daily dose of an antibiotic is effective in controlling *turista* — ask your doctor before you leave.)

You will not need any special shots to enter Mexico; however, if you plan a trip to the more remote parts of the Southern Highlands or the Pacific Coast around Puerto Escondido (south of Oaxaca), ask your doctor to give you a typhoid shot and take along quinine pills. There have been some reports of malaria along the remote coastal areas.

LEGAL PROBLEMS

Mexico operates under the Napoleonic Code of Justice, guilty until proved innocent. This means any entanglements with the law can be time-consuming and confusing. The first thing you should do if you find yourself in a legal hassle is contact the US Embassy in Mexico City or the nearest US consulate. The Mexican tourist office in Mexico City also can help you find legal counsel.

If you are driving, read the following chapter on driving in Mexico for advice on what to do if you are involved in an accident.

It is wise to keep all valuables either with you or in a hotel safe. Also, in larger cities, watch out for pickpockets; they are the bane of tourists from New York to New Delhi. Keep your purse closed with any opening toward your body; men should keep their wallets in an inside coat pocket.

Illegal drugs are available in Mexico, and you may be approached by sellers, particularly at the border and in the resort areas. Many sellers are also informants, so you buy at your own risk. The wheels of justice turn a little slower in Mexico than in the United States, and penalties for drug possession can be harsh. The Mexican Secretaria de Turismo publishes a guide containing excerpts from the Citizen's Code of legal rights. You may obtain a copy by writing to the Mexico City tourist office (see Mexico City "Tourist Services" for the address) and asking for the "Codigo del Ciudadano Version por a Turistas."

KEEPING IN TOUCH

You may want to know what's going on in the world, or you may want to forget for a couple of weeks. Naturally, Mexican newspapers feature Mexican news, and as most of the print and electronic media are under the direct control or influence of the government, what you read in most Mexican newspapers and see on television will be colored by the official view. Newspapers and television concentrate heavily on Latin and South American news with good coverage of European affairs, particularly Italy and Spain.

The *Miami Herald* sells its Latin American edition in English in Mexico's larger cities, and *The New York Times* weekly supplement of the news is also available. One English-language newspaper, *The News*, is published in Mexico. There are three major national dailies: *Excelsior*, considered to be the best newspaper, moderate to conservative in tone; *La Prensa*, a liberal daily; and *El Nacional*, the government organ.

Many of the larger, deluxe hotels in Mexico City subscribe to US Cablevision, and there are also two English-language radio stations in Mexico City with US news broadcasts—1560 AM and 105 FM.

Mexican television features many regular US shows with Spanish dubbing, and old Hollywood movies are often shown with Spanish subtitles—a great way to learn Spanish.

Don't send packages either to or from Mexico unless you absolutely have to, because customs regulations are very stringent. Always send postcards and letters by airmail—1.60 pesos a gram. Many hotels sell stamps, and post offices are open from 9 A.M. to 7 P.M.

Telegrams can be sent from your hotel. There are several classes of telegrams, all inexpensive, so send the most expensive if you want the telegram to arrive before you do.

Local telephone calls are inexpensive, especially if you make them from a phone booth, only 20 centavos. Most hotels charge for local and long-distance calls, as much as 60 pesos in resort areas. *Never* charge a long-distance call to the United States to your room. *Always* call collect; otherwise the charge could be as much as the cost of the room. (See "Mamá Bell" on the next page for more information.)

Most church denominations are represented in the larger cities. Ask at your hotel desk, the tourist office, the US Embassy or the US consulate, or check the phone book. The Roman Catholic Church is still the predominant faith in Mexico, and visitors are always welcome at church services. Although women no longer need a head covering, many of the Mexican women still wear one; always dress appropriately.

Mamá Bell

Follow this easy guide for placing calls to Mexico, or from city to city within Mexico.

To call Mexico: First, call 1-800-874-4000, the international information number, and ask the operator for the city code of the place you are calling in Mexico. For example, the city code for Acapulco is 748; for Mexico City the city code is 5. (Many cities in Mexico cannot be dialed directly. For those cities, you will have to go through an operator. Dial O and give the operator the country, city, and local phone number you wish to reach.)

If the city has a city code, you may dial directly:

1. Dial international access code 011.
2. Dial country code 52.
3. Dial the city code.
4. Dial the local number (this may be seven digits or fewer).

To call city to city within Mexico: Long-distance calls may be made only from private phones or from special long-distance public phones clearly marked *Servicio de Larga Distancia.* These are located in post offices, telephone company offices, bus terminals, airports, and other public places. We recommend that you avoid making long-distance calls from your hotel room — rates, surcharges, and taxes are excessive. (If you must call from your hotel, *always* call collect.)

Access codes are called *ladas* in Mexico. You must dial different codes for different types of long-distance calls. For example:

91 — station to station (*á quien contesta*)
92 — person to person (*persona á persona*)
95 — station to station from Mexico to the United States or Canada

To place a long-distance call from a public phone, follow this procedure:

1. Have plenty of change on hand. Long-distance calls are not cheap in Mexico. If you plan to call collect (*por cobrar*), you may still have to pay a small service charge.
2. Look up the city's area code in the phone book or dial 01 for information assistance. You will find area codes are also listed in this guidebook in city listings under "Vital Statistics." Mexican area codes are two- and three-digit numbers. To call unlisted cities, dial 02 for assistance. Tell the operator the city and the local number you wish to call. For assistance with calls to Canada and the United States, dial 09. Again, we recommend calling collect.
3. Dial the appropriate *lada.*
4. Dial the city's area code.
5. Dial the local number.

Other helpful numbers to remember are 06 for police and 07, a general assistance number for everything from finding lost babies to calming disoriented tourists.

TIPS FOR PHOTOGRAPHERS

If you are a professional photographer or a rabid amateur with more gear than Ansel Adams, you may encounter some problems entering through Mexican Customs. One expert suggests you limit your gear and distribute film in several locations throughout your luggage. (Strictly speaking, each person may carry only 12 rolls of film.) It's really only necessary to obtain permits if you are carrying a great amount of photographic gear, particularly movie and video equipment. Check with the Mexican tourist office or Mexican consulate to obtain any necessary import permits. It is wise to keep a list with serial numbers of your camera gear. If you don't want to carry around a bag full of lenses, leave them in the hotel safe. Most hotels rent small safes that require two keys to be opened. One key is kept at the desk; the other will be checked out to you.

Tripods, models, and flash units are forbidden in most museums, art galleries, archaeological zones, and protected colonial areas. Take plenty of fast film and take enough film — it's expensive in Mexico.

There are certain areas of Mexico where photography is forbidden. Zones guarded by Mexican Army officers — dams, docks, certain ferries — may be off-limits. Some government buildings are verboten, and then there are other buildings where photographers will be shooed away for no apparent reason — for example, the national pawnshop in Mexico City, called Monte de Piedad, Mountain of Pity. If you are warned not to photograph, don't.

TRAVELING WITH PETS

Don't travel with pets. In a country where there is poverty, taking the pampered family pet with you can be culturally insensitive, and chances are Fido won't enjoy himself anyway — there's not a whole lot for a dog to do in Mexico.

As Mexico's middle classes grow, more and more pets are being kept in the cities, but you will rarely see them on the streets or in the parks. In the Southern Highlands and Yucatán, dogs and cats roam freely in the Indian villages. The Mesoamerican Indian domesticated the dog hundreds of years ago. The Aztecs even enjoyed eating a certain small breed.

If you must take the family pet along, secure a certificate of good health from your veterinarian and a letter stating the dog has been vaccinated against rabies within the last three months. This information must be presented to the nearest office of the Mexican consulate before you leave. You will have to pay a small fee for your dog's entry papers. And a certificate proving the animal has been vaccinated against rabies within the last 30 days is necessary to reenter the United States. (Please note: If you plan to keep your pet in Mexico longer than 30 days, you will be required to have the animal vaccinated against rabies before returning to the US in order to meet the US authorities' 30-day vaccination requirement.)

Dog and cat food are hard to find in Mexico, except in some of the modern supermarkets in the larger cities. Unless you plan to stay in Mexico for an extended period, it's best to leave the family pet at home; but remember to bring him a souvenir. Cat owners go crazy over those little sombreros sold in the markets; cats don't seem to be too crazy about them, however.

COMING HOME — US CUSTOMS

The same universal rule applies — smile, say hello, do as you are told, and no jokes about the kilo of dope you have in your bag.

The US Customs Service provides all travelers with a booklet with the catchy title *Know Before You Go*. You can find one at the post office, federal building, or for a free copy, write to US Customs, Box 7118, Washington, DC 20044. The booklet lists all the do's and don'ts.

You are allowed to bring $400 worth of purchases each month per family member into the United States. You may also bring back unlimited amounts of certain items, such as pottery, stoneware, and basketry, under the Generalized System of Preferences (GSP), a system designed to aid the underdeveloped countries, like Mexico. All those U-Haul trucks you see headed north through Texas loaded with wrought iron chairs and plant racks are taking advantage of the duty-free GSP list. Items allowed under the GSP vary; call US Customs for more information.

In addition, you may bring back duty free one quart of liquor and 200 cigarettes. If you are driving, or visiting a border town, you may want to bring back a case of Mexican beer in addition to the obligatory bottle of tequila — this is usually allowed.

Anything over the $300 limit will be taxed at 10 percent on the next $600 worth. If you have a special question while you are in Mexico, call the US Embassy in Mexico City, 553-3333.

You may not bring back certain fruits or vegetables, stilettos, Cuban cigars, or Cuban rum; and the Mexican government will throw you in jail if you try to bring back an archaeological or colonial artifact. On the other hand, the US government will throw you in jail if you smuggle in dope or guns. If you do buy an antique or one of the very good reproductions available of pre-Hispanic works, ask for a receipt giving the description and listing the value.

Keep all your receipts in one place. If you fly back, you will be given a customs declaration form to fill out before you land. Have your papers ready.

4

MEXICO AND THE WHEEL

TAKING TO THE ROAD

In 1790 Queen Marie Antoinette, finally awakening to the horrid possibilities the future might hold for her, fled Paris in a large, cumbersome coach and journeyed to Varennes, where she was captured while taking an unscheduled rest stop. After she was returned to Paris, it was reported that her hair had turned pure white overnight. Travel can be disconcerting even for the privileged classes.

There is no recorded instance of a returning motorist driving the last yards over the old International Bridge in Laredo and collapsing, white-haired and broken, at the feet of an unsympathetic US Customs agent; however, some say, there hangs in the air over the northern banks of the Rio Grande the vast echo of a million sighs uttered by returning tourists who have ventured south of the border in the family car.

While the average American driver is accustomed to order and control, the Mexican driver marches to the tune of a different drummer. Not so much marches, that is, but charges willy-nilly to the chorus of Volkswagen horns playing the opening bars from "La Marseillaise," or "La Cucaracha," or even the theme from *The Godfather*.

Driving in Mexico is not for the fainthearted. It takes a free spirit, a willingness to meet adventure head-on, six eyes, fast feet, and a large bottle of tequila for the journey's end. It is the best way to see the country and to test your mettle. If you follow our guidelines, keep your wits about you, and use common sense, you should have few problems; however, if you find yourself whistling "La Cucaracha" and passing cattle trucks on mountain passes, it's time to let someone else drive.

Before You Go

Before driving in Mexico consider whether or not your car is suitable for such a trip. Many US car companies have branches in Mexico that manufacture models for the Mexican market — Ford, Chrysler, General Motors. If you have a standard, midsized American car, chances are you won't have too many problems finding parts in Mexico. Luxury models and large American cars are unsuitable because they are too big to maneuver in some colonial towns, and because parts can be hard to find. The wonder of an electronic ignition may be beyond the realm of experience of the average Mexican mechanic and is certainly beyond the expertise of most US motorists.

You will have no trouble finding parts in Mexico for the ubiquitous Volkswagen, particularly the Rabbit and Beetle models. Renault is also producing large numbers of compacts in Mexico that seem to have been bred with the same fervor as their German cousins. Japanese compacts are ideal for travel in Mexico; however, parts may be hard to find. And if you own an exotic, cherished automobile, don't take it south — some well-meaning parking lot attendant may wash it and destroy a $100 wax job.

You are forbidden by the Mexican government to sell your car in Mexico, and if anyone expresses interest in your car, discourage him immediately. The US Embassy has suggested that American motorists should not allow strangers, including policemen, to drive their cars. If a policeman makes that suggestion, write down the number from his cap badge and tell him you will follow him to the station.

The two essential things to do before you leave are, first, check your car to make sure everything, spare parts as well, is in working order; and, second, purchase Mexican car insurance. Insurance is an absolute necessity; your US insurance will not cover you. (Some Texas policies cover Texas drivers in the border zone of Mexico — the twelve-mile strip that runs along the border in northern Mexico.) Mexican car insurance policies usually provide access to a Mexican lawyer in case of an accident or police action — important in a country that operates under the Napoleonic Code, guilty until proved innocent. Insurance can be purchased through an automobile club or at one of the border agencies. Sanborn's Travel, a Texas institution along the border, provides free driving guides with the purchase of insurance. (For more information, write to Sanborn's Mexican Insurance Service, P.O. Box 1210, McAllen, TX 78501, or call 512-682-3401.) Costs for insurance average about $6 a day, depending on the year and make of your car.

When you purchase your policy, it's best to overestimate your stay by a few days.

Check with your mechanic to see which of the following items you should take on your trip to Mexico. If your car is new, not everything on this list will be necessary.

- Spare tire
- Gas can — empty
- Army shovel (available at army-navy surplus stores)
- Flashlight
- Fuel pump kit
- Generator kit
- Plugs, points, and a condenser
- Tire pump
- Fan belt — take a couple
- Oil — a couple of cans
- Fuses
- Oil filter
- Gas filter
- Flares
- Radiator hose
- Water jug (two) — one for the car, one for you
- Duct tape
- Baling wire
- Electrical tape
- Tire gauge
- Wrenches, pliers, tools
- Windex, paper towels
- Toilet paper

Mexican Customs

You will need your car title or proof of ownership to take your car into Mexico. Customs officials will issue your car importation permit at the border and will attach car stickers to your front, side, and rear windows, indicating you are a tourist. Your tourist card will be marked to show you entered by automobile, and everyone in your party will be expected to leave Mexico the same way he came in, although not necessarily at the same port of entry.

Driving into Mexico is a little different from flying in commercially. Customs procedures are more bureaucratic; there's more red tape and even a little bribery involved. As you pull into the customs dock, a porter will either take your bags out and into the customs building or stand by to assist a customs official. You should tip the porter, who will then pass this on to the customs official, which means you must tip the porter again, only less, when he returns with your bag. Give

$1 the first time, followed by 50 cents, and you will be surprised how quickly you will clear customs. Remember, *don't* try to tip the US Customs agent when you return.

Approximately 12 miles into the interior, you will cross another checkpoint. Stop and have your papers checked. On the way back, you will surrender your papers here.

Maps

Several US travel clubs, gas companies, and bookstores stock good road maps of Mexico. Distances are usually marked in both kilometers and miles. Don't worry if a highway sign occasionally doesn't match the map; this happens once in a while.

The Mexican government's tourist offices offer free, excellent road maps. Usually, the location of the tourist office is marked on a blue sign, which you will see as you drive into town; if not, ask a policeman.

Gasoline

Leave your credit cards at home. In Mexico, the petroleum industry is nationalized and all gasoline is sold under the auspices of PEMEX, Petróleos Mexicanos. PEMEX stations are found throughout the country; however, in some remote areas not all grades of gasoline are available, particularly unleaded. Regular, an 81-octane gas, is called Nova and is in the blue pump. Unleaded gas, Extra, is in the silver pump — it's rated at 91 octane. Remember to brush up on your metrics, because all gas is sold by the liter. (In the past, gasoline was a bargain and diesel fuel still is. However, in December 1982, prices were raised to approximate US prices. Subsequent drops in the value of the peso have increased the buying power of US and Canadian tourists and gasoline prices may reflect this, but be prepared to spend the dollar equivalent for gasoline.)

PEMEX stations accept only hard Mexican currency — no dollars, no traveler's checks, no credit cards. If you are not fluent in Spanish, always try to buy the same amount of gas at each stop. Fill up when you reach half a tank. Figure your tank's capacity in liters and how much a fill-up would cost, divide that by two, round it off, and always get that amount. When you pull into a PEMEX station, watch carefully. Tourists are easy marks, and sometimes you will be distracted by vendors, little boys offering to wash your windshield, and the curious. Watch the man pumping the gas. A locking gas cap is a worthwhile investment.

PEMEX stations do only minor repairs, such as fix flats and recharge dead batteries. You have to go to a *refaccionaria* for major repair work or for coolant.

Rules of the Road

Never drive at night. Driving in the daytime in Mexico requires all your wits; driving at night can be dangerous. If you are forced to drive at night, install airplane landing lights and post a lookout. Be prepared to meet wandering animals, buses going 90 mph with all their lights blazing, buses with no lights going 9 mph, herds of goats migrating west, and caravans of huge, intimidating trucks. For some reason, known only to them, many Mexicans drive at night with their lights off; conversely, some drive with bright lights and refuse to dim them. "A foolish consistency," as Emerson said, "is the hobgoblin of little minds."

During the daytime, always keep alert for animals and people on the road. Perhaps it's the gasoline fumes, but the animals seem to enjoy the grass next to the highway best of all. Sometimes animals will be tethered, but more likely they will be roaming free. Be on the lookout as you drive through villages — burros, small pigs, and chickens take on suicidal tendencies when they see a gringo approaching — and the trucks and buses breathing down your neck won't understand your Humane Society approach.

Many of the smaller towns and villages have bumps in the road called *topes*, which are designed to make you slow down — they work. As for speed limits, they are posted, but no one seems to notice them too much. At first, you will obey the signs, but this soon wears off. The same goes for Stop signs, especially at railroad crossings. If no one is around, stop; but if there's a cattle truck equipped with a large rock scooper behind you, think twice. It is better to slow down and cross carefully; the truck will probably roar past you as you cross. That Mexican trains travel as fast as, if not faster than, Mexican cattle trucks is just one of the dilemmas you will face on Mexican highways.

Bridges pose another dilemma. It is the custom in Mexico for a driver to race toward a one-lane bridge, flash his lights before the oncoming driver flashes his, and claim suzerainty — a sort of modern remake of the Little John–Robin Hood battle. If you find yourself gnashing your teeth and trying to flash first, you are taking all this too seriously.

Stay on paved highways, unless you plan a short sight-seeing trip to a nearby village. But watch out for those heavy afternoon rain showers. That dry creek bed you crossed earlier in the day could turn into a raging torrent in a matter of hours.

Small mounds of rocks in the road mean that a driver is having a mechanical problem ahead — why buy flares when all you need is a few rocks, a scrap of handkerchief, and rudimentary building skill?

Watch your gestures when you drive. An innocent wave of the hand or arm may take on new meaning south of the border.

Horn honking is basically a Mexico City habit. Avoid honking; gringos tend to look silly doing a poor imitation of an angry Mexican driver.

Don't drive in the city. Park the car and take a cab. If you must drive in a city, watch out for cab drivers, kids washing windshields at stoplights, and policemen. Mexican traffic cops don't use hand signals, but their body positions will tell you whether you can go or must stop. If the policeman is facing you or if his back is toward you, stop. When he turns sideways, you may go. Many cities, particularly Mexico City, have circles called *glorietas*, usually with a large monument in the middle. Six or seven streets might empty into this large open circle, with little or no traffic regulation. If you are driving, keep going around the monument until you fiure out which way you would like to go. If you are walking, watch out.

Toll Roads

Most of the highways in Mexico are free; however, around Mexico City there are several four- and six-lane highways called *cuotas* (tolls). Tolls range from 20 to 40 pesos, and you may have to pay at both ends. The slower, older highways are beside the toll roads and are often more scenic.

Roadside Picnics

You won't find picnic tables, but you will find a million glorious spots along the road that are perfect for a picnic lunch. A large, sturdy ice chest is ideal for automobile travel in Mexico. You can buy ice (and beer) from the local *cervecería*, and wine is sold at liquor stores and grocery stores (*tiendas*). Stock up with canned snacks—smoked oysters, pâté, crackers, and olives. You can buy fresh fruit at the market and restock your munchie basket at one of the large supermarkets, often called Conasuper, in the major cities.

But remember, if you drink and drive, your insurance will be invalid if you have an accident.

Accidents

If you are involved in a minor fender bender, do as the Mexicans do —drive away. Under Mexico's laws, involving the authorities could mean hours, if not days, of hassles. Of course, if you are in a major accident, you will have little choice. Contact the lawyer or insurance representative listed on your Mexican insurance policy and, if necessary, a representative of the US government.

Watch out for signs warning of rockfalls, fog, or ice. If there's a sign in Mexico, the problem must be serious. Driving in the mountains, especially east and west of Mexico City, in the fog and rain can be hazardous. Always account for the slowness of mountain travel when you estimate arrival times.

Be alert at all times, especially for new and unexplained signals. For example, if you are behind a car and want to pass it, watch for a signal from the back lights—if the driver signals with his left turn signal, that means go ahead and pass, or it could mean he's turning left; if he signals with his right turn signal, that means don't pass, or it could mean he's turning right. . . .

And don't be fooled into thinking one-way streets alternate like they do in the States; you may cross two or even three northbound streets before you find one southbound.

The Green Angels

The Mexican government provides a great service for tourists who drive south, the Green Angels. These teams of English-speaking mechanics patrol the major highways in Mexico, particularly the Pan American Highway from Nuevo Laredo to Mexico City and on through Oaxaca to the Guatemalan border. If your car breaks down, ask a passing motorist to call them for you. The Angels make regular passes on most major highways.

Military Patrols

You may be stopped at military roadblocks where your car will be briefly searched for weapons or drugs. These searches take place mostly south of Mexico City, particularly in the mountains of Guerrero and along the Pacific Coast where drug and gun traffic is heaviest. There are insurgents in the Southern Highlands who are opposed to the present government, but if you stay on the major highways, you will have little chance of any contact with them.

The best way to deal with military searches is to be polite and cooperative. Usually, the soldier will ask you to open your trunk and your glove compartment. He may also ask you for your papers and if you have any guns, marijuana, or other illegal items. Just say no (assuming you have none of these), and don't try to engage in any personal conversation, unless he does.

Parking

Try to find a hotel with a guarded parking lot. Tip the attendant when you leave. (He will probably wash your car without asking you.)

When you park on the street, always lock your car and take papers and valuable items with you. If your hubcaps are removable, take them off or leave them at home, but remember to check your lug nuts when you return to the car.

No Parking signs, both official and handmade, are generally ignored by Mexican drivers. In most Mexican cities, the parking meters don't work, but check before you walk away. If you return and find your license plates missing, you have been caught by a Mexican traffic cop —these policemen take offenders' license plates down to the local station, thus ensuring that a fine is paid immediately.

Many businesses hire parking attendants who wear old, official-looking uniforms, purchased at the local army-navy surplus. These "guards" will allow you to park in their assigned area for a small tip, a peso or two. Small boys will also offer to watch your car; it's not a bad idea to give one this task and tip him when you return.

ROADHOUSES

Finding the right place to rest on a long journey into the interior is important. We have picked some of the best hotels in Mexico, and some of the best in town (not always the same thing). The cities included in these listings are Chihuahua, Durango, Monterrey, Querétaro, Saltillo, San Luis Potosí, Torreón, and Zacatecas.

If you are heading south from Nuevo Laredo to Mexico City, you may want to break your journey at San Miguel de Allende. You will find listings for that town in the chapter **Mexico of the Colonials.** Border town hotels and motels are listed in the chapter **The Best of the Border.**

For a mile-by-mile guide, we recommend Dan Sanborn's driving logs, which are given to all Sanborn's customers who buy their Mexican car insurance from the famous travel agencies in the Rio Grande Valley. For information call 512-682-3401.

If you're making reservations in advance by phone, you'll need the telephone routing codes that when combined with the international access code allow you to dial directly your favorite hotel reservations desk. For the cities with roadhouses listed in this chapter the routing or city phone codes are Monterrey, 83; Saltillo, 841; San Luis Potosí, 481; Querétaro, 463; Chihuahua, 41; Durango, 81; Torreón, 171; and Zacatecas, 492.

MONTERREY

Monterrey used to be a popular place to spend a couple of days, but industrial pollution has made this city a place to avoid, if possible. An overnight stay can be combined with a quick shopping trip. Then head south, open up your windows, and enjoy the clear mountain air south of the city.

HOTELS

Gran Ancira Hotel, southwest corner Plaza Hidalgo (43-20-60). An old revered landmark of a hotel with a grand lobby. (Everyone knows the story that this is the lobby where Pancho Villa parked his horse.) The rooms are aging, but the hotel still has the luxury touch. A. Cr.

Holiday Inn, Hwy. 85 (52-24-00). Good spot to stay if you don't want to fight the traffic downtown. Just like the Holiday Inns north of the border. A. Cr.

Ramada Inn Monterrey, atop Topo Chico Hill, one mile off Hwy. 85,

west on Blvd. Lope de Vega. Located six miles north of the city this is a good place to stop if you had a late start at the border. Unfortunately, because of the pollution, you probably won't be able to see the city lights. A. Cr.

Cabins, Cola de Caballo (Horsetail Falls). If you are making your way south at a leisurely pace, consider a night in a mountain cabin at the Cola de Caballo National Park. Head south on Hwy. 85 out of Monterrey, drive through Santiago and El Cercado, and take the turn-off marked Cola de Caballo. The curving mountain road is slow going and can be dangerous in fog. Don't drive it at night. The cabins overlook a deep ravine and cost about $1,000 (pesos) a night. There's a restaurant next door.

RESTAURANTS

There are three excellent restaurants located downtown on Plaza Hidalgo within walking distance of the Gran Ancira: Luisiana (43-15-61), continental cuisine in posh surroundings; Santa Rosa (42-71-11), Mexican specialties in a colonial setting (wear a jacket); and Café Flores (43-62-50), a small café popular with students that serves *cabrito* and grilled meats — informal. Luisiana and Santa Rosa are moderate to expensive and Café Flores is inexpensive. All accept credit cards.

SHOPPING

Cristalería Kristalux, Doblado and Progreso. It's worth making a quick stop at the glass factory. Order custom-made work and pick it up on your way home.

POINTS OF INTEREST

Cuauhtémoc Brewery. The beer that made Monterrey famous . . . and rich can be tasted at the brewery located on Hwy. 85, conveniently the road to Mexico City. Stop in for a sample. Open weekdays.

SALTILLO

You may want to bypass Monterrey and stay in Saltillo, a city quieter than its industrial sister.

HOTELS

Camino Real, Hwy. 57, southeast of the city (3-81-90). Modern hotel with a dining room and coffee shop. Centrally heated and air-conditioned. Heated pool. C. Cr.

Motel El Paso, Blvd. V. Carranza Norte (4-13-97). Downtown motel with large rooms, not heated but plenty of blankets. Adjoining restaurant. D. Cr.

If you are heading west toward Torreón from Saltillo, you might want to stay in Parras, 40 miles west of the city.

Hotel Rincón del Motero, Hwy. 2, Parras (2-05-40). Cabins and rooms available; golf, horseback riding, tennis, and gardens. Parras is the hometown of revolutionary Francisco I. Madero and is surrounded by vineyards. Nearby Hacienda de San Lorenzo is open for tours daily, except Sunday.

RESTAURANTS

Colonel Sanders Kentucky Fried Chicken, Hwy. 40 at Hwy. 57. The same old colonel serving up his "pollo frito."

Muchoburger, next door to Colonel Sanders on Hwy. 40. Burgers to go. Plus pizza and tacos.

Tena, Hwy. 40 at Hwy. 57. Sandwiches and Mexican lunches.

TOURIST SERVICES

Tourist Office (Subdelegación Federal de Turismo), Blvd. Francisco Coss and Manuel Acuña (3-91-43 or 2-88-78).

SAN LUIS POTOSI

Most tourists pass San Luis by, but it's worth staying a day or two. There are several excellent restaurants in the city, and the colonial architecture is notable.

HOTELS

Cactus Motel, just south of Benito Juárez Circle, Hwy. 57 (2-18-71). Motel located on the main highway to Mexico City. Air-conditioned, set back away from highway, traffic noise minimal. C. Cr.

Imperial Motel, just south of Benito Juárez Circle, Hwy. 57 (2-93-11). Typical motel decor, comfortable rooms, little traffic noise, especially in rear rooms. C. Cr.

Panorama Hotel, two blocks west of main plaza, Hwy. 80. Modern ten-story downtown hotel. Comfortable rooms. Dining room on top floor with panoramic view of the city — hence the hotel name. Parking lot with guards. C. Cr.

RESTAURANTS

La Fogata, just south of Benito Juárez Circle, Hwy. 57, next door to the Cactus Motel. Northern-style grilled meats. Moderate. Cr.

La Madrileña, three blocks west of the main plaza on Calle Morelos. Spanish restaurant located across from the Hotel Filher. Paella is a house specialty. Open until 2 A.M. Moderate. Cr.

La Virreina, Blvd. Carranza 830, Hwy. 80, just past Blvd. Jiménez. One of the best restaurants in Mexico. Located in a nineteenth-century mansion. Continental cuisine. Open until midnight. Special smorgasbord on Sunday afternoon. Expensive. Cr.

TOURIST SERVICES

Tourist Office (Delegación Federal de Turismo), Av. Jardín Hidalgo 20 (2-31-43).

QUERETARO

Querétaro is a growing industrial city that still has a colonial charm about it. The city is famous for its Hill of the Bells, the execution site for Emperor Maximilian.

HOTELS

Hotel La Mansión and Hacienda Galindo, south of Querétaro (1-800-228-9000). These two hotels, which are owned by the Hyatt chain, have got to be the best roadhouses in Mexico. The famous Galindo fighting bulls were once raised on the hacienda, and an old granary has been converted to beautiful public rooms. Located just north of San Juan del Rio (noted for baskets and rebozos) and within easy driving distance of the wineries at Tequisquiapán and the ruins at Tula, the resort is a good place to spend a weekend or several days exploring the region. It can serve either as a refreshing break from a long drive or as a restorative after a busy few days in the capital. Very popular with capital residents on weekends. Call the Hyatt toll-free number (above) and ask for brochures and information. A. Cr.

TOURIST SERVICES

Tourist Office (Delegación Federal de Turismo), Escobedo 22, Querétaro (2-27-02).

CHIHUAHUA

It took the Spaniards longer to tame the Chihuahuan desert and the Apaches than it did to conquer the Aztec empire. In 1709 a settlement was finally established. Chihuahua is famous as the home of Pancho Villa, the revolutionary bandit. Villa's palace, Quinta Luz, can be seen at Calle 10 Norte 3014.

This is also the city to which tourists flock to take the famous Copper Canyon train (see the chapter **The Unique and the Random**). The Chihuahua Pacific Railroad is located at Mendez and Calle 24 (2-22-84). Hotels may allow you to leave your car for several days, at a nominal fee, in their parking garages.

HOTELS

El Dorado Hotel, Julian Cabrillo and Calle 14 (2-57-70). Located half a mile northwest of the main plaza. Very inexpensive yet pleasant. Street parking. D. Cr.
Hotel El Presidente, Calle Libertad and Segundo, on the main plaza

(2-68-83). Modern hotel with parking garage. Rooftop steakhouse. C. Cr.

Posada Tierra Blanca, Av. Independencia y Niños Héroes (5-00-00). Located two blocks north of the main plaza. Comfortable motel; most rooms air-conditioned. C. Cr.

TOURIST SERVICES

Tourist Office, (Delegación Federal de Turismo), Av. Carranza 505 (2-63-63).

DURANGO

This quiet colonial town occasionally comes to life when movie companies invade to make the latest Western. The movie sets can be visited — they are located on Hwy. 45, just north of the city.

HOTELS

Campo Mexico Courts, just south of the intersection of Hwys. 40 and 45 (1-55-60). "Campo" may be the adjective here. Pleasant, comfortable, and billed as a "super motel." Great value for the money. D. Cr.

Posada Duran, Av. 20 de Noviembre, just off the main plaza (1-24-12). This pleasant colonial-style inn is a quiet haven after a day of mountain driving. The rooms are centrally heated against those cold mountain nights. Dining room and bar. D. Cr.

TOURIST SERVICES

Tourist Office (Delegación Federal de Turismo), Palacio Municipal (1-21-39 and 1-23-83).

TORREON

Torreón, like Monterrey, is basically an industrial city with little to attract the tourist except a good night's sleep.

HOTELS

Hotel Palacío Real, Av. Valdez Carrillo and Calle Morelos (2-64-22). Located on the main plaza, this comfortable hotel offers air-conditioned rooms, a guarded parking lot, a dining room, and a sidewalk café. C. Cr.

Motel Paraíso del Desierto, on Hwy. 30 at Blvd. Independencia and Calle Jiménez. Relatively new hotel and motel with air-conditioned rooms, heated pool, garage, and restaurant (open until midnight). C. Cr.

ZACATECAS

Zacatecas is a pleasant colonial city rarely visited by tourists except those who drive through on their way to Guadalajara and points south. Originally a silver-mining center, it is rich in colonial architecture, and the cathedral is considered one of the best examples of Churrigueresque architecture in the country. The city is also in the center of the Huichol Indian lands, and there is a museum of their arts and crafts in the city.

HOTELS

Hotel Aristos Zacatecas, about two miles west of the city on Hwy. 45 (2-17-88). This motel has a commanding view of the city. Comfortable, modern rooms. Excellent dining room. B. Cr.

Motel del Bosque, two miles west on Hwy. 45; follow signs for one mile. Located on a hilltop, the motel has an excellent view of the city. Modern rooms, restaurant, and bar. C. Cr.

TOURIST SERVICES

Tourist Office (Delegación Federal de Turismo), Blvd. López Mateos 108 (2-01-70 or 2-41-70).

5

IN THE HEART OF THE COUNTRY
MEXICO CITY

When the conquistador Bernal Díaz del Castillo viewed Tenoch-titlán from the mountains surrounding Lake Texcoco, he marveled at the sight, dubbing the island city with its causeways and canals the "Venice of the New World."

Mexico City may have been the Venice of the New World back when Bernal was bent on conquering it, but it will be obvious to any visitor sitting in the back of a cab during rush hour that no one in this city of 15 million is pushing a gondola down flower-strewn canals anymore. During rush hour, every day, it is estimated some two million vehicles are on the loose in the capital. If you sit long enough in a traffic jam, pondering the thought that half of the drivers around you are cabbies, it's easy to imagine that had they been gondoliers in Moctezuma's time they might have beaten back Cortés's warships.

The only sane way to view the capital's traffic is from the Muralto Bar on the 41st floor of the Latin-American Tower downtown. The view from the city's highest building is awesome. The metropolitan area covers some 150 square miles. Include the suburbs and you have a city of 800 square miles, most of it resting on a dry lake bed that is causing the city to sink at an alarming rate—some 20 feet in this century.

Mexico City is a fitting symbol of the Third World, rich in history and pulsating with the voices of millions. But, in spite of its size,

Mexico City is one of the world's most captivating cities, a city massive, yet intimate. Bernal Díaz, if he could survive the shock of the cab ride from the airport, would find this is still a city open to exploration. In fact, a visitor equipped with a map of downtown can rely on his own two feet or an occasional subway ride to see most of the sights.

The heart of the city, as it has always been, is the Zócalo, the square where the Great Temple and Moctezuma's Palace stood. Cortés razed the temple following the battle for Tenochtitlán but retained the great plaza as the heart of his capital. (Excavations near the Zócalo have uncovered some of the debris from the Great Pyramid.) Throughout the city's history, the Zócalo has been the stage for many important events. In Indian times, the gutters ran red with the blood of victims; the Spanish priests erected the stake of the Inquisition here, bullrings and fountains decorated the square, and the cries of revolutionaries echoed off the walls of the surrounding government buildings. Now the plaza is bare, except for a huge Mexican flag flying from a tall flagpole in the center of the pavement. The traffic of Mexico City whirls all around in a never-ending cacophony of horns and rushing engines.

This is the heart of the capital, the only capital city in the world that bears the name of its country, the only major city in the world completely landlocked by mountains with no major river running nearby. Mexico City was built here because this was once Tenochtitlán, the heart of the Aztec empire. According to some historians, the Aztecs built their city here because when they were outcasts the best land belonged to more powerful tribes. So they built their *chinampas* ("floating gardens") on rafts around a small island in Lake Texcoco. Whatever the history, the myth is more popular. The Aztecs, according to legend, were told to settle on an island in a vast lake, on an island where they would see an eagle hovering above a cactus with a snake in its talons. It is that symbol, displayed on a field of white, that flies on the flag in the Zócalo.

Whether it was by vision or necessity that the Aztecs built their city here, it was an act of political shrewdness that led Cortés to raze Moctezuma's capital and build his own. All those who had looked to Tenochtitlán would look to Mexico City. Consequently, the heart of Mexico City is essentially colonial, but each time a city worker digs a ditch for a gas pipe or a telephone line, his shovel inevitably strikes the past. It was a utility crew that uncovered the great disc showing the dismembered moon goddess, unearthed near the Zócalo.

One of the best ways for you to contemplate the city's past and present is with a bottle of Hidalgo Cabernet Sauvignon from the mountains north of Mexico and a bowl of sopa azteca while sitting in the roof garden of the Hotel Majestic, overlooking the Zócalo. However, if you are not staying in the Majestic or the nearby Gran Hotel, you will have to get your Mexico City bearings before you tour the city:

Most tourists stay in one of three areas in Mexico City — along the Reforma and Avenida Juárez, the Chapultepec Park area, or in the Zona Rosa. Chapultepec Park, a vast parkland approximately three miles west of the Zócalo, is the farthest from the main plaza. The park is filled with museums, gardens, and pathways; has a hotel or two; and is bordered by old neighborhoods. It is the site of Mexico City's answer to River Oaks, Lomas de Chapultepec, where many of the capital's richest citizens live. A tree-lined boulevard, the Paseo de la Reforma, runs through the heart of the park, and as it emerges at the eastern end, it widens into an eight-lane boulevard. This boulevard, usually called the Paseo or just the Reforma, curves gently to the northeast. A few blocks east of the park and south of the Reforma is the Zona Rosa, a chic neighborhood where the streets are named after European cities and are lined with galleries, cafés, and hotels.

Continuing to the northeast, the Reforma is a prestigious address shared by embassies, banks, the exclusive University Club, government buildings, airline offices, restaurants, and hotels. Each intersection is marked by a circle and a monument — the angel of independence, Christopher Columbus, the Aztec leader Cuauhtémoc. Approximately two miles east of the park, at the circle marked by the equestrian statue of Carlos IV, Avenida Juárez intersects the Reforma. The Reforma continues northeast; Juárez leads the visitor downtown. At the intersection of a wide north-south street, San Juan de Letrán, Avenida Juárez narrows and becomes Avenida Madero. It is this narrow street that leads to the Zócalo — and the roof garden of the Hotel Majestic.

Within this three-mile journey are most of the museums, shops, hotels, and historical sites visited by tourists in Mexico City. Of course, there are things to see in the suburbs and outside the city, but this is the heart of the city. All you will need to get around is a good pair of walking shoes, a map of the city, an umbrella or raincoat for afternoon showers, and, in case you get tired of walking, a passing knowledge of the city's subway system.

Mexico City has one of the world's best subway systems. It's cheap — five tickets for five pesos; buy them in batches of five at a time — and it's efficient, running every few minutes along the three routes from 6:00 A.M. to 12:30 A.M. It's packed during rush hours but easy to use at other times. The three lines intersect, allowing you to transfer from one to another. Line 1 runs east-west; Line 2 originates in the northwest, bends around the Zócalo, and heads south; Line 3 runs north-south through the heart of the city. The stations are all marked by a name and a symbol; for example, Chapultepec Station has a grasshopper for a symbol because Chapultepec means "hill of the grasshoppers."

One subway station serves La Merced market, the huge central market located southeast of the Zócalo. (Don't try to take any large packages on the subway; they are forbidden.) If you want to walk from the Zócalo, take Pino Suárez out of the southeast corner of the

MEXICO CITY

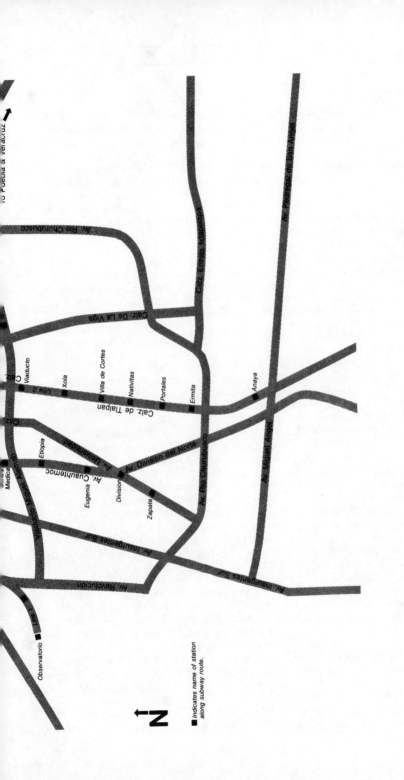

To Puebla & Veracruz

Av. Rio Churubusco

Av. Pedregal de San Ángel

Calz. Ermita, Ixtapalapa

Calz. De La Viga

Calz.
Viaducto

Line 2

Villa de Cortes

Xola

Nativitas

Portales

Calz. de Tlalpan

Ermita

Anaya

Calz.

Etiopia

Av. Universidad

Av. Río Churubusco

Av. Miguel Ángel

Viaducto Miguel Alemán

Medica

Av. Cuauhtemoc

Eugenia

Av. División del Norte

Division

Zapata

Av. Insurgentes Sur

Av. Insurgentes Sur

Av. Revolución

Observatorio

N

■ Indicates name of station along subway route.

square and turn left at Fray Servando. La Merced is only one of the many markets that dot the downtown area — there is a crafts market, an exotic food market, a flower market, and an herb market. One of the most interesting markets is La Lagunilla, located a few blocks northeast of the Zócalo near Plaza Garibaldi, the gathering place for Mexico City's mariachis. Lagunilla is a rambling collection of antique shops, which feature an assortment of genuine antiques and second-hand junk. On Sunday there is a thieves' market in the neighborhood.

If you are interested in other people's discards, go back to the Zócalo and visit the Nacional Monte de Piedad (Mountain of Pity), the national pawnshop, located on the northwest corner of the plaza. Jewelry, antiques, furniture, and family heirlooms are sold here, should their owners not claim them after a prescribed length of time.

On the north side of the Zócalo is the National Cathedral, which was started in 1573 and finished in the last century. It's a mélange of styles, with an interior more impressive than the recently renovated exterior. Inside, English-speaking guides offer their services for a small fee. Outside, small dance groups dressed in Aztec costumes often perform for the tourists. Some of the dancers are Aztec, many of whom live in poverty in the barrios of the capital. The Mexican government has attempted to discourage rural Mexicans from flocking to the capital, and new businesses are being encouraged to locate in other cities. Much of Mexico's industry is concentrated in the capital, Guadalajara, and Monterrey.

On the east side of the Zócalo is the National Palace, which was begun by Cortés in 1524 on the site where Moctezuma's palace once stood. Inside the main entrance hangs Mexico's Liberty Bell, and behind the palace is the seldom-visited museum dedicated to Benito Juárez. Two more government buildings, the old and new Municipal Palaces, stand on the south side of the square, and on the southeast corner is the national Supreme Court building with José Clemente Orozco's biting, satirical mural of the judiciary.

Avenida Madero leading out of the northwest corner of the Zócalo passes some of the best examples of colonial architecture in the capital: the Church of La Profesa, the Palace of Iturbide, and the Church and Monastery of San Francisco. At the end of Avenida Madero, just before the busy San Juan de Letrán intersects the narrow street, is a Mexico City institution, Sanborn's House of Tiles. This US-style drug-store, located on the north side of Madero, is housed in a colonial mansion once owned by the counts of Orizaba and covered with blue and white Talavera tiles. Sanborn's is a haven for US tourists and *capitalinos* alike. Maps, Band-Aids, ice cream, good coffee, US magazines and newspapers, *bolillos* covered with beans and cheese and toasted — all these and more are sold here. There are several other Sanborn's stores throughout the city.

Across the street from the House of Tiles, on the second floor of the Guardiola Building, is the Numismatic Museum, which has an extensive collection of Mexican coins, including some gold-filled quills used by the *pochteca* ("Aztec merchants").

At the corner of Madero and San Juan de Letrán is the Latin-American Tower — there's a mirador on the forty-second floor, or you can have a drink or dinner in the Muralto Bar on the floor below. Don't worry about sinking into the lake bed; the skyscraper is set on pilings deeply embedded in the rock below. Given Mexico City's altitude, the tower is the tallest building in the world.

Once you cross San Juan de Letrán, the street widens and becomes Avenida Juárez. On the north side of the street are two of the city's most prominent landmarks, the Palacio de Bellas Artes (Palace of Fine Arts) and Alameda Park. The former is a glittering example of the architecture of La Belle Epoque. Begun under the Díaz regime at the turn of the century, the Palace of Fine Arts wasn't completed until the 1940s. The palace is the home of the National Ballet Folklórico, and no one should miss an opportunity to see the company perform. The palace also houses some of the finest examples of Mexican mural painting.

Next door is Alameda Park with its huge monument to President Benito Juárez. The park was once the site of the Inquisition and at another time was off-limits to the unfashionable. The Hotel Del Prado, across the street, houses a mural by Diego Rivera called *Dream of a Sunday Afternoon in the Alameda Park*. Sit down in the lobby, order a drink, and look it over.

Two of the best government-owned crafts stores are located on Avenida Juárez, one next door to the Hotel Alameda and the other across the street. Both offer an excellent selection of crafts from throughout Mexico; the store next door to the hotel on the south side of the street has good examples of copper work from Michoacán and pottery from Guanajuato. Don't be fooled by the signs that say Museo, because both are exhibition halls and salesrooms.

As Avenida Juárez intersects with the Reforma, look at the southeast corner for the city's main tourist office. Free information, maps, and brochures are here for the asking, and there is an ever-changing exhibit and sale of various crafts.

Turning onto the Reforma, you will see many of the banks, airline offices, bus companies, travel agencies, and rental car offices you may need during your stay. Stationed along the Reforma are blue-suited police officers, wearing various national flags on their lapels. The officers may approach you and ask if you need any assistance; they enjoy speaking English and can give directions if you need them. They may also assist you in finding a cab.

The Reforma widens as it approaches the park, and several embassies and luxury hotels are located along the western portion of the boulevard. The US Embassy is located near the Monument to Independence (the golden angel atop a pillar) on the north side of the Reforma. On the south side of the Reforma is the Zona Rosa, a neighborhood of galleries, hotels, sidewalk cafés, a deli or two, restaurants of every possible ethnic cuisine, and boutiques. This is where Mexico City's smart set, students and businessmen, tourists and diplomats, gather after dark. Most of the city's best restaurants are located in the Zona Rosa, and you can dine on a different fare each night.

West of the Zona Rosa, the Reforma passes over the Periférico, the circular highway that carries most of Mexico City's commuters home. By five o'clock in the evening, traffic on the highway is bumper-to-bumper, but there are bridges leading over to the park. Chapultepec has its own Metro station, also. At the entrance to the park is the monument to Los Niños Héroes, the military cadets who defended Chapultepec Castle in the 1847 US–Mexican War. Rather than surrender, the children threw themselves from the castle's ramparts. The marble pillars and the gilded statues are located at the bottom of the hill leading to the castle. The Reforma passes through the park, and it's difficult to cross during rush hours. The National Museum of Anthropology is located on the north side of the Reforma; the castle, and other museums are to the south.

Sunday is the best day to visit the park and the castle, but visit the museums on other days when they will not be as crowded. (Most museums are closed on Monday.) On Sunday, the only day off for many Mexicans, prices are lower at the museums and the park attractions, so the working people of the city bring their families to enjoy the sights. The park is filled with children, grandmothers, balloon vendors, pushcarts with cotton candy and snow cones, fortune tellers, magicians, and puppet shows. But it is in the castle where the visitor captures the feeling of modern Mexico. This is no stately, hushed museum, a place where mute citizens file meekly in orderly fashion behind tyrannous guides. This is a people's museum: men carrying buckets of water lead their families from one exhibit to another; bags filled with tortillas and fruit are carried out on the ramparts for lunch; a curious mob gathers around the death mask of Maximilian. There are no arrows on the floor to guide the way, no signs admonishing silence, no Keep Off The Grass or Please Do Not Touch signs. Here the working men and women of modern Mexico stare at the gilded furniture of Maximilian and Carlota, inspect the portraits of the viceroys, and stand in front of the revolutionary murals, pointing out the familiar faces of the heroes to their children.

On Sunday, Chapultepec is a people's park. Once a favorite haunt of Moctezuma, now an island of greenery studded with ancient *ahuehuete* ("cypress trees") and riddled with pathways and streams, Chapultepec is one of the most beautiful parks in the world. And it is filled, like the city surrounding it, with a feast of delights for the spirit and the mind.

Mexico City is a cosmopolitan city that has grown around and eventually absorbed old Indian fishing villages, rural colonial haciendas, and Moctezuma's hunting grounds. Although modern concrete barrios, like Nezahualcóyotl, romantically named after the great poet-king, have been erected on the outskirts of the city, some of the city's colonial neighborhoods have survived and, like small towns, have a unique atmosphere of their own. Some of these suburban sights can be reached by taking the Metro; others involve cab or bus rides — ask your hotel desk clerk or bell captain for directions, and determine the cab fare before you get in.

A colonial enclave in the midst of some of the most modern neighborhoods in the city, Coyoacán is in the southern part of the city, south of the University of Mexico campus. It was the home of the conquistadores while the city was being rebuilt. The center of the neighborhood is Plaza Hidalgo and the adjacent Jardín Centenario. A sixteenth-century church stands on one side of the plaza. Several homes in the area bear the names of the conquistadores, although the actual structures date from the seventeenth century. Coyoacán has been home for several famous people including Leon Trotsky, who was assassinated here. (His home is a museum.) The Museo Frida Kahlo is located in the neighborhood. Kahlo, an artist of some note, was married to Diego Rivera, one of Mexico's great muralists. Their home, which had been Kahlo's since childhood, is located at the corner of Londres and Allende and is filled with works and mementos of both artists. (For more examples of their work, visit the National Museum of Modern Art in Chapultepec Park.) A small museum of interest to US visitors is the Churubusco Museum at General Anaya and 20 de Agosto (streets in Mexico are often named after historical dates of importance). Housed in an old monastery, the Churubusco features relics of the 1847 US–Mexican War.

Like Coyoacán, San Angel is a colonial suburb filled with old churches and homes built by the colonial elite. Located in the southwest quadrant of the city, San Angel is a popular tourist spot on Saturdays, when the Bazar Sábado, an art show and sale, is held in the heart of the quarter. The show, which features a variety of traditional and avant-garde works, is held in an old mansion on the west side of San Jacinto Plaza. After shopping or browsing at the bazaar, it is customary to relax over lunch at the famous San Angel Inn, a restaurant operated in what was once the main house of a huge hacienda. The inn is located at Palmas 50, and the patio is a favorite spot for lunch. Other sights you will want to see in San Angel include El Carmen Convent and Church — you can buy reproductions of colonial art in the restored convent, all printed under the auspices of the National Institute of Anthropology and History. San Jacinto Plaza is the heart of the neighborhood and was the fashionable place to live in colonial times. On the west side of the plaza, one home bears a bronze plaque commemorating the Irish martyrs of St. Patrick's Battalion. These men, the plaque states, gave their lives in the "unjust" invasion of Mexico by the United States in 1847. Members of the battalion were from San Patricio, Texas, and when the US captured them they were tried as deserters — 23 were hanged and 24 were dishonorably discharged and branded on the cheek with a *D*.

UNIVERSITY OF MEXICO

Located just south of San Angel, atop a lava bed, the University of Mexico has an outdoor gallery of work by Mexico's best modern artists. The library is covered with a mosaic mural by Juan O'Gorman depicting the history of Mexico. David Siqueiros's mural, showing the students of Mexico going out into the countryside to spread knowledge, graces the exterior of the Administration Building, and Diego Rivera's work dominates the Olympic Stadium. The university's botanical gardens, south of the stadium, include large collections of orchids and cacti. West of the university, built on the same lava bed, is the Jardines del Pedregal, a neighborhood of remarkable homes, built during the 1940s and owned by some of the capital's most affluent citizens.

XOCHIMILCO

You might consider combining a trip to the Floating Gardens of Xochimilco with a tour of the university. Xochimilco is south of the campus on the road to Cuernavaca. The somewhat jaded gardens are the remnants of what was once a remarkable transportation grid, a network of canals that served the old city of Tenochtitlán. In addition to serving as transportation routes, the canals were utilized for agricultural purposes. *Chinampas* ("floating gardens") were covered with soil and planted and floated in the waters of Lake Texcoco, providing fresh fruit, flowers, and vegetables for the nearby cities. Now tourists and *capitalinos* on a Sunday outing can take a ride in a flower-bedecked (sometimes plastic flowers) boat through the canals.

THE SHRINE

The Basilica of Our Lady of Guadalupe is the most revered spot in all the Americas for Catholics in the New World, for it is believed to be here, in 1531, that the Virgin revealed herself to a poor Indian named Juan Diego. On three separate occasions, the Virgin appeared to Diego who, after the first visit, told the bishop of his vision. The bishop did not believe him until Diego returned with his cape filled with roses; as the roses tumbled out of the cape, all present saw that the image of the brown-skinned Virgin had been imprinted on his robe. That image remains on the cape hanging in the basilica, its creation a mystery unsolved by scientists. The picturesque old basilica is slowly sinking into the lake bed, and a circular, modernistic shrine has been built next door. Thousands flock here especially at Christmas to seek the intervention of the Virgin. To visit the shrine, drive out Insurgentes Norte, turning west on San Juan de Aragon, or take the Metro to the end of Line 3 and walk several blocks to the shrine. You might combine a trip to the shrine with a visit to Tlatelolco, the twin city of Tenochtitlán. The center of Tlatelolco is the Plaza of the Three Cultures, named for the three examples of architecture represented there: a small pyramid, the sixteenth-century Church of Santiago Tlatelolco, and the modern Tlatelolco Housing Project. The College of Holy Cross also stands there. It was once a school operated by Fray Bernardino de Sahagún for the sons of Aztec nobles, and it was here, with their assistance, that Sahagún compiled his history of the Aztecs. To get to the plaza, take San Juan de Letrán north from Avenida Juárez, or take Metro Line 3 and get off at the Tlatelolco station.

THE BULLFIGHTS

The *corrida de toros* ("bullfight") is an intrinsic element of Mexican culture and one little understood by the gringo. To the aficionado it is not a sport but rather something akin to an artistic happening, a work of art performed rather than painted. A corrida is theater and art; even the costumes worn by the players were created by master artist Francisco José de Goya y Lucientes.

A corrida is not for everyone; cultural barriers and sensitivities preclude some from watching, but any serious visitor to Mexico, intent on exploring the culture and national psyche, should attend a corrida.

The term *bullfight* is misleading; it is not a fight, and the Spanish term *corrida de toros* means "the running of the bulls." It is a spectacle that has its origins in the Dark Ages of Spain. The bulls are the descendants of the Auroc, the savage wild bulls that roamed the forests of the Iberian peninsula long before Roman times. Historians note that the Celtic Iberians danced before the bulls to show their valor, killing them at the last minute with an ax. As each wave of invaders came to the peninsula, the spectacle surrounding the corrida was enhanced — the Visigoths were famed for their strength before the bulls; the Muslims brought expertise on horseback. The spectacles were held in Spain's ancient Roman amphitheaters.

Legend says Rodrigo Díaz de Bivar, El Cid, was the first Castilian to lance a bull on horseback. During the Middle Ages and until the eighteenth century, it was the custom of the nobles to lance the bulls from horseback; however, alarmed by the deaths caused by the corridas, the Church forbade nobles to participate, thus resulting in the creation of a new class of toreros, men from the lower classes who rose to great fame as matadors. Because the lance was considered an aristocratic weapon, these new toreros used the short sword, the *estoque,* and the short cape, the *muleta.* In the subsequent two hundred years little has changed in the corrida except for the refining of the style and manner of approaching the bull.

Bulls are raised on special farms (*ganaderías*) exclusively for the bullring. Young ones are tested, and those showing good breeding attributes are put out to stud; the rest are run through a series of preliminary tests to determine if they are destined for the ring or the slaughterhouse. Bulls only enter the ring once; a particularly brave bull, a bull with heart, may survive and live out his days as a stud on the ranch. However, it is the bull's destiny, aficionados declare, to meet his fate in the ring. Bulls also have good memories and would be of little use in a second corrida. They are color blind, and the fact that the muleta is pink is of no interest to the bull at all.

Mexico City has one of the largest bullrings in the world. The Plaza de Toros on Insurgentes Sur seats 50,000 people, and the formal season begins in December, lasting for three months. During the rest of the year, the novilleros, apprentice toreros, appear in the plaza. Only when a novillero has passed a test in the ring, his *alternativa*, can he call himself a matador.

In Mexico City corridas begin precisely at 4:30 P.M. every Sunday. The best seats are those in *la sombra* ("the shade"). If you are not an aficionado, refrain from any comment about the corrida; it's considered very gauche for foreigners to express their feelings about bullfighting in public. The day's spectacle begins with a parade as the cuadrillas, the troops of toreros, march into the ring. Each cuadrilla consists of banderilleros (those who place the banderillas ("stakes") in the bull's shoulders), picadors (toreros on horseback), and the matadors. The banderilleros wear no gold braid on their costumes, distinguishing them from the matadors. The parade is led by the *alguaciles* ("bailiffs"). The president of the corrida, usually the mayor or another politician, tosses the keys to the bull pen to an *alguacile*, who prepares to let the first bull into the ring.

A corrida is divided into three *tercios* ("stages"). The first cuadrilla remains in the ring while the others leave, and the bull is allowed to pass into the ring. As he runs through the gate, a rosette showing the colors of the ranch is attached to his neck.

Before the first *tercio*, a banderillero tests the bull to see if he favors one horn over the other; then the matador enters to make a series of preliminary passes called *quites*. The most basic move is the *verónica*, a sweeping motion executed as close to the horns as possible.

The first *tercio* begins when a horn sounds and the picadors enter the ring and attempt to lance the bull in the shoulder muscles. Between the first and second *tercios*, the matadors who are performing that day take turns with the bull. The second stage is taken up by the banderilleros, who charge the bull, planting the banderillas in the bull's shoulders to weaken the shoulder muscles and lower the head.

The final *tercio* is called the "hour of truth." The matador first asks permission to dedicate the bull, and when such permission is granted, he tosses his *montera* ("hat") to the person being honored. The *estoque* is hidden beneath the cape, and after a series of passes, each close to the bull's horns, the matador plunges the *estoque* into the bull's neck. Done properly, this last act severs the bull's aorta and he dies instantly.

If the matador has performed well, he is given one ear; two ears denote an excellent performance; two ears and a tail mean his performance was superlative. The bull's spinal cord is severed in the ring and the carcass dragged away. Usually, the meat is sold outside the plaza.

The corrida is not a fight between two forces but a test of the man. Aficionados say the bull knows he is destined to die, and the toreros themselves face danger at every minute. Almost half of the major matadors in the last two and a half centuries have died in the ring. The corrida is not a tourist attraction.

BEYOND THE CAPITAL: DAY-TRIPPING

If you tire of city life and long to get away from the hubbub of the capital, a wide selection of day trips can be made either by bus or rental car in the region around Mexico City. Several tollways lead from the city to nearby towns; however, the older highways offer the most scenic views through the ring of mountains surrounding the capital.

TOLUCA

It's a picturesque drive through the pine-covered mountains to Toluca, at 8,760 feet the highest city in Mexico. Located some sixty miles west of the capital, Toluca is famed for its Friday market, although you can find good buys here any day of the week. Look for the bulky white sweaters made in this area (you will probably need one in this cool mountain city), pottery from nearby Metepec, and rebozos from Tenancingo, a village at the foot of the nearby extinct volcano, Nevada de Toluca. The market is located on the eastern outskirts of the city. On the main square, in the center of Toluca, is the Museum of Popular Arts, one of those government-owned stores that exhibit the best examples of the local crafts — this is a good place to visit before you go to the market. West of the city on Hwy. 15 is the popular spa of San José Purúa, and south of Toluca, on Hwy. 55, is another spa favored by *capitalinos*, Ixtapan de la Sal. About eighty miles southwest of Toluca is the popular weekend resort Valle de Bravo, located in a national park. Many residents of the capital go on weekend retreats to this lakeside town, and it has become something of an artists' colony. Take Hwy. 15 to Toluca and then follow the signs to Valle de Bravo.

THE VOLCANOES

There was a time when the twin snowcapped peaks of Popocatépetl and Iztaccihuatl could be seen from the capital, but now it is a rare sight in the smog-plagued city. Usually called "Popo" and the "Sleeping Lady," the two volcanoes are both over 17,000 feet high. The government has created the Izta-Popo National Park, an unspoiled area just a short ride from the capital. Take Hwy. 190 (not the tollway, 190D) toward Puebla, turn right onto Hwy. 115, and follow the signs to the park.

TEXCOCO

It was in Texcoco in 1521 that Hernán Cortés assembled his warships that had been built from logs his men and their Indian followers had hauled across the mountains from Tlaxcala, and it was from Texcoco, then a lakeside town, that the assault on Tenochtitlán was launched. Cortés had been ejected from the city the year before, but in four months he managed to seize and raze the capital. The lake bed is dry now, and the Mexican government is trying to reclaim the land in an attempt to thwart the dust storms that plague the area. Texcoco is a city of 70,000 and a popular spot on Sundays and Mondays when the market is at its busiest. There's no direct road across the lake bed from the capital, although one is planned. Take Hwy. 190 toward Puebla, turn north at Los Reyes, and drive into the city. Just north of Texcoco is the small town of Chiconcuac, famed for its textiles.

PUEBLA

Once you are clear of city traffic, it's a scenic three-hour drive to Puebla through some of the most impressive mountain scenery in Mexico. There are two routes: Hwy. 190D, a toll road; the other, the old highway, Hwy. 190, which is slower and more picturesque. Puebla is the place to go for onyx and Talavera tiles. The main market, El Mercado Victoria, is four blocks north of the central zócalo. The tile factories are located along a street named 4 Poniente near the market. Most of them will ship tiles to the United States. And there is an artists' district, Barrio de las Artistas, located on Calle 8 Norte just off 4 Poniente. For lunch try the local specialty *mole poblano* at either the Hotel Royalty, the Hostería de los Angeles, or Charlie's China Poblano — all downtown. (For an in-depth look at the colonial city of Puebla, see the chapter **Mexico of the Colonials.**)

THE CAVES OF CACAHUAMILPA

The spectacular caves of Cacahuamilpa are one of Mexico's best-kept secrets. They are located about a hundred miles south of the capital in a national park. Take Hwy. 95 or Hwy. 95D to Cuernavaca and then Hwy. 421 to the park. The guided tour takes four hours, and there is a restaurant at the entrance.

TLAXCALA

Tlaxcala is the smallest state in Mexico and the home of Cortés's most faithful allies in the war against Tenochtitlán. The state capital, also called Tlaxcala, is a good place to buy rugs and serapes. In several of the nearby towns and villages, notably Villa San Martín and Texmelucan, excellent textiles are made. Take Hwy. 150 east out of the capital and turn north on Hwy. 119.

CHOLULA

Cholula is a city of churches; one is built atop a huge mound that is thought to have been an immense pyramid or platform in pre-Hispanic times. Tunnels running through the mound are open to the public, and the walls are covered with frescoes. Cholula was the site of a massacre by Cortés, who was alarmed by reports from his Indian mistress, Doña Marina (La Malinche), that the locals were gong to rise up against him. Take Hwy. 190 east toward Puebla and turn south at Hwy. 117 just before reaching Puebla.

TEPOTZOTLAN

The Church of San Francisco de Javier in the town of Tepotzotlán is, undoubtedly, one of the most magnificent churches in a land of magnificent churches. The adjoining monastery has been restored and houses the National Museum of Colonial Arts and Handicrafts. During the Christmas season a *pastorela*, a medieval Spanish passion play, is held on the patio of the church. Travel agencies in the capital sell tickets to the popular event. Dinner is included. A restaurant on the patio is open for lunch every day. Take Hwy. 57D, a toll road, north out of the city; watch for the Tepotzotlán signs, about 25 miles beyond the city limits.

THE PYRAMIDS

The most popular day trip from the capital is an outing to the ancient city of Teotihuacán, located northeast of the city in a wide valley. Plan to spend a full day at the site and brush up on your archaeology before you go. Several smaller sites surrounding the ancient city are worth including in your visit. Take Hwy. 85D, the fast toll road, out of the city or the slower old road, Hwy. 85, which passes the sixteenth-century Monastery of Acolman, about six miles south of the ancient city. From October to May there is a sound and light show at the pyramids each night at seven in English — there's a later show in Spanish. Travel agencies in the city sell tickets to the show. A word of warning: many curbside tour companies operate in the capital offering day trips to the pyramids — check at the tourist office, your hotel desk, or a respectable travel agency before signing on. Guided tours are available at the site.

TAXCO AND CUERNAVACA

Unfortunately, too many tourists sign up for one-day visits to Cuernavaca or Taxco and when they get to these colonial havens of peace and perfect weather realize that they could easily spend the rest of their lives there. Both towns are unmatched for their beauty and atmosphere. (The two towns are profiled in the chapter **Mexico of the Colonials.**) Cuernavaca is larger and has several restaurants and hotels that rank among the best in the world; Taxco is smaller, a maze of cobbled streets and geranium-laden balconies. Both towns make an ideal getaway from the capital, a place to unwind for those few final days of your trip before you fly back to the humdrum of the real world.

Both towns are easily reached from the capital, either by car or bus, and you won't need a car to get around once you are there. In Taxco, it's hard to maneuver anything larger than a bicycle anyway. However, you may want to rent a car in the capital so that you can stay in one town and still visit the other. Make your hotel reservations well in advance.

How to choose between the two? Taxco is for strolling, shopping for silver, sitting in Paco's Bar or Berta's, and watching the tour groups come into town. Cuernavaca is filled with sidewalk cafés, old posadas equipped with tennis courts and swimming pools, rambling gardens, and rich gringos. In Taxco, you go to bed early and listen to the local brass band as it practices for a fiesta; in Cuernavaca, you spend the afternoon in a café, wander to the market to buy some huaraches, and dine late. Cuernavaca is larger, busier, while Taxco is quiet and is certainly one of the most beautiful towns in all Mexico. Stay in one and visit the other, but do stay in one of them. To get there, take Hwy. 95D, a toll road, out of the city, or take the more leisurely Hwy. 95. Both highways go to Cuernavaca, but the toll road bypasses Taxco. The road to Taxco is very scenic but narrow and full of curves. Cuernavaca is approximately 100 miles south of the capital; Taxco is another 75 miles beyond that.

BOCADITOS

In a giant metropolis of 15 million people, it's not always easy for the visitor to find the best spots in town to relax and unwind. To help you feel at home in the capital, we've assembled a list of *Texas Monthly* favorites, including restaurants, hotels, museums, and retreats. For more information, check the Mexico City listings that follow in this chapter.

The best "I can't eat another enchilada—I need meat" restaurant: **The Picadilly Pub, Copenhague 23, in Mexico City's Zona Rosa.** This popular café-pub is located on the Copenhague pedestrian mall, a narrow cobbled street just off the Paseo de la Reforma. Popular with businessmen for lunch and crowded at night, it serves British specialties including authentic, outrageously expensive (but good) Scottish salmon, steak and kidney pies, an excellent *filet moutarde*, London grill complete with English sausages, and Yorkshire pudding. The owner's wife is English, and the atmosphere reminiscent of a London pub.

The best "Let's have another bottle of wine for lunch" restaurant: **The rooftop, open-air restaurant in the Hotel Majestic, on the Zócalo.**

If it's midsummer, beware. The temperature inversions may keep the fumes from Mexico City's two million vehicles trapped over the city, but on a clear day this is one of the best spots to watch the traffic fly around the heart of Mexico, the Zócalo. Right across from the government offices, the restaurant attracts politicians and bureaucrats during those long, leisurely lunches favored south of the border. Try the sopa azteca.

The best gringo hotel hangout: **The Geneve** is where you will find Texans, not the Highland Park–River Oaks set, but UT professors, Garden Club members from Abilene, and young professionals with a taste for the quaint and inexpensive. The Geneve is something of an institution, and it has a loyal following. The Geneve is in the heart of the Zona Rosa at Londres 130.

The best tequila high: **Margaritas in the Muralto Bar** on the forty-first floor of the Latino-Americano Tower, the highest building in Mexico and tallest in the world, considering the capital's altitude. Sit and watch the sunset, the traffic jams, and the jets landing at the airport. Don't worry about earthquakes—the tower is anchored in the rock bed. There is also a restaurant in the Muralto, but the food is expensive and not as good as that at more down-to-earth places. Keep the plastic swizzle sticks as souvenirs.

The best Mexico City bagel: **The Kinaret deli** at the corner of Génova and Hamburgo in the Zona Rosa—it's always packed.

The best corn fungus crepes: Try 'em. *Crepas de huitlacoche,* a Mexico City delicacy, are served in style at the **San Angel Inn, Palmas 50, in the suburb of San Angel.** The corn fungus is gathered from the ears at a certain time of year, wrapped in a delicate crepe and sauced. The San Angel is a must stop for any serious gourmand interested in exploring the intricacies of Mexican cuisine.

The best retreat from all that noise: **The suburb of San Angel** where on Saturday you can enjoy the Bazar Sábado, an arts and crafts show featuring traditional and modern work by some of Mexico's finest artists. There's a small Indian market nearby and several quiet parks and courtyards.

The best place to find fellow gringos: Aside from the US Embassy on the Reforma, it's **Sanborn's House of Tiles on Avenida Madero,** near the intersection of San Juan de Letrán and Avenida Juárez. Sanborn's features an American-style soda fountain, US newspapers and magazines, paperback books in both English and Spanish, drugstore essentials, and an excellent selection of maps—look for the blue and yellow Patria maps.

The best market: **The Sunday thieves' market in Lagunilla, Calle Comonfort,** adjacent to Plaza Garibaldi off San Juan de Letrán. From 10 A.M. to late afternoon, the streets are filled with vendors selling junque, antiques (both authentic and reproduced), black-market items like Swiss cheese, and items of dubious origination (i.e., stolen). There are also several good secondhand junk shops in the area.

The best museum off the tourist track: **The Museo de la Ciudad de Mexico** (the Mexico City Museum) is located in a mansion built by the counts de Santiago de Calimaya at Pino Suárez 30. Open Tuesday through Sunday from 9:00 A.M. to 7:30 P.M., the museum features several exhibits depicting the history of the capital.

The best maguey worms in town: You can settle for good seafood instead at **Prendes, the restaurant at 16 de Septiembre 10** that is popular with celebrities and businessmen, tourists and politicians. If you are brave, try the fried maguey worms—those are the little worms you find in the mescal bottles.

The best time to go: Mexico is alive and kicking all year; however, in the summer months the pollution levels do become dangerously high on certain days. Be prepared to move on to greener pastures if your eyes begin to sting and your shirt collar is black by the end of the day.

AROUND MEXICO CITY

VITAL STATISTICS

Climate. The high altitude spares the capital from the torrid temperatures commonly found at the same latitude. Summer days can be warm, though daytime temperatures year-round hover in the 70s. Nights are sometimes chilly as temperatures dip into the low 50s or 40s. The city is ringed by mountains once visible from the city's center but now usually blocked from view by the city's pollution. In the summer, light rain showers or an occasional thunderstorm clears the air. Pollution does cause temperature inversions during the summertime, and persons suffering from respiratory problems are advised to leave the city.

Population. In 1980, the population was estimated at 15 million.

Altitude. 7,350 feet.

State. Distrito Federal (DF).

City phone code. 5. (Residents of Canada and the United States may dial Mexico City directly by dialing 1-905 followed by the local number. This method is shorter than the conventional international dialing method that may be used also—011 (international access code), 52 (country code), 5 (the city access code), and the local number.

HOTELS

Camino Real, Mariano Escobedo 700 (545-6960). An example of Mexico's modern, concrete block architecture, the rooms here are surprisingly cozy once you're past the huge, stark halls and large public rooms. It is easy to get lost in the maze of restaurants, coffee shops, a disco, boutiques, and convention rooms. Tennis and swimming facilities are available. There is a complete wing of luxuriously appointed two-floor suites clustered around a pool, where visitors are so isolated they forget they are staying in Mexico City. Close to major shopping areas and the Polanco residential district. A. Cr.

El Presidente Chapultepec, Campos Eliseos 218 (250-7700). The newest large hotel in Mexico City, this one is now a landmark skyscraper in the Polanco neighborhood. A modern structure towering over Chapultepec Park, it is located close to the Anthropology Museum. Inside is like a small city — different levels with bars, restaurants, coffee shops, Maxim's of Paris upstairs, and one level devoted to boutiques. The halls are quiet and the rooms decorated with minimum-fuss modern. The rooms were planned for the medium price range; the downstairs with its luxurious public rooms was tacked on later. For afternoon tea, a string quartet plays in the bar; at night the tempo changes to jazz and the place swarms with singles. A. Cr.

El Presidente Zona Rosa, Hamburgo 135 (525-0000). Recently remodeled, the Zona Rosa Presidente is not as deluxe as the one in Chapultepec, but it still offers numerous creature comforts for travelers as well as the advantage of a central location. There are several bars: one with nightly entertainment, one for quiet talks, and a lobby bar by an indoor pool. Rooms and suites have televisions and refrigerators. A. Cr.

Galeria Plaza, Hamburgo 195 (286-5444). The lovely new ultramodern member of Mexico's Camino Real chain and a cousin to the Galleria Plaza and Houston Oaks in Houston. The rooms are tastefully done in earth tones and wicker; the service is very attentive. In the Zona Rosa but on a relatively quiet street on the edge of a residential area not far from Chapultepec Park. A. Cr.

Gran Hotel de la Ciudad de Mexico, 16 de Septiembre 82 (510-4040). For fans of turn-of-the-century architecture, this hotel is one of the most visually pleasing in Mexico City. An ornate stained-glass ceiling covers the central lobby, where you travel to your floor in open cage elevators. The large rooms have comfortable old-style furnishings. B. Cr.

Hernán Cortés, Av. Hidalgo 85 (585-0322). A lovely patio is the heart of this refurbished eighteenth-century Dominican hostelry. Authentic colonial touches make the setting relaxing and picturesque. The rooms are nicely furnished. C. Cr.

Hotel Alameda, Juárez 50 (518-0620). A well-located, modern hotel with pool and exercise facilities, restaurants, coffee shops, and bars. B. Cr.

Hotel Aristos, Paseo de la Reforma 276 (533-0560). A lively hotel, now on a pedestrian mall filled with outdoor restaurants. Bars, a disco, restaurants, and coffee shop. The rooms are modern, and there is a sun terrace and a sauna. B. Cr.

Hotel Bristol, Rio Pánuco and Rio Sena at Plaza Necaxa 17 (533-6060). A smaller, modern hotel with a Denny's restaurant on the ground floor. Close to business areas, in the Cuauhtémoc district, the rooms are comfortable and modern. B. Cr.

Hotel CanCun, Donato Guerra 24 (566-6488). Small rooms, a moderately priced restaurant, and lots of quiet. The rooms come with spartan furnishings and television. C. Cr.

Hotel Casa Blanca, Lafragua No. 7 (566-3211). A pleasant, air-conditioned, reasonably priced businessmen's hotel situated just off the Reforma between the Alameda area and the Pink Zone. The kitchen is adequate and the service attentive. There's a roof garden with a bar and a small swimming pool. B. Cr.

Hotel Del Prado, Av. Juárez 70 (518-0040). With its elegant entrance and a spectrum of shops and boutiques on the lower arcade, the Del Prado is one of the city's older hotels. It's now totally remodeled, and the special attraction is the artwork by Mexican artists. The Diego Rivera painting *Dream of a Sunday Afternoon in the Alameda Park* now hanging in the lobby was once kept behind a curtain in the dining room after public furor about its antireligious overtones. B. Cr.

Hotel Fiesta Palace, Paseo de la Reforma 80 (566-5655). Another of the large hotel "cities," the Fiesta Palace has the usual mix of restaurants, coffee shops, and bars with the added feature of a nightlife that really swings. In fact, many visitors say that the nightlife is the true attraction, since the rooms are well worn, including patches of threadbare carpets. Rooms are equipped with cable American television and refrigerators. A crowded and busy hotel, the favorite of many charter groups and tours. A. Cr.

Hotel Geneve, Londres 130 (525-1500). Visitors come back time and again for the unassuming appearance and good service of this older hotel. Under new management and recently redecorated. The dining room is now located in the lobby and a glass-roofed bar filled with plants connects two wings of the hotel. Rooms have spartan furnishings. You can find small, inexpensive rooms here, but they cannot be reserved in advance. B. Cr.

Hotel Maria Cristina, Lerma 31 (546-9880). The older Spanish architecture also includes a lovely and peaceful garden behind the hotel walls. The hotel itself reflects the toned down calm formerly found in Mexico City, and the service is very attentive. The rooms are charming and recently remodeled. B. Cr.

Hotel Montejo, Paseo de la Reforma 240 (511-9840). The Montejo blends into the buildings along the Reforma so well that the colonial-style building is easy to miss. The colonial theme is carried throughout down to the details of the pleasing medium-sized rooms and the rooftop dining room and bar. C. Cr.

Majestic, Madero 73 (521-8600). This old-fashioned hotel with its muted elegance is near the Zócalo. The marble floors and fixtures and the personable service hark to years gone by. A charming roof restaurant looks over the Zócalo; on Sundays, mariachi music and a generous buffet bring it alive. Rooms are comfortable with few frills. C. Cr.

María Isabel Sheraton, Paseo de la Reforma 325 (525-9060). In the heart of the Zona Rosa, the María Isabel is a longtime favorite of visitors who want to be within walking distance of the shopping and restaurant area and most sights. Has a rooftop swimming pool, ground floor shops, a small movie theater, cafeterias, restaurants, and bars. Comfortably decorated rooms. A. Cr.

Park Villa Motor Hotel, Gomez Pedraza 68 (515-5245). Drive your car right to your comfortable room. The pleasant garden with café, mildly spicy Mexican food, and pleasant service (all hidden behind concrete walls) make this a real find for tourists who want to drive their own cars. The motel looks across the street to Chapultepec Park and is within a ten-minute subway ride or drive to major sight-seeing areas. The Juanacatlán subway stop is just a few blocks away. C. N.

Ritz, Madero 30 (518-1340). A quiet sophistication has settled over the Ritz, where large comfortable rooms provide peace from the teaming downtown. Large suites and a penthouse are available. Also a good restaurant and a bar with live entertainment. C. Cr.

Vasco de Quiroga, Londres 15 (546-2614). From the small lobby to the small but cheery rooms, the Vasco de Quiroga wraps you in its cozy atmosphere. The restaurant/bar is usually empty except at mealtime, and customers often chat with the waiters there. B. Cr.

RESTAURANTS

Bar Tijuana, Heroes Ferrocarrileros and Buena Vista. This seafood restaurant offers typical luncheonette decor, complete with plastic-covered chairs, but looks prove unimportant once you try the food. You can choose practically any fish or seafood from a glass display and have it prepared to your taste. A Spanish-seafood lover took us here our first time and introduced us to squid *bilbaína* style, served hot and sprinkled with olive oil, salt, and paprika. Bar. Inexpensive. Cr.

Bellinghausen, Londres 95 (525-8738). The uptown version of downtown's Prendes (see below). The *filete chemita* is a house specialty, a Mexican cut from the heart of beef loin, grilled to taste. This is also one of the few places where you can find brook trout in Mexico. Patrons make their choice from a tank full of swimming fish. Full bar, but the best choice here is the draft beer. Moderate. Cr.

Café de Tacuba, Tacuba 28 (512-8482). Of the old downtown cafés, this is one of the ones with the most tradition and atmosphere. The *mole*, enchiladas, and soups are tasty. The *pozole* is a heavy blend of corn and pork soup topped with cabbage and radishes. The enchiladas in *pipián* sauce, pumpkin seeds, and chile are another interesting specialty. At night sweet breads, French-style hot chocolate, or even richer Spanish-style hot chocolate is a delightful treat. Bar. Inexpensive to moderate. Cr.

Café Viena, Amberes 4 (511-3486). Little effort has gone into the decor, but much care goes into the preparation of German food and kosher sandwiches. The hot pastrami and the chopped liver with cream cheese come piled high or spread thick on white or dark breads. The full meals are filling—large servings of stuffed cabbage or pepper, or goulash. Passing up the pastry cart requires Herculean willpower. Give in and order *cappuccino* or espresso. Bustling at lunch. Beer only. Moderate. Cr.

Chalet Suizo, Niza 37 (511-8807). A small place with a limited menu, this restaurant does very well with what it serves. The fondue is thick and cheesy, and we recommend the German sausage with sauerkraut. Bar. Moderate. Cr.

Champs-Elysées, Amberes 1 (514-0450). Currently one of the more popular restaurants in the city, this French restaurant was favored by Carmen López Portillo for lunch. The exiled Shah of Iran was known to drive in from Cuernavaca for a meal here. Several floors for dining and cocktails, including a balcony overlooking Paseo de la Reforma, are usually jammed for lunch and dinner. Bar. Reservations. Expensive. Cr.

Cicero's, Londres 195 (525-6530). One of the more recent additions to Mexico City's expensive restaurants, Cicero's has a poolroom where patrons sip champagne. Decorations include an elaborate mix of San Francisco stained glass windows, greenery, high ceilings, and mirrors everywhere. The crowd ranges from couples having intimate dinners to celebrities who show up here to be seen. As for the food, the steaks are a good choice; and although the seafood platter sounds pedestrian, it is anything but. Cocktail lounge. Reservations. Expensive. Cr.

Circulo del Sureste, Lucerna 12 (535-2704). A favorite haunt of Mexican gourmands who enjoy the specialties of the Yucatán peninsula. A typical meal might begin with Cenote Sagrado, a honey drink, and end with Xtabentun, a Yucatecan liqueur. In between, try the barbecued pig or the octopus in its own ink. Moderate to expensive. Cr.

Daikoku, Rio Pánuco 170 (514-8257) and Michoacán 25, Colonia Condesa (584-8557). Frequented by Mexico City's Japanese community, the Rio Pánuco restaurant is next door to the Japanese embassy. The sobas and ramen soups are served steaming and have to be slurped in the true Japanese style. Customers prepare a large number of dishes themselves on individual grills—frying the meat, fish, and vegetables to taste and dipping the results into a soya-based sauce. Beer only. Moderate. Cr.

Da Raffaello, Londres 123 (525-1343). We have returned time and again to eat *ostiones rasurados,* making a whole meal out of several plates of them. These oysters arrive on the half shell with onions, oil, salt, and Tabasco and Worcestershire sauces piled on top. After oysters or the sliced abalone, it is easy to overlook the Italian specialties, including remarkable canneloni and spaghetti. The pastry cart holds excellent cakes for dessert. Bar. Moderate. Cr.

Delmonico's, Londres 87 (514-7003). This elegant restaurant offers spareribs in a hearty and tangy sauce. The T-bone and sirloin steaks are unfailingly well cut and prepared. For dessert try the baked Alaska. Recently the restaurant added breakfast to its lunch and dinner menu. Large Sunday brunch. Bar. Reservations at lunch and evening. Expensive. Cr.

Denny's, various locations. Just like back home. Burgers and fries, hotcakes and sausage. All locations are open 24 hours a day. Inexpensive. N.

Estoril, Génova 75 (511-6970). Dine in understated surroundings and admire the paintings offered for sale throughout. The menu selection is limited but excellent. The escargot a la bourguignonne is superb, and the red snapper comes stuffed with eels. Another house specialty is the filet covered with morille sauce. For dessert, try the almond meringue. Bar. Reservations recommended. Moderate to expensive. Cr.

Flor de Lis, Huichapan 21, Colonia Condesa. A little off the main tourist track, this restaurant is a favorite among grandparents who want to take their grandchildren out for Mexican food and ice cream. Frequent patrons say that service and food have slipped over the past few years, but even so it still rates high. Tamales are the house specialty. The enchiladas in green chile or *mole* sauce are not overly *picante* and are topped with cream and cheese. Lunch and dinner. Inexpensive. N.

Fonda del Recuerdo, Bahía de las Palmas 39-A, Colonia Anzures (545-7260). Both the food and the mariachi music here are of the Veracruz variety. The red snapper *à la veracruzana* with jalapeños, olives, and tomatoes endures as the state's specialty. Moderate to expensive. Cr.

Fonda del Refugio, Liverpool 166 (528-5823). On our first visit here we enjoyed a delightful and tasty Mexican lunch. The chiles rellenos were covered with a delicious green chile sauce and thick melted cheese, and the mixed platter offered the full spectrum of enchiladas, tacos, and guacamole. The *puntas de filete,* tenderloin tips, were tender in a toned down chile sauce. But on another occasion we found that the *chiles en nogada,* a Mexican specialty only available in late summer and early fall, were not up to par with the rest of the menu. Mexican decor and music make for an appealing atmosphere. Lunch and dinner. Moderate. Cr.

Fouquet's de Paris, Hotel Camino Real, Mariano Escobedo 700 (531-7279). Another of the well-known and frequented French restaurants in the city, this one stages a French chef's fortnight twice a year. Write or call to find out the dates when chefs from different regions of France descend on Fouquet's to cook up a French storm. On our last trip, the *sepes à la provenzal* proved admirable. Fish specialties include red snapper and sole. An extensive wine selection. Closed Sundays. Reservations. Expensive. Cr.

Hacienda de los Morales, Av. Vazquez de Mella 525 (540-3235). The opportunity to see the inside of this restored hacienda—a private residence until a few decades ago—draws us back repeatedly. The food is excellent, especially the *mole*, an elaborate sauce blended from ten different chiles, nuts, tomatoes, and chocolate, and served over chicken breasts. Two other specialties include Rocky Mountain oysters in green chile sauce and *tournedos* covered with pepper sauce. We also like the Mexican desserts, including *cocada*, a sweet coconut cream. Music by mariachis. Valet parking. Reservations required. Expensive. Cr.

Happy's Pizza, Tolstoi 17. A cheerful place favored by teenagers and families on weekends, featuring pizza with a thick crust and lots of cheese, but scant on the tomato sauce as is the Mexican style. Beer and soft drinks served in icy mugs, and deep booths where you can spend the afternoon talking. Inexpensive. N.

Hotel Majestic, Zócalo (521-8600). The rooftop bar and terrace restaurant is a popular luncheon spot with local bureaucrats who drop in from Government Palace across the square. The food is pleasant, the view on a clear day is exhilarating, and the traffic below is always busy. Breakfast and lunch are good buys. Or just drop in for a bowl of sopa azteca and a drink midafternoon. Moderate. Cr.

Kinaret, corner of Génova and Hamburgo. This deli in the heart of the Zona Rosa is always packed. In the morning it's coffee and bagels, and late at night it's time for kosher corned beef and dills. Inexpensive. Cr.

Focalare, Hamburgo 87 (511-2679). This is the place where the famous Violins of the Villa Fontana perform. Good Italian food, served to the tune of romantic violins. Reservations advised. Expensive. Cr.

Konditori, Génova 61. A soup and sandwich visit to this quiet café makes an ideal shopping break. The chicken and vegetable soup is a house specialty and good enough to be worth a takeout visit. Inexpensive. N.

La Calesa del Londres, Londres between Génova and Niza (533-6625). Located in the former American ambassador's residence. Elegant atmosphere. Everyone comes here for the steaks and a large, tender filet prepared with roquefort sauce (a la Calesa) is a bargain at 150 pesos. Expensive. Cr.

La Gondola, Génova 21 (511-6908). Whenever we find ourselves in the

Zona Rosa with a hankering for Italian food, we end up at La Gon-dola. We have never been disappointed. The fettuccine alfredo; spag-hetti a la carbonara with ham, bacon, cheese, and egg sauce; and the spaghetti Vivaldi with a spicy meat and tomato sauce never fail to arrive *al dente* and delicious. The roast beef is usually moist and tender, although we have seen it slightly overdone. Mixed or Caesar salads round out the meal. This is one of the few places in Mexico that serves zabaglione. Bar. Moderate. Cr.

La Marinera, Liverpool 183 (511-2466). A seafood feast is a traditional favorite of many Mexicans, and this is just one place in the capital to enjoy the country's seafood harvest. There are eel omelets, whitefish from the Yucatán, abalone, squid, and local beer served in earthen-ware jars to wash it all down. Moderate to expensive. Cr.

Las Cazuelas, Av. San Antonio 143-E (563-3956). The real thing. Chicken with pumpkin seed sauce, chicken in mole sauce, stuffed chiles . . . whatever can be cooked in a cazuela, a large earthenware pot. There are rows of the bubbling dishes at the entrance to the res-taurant, which is located a few blocks north of the Zócalo, off the beaten tourist track. Noisy, bustling, and popular with the locals. Inexpensive. Cr.

Las Fuentes, Rio Tiber and Rio Pánuco (525-0629). A large vegetarian restaurant with the look of a chain restaurant, large booths with plastic-covered seats, and fast service. The long menu includes sandwiches and hot meal combinations, all served with soups and salads. The potato soup had a delightful taste of garden fresh vegetables. The fruit salad was also fresh and covered with a delicious honey-cream sauce. But the avocado and cheese sandwich arrived with the bare minimum of ingredients stuck between two slices of whole wheat bread, and the soybean croquettes lacked flavor. Inexpensive to moderate. Cr.

La Veranda, María Isabel Sheraton Hotel, Paseo de la Reforma 325 (525-9060). Most hotels offer buffet breakfasts with some regional touches, but at the María Isabel you can get a bowl of Sonoran menudo (good hangover cure) served with your hot chocolate. An-other menu specialty is *machacado con huevos* (scrambled eggs with beef jerky). Reservations are necessary after 9 A.M. during the week because this is a popular breakfast spot with Mexican businessmen. Moderate. Cr.

Loredo, Hamburgo 29 (566-3433). The owner, José Loredo claims to be the originator of *carne asada a la tampiqueña*, a popular dish of grilled steak served with Mexican trimmings that has become a tourist standby. But be adventurous — try some of the other authentic and delicious offerings, like bone marrow soup with chipotle peppers or soused pigs' feet or spotted avocado stuffed with eels. A Mexican gourmet treat and an adventure. Expensive. Cr.

Luau, Niza 38 (525-7474). The savory food prepared here is the closest to Cantonese cooking to be found in Mexico. The *moo goo gai pan* and Cantonese duck stand out as excellent dishes. Popular. Expect to line up outside, especially on weekends. Fixed price dinners are also available. Bar. Lunch and dinner. Moderate. Cr.

Les Moustaches, Rio Sena 88 (533-3390). Charming chandeliers hang from the ceilings of rooms clustered around an interior courtyard, New Orleans style. The sole Veronique, the house specialty, is a nicely done filet of sole covered with béchamel sauce and grapes. Another specialty is the tenderloin tips in *albañiles* (bricklayers) sauce, a hearty but not too heavy hot sauce. Other choices range from Oysters Rockefeller to chicken curry. Bar. Reservations. Expensive. Cr.

Los Panchos, Tolstoy and Dante. When Mexicans feel like eating fast food, they head to a taco restaurant where they consume small corn tortillas wrapped around diced meats sprinkled with cilantro, onion, and for the intrepid, hot chile sauces. There is little besides tacos, *quesadillas* (grilled tortillas with cheese inside), and beer and soft drinks. A specialty is the tacos *al pastor*, with meat sliced from the stacks of steaks grilling at the counter. Beer. Inexpensive. N.

Maxim's, Hotel El Presidente Chapultepec, Campos Eliseos 218 (254-0025). In red velveted and mirrored elegance, Mexico's own version of the famous Paris restaurant has become a place for the elegant to see and be seen. The meal can be as entertaining as it is delicious; if you want your dinner flambéed, you won't be short on choices. The sweetbreads are prepared with a cream sauce, and the Grand Marnier soufflé and crepes suzette rival one another for first place in the dessert stretch. Bar. Reservations. Expensive. Cr.

Mauna Loa, San Jeronimo 240, Pedregal de San Angel (548-6884). Hawaiian dancing on stages throughout the restaurant; Polynesian music; and a polyglot menu of Indian curries, Hawaiian shish kebabs and oriental dishes make eating here a theatrical production. Even the exotic drinks come flambéed to your table, if you are in the mood for a private show. The smoked spareribs are succulent. Dancing at night. Lunch and dinner. Expensive. Cr.

Mesón del Caballo Bayo, Av. de Conscripto 360 (589-3000). A country inn atmosphere where friends meet for lunch and end up canceling their afternoon at the office. Far from the downtown area, it is worth spending several hours once you get there. The restaurant tables are scattered over courtyards, around a fireplace, and throughout several dining rooms. The hors d'oeuvres are so good that they can easily become a full meal. Service is difficult on busy afternoons. Cocktail lounge, takeout service, and parking. Breakfast, lunch, and dinner. Moderate to expensive. Cr.

Mesón del Cid, Humboldt 61 (512-7629). An immense fireplace, rustic wooden tables, and costumed waiters set the scene to Spain in the Middle Ages. Strictly Spanish, the emphasis is on hearty food and large servings. The pheasant arrived with a succulent vegetable and fruit stuffing, and the milk-fed kid goat is a rare treat. There are also Spanish traditionals, paella, and seafood dishes. On Saturday nights, the restaurant stages a medieval banquet at which the wine flows and enormous roasts cook in the hearth. Bar. Closed Sunday. Expensive. Cr.

Museo Restaurant, National Museum of Anthropology, Paseo de la Reforma. A good way to take a break between the Mayan Salon and the Mixtec. The museum's small restaurant serves excellent luncheons. Inexpensive. N.

Picadilly Pub, Copenhague 23 (514-1515). The maître d' looks and acts like Arthur Treacher. The penultimate English butler. The food is so English Charles Dickens would feel at home. Try the London grill, the beefsteak and oyster pie, or the Welsh rarebit. Begin with a traditional English cocktail — Pimm's No. 1. The steak in a mustard sauce is a favorite. You can eat inside — all plaid and pewter — or outside, under the stars, where you can watch the world pass by on cobbled, traffic-free Copenhague. Closed Sunday. Moderate to expensive. Cr.

Piccolo Suizo, Mariano Escobedo 539 (531-1298). On weekends this is a traditional family restaurant, but it doubles as a favorite of nearby office workers during the week. The cheese fondue is filled with rich Gruyère. Steaks, especially with morille sauce, are excellent. Bar. Moderate. Cr.

Prendes, 16 de Septiembre 10 (585-4199). So full of politicians and businessmen that it may be hard to attract attention, Prendes rates high marks for Mexican food and fish. We have eaten an excellent *ceviche* (fish marinated in lime and mixed with tomato, avocado, and jalapeños), and the bone marrow soup is worth making a special trip. For the really adventurous the *gusanos de maguey* (worm from the maguey cactus, fried and prepared with a special sauce) are a must. Bar. Moderate. Cr.

Restaurant del Lago, Nuevo Bosque Chapultepec Park (515-9585). The decoration is ultramodern, yet Del Lago manages to achieve something akin to intimate dining. There are large expanses of mirrors, tables lit by candles, a subdued dance floor, greenery, and a window view of a sparkling fountain and Chapultepec Park outside. The *ceviche* is a good way to start a meal. The sea bass and the tenderloin tips in chile sauce are also well prepared. Food is overpriced, but the surroundings are stark and lovely. Bar. Closed Sundays. Reservations. Expensive. Cr.

Rivoli, Hamburgo 123 (525-6862). Many Mexicans rank this as Mexico City's number one restaurant in tradition, price, service, and food. The mirrored and chandeliered interior is small enough for patrons (often Mexican celebrities or politicians) to eye each other. We had a hard time choosing among the entrées, but the Chicken Kiev was juicy and cooked to a crisp finish. The lobster soufflé is light, moist, and blended with generous quantities of lobster. Another house specialty is *huachinango empapelado,* red snapper cooked in paper, and the pepper steak is also tender and juicy. The dessert soufflés are the smashing pièce de résistance. There is a cocktail lounge, a large wine selection, and soft music in the evening. Closed Sundays. Reservations required. Expensive. Cr.

San Angel Inn, Palmas 50, San Angel (548-6746). We try to eat here in late summer or early fall just to savor the *chiles en nogada,* an amazing dish of chile poblano stuffed with chopped meat, nuts, and raisins and covered with sauce and pomegranate seeds, which we consider Mexico's unsung contribution to world cuisine. But even when the *chiles en nogada* season is over, the food and service in this lovely hacienda are impeccable. Red snapper dishes include the impressive Veracruz style. Another Mexican specialty not to be missed is the crepes of *huitlacoche,* a black mushroom that grows on corn, sautéed with onions. Desserts are sinfully rich, like the *cocada* made of coconut and milk or the two cream puddings of almonds and piñon nuts. The restaurant includes a chapel, gardens, and courtyards. Daily buffet. Bar. Mariachi music on weekends. Reservations. Expensive. Cr.

Sanborn's, various locations. Basically Sanborn's offers slightly expensive drugstore food; the chain is a subsidiary of Walgreen's. Other than excellent *enchiladas suizas* (enchiladas topped with melted cheese), the food is only passable and the service is slow. The downtown Sanborn's on Madero is in the landmark colonial House of Tiles and is worth a visit just to admire the building — open 24 hours a day. The Sanborn's milkshake is Mexico's best, whipped thick with a generous helping of ice cream. Cocktail lounges at some locations. Inexpensive to moderate. Cr.

Shirley's, various locations. Another favorite among tourists, this chain restaurant has two choice items on its Mexican-to-American-food menu: the only Reuben sandwich we have found in Mexico and lemon chiffon pie. Otherwise the food, including hamburgers, is mediocre, chain-restaurant fare. Lunch buffets. Inexpensive. N.

Sir Winston Churchill's, Blvd. Avila Camacho 67, Periferico Norte (520-0585). Years ago an Anglophile family living in Mexico hired an English architect to build them an authentic Tudor mansion. Now the mansion is a restaurant with paneled rooms and timbered ceilings, and the English menu includes steak and kidney pie. The sliced abalone with a special sauce is a house specialty. For dessert: pumpkin pie if they have it or flambéed mangoes. Bar. Closed Sundays. Reservations. Expensive. Cr.

"Suntory," Torres Adalid 14 (536-7754). The most luxurious Japanese restaurant in Mexico, with prices to match. The dining rooms vary, and the food in one room is cooked at the table on grills resembling samurai helmets. The *sushi* bar offers overpriced *sushi* and not much variety. The warm sake flows from little jugs. Bar. Reservations. Expensive. Cr.

Taqueria Beatriz, Londres 148-A and El Salvador 44-D. A taco chain where the tortillas are handmade. Soft drinks only. Inexpensive. N.

Tecamacharlie's, Fuente Trevi 4, Tecamachalco (294-0448); Anderson's, Paseo de la Reforma 400 (511-5187); and Carlos 'n Charlie's, Calzada del Desierto 67, San Angel (548-1265). These three restaurants, all run by the same owner, have funky decorations and an atmosphere to match. The Tecamacharlie's is filled with baskets of all shapes and sizes; at Anderson's the walls and ceiling are plastered with hats. People go here to drink and have fun. The waiters (often American) themselves sometimes stumble out the door at six in the morning. For such a wide menu selection, the food is amazingly good. Nowhere in Mexico have we eaten such a savory plate of barbecued spareribs. And the shrimp bisque with just a touch of chile was so tasty we had to ask for seconds. Bar. Moderate to expensive. Cr.

Tel Aviv, Paseo de la Reforma 105 (546-8205). We were served a rather dry corned beef sandwich, although the coleslaw was crunchy and its dressing creamy. The price-fixed meal offers a lot of food for a very low price. One of the few sidewalk cafés along Paseo de la Reforma. Inexpensive. Cr.

Vips, various locations. We have tried their *pozole* (a pork and corn stew) late on a chilly night, and it deserves high marks, as does another soup called *caldo tlalpeño*. For those who are less enthusiastic about such heavy Mexican soups, there are the not-too-*picante enchiladas suizas* and ordinary sandwiches. Beer. Inexpensive. Cr.

NIGHTLIFE

Ballet Folklórico, Palacio de Bellas Artes, Juárez and Angela Peralta. The magnificent opera house is the home of the National Ballet Folklórico, a talented company of dancers who perform the country's native dances. No visitor should miss a chance to see a performance: shows each Wednesday at 9:00 P.M., Sundays at 9:30 A.M. and 9:00 P.M. Tickets may be purchased the day before the performance at the box office on the ground floor of the theater. Prices vary.

Café Toulouse-Lautrec, Londres 104. Located in the arcade between Génova and Niza, this café is hidden beneath its awnings. Popular with students, businessmen, bohemians. Good place to go for a pre-dinner drink or a late espresso. Inexpensive. Cr.

Concerts, various locations. Mexico City has a symphony orchestra and several smaller ensembles. National and international stars perform in the capital frequently and tickets, particularly at University of Mexico functions, can be very reasonable. Look for posters on walls or check the daily cultural column in *The News*, the capital's English language paper.

Dancing, various locations. For touch dancing a la Fred Astaire, as opposed to disco, try El Camichia in the Hotel Alameda, Juárez 50, or the Stelaris in the Hotel Fiesta Palace, Paseo de la Reforma 80 at Colon Circle. If it's plain old rock 'n' roll you want, try the Quorum at the Hotel Fiesta Palace; La Lechuga in the Hotel Aristos; or El Circo in the Holiday Inn Zona Rosa, Liverpool and Amberes.

Discos, various locations. Disco is popular in the capital, especially among the upwardly mobile middle class. Here's a sampling: Cero-Cero in the Camino Real, Mariano Escobedo 700; El Chapulin in El Presidente, packed but closes early at 2 A.M.; Chapultepec in the park; Cancan in the Zona Rosa, Hamburgo and Génova; Marrakesh, Florencia 36, in the Zona Rosa, three clubs in one. Most clubs have cover charges and are expensive. Cr.

Movies, various locations. You can't beat the price of a movie ticket in Mexico — as low as 25 pesos. Most of the English language films being shown in the capital are not dubbed, but have Spanish subtitles — a good way to polish your Spanish. Check *The News* or other newspapers for the movie listings.

Muralto Bar, Latin-American Tower, San Juan de Letrán and Madero (the extension of Juárez). The view from the 41st floor is unmatched. Sit here and unwind, watch the traffic spread out to the mountains, and contemplate the fact that this is a city of some 15 million souls. Usually busy, especially during cocktail hour. Drinks are reasonably priced; food is more expensive and not particularly outstanding. Moderate Cr.

Opera, various locations, usually the Palacio de Bellas Artes. There are two seasons in Mexico City, the national season in summer and the international season in winter. Mexico has given the world some of the best singers and so both seasons are worth attending. Check *The News* for performance dates and times, or go by the ticket office in the Palacio de Bellas Artes (Palace of Fine Arts) on Avenida Juárez for information.

Plaza Garibaldi, off San Juan de Letrán, a few blocks north of Juárez. This is Mexico City's famed mariachi square where bands begin to assemble about eight or nine in the evening and play until the early hours of the morning. There are several bars on the plaza where tourists are welcome. Tenanapa is a Mexico City institution famous for its *ponche granada* (pomegranate punch laced with tequila). Guadalajara de la Noche has a dance floor for exuberant gringos. Both clubs open until early morning. Inexpensive. Cr.

Theater, various locations. In a city the size of the capital, there are numerous performances by dramatic groups, both professional and amateur. Of course, most productions are in Spanish; however, everyone can enjoy the variety show at the Teatro Lirico, Cuba 46.

The Zona Rosa. The capital's cosmopolitan restaurant-boutique district comes alive at night when student mummers, lovers, hot dog vendors, window shoppers, and flower ladies take to the streets and arcades of the city's "Pink Zone." There are several cafés for people-watching, many of the restaurants stay open until midnight or 1 A.M., and the streets are safe late into the evening.

SHOPPING

Avalos Brothers, Carretónes 5, downtown. The best-known glass factory — right by the crowded and bustling Merced market in downtown Mexico City. The craftsmen blow glass as you watch and the shop has dishes, glasses, and pitchers in clear and colored glass. Fixed prices.

Bazar Sábado, Plaza San Jacinto 11, San Angel. A very artsy-craftsy bazaar held in a seventeenth-century mansion in San Angel, a quiet suburb of the city near the southern highway to Cuernavaca. Don't miss the dancing flea exhibits. Next door in La Casona, Plaza San Jacinto 9, modern craftsmen hold a sale every Saturday, also. There are a couple of restaurants on the plaza, including an Indian one. Saturday 10–8.

Centro Artesano, Ayuntamiento and Dolores. Part of the remodeled San Juan Market. Lots of arts and crafts are found in this market, usually at good prices. Be sure to bargain.

Ciudadela Handicrafts Market, Balderas between Ayuntamiento and Dondé. Over 200 independent craftsmen are housed in this modern building. They work here and sell their crafts 9–9 Monday through Saturday. Open on Sunday irregularly.

Del Angel, Rio Lerma and Sena. Located just a couple of blocks north of the Reforma and the Zona Rosa, this pastry shop is a favorite among the more affluent in the capital. Drop in for some supplies on your way to Chapultepec Park.

Department stores, various locations. You will see Mexican branches of old faithfuls like Woolworths and Sears, but try Puerto de Liverpool and Palacio de Hierro, two popular department stores on 20 de Noviembre, just one block south of the Zócalo.

FONART Museum of Popular Arts, Juárez 89. This government store has a good selection of handicrafts from around the country at quite reasonable prices. Across the street at Juárez 92, the Ministry of Tourism building also has an exhibit and sales area.

El Caballo, Pino Suárez 27. This exclusive store just south of the Zócalo is the place to go if you are a charro, a Mexican gentleman cowboy or lady cowperson. Custom-made boots, chaps, etc.

El Valle de Mexico, Tonalá 133-A (584-0239). This is where you will find *puros* — handmade, hand-rolled cigars. El Valle is tucked away behind old, hand-carved doors in a dowager neighborhood just south of the Zona Rosa. You can arrange to have your favorites shipped back home on a regular basis.

La Lagunilla, Comonfort. This is Mexico City's traditional flea market, where you can find just about any imaginable knickknack or piece of junk, a passable or valuable painting, or wooden images of saints. The market bustles with veteran sellers, Indians who barely speak Spanish, tourists, and knowledgeable collectors who come weekly to browse. A longtime tradition is the demonstrating vendors who repeat their sales pitches countless times. Be sure to bargain at La Lagunilla. Every Sunday 10-4.

Market on Londres, No. 160, Zona Rosa. The covered market is hung roof-high with traditional Mexican clothing and tapestries. The emphasis is on dresses, shirts, wall hangings, leather goods, and baskets. Vendors are willing to bargain at this market, well located in the Pink Zone.

Mercado de Curiosidades, Ayuntamiento between Buen Tono and Aranda. This new building houses crafts from all over the country. A continuous spiral ramp leads to all the floors. Monday through Saturday 10-6.

Museo Nacional de Artes y Industrias Populares, Juárez 44. If you hate to bargain and are short on time, you can just about make this store your first and last stop for handicrafts. Items are carefully selected, the prices are fixed and reasonable, and the exhibits of prize-winning handicrafts change constantly. Fixed prices. Closed Sundays.

Polanco Market, Homero and Musset. Many of these same vendors go to La Lagunilla on Sunday. But the prices are higher here. The market stalls show the same knickknacks as La Lagunilla plus blue jeans, shirts from India, baskets, Mexican handicrafts, jewelry, paintings, and hundreds of other items. The park is clean and the atmosphere is pleasant. Bargain. Every Saturday 10-4.

Salchichoneria Polano, Virgilio 8. This popular deli is located just north of Chapultepec Park in one of the city's chic neighborhoods, just west of the Museum of Anthropology. Look for the streets named after famous writers — Oscar Wilde, Charles Dickens, T.S. Eliot, and "Virgilio" or Vergil. The shop sells all kinds of sausage (hence the name) and cheeses. Good place to stock a picnic basket before you leave for a day trip.

San Juan Food Market, Ernesto Pugibet 21. San Juan is the capital's gourmet market where many of the top restaurants buy their daily supplies. Imported as well as domestic delicacies.

Sonora Market, Fray Servando Teresa de Mier and San Nicholás. This is a section of the city's unbelievable main market, Merced, and this is where you will find herbal remedies; pottery; birds; and at Christmas, nativity scenes.

Siqueiros Polyforum, Insurgentes Sur and Filadelfia. Built by David

Siqueiros, the Cultural Polyforum is on the grounds of the unfinished Hotel de Mexico. With a handicrafts store in the basement, exhibits by contemporary artists on the ground floor, and the huge Siqueiros mural portraying Mexico's history upstairs, this is a good stop for fans of Mexican murals. Fixed prices. Open daily 10–9.

Zona Rosa, south of Paseo de la Reforma between Chapultepec Park and Niza. This is the heart of the boutique and gallery district, where you will find everything from Paris fashions and English shoes to French perfume and original Mexican art. Some prices, particularly on imported fashions, leather, and jewelry, are cheaper than in the United States, especially since the devaluation of the peso. Always compare before you buy. Although shops named Gucci and Cartier sell excellent merchandise, they are not affiliated with the European originals. Here's a sampling of stores in the Zona Rosa: Misrachi Gallery, Génova 20, modern Mexican masters; Sergio Bustamante, the popular artist from Guadalajara, has a gallery in the Copenhague arcade, just south of the Paseo de la Reforma; Antil, Florencia 22, Mexican leathers and suedes; Flato, Amberes 21, exotic and rare jewels; Jossclaude, Londres 112, a chic hair salon; Flamma, Hamburgo and Londres, candles, soaps, etc.; Artel, Estraburgo 31, pillows, throws, and fabrics from Chiapas; Girasol, Génova 39-A, Gonzalo Bauer's popular dresses, shirts, and blouses, influenced by Mexican folk art; La Aguila Descalza ("The Barefoot Eagle"), Copenhague 311, designs for romantic or casual dressing by the famous Mexican designer Josefa.

POINTS OF INTEREST

Alameda Park, Av. Juárez, just west of the Palace of Fine Arts. This once beautiful park is beginning to show the signs of heavy pollution, but in summertime it's still a good place to sit and watch the world go by, especially on a Sunday afternoon when Mexico's parks are always filled with workers enjoying what is probably their only day off. There is a large monument to President Benito Juárez facing the avenue that bears his name. One interesting historical note — the park was once the site of the Inquisition's infamous *auto de fé* (burnings). Across the street, the Hotel del Prado, Juárez 70, boasts a lobby decorated with a famous mural by Diego Rivera. Titled *Dream of a Sunday Afternoon in the Alameda Park*, the mural depicts many of the big names in Mexican history — not always in a complimentary way. Rivera, whose murals often caused great controversy, was obliged to paint out an offending phrase on the painting. The phrase "God does not exist" caused the painting to be covered for ten years. Rivera finally conceded and he painted over the phrase in 1958.

Bullfights, Plaza México. Located on Insurgentes Sur between Holbein and San Antonio, the capital's bullring is the largest in the world and seats over 50,000. The bullfight, as it is called in English, is more theater than sport, and no one should approach it as a tourist attraction. Read up on the spectacle before you go, and don't go if you feel you will not enjoy or understand the bullfight. There are two seasons each year — the "little" season, usually from mid-March to November when the new hands, the "rookies," face the bulls, and the "big" season, from December 1 to March or April when the old hands enter the ring. Bullfights are always on Sunday at 4:30 P.M. and are one of the few things in Mexico that start on time. Tickets are on sale at the plaza; however, reservations are recommended for tourists. Your hotel will usually help you make arrangements.

Chapultepec Castle, Chapultepec Park. This eighteenth-century castle built by one of the viceroys is more than a museum — it's a step back into the past. The grounds are open to the public, and there is a good view of the city from the terrace. In the days before pollution, Maximilian and Carlota were able to look out over the lake bed to the snowcapped volcanoes on the horizon. Much of the furniture was brought over by the ill-fated couple, but there are also extensive exhibits from the colonial period and the wars for independence and the Revolution. One grisly item that attracts a great deal of attention is the death mask of Maximilian. This is a "people's" museum, and on Sundays it is packed with working-class Mexicans, some carrying buckets of water and their lunch, who look eagerly at all the exhibits from their tumultuous past. Daily 9–6; closed Tuesday.

Chapultepec Park, Paseo de la Reforma. This huge park is home to several museums and galleries, including the incomparable National Museum of Anthropology. But it is also a place to stroll, to visit the amusement park or the zoo (see the pandas), to ride the miniature train, or to rent a rowboat on the lake. The tall *ahuehuete* trees, or Moctezuma cypresses, made this a favorite haunt of Aztec leaders. Relatively quiet during the week, but go on Sunday and see everyone and anyone.

Churches, various locations downtown. There are several examples of Mexican-style architecture in the downtown area. Church of San Francisco on Avenida Madero is noted for its Churrigueresque doorway — an eighteenth-century remnant of the convent that stood on this spot. Cortés's remains were said to have been kept here until 1794, when they were moved to the nearby Hospital of Jesus. Church of La Profesa, Madero and Isabel de la Católica, a baroque church built in 1720. Church of Jesus Nazareno, Avenida República de El Salvador and Pino Suárez, a seventeenth-century baroque church with modern frescoes by Orozco. Other churches around the downtown area are open to the public for viewing.

Church and Hospital of Jesus, southwest corner of Pino Suárez and República de El Salvador. Legend has it that this church stands on the spot where Moctezuma greeted Hernán Córtes in 1519. In 1524, Cortés ordered a hospital to be built on the spot and he endowed it, making it the oldest hospital in the Americas. It is still in operation. In 1794, Cortés's bones were interred in the church. A mural by the revolutionary José Clemente Orozco arches the nave.

Latin American Tower, Madero and San Juan de Letrán. This 580-foot, 43-story skyscraper is the tallest building in the capital. The top floor serves as a viewing terrace, and just one floor below is a bar and restaurant with panoramic views of the city. There's a small charge to enter the viewing terrace.

The Metropolitan Cathedral, Zócalo, north side. The original building was constructed on part of the site of the Great Aztec Temple, on the Wall of Skulls and the Temple of Xipe Totec, whose spring rites were particularly gruesome. The original building, begun in 1525, was partly demolished and the building we now see was begun in 1563. For over 250 years, builders have added to the structure making it a mixture of styles. Guides roam the Cathedral grounds, and it's worthwhile hiring one if you want a detailed history of the church. On the east side next door stands the Sagrario Metropolitano, a parish church built in 1768. It is an outstanding example of Mexican Churrigueresque architecture.

National University, southern section of the city on both sides of Insurgentes Sur. Mexico's great muralists were commissioned to execute vast outdoor works on the campus, including mosaics, murals, and sculptures. A walk through the campus is a lesson in art history. Amateur botanists might want to visit the university's cactus and orchid collections housed near the stadium.

Palacio de Iturbide, Iturbide and Madero. Originally built and occupied by the Condé de San Mateo de Valparaiso in the eighteenth century, this baroque palace was occupied by Mexico's first emperor, the ill-fated Agustín de Iturbide.

Plaza of the Three Cultures, Colonia Tlatelolco. You can take the subway to this remarkable plaza just north of Paseo de la Reforma. In the plaza are excavated remains of an Aztec ceremonial center; a sixteenth-century church dedicated to Santiago Tlatelolco with its adjoining college, Holy Cross College, built in 1536, where the sons of Aztec nobles were educated; and a modern 24-story high rise. The Colonia (suburb) Tlatelolco takes its name from the famous Aztec market that stood here when Hernán Cortés arrived. It was here, also, that Cuauhtémoc, last of the Aztec kings, was captured after an 80-day siege in 1521.

Pyramids, Teotihuacán, about 35 miles north of the capital. Take Insurgentes Norte to the toll road and follow the signs, or join one of the many tours offered throughout the city. There is also bus service to the ruins, or you can contract with a taxi for the day. Check at your hotel desk or the central bus station on Avenida de Cien Metros. That the pyramids are one of Mexico's most popular sights doesn't detract from their magnificence. Read the chapter **Mexico of the Ancients**

before you go. Each Wednesday from October to May a sound and light show is held at the pyramids, first in English at 7:00 P.M. and then in Spanish at 8:15 P.M. Tickets sold at the site, or ask at your hotel.

Santo Domingo Church and Plaza, Av. República de Brasil, three blocks north of the Cathedral. This church, built in 1736, is an outstanding example of Mexican baroque. The most beautiful part of the church, left of the entrance, was razed during the anticlerical Reform Era, then rebuilt in 1968. The Tribunal of the Holy Inquisition was housed in the building on the east side of the plaza. At one corner of the square, Calle Cuba 95, is a historical marker that notes that the infamous La Malinche, Cortés's Indian mistress, lived here in 1527. The square has retained its colonial atmosphere — under the arches are the *evangelistas*, professional scribes who write letters for the illiterate.

Shrine of Our Lady of Guadalupe, north of downtown off Insurgentes Norte. Take the Basilica exit on Line 3 of the subway and follow the signs and crowds. The most revered shrine in the Americas. A must for any visitor, particularly in December when the faithful flock here to honor the Virgin on December 12 and throughout the Christmas season. The original basilica, begun in the sixteenth century, is sinking into the lake bed; a new, modernistic shrine was built in the seventies. A moving sidewalk takes the faithful and the curious past the cape that bears the miraculous image of the Virgin.

Xochimilco, southern edge of the city. To reach the so-called floating gardens, take Calzada Tlalpan south and follow the signs, or join a tour. Mexico City was originally served by a network of canals. Few remain, but in Xochimilco you can stretch out in a flower-bedecked boat and with a great deal of imagination think back to the days of Tenochtitlán when the city was a maze of canals, some for transport, others as floating vegetable and flower gardens. A popular Sunday outing.

Zócalo, Plaza de la Constitución. This is the heart of the city and the country. This vast square, empty except for a massive Mexican flag, was the heart of the old Tenochtitlán and is the heart of the new city. The National Palace, on the east side of the plaza, stands on the ruins of Moctezuma's Palace. On the north side is the Metropolitan Cathedral, standing on the ruins of the Great Temple. National parades are held here and Mexico's president often addresses the people from a balcony in the National Palace. The Hall of Justice stands on the south side, and on the east is the Monte de Piedad, the state pawnshop. There's a subway station under the square.

MUSEUMS

Anáhuacalli (Diego Rivera Museum), Calle Museo off División del Norte. Diego Rivera bequeathed this museum to Mexico. Except for one room showing his last studio and sketches, the museum's three floors contain his excellent collection of pre-Hispanic ceramics, figurines, masks, reliefs, and artifacts. Tuesday through Sunday 10–6.

Chopo Museum (Museo del Chopo), E. González Martinez 10 (546-5484). One of the few art nouveau buildings in Mexico, this was the first prefabricated construction in the country. Now it specializes in temporary exhibits with emphasis on contemporary Mexican culture. Daily 10–2 and 4–7.

Colonial Museum of Acolman, Ex-Convento de San Augustin, Acolman. A lovely — albeit run-down — early sixteenth-century convent built by the Augustinian friars about five miles from the Teotihuacán pyramids. Saturday through Thursday 10–5.

El Carmen Colonial Museum (Museo Colonial del Carmen), Av. Revolución 4, San Angel (548-2838). The innter courtyards of this former Carmelite convent are a welcome relief after the bustle of Mexico City's streets. Much of the building has yet to be restored, but the museum contains some interesting frescoes, decorative tiles, colonial furniture, and that favorite of Mexican museums — mummies on display in the crypt. A shop on the premises sells reproductions of some choice pre-Hispanic pieces from the National Anthropology Museum. Tuesday through Sunday 10–5.

El Desierto de los Leones, Desierto de los Leones National Park, Toluco highway. On Sundays, families flock here to escape from metropolitan Mexico. In colonial times the park and monastery were a Carmelite religious retreat. The park has picnicking and hiking areas as well as the large monastery, where the courtyards, chapels, living quarters, and even the whispering chapel retain their former serenity.

Palace of Fine Arts (Palacio de Bellas Artes), Juárez and Angela Peralta (512-5404). The interior of this museum and performing arts center is often described as art deco but is actually an eclectic mix of styles that took decades to finish. The building was designed by Italian architect Adamo Boari. Main attractions inside are murals by Diego Rivera, José Clemente Orozco, David Alfaro Siqueiros, Rufino Tamayo, and Jorge González Camarena. The Rivera mural is a copy of the one done for the Rockefeller Center in New York City, which was rejected and destroyed because of its political content. There are usually temporary exhibits — often the choicest in town. Tuesday through Sunday 11–7.

Frida Kahlo Museum (Museo de Frida Kahlo), Londres 247, Coyoacán (554-5999). Frida Kahlo was married to Diego Rivera and their blue-painted house in Coyoacán has been turned into a museum. It contains a small collection of Rivera's works and some by his contemporaries, but the focus is on Frida Kahlo. One room is hung with her surrealistic paintings, many dealing with her own life (she was partially crippled in a bus accident), and there are displays of her Mexican costumes and memorabilia, including her diary, notes from her and from Rivera, and even the household budget ledger. Tuesday through Sunday 10–6.

Great Temple Excavation (Proyecto Templo Mayor), Seminario and Guatemala (522-4367). It has been known for centuries that fifteenth-century Aztec temples lie under buildings and streets in the Zócalo. But when subway excavations bumped into the ruins in 1976, the government decided to unearth them and turn the center of town into a major archaeological complex. Archaeologists have had to battle with historians who want to save colonial architecture and with motorists who want to use the streets, but archaeologists seem to have won half the battle. The surrounding streets are now closed and will reopen as pedestrian malls around the outdoor complex. Excavators have found thousands of Aztec ceramic treasures and have excavated layered pyramids. Some are so well preserved that the paint remains. The diggings are usually closed to the general public, but tours can be arranged through the National Anthropology Museum.

Mexico City Museum (Museo de la Ciudad de México), Pino Suárez 30 (547-0487). The mansion that once belonged to the Counts de Santiago de Calimaya now serves as Mexico City's own museum. Models, maps, and murals trace the civilizations that have settled in different locations in the Valley of Mexico, from pre-Hispanic to Spanish colonial and finally modern Mexico — an interesting case history on the lack of urban planning. Tuesday through Sunday 9:00–7:30.

Museo Nacional del Virreinato, Tepotzotlán. Located about 25 miles north of Mexico City on the Querétaro highway, the former church and monastery in Tepotzotlán are among the most outstanding and best preserved examples of colonial architecture. The church is one of the few examples in Mexico of Churrigueresque architecture, a type of exuberant baroque. There are often concerts in the museum and during December the traditional pageants called *las posadas.* Tuesday through Sunday 10–4.

National Museum of Anthropology, Paseo de la Reforma, Chapultepec Park. Undoubtedly, one of the finest museums in the world. An architectural masterpiece and the sanctuary for many of Mexico's most treasured Mesoamerican artifacts. The interested visitor can spend an entire day here. The center of the museum, an open patio, is partially covered by a huge concrete mushroom that serves as a fountain said to symbolize the eternal cycle of life, an essential element in Mesoamerican religious thought. There is a book shop in the entrance hall, and serious visitors are advised to purchase a detailed guide to the museum — all signs are in Spanish. The ground floor features artifacts, including the massive so-called Aztec calendar, all set in dramatically lighted surroundings. The upper floors show dioramas depicting present-day Indian life. There is a pleasant restaurant in the museum. Tuesday through Saturday 9–7; Sunday 10–6; closed Monday.

National Museum of Cultures, Moneda 13. A complete ethnographic collection of artifacts, artwork, and models (mostly replicas) showing different world cultures from the distant and not-so-distant past. Especially interesting is the attempt to place pre-Hispanic culture in the scope of world history. Monday through Friday 9:30–6:00; Saturday 9:30–3:00; closed Sunday.

National Museum of History, Chapultepec Castle, Chapultepec Park. Houses furniture, paintings, and artifacts from the colonial period, including a room filled with portraits of the viceroys; furniture from the Second Empire (Maximilian and Carlota); and artifacts from the wars of independence and the Revolution. Popular on Sundays when the admission price is reduced. Daily 9–6; closed Tuesday.

Pinacoteca Virreinal de San Diego, Dr. Mora 7. A charming and unique collection of religious art painted by colonial artists in the sixteenth, seventeenth, and eighteenth centuries. The building is a former convent. Tuesday through Sunday 10:00–4:30.

Polyforum, Insurgentes Sur and Filadelfia. (See Shopping.)

San Carlos Museum (Museo de San Carlos), Puente de Alvarado 50 (566-8550). Right by the Revolución subway stop, the oval mansion itself is a major example of Manuel Tolsá's neoclassical architecture. The galleries hold a small but interesting group of paintings by European artists of the classical period and another collection of work by colonial artists. Tuesday through Sunday 11–5.

Technological Museum (Museum Tecnológico), Nuevo Bosque de Chapultepec. This is a museum for those who love to touch and work exhibits. The electricity and electromagnetic experiments all work at the touch of a button. The museum has opened petroleum, transportation, and physics exhibits. Tuesday through Saturday 10–5; Sunday 10–2.

Teotihuacán Archaeological Museum, Teotihuacán. A small museum on the pyramid site displays pottery and tools used by the civilization that built Teotihuacán. Daily 8–6.

Tepexpan Prehistoric Museum, kilometer 11 on the Mexico City–Teotihuacán highway. The small museum is located on the site where the remains of a prehistoric hunter called the Tepexpan man were discovered. The remains are dated to somewhere between 11,000 and 9000 B.C. Tuesday through Sunday 10–7.

Wax Museum (Museo de Cera), Londres 6. An old mansion was renovated several years ago and now bursts with the wax figures of contemporary celebrities and famous people from Mexican and world history. Daily 11–7.

SPORTS

Auto racing, Mexico City Autodrome, Sports City. Southeast edge of the capital. Check the newspapers for schedules.

Horse racing, Hipódromo de las Américas, north of the city on the

Periferico. The track is one of the best in the world. The season begins in late October and ends the following early September. Open from 2 P.M. each Tuesday, Thursday, and Saturday. (Closed Tuesdays in summer.) There's no off-track betting in the capital, but you can drop all the pesos you want at the track. Tourists can eat at the Gay Dalton Club (show your tourist card) where there is a 150-peso minimum for drinks or food. Your hotel may also make arrangements at the exclusive Jockey Club.

Jai alai, Frontón Mexico, north side of the Plaza de la República, and the Frontón Metropolitano, Bahía de Todos Santos. Men play at the Frontón Mexico, women at the Metropolitano. A fast-paced Basque game popular in Hispanic countries and Florida. You may want to watch a few games before you bet. The men play from 7:30 P.M. daily except Monday and Friday. Women play from 4 P.M. daily except Sunday.

Soccer, Aztec Stadium, Calzada Tlalpan. Latin American soccer should not be missed. While US football is fast gaining fans by cable television, soccer is still the national sport in virtually every country south of the Rio Grande — wars have even been fought over a lost game. Check the sports section of *The News* for game times.

FIESTAS

The capital celebrates all national holidays with a special fervor, given its size and the millions of people who live in the federal district. Special fiestas to take note of when making reservations include

Holy Week, week before Easter. Many shops and restaurants closed.

May 1, Labor Day. A parade of workers through the Zócalo and downtown that cripples traffic.

September 1, President's State of the Union address. More parades and some closings.

September 16, Independence Day. The biggest holiday of the year. The Zócalo is packed at midnight on the fifteenth for the president's "grito" — the famous cry for independence. Fireworks, parades, revelry. Reservations a must.

October 12, Día de la Raza. Our Colombus Day. Parades, revelry.

November 2, Day of the Dead. Look out for pastries and candies shaped like skulls and graveyards.

November 20, Day of the Revolution. A huge sports parade through downtown.

December 12, Our Lady of Guadalupe festival. Thousands flock to the Shrine of Our Lady of Guadalupe to honor the Virgin Empress of the Americas. The celebrations keep up through the Christmas season.

January 6, Day of the Three Kings. Gift giving and fiestas that close the Christmas season.

TRANSPORTATION

Airport. Individual passenger taxis or minibuses (SETTA) operate from the airport to the downtown hotels. Traffic congestion varies, but the airport is approximately 30 minutes from downtown. The SETTA minibuses are the cheapest way to get downtown if you have luggage. If you are traveling light, take the subway. No large bags are allowed on the subway, and you may be stopped during rush hour if you are carrying even a backpack.

Buses. Tourists should take only luxury and first-class buses. The luxury buses, Dolphins, have a silver dolphin beside the door. Fare is two pesos and the buses operate on the main thoroughfares. First-class buses are blue and white. The fare is 1.50 pesos. No transfers. Buses operate from 5 A.M. to midnight. Ask your hotel bell captain for assistance on routes. If you get lost, board the nearest bus that says "Reforma" or "Zócalo" and you will eventually arrive downtown. Buses are packed during rush hour.

Bus terminals. There are four bus terminals in Mexico City, each serving a different section of the country. Check in the Yellow Pages under "Camiones" for the appropriate terminal. Most are served by the subway or city bus service.

Car rental. There are numerous car rental agencies throughout the city. For a complete listing, consult the yellow pages of the phone book. Agencies include Avis — at the international airport (domestic arrivals 762-8111, international arrivals 762-0099), in Hotel Del Prado, in Hotel El Presidente Chapultepec, in Hotel Fiesta Palace, and at Paseo de la Reforma 322-A (511-4613); Hertz — at the international airport (domestic arrivals 571-3239, international arrivals 571-3229), in the Camino Real and the Hotel Aristos, in the Zona Rosa at Versailles 6 (566-0099), and at Insurgentes Sur 725 (543-1324); and National — at the international airport (domestic arrivals 762-8426, international arrivals 571-8710), at Paseo de la Reforma 219 (556-6055), and in the Hotel Krystal at Liverpool 155 in the Zona Rosa (533-3500).

Subway. Built in 1968 and recently expanded, Mexico City's subway system is one of the best in the world. Clean, fast, and cheap — five tickets for five pesos, transfers included. You only have to wait two or three minutes between trains. Read the section on subway travel and check the map in this chapter. Wall maps in all stations. Avoid rush-hour travel. Closes at midnight and reopens at 6 A.M.

Taxis. Two types of cabs are available, red *sitio* cabs and yellow cruising cabs. *Sitio* cabs usually park in front of major hotels and restaurants and are the most expensive. Always set the price before getting in. Cruising cabs charge a base price of four pesos. Small Volkswagen cabs are called *peseros* because they used to charge a peso. Now *peseros* cruise busy streets and carry up to five passengers in close comfort for three to six pesos a person.

Trains, Buenavista Main Terminal, just north of Paseo de la Reforma off Insurgentes Norte. You can travel to just about any spot in the country from the main terminal and at ridiculously low prices. There's a special booth at the station manned with an English-speaking information person to assist you. If you arrive by train, there's a cab stand outside the terminal. You are just a few blocks from the Zona Rosa and only a dozen or so from downtown, so watch out for price gouging by taxi drivers. If your load is light, you can walk to the Paseo de la Reforma. For schedule and fare information call 547-1084, 547-1097, or 547-6593.

TOURIST SERVICES

American Express Office, Hamburgo 75, Zona Rosa (533-0380 and 528-7084). The usual services — credit card loss reports, money orders, travelers checks, messages for card holders — are available here.

Bilingual police officers. Stationed along the Paseo de la Reforma and in the Zona Rosa. These officers will approach you in a friendly manner and ask if you need assistance. The languages they speak are represented by flags on their uniforms. Usually eager to help and to practice their foreign languages.

Churches. There is a large diplomatic and foreign business community in the capital. Many churches hold regular services for visitors. Check the listings in *The News* for that week's schedule.

Embassies. The US Embassy is located at Paseo de la Reforma 305 in a beautiful building (553-3333). The Canadian Embassy is located at Melchor Ocampo 463-7, just off the Paseo de la Reforma (533-0610). If you need any assistance, don't hesitate to call your embassy. Lists of local doctors are kept current by embassy personnel. If you plan to travel into remote regions of Mexico, it's wise to check with the embassy before you go. The US Embassy keeps up-to-date travel advisories on local conditions, particularly infrequent political or criminal disturbances.

Tourist information. The Secretaria de Turismo mans an information booth at Av. Juárez 92 (585-3066), where you can obtain free maps of the city and the country. The main office is located at Av. Presidente Masaryk 172 (250-8585). Report any problems to the secretary, particularly dishonest guides and taxi drivers or hotels that don't follow the posted rates. Menu prices are also subject to regulation by the secretary. For information about goings-on in the capital, tourist services, or other related activity, dial 07 at any public 20-centavo phone booth.

Tours. There are several tour groups operating in the capital. Gray Line tours has its headquarters in the American Express office in the

Zona Rosa, Hamburgo 75 (533-0380). Check at your hotel desk or ask other tourists about other tour companies.

COMMUNICATIONS

Newspapers. *The News*, the capital's English language daily is free and is distributed to many of the major hotels. Daily events are listed in the "What's on Today" column. Other newspapers feature daily entertainment listings much like their US counterparts. US magazines and major dailies are sold at Sanborn's drugstores throughout the city.

Post office. Most hotels sell stamps ("timbres"), and the main post office (*Correo Mayor*) is located just east of the Palace of Fine Arts at Av. Ruiz de Alarcon and Calle Tacuba. An airmail stamp is four pesos.

Radio news. The CBS news is broadcast on the hour from 7 until midnight on Radio VIP, 1560 on the AM dial.

Telegrams. The main telegraph office is located at Balderas 7 and is open from 8 A.M. to midnight. There are several classes of telegrams. Always purchase the most expensive, although it will be relatively cheap by US standards, to ensure that the telegram gets there as quickly as possible.

Telephones. Calling long-distance from your hotel room may be prohibitively expensive owing to service charges. Always call collect back to the United States or Canada. You can make long-distance calls only at special phones. In the street are 20-centavo phone booths that are for local calls only. To make a long-distance call outside your hotel, go to Sanborn's, Paseo de la Reforma 333, open 24 hours; the airport (two telephone offices); the main telephone company, Parque Via 198, 8–11; the downtown telephone branch, Victoria 58, 8–11; or the telephone office on the Paseo de la Reforma 122-B, 8:00–8:30.

Television. The news is in Spanish and there's lots of it; however, you will find English movies and television shows on Mexican television, sometimes dubbed in Spanish but more likely with Spanish subtitles.

6

THE CITY OF ROSES
GUADALAJARA

Much of what we consider to be "Mexican" has its roots in the soil of Jalisco, the 30,000-square-mile central Mexican state that has as its heart the city of Guadalajara. Mariachis, sombreros, the siesta, *charreadas,* and bullfights are all part of the Guadalajara experience. The most Mexican of the country's large cities, Guadalajara has none of the urgent air of the huge capital, and it shares little with Monterrey, a city comparable in size, where the dons of industry send their sons and daughters to US universities and their wives on shopping sprees in Houston and San Antonio.

Founded as a Spanish outpost in the early years after the conquest, Guadalajara struggled to survive amid fierce opposition from the Indians. This was the home of the Jalisco tribes and part of the kingdom of Chimalhuacana, "Shield User's Land." The Aztecs, some miles away in Tenochtitlán, now Mexico City, had difficulty conquering the tribes in the west, and the infamous conquistador Beltran Nuño de Guzmán faced a similar dilemma when he arrived to settle Spanish claims to the land. Carlos V of Spain was to call the area New Galicia when Guzmán finally conquered the Indians in 1532 and founded Guadalajara, naming it after his birthplace in Spain. Ten years later, Spain sent supplies with instructions that a great city of plazas, fountains, wide boulevards, and churches should be built on the site. Some call it a

Spanish city — its ties to Spain have always been strong — but it is truly a Mexican city, a synthesis of Indian and Spanish. The citizens of Guadalajara are proud of their origins and their city. They call themselves *tapatíos,* a word of disputed origin that has come to mean culture, pride, honor, gentility, and beauty.

The city, Mexico's second largest with a population of a little over one and a half million, has managed to retain its beauty in spite of industrialization. However, as in Mexico City and Monterrey, pollution can be a problem. Dominated by wide boulevards and plazas filled with fountains and flowers, Guadalajara is also a city of freeways and factories. With a year-round average daytime temperature of 75 degrees and a citywide penchant for gardening, Guadalajara is known as the "City of Roses." The city's climate, shopping, and location help it attract more tourists each year than any other city in Mexico. Indeed, Jalisco is the country's leading state in tourism. A few miles to the east of the city are lakeside villages filled with American retirees and artists; to the west is Puerto Vallarta. Making Guadalajara your base, you can discover many aspects of Mexican culture and life.

The state of Jalisco is one of the most beautiful in Mexico, a place of pine woods and lakes, lagoons and beaches, fertile river valleys and mountain ranges. Sportsmen hunt for deer in the hills; the weary visit the health spas and baths; collectors tour the craft-rich region; and escapists head for the beach. The mile-high city of Guadalajara offers the first-time visitor to Mexico an overview of the country. Railway lines, highways, and air traffic routes all converge at the city. (There's air service between Guadalajara and Puerto Vallarta, making PV a good place to wind up your trip.) Getting around in the city is no problem — many sights can be reached on foot or by a short, inexpensive cab ride. A rental car is not necessary in the city; however, there is much to see in surrounding towns and villages.

Guadalajara has an ideal climate for sight-seeing — daytime temperatures hover in the high 60s and 70s in the fall and winter, rising to perhaps the low 80s in the summer. Be prepared for afternoon showers and cool evenings, and remember Guadalajara is a conservative and genteel city, so dress appropriately.

ON THE TOWN

Guadalajara is best known as the home of the mariachis, the strolling players who have become symbols of the Mexican culture. Again, the origin of the word is disputed, but most experts say *mariachi* comes from the French word *mariage* meaning marriage. French culture infiltrated Mexico with the invasion of Napoleon III in the last century. Mariachis may have performed at the wedding of some French officer to a young Mexican woman. The musicians dress in the regional costume of the state of Jalisco, a combination of the Spanish riding costume and the working clothes of the vaquero. Mariachis, outfitted in these distinctive clothes, gather in the Plaza de Mariachis, which is located near the Mercado Libertad in the heart of Guadalajara.

Many of the city's major attractions are located in the immediate downtown area. The three main thoroughfares are Avenida Juárez, which runs east-west and intersects Avenida Alcalde, the major north-south street, and Calzada Independencia, which runs northeast-southwest, eventually intersecting Avenida Juárez. (Remember, in many Mexican towns and cities, street names change at major intersections.) Maps are available at the local tourist office, downtown shops, and hotels.

The heart of the city is the Plaza de los Laureles. The Cathedral Guadalajara is located on the east side of the plaza, and the church bell tower offers a panoramic view of the city. The cathedral was begun in 1571, and additions in a variety of styles have been made through the years. The church's twin towers were destroyed by an earthquake in the early years of this century, though they have been rebuilt. The architectural mixture of Byzantine, Corinthian, Moorish, Gothic, and Tuscan styles has a somewhat unsettling effect; however, the interior boasts some of the most beautiful *retablos* to be found anywhere – the altar of Our Lady of the Roses is particularly beautiful. One of the cathedral's most valued artworks is Estebán Bartolomé Murillo's painting *The Assumption of the Virgin,* which is on view in the sacristy.

Guadalajara, like so many Mexican colonial towns, is famous for its churches. Two of the most beautiful, the Church of St. Francis of Assisi and the Church of Our Lady of Aranzazu, are located near San Francisco Park, just a few blocks south of the zócalo.

On the west side of the Plaza de Armas is the Palacio del Gobierno, the Government Palace, and inside are murals painted by one of Guadalajara's most famous favorite sons, José Clemente Orozco. Orozco was born in Jalisco in 1883 and died in Mexico City in 1949. His work is hailed as significant both within Mexico and in the world community of artists. His murals were an attempt to reach the masses. He is quoted as saying, "Good murals are really painted Bibles and the masses need them as much as spoken Bibles. Many people cannot read books; in Mexico, this is a majority." He painted murals to show the people of Mexico their history, and his most famous ones are in Guadalajara, his hometown. Orozco lost his left hand as a child, an event that probably contributed to his melancholia throughout his life. He graduated as an agricultural engineer, but he began drawing cartoons in the early years of this century for a revolutionary paper. The revolution began in 1910. In 1913, Orozco executed a canvas showing the retreat of the Spanish Army in 1822, considered a revolutionary subject. Following the Revolution, he began to paint murals in Mexico City. For a time in the late twenties and early thirties, he painted in the United States, and his paintings from that period can be found in Dartmouth College in New Hampshire and Pomona College in California. Orozco's bold, colorful murals and paintings are angular

GUADALAJARA

To Zapopan

Calzada A. Camancho

Circunvalación

GUADALAJARA

To Mazatlan & Nogales

Av. Vallarta

The Archway

Chapultepec

Av. N

N

Av. López Mateos

Calzada M. Otero

To Morelia

in style and rich in symbolism. They emphasize struggle. No visitor to the city should miss an opportunity to view his works.

The artist's workshop is now a museum and can be visited daily. (Follow Avenida Juárez west – the workshop is located just before Avenida Juárez intersects Avenida Presidente López Mateos.) More of the artist's work, *Man of Fire* and *The Four Horsemen of the Apocalypse*, can be viewed at the Hospicio Cabañas, an orphanage just two blocks east of Calzada Independencia Norte, near the market.

Guadalajara is a good place to buy pottery and glassware – for an overview of all the crafts of the region, visit the Casa de las Artesanías de Jalisco. This shop is a government owned and operated crafts center and sells various crafts at fixed prices – it's a good idea to visit the center before shopping in the market to get an idea of comparable price and quality. The center is located near Parque Agua Azul, south of the zócalo on Calzada Independencia Sur. (Don't get your Independencias mixed up – the main street is Calzada Independencia; another Independencia, Calle Independencia runs east-west joining the Calzada and Avenida Alcalde.) Parque Agua Azul is a popular Sunday spot where *tapatíos* gather with their children to enjoy the flower garden, amusement park, zoo, and the birds in the tropical aviary.

Guadalajara's main market is called Mercado Libertad and is located on Independencia, across from the Plaza Liberacion and the impressive Teatro Degollado, home of the city's symphony orchestra. Libertad is a huge, modern marketplace featuring everything from food staples to magic herbs. On Sundays take a cab to El Baratillo, the flea market, which is held in a maze of streets and is about a five-minute drive from downtown.

One of the largest shopping centers in Latin America is located in the southwestern part of the city (you will need a cab unless you happen to be staying at one of the hotels in that area) and it's called the Plaza del Sol. Located between Mariano Otero and Avenida López Mateos, the center features many boutiques and art galleries.

You will find more nightlife in Guadalajara than in most of Mexico's colonial cities, but not the variety offered in the capital or Acapulco. Of course, one of the best ways to spend an evening is in the Plaza de Mariachis, where the bands begin to play in late afternoon and really get going by the late evening hours. And Guadalajara has the usual selection of bars and discos.

Special fiestas and celebrations include Octoberfest, a month-long festival of music, dance, theater, bullfights, and other special events. A colorful fiesta is held in the suburb of Zapopan every October 12 when the revered Virgin of Zapopan returns to her home church after touring the city's other churches. Of course, the national holidays, particularly Independence Day, are celebrated in Guadalajara with typical Mexican exuberance. Unlike Mexico City, Guadalajara observes the siesta; however, many large businesses are abandoning the practice.

BULLFIGHTS AND CHARREADAS

In a country where many people work six days a week, Sundays are special days, and in Guadalajara bullfights and *charreadas*, Mexican rodeos, are the order of the day. Bullfights are held every Sunday from November to May in the Plaza de Toros, located in downtown Guadalajara. Called both a "dance of death" and a "ballet," bullfighting often seems alien to foreigners, but if you want to see a well-executed bullfight (as opposed to some of the butcherings that take place in smaller, tourist-oriented rings), then Guadalajara is one of the best places to go. If you don't enjoy the spectacle, refrain from expressing your opinions and leave quietly.

Second only in popularity nationwide to bullfights, *charreadas* are more popular among the *tapatíos* of Jalisco than anywhere else in the country. Many of the best *charros*, riders, are found here. Complicated rules govern a *charreada* as in the bullfight. Even the costumes must follow certain rules. *Charro* costumes originated in Salamanca, in Spain, and the conquistadores brought *charro* tradition with them. There are several classes of costumes, the grandest being the *gran gala* suit. The sombrero is made of felt or woven palm and has a wide crown and brim. It may be worn plain, or decorated with braid, gold or silver. The shirt is usually cotton or linen, perhaps discreetly embroidered. The *charro* wears his tie in what is called the "butterfly" style, knotted at the throat with long, flowing tails. The tie should be red, brown, or gray — serious colors. Frivolous colors like pink or baby blue are not considered manly. The *charro's* trousers are tightly fitted and decorated with gold or silver buttons along the outer seam, and his boots are made of a single piece of leather.

The Federation of Charros sets out the rules for *charreadas* and the *charro*, in spite of his peacock appearance, must be able to meet a demanding test of his skill as a horseman. There are ten basic contests in a *charreada*, including the horse position, riding expertise, lassoing, wild bull or wild horse riding, a tail-pulling competition, and the dangerous *paso de la muerte*, the pass of death. Several of the tests of skill are similar to those seen in US rodeo arenas since many cowboys learned their skills from the Mexican vaquero. The *charro*, though, must execute his moves with the grace of a ballet dancer.

The horse position contest begins with the *charro* astride his mount facing the judge. He then turns the horse as quickly as possible in a tight circle, to face the judge again at the end of the turn. Judging is based on the cleanness of the turn and the responsiveness of the horse.

To test riding expertise, mounted horsemen line up at the farthest point of the ring and then, following a signal, race full speed to the judges' stand. Again, responsiveness is the test.

Charros rope both bulls and horses in the lassoing contest, on horseback and foot. They also perform rope tricks, some of which have been incorporated into ballet folklórico performances.

The wild bull and wild horse contests are similar to those held in the United States. Points are given for length of time on board, and the *charro* is not allowed to hold the rail as he dismounts. One-handed rides win him extra points.

In the tail-pulling contest, the *charro* on horseback chases down a wild bull, grabs his tail, and twists it to turn the animal over. Sometimes part of the tail is torn loose — the weak-hearted may want to avoid the tail-pulling contests.

The *paso de la muerte* is the *charro's* moment of truth. This is the true test of horsemanship, in which man and horse must rely on each other. A wild horse is set free in the ring, and the *charro* must follow him. At the right moment, the *charro* jumps from his own animal to the wild horse.

Given its color and similarity to our rodeo, the weekly *charreada* is something visitors should try to attend. The spectacle has the inevitable atmosphere of fiesta found at any Mexican celebration. If you don't think you can cross the cultural bridge to watch a bullfight, a *charreada* is the next best Mexican experience.

Charreadas are not unfamiliar to Texans, especially South Texans who are familiar with the so-called Mexican rodeo, which includes displays of riding skill and the arts of the vaquero. Each Sunday afternoon, *charreadas* are held in Parque Agua Azul. The *tapatíos* also display their riding skills on the first Thursday of each month in a *serenata tapatía* in the Plaza de Armas. *Charros* ride around the square either on horseback or in carriages courting costumed ladies. The *serenata* begins at 6:30 P.M.

IN THE SUBURBS

TLAQUEPAQUE

It's pronounced Tlah-keh-pah-keh, and it's one of Guadalajara's prime attractions. A shopping mecca for tourists, San Pedro Tlaquepaque is located in the southeast quadrant of the city and, like most Mexican suburbs, is a town within itself. A cab ride from downtown will cost you approximately 60 pesos (rates are fixed in Guadalajara), or you can drive your car and park it in the municipal parking garage at Obregon and Morelos. To reach Tlaquepaque, head south on Boulevard Tlaquepaque, turn left onto Florida, drive five blocks east, and turn south onto Francisco Madero; turn left again onto Morelos and look for the parking garage entrance.)

It's easy to spend a whole day in Tlaquepaque and fortunately, there are plenty of restaurants and cafés where you can rest your feet — wear good walking shoes.

You may wish to begin your tour at the Tourist Office located in a pedestrian arcade just one block from the parking garage. The easiest way to find the office is to look for the parish church, El Templo Parroquial de San Pedro. Running through the heart of the suburb and one block south of the parking garage is Independencia, a pedestrian mall. Head for the mall, walk west for one block, and turn north onto P. Sanchez. On your right, midway through the block is Guillermo Prieto, an L-shaped arcade where you will find the Tourist Office and the main entrance to the church. The Tourist Office is open from 9 A.M. to 8 P.M. during the week, from 9 A.M. to 1 P.M. on Saturdays, and closed on Sundays. Maps and tourist information are available. In addition, many of the local shops give away maps of the area. The post office is located in the arcade, and you may mail small packages from there.

Most of the shops and restaurants are located on Independencia; however, one of the best restaurants in Mexico is located just one block east of the Tourist Office at Francisco Madero No. 80. To help confuse everyone, the restaurant has no name, so it's known as "The restaurant with no name." There is not a sign, either; however, you can make reservations by calling 35-45-20. Open every day from noon until midnight, the restaurant has been hailed by food critics as one of the best in Mexico. It is housed in an old colonial mansion, and patrons dine in a variety of rooms or on the patio where an orchid collection is displayed and exotic birds wander. The menu is a mixture of classical Mexican and French cuisine; dress is casual and reservations are recommended. In keeping with the neighborhood, the restaurant with no name also houses the art gallery with no name — you may be given a table in the gallery. A variety of work by Mexican and foreign artists of note is displayed for sale in the gallery.

Next door to the restaurant with no name, is the gallery called K. E. de Tonala. K. E. stands for Kenneth Edwards, the American who urged the potters of nearby Tonala to adopt new techniques in order to produce sturdy stoneware. The pieces are known for their brilliant glazes.

Back on Independencia is a multitude of galleries and small craft shops. At the east end of the mall is El Parian, a block of cafés and bars, a few stores, and patios where mariachis are for hire. Across the street are two well-known jewelry stores, Joeria Rodríguez and Plateria Magda. Walking west on the mall, the visitor sees on the north side El Jardín, the suburb's main square, which is often the scene of some fiesta. West of the square, is Leo y Hijos, a leather goods shop that can produce special orders within a few hours. On the north side of the next block is Girasol, featuring designer clothes by Gonzalo Bauer; Bazar Hecht, where you will find furniture and objets d'art; El Balcon, selling contemporary ironwork, leather furniture, and cotton by the yard; and Galeria d'Mama Carlota, where Victor Camaerena's designs for women are sold. Across the street, Mis 4 Reales sells glassware and ceramics. Next door is Camarasa, where you can buy some of the famous red glassware.

Between Cruz Verde and C. Medelin on the north side of the mall is the gallery of Sergio Bustamante whose work has become very well known in the United States and much-copied in Mexico. You can buy an original, signed, and numbered piece for about half what you would pay in the United States. Bustamante's whimsical papier-mâché and metal animals sell for hundreds of dollars in stores like Blooming-dale's, Gump's, and Macy's in the United States. Even if you can't afford to buy, browse through the delightful gallery.

Next door is Rosa de Cristal, the suburb's oldest glass factory. You can watch the glass blowers at work every day until 3 P.M., except on Sunday. Many of the glass factories will take custom orders and ship.

Across the street from the Bustamante studio is a ceramic museum, Museo Regional de la Cerámica. Open Tuesday through Saturday from 10 A.M. until 4 P.M., and Sunday from 10 A.M. until 2 P.M., the museum is free, and there are displays of pottery, with pictures of the area's most famous artisans. Also on this block is the Alfareria la Colonial which sells lamps and carved stone fountains. Many of the Tlaquepaque stores will ship large items back to the United States for a reasonable fee. The shipping is reliable, but don't expect your purchases to arrive back home before you do.

On the final block of the pedestrian mall are a couple of restaurants, one of which serves hamburgers and Texas barbecue. If you are hungry for a taste of home, Mariachi, the open-air café on the north side, is the place to go. It's open Monday through Saturday. On the south side of Independencia is Los Ocho Soles a restaurant-bar which features Mexican food. It's open daily. At No. 295 on the south side of the mall is Maximilian, a leather shop which also features a large stock of Jorge Wilmot's well-known ceramics — you may have seen his animal-shaped pieces in brown and pale blues, painted with flowers, in many of Mexico's better shops. For antique furniture, visit Antigua de Mexico at No. 255 on the south side of the mall, closed on Sundays.

There are several more stores worth visiting one block south of the mall on Avenida Juárez. Look for the Barefoot Eagle at No. 120 for dresses by Josefa; Jimenez Hermanos at No. 145 for leather; Mia, No. 145-5, sells hand-woven rugs; Cristal Tlaquepaque, No. 315, for glass-ware; Cerámica Guada, No. 347, for handmade tiles; and El Tular, No. 417, for furniture and *equipales*, the leather patio furniture popular in the Southwest.

Because many of the stores in Tlaquepaque are closed on Sunday, and a few are closed on Monday, Saturday is a good day to visit.

TONALA

A few miles beyond Tlaquepaque is Tonala, where many of the artisans whose work is sold in Tlaquepaque have their *tallers* ("workshops"). Prices here are lower than at the tourist shops in town. Mexican *tallers* are much like the workshops of medieval craftsmen; home and work place are combined, and goods are displayed in the central courtyards of each compound. As you park your car or leave your cab, young boys will offer to give you a tour of the *tallers*. Offer a small tip if you accept, or strike off on your own. Many of the *tallers* are hidden behind walls and there are few signs, but it's perfectly acceptable to wander into the inner courtyards and watch the artisans at work. The Tonala craft market is on Thursdays and Sunday mornings.

ZAPOPAN

This is the home of one of Mexico's most revered religious icons, the tiny Virgin of Zapopan. The ten-inch statue of the Virgin, called *la zapopanita*, is the central figure in one of Jalisco's major fiestas. From June to October, she tours the city's churches, bringing her blessings. Then, on October 12, she returns to her home in Zapopan. The legend surrounding the Virgin says that in 1531, as the Spaniards battled the Chimalhuacano Indians, Fray Antonio de Segovia, a Franciscan friar, climbed a hill above the battle and held the Virgin's image before the Indians. They surrendered and converted to Christianity. Now, *la zapopanita* is revered, particularly among the Indians, and she is kept in a special silver cup inside the basilica on the main plaza.

To get to Zapopan, take Avenida Alcalde past the cathedral in downtown Guadalajara, and turn left onto Avila Camacho, which leads into the main square of Zapopan. There's also a museum in the suburb featuring the work of the Huichol-Cora Indians. The Huichols and their brother Coras revere the peyote plant, and the colorful, fanciful wool paintings and so-called "God's Eyes" that are displayed and sold here are no doubt inspired, in part, by their ritual peyote-taking.

BARRANCA DE OBLATOS

Mexico's city planners may not have prepared for the automobile, but they did have the foresight to plan large parks where Mexicans could escape the crowded barrios and streets. The Parque Independencia, located at the north end of Calzada Independencia, encompasses a rugged, natural *barranca* ("canyon"). Much of the land has been left in its natural state, and the park is a favorite spot for alfresco picnics on Sundays, the only day off many Mexicans enjoy. There are also an outdoor amphitheater and snack bars. There's a five-peso admission.

DAY TRIPS

TEQUILA FACTORIES

There are several tequila factories located in Guadalajara; however, a trip to the factories in the nearby town of Tequila affords the visitor a chance to see the Jaliscan countryside and the vast fields where the tequila-producing maguey is grown.

Tequila is approximately 36 miles northwest of Guadalajara on Highway 15. Free samples of virgin tequila, 120 proof, are offered—

drivers beware. Made from the maguey cactus, a blue-green plant that looks much like a huge aloe-vera, the first tequila is said to have been distilled in the early seventeenth century by the Spanish. The Sauza and Cuervo families established their distilleries in the late 1800s.

The tequila factories in Guadalajara are located in the western section of the city. Tequila Orendain is located at Vallarta 6230; Tequila Sauza offers tours at its city plant at Vallarta 3273. The four most well-known brands of tequila are Cuervo, Sauza, Orendain, and Herradura.

EL SALTO DE JUANACATLAN

Beyond the Guadalajara airport, some 30 miles from the city is Lake Chapala. On the road to the lake and along its shores are several interesting sights which can either be combined into a single, somewhat hurried day of sight-seeing or extended over a period of several days. A rental car is the best way to get around, but if you prefer not to drive there are guided tours of the area (check with the Tourist Office) or you can rent a cab for the day.

Follow Hwy. 90 out of Guadalajara and look for the Juanacatlán turnoff, approximately four miles beyond the airport. El Salto means *falls*, and the waterfall at Juanacatlán is billed as the "Niagra Falls" of Mexico. In the wet season, the horseshoe-shaped falls are spectacular as they plunge 150 feet to the valley. Even in the winter (the dry season) the falls are impressive, and it is possible to get even a closer view of them.

LAKE CHAPALA

This 50-mile-long lake is the largest in Mexico and along its banks are some of the most popular retirement havens for US and Canadian citizens. Swimming in the lake is not recommended. However, you may want to take one of the boat trips to Isla de los Alacranes (Scorpion Island) which is located in the middle of the large lake. You can also rent boats in Chapala. All the restaurants in the area serve *pescado blanco*, the famous and delicious highland lakes whitefish.

CHAPALA

The highway leads right into this lakeside town where many of the residents are retirees and artists. The climate, the beautiful countryside, and the relaxed atmosphere make the north shore of Lake Chapala a favorite with tourist and settler alike. The adjoining community of Chula Vista is heavily populated with Americans. There are several golf courses in the area, as well as facilities for swimming, fishing, waterskiing, tennis, and horseback riding.

Chapala is 5000 feet above sea level and enjoys a year-round balmy climate. The town was founded by an Indian leader, Chapalac—hence the name. There are a promenade and beer gardens on the lakeshore where Chapalac established his settlement. Many *tapatios* leave

Guadalajara for the weekend lakeside homes every week, and the town is crowded on weekends and holidays. There are excellent restaurants along the seafront. If you want to spend the night, there are several budget hotels in town.

AJIJIC
Pronounced Ah-hee-hic, this lakeside town west of Chapala is a haven for artists and writers. It's also a good place to buy native crafts. If you are looking for a place to get away from the hustle of Guadalajara for a day or two, book a room at the Posada Ajijic, a colonial-style hotel on Avenida 16 de Septiembre. The hotel has an excellent restaurant.

SAN JUAN COSALA
West of Ajijic is the spa San Juan Cosala. It's a popular spot on weekends. You can take the waters in the public baths where the thermal waters are pumped. There's also a geyser that sends hot water into the air. Dressing rooms, a bar, and restaurant are located near the baths.

JOCOTEPEC
This is one of the prettiest villages on the north shore of the lake; however, there are limited tourist facilities. Posada Ajijic runs La Quinta hotel, which is the best place to stay in town. The big attraction in Jocotepec is the white serapes that are sold everywhere. Carefully examine the serape before buying, and check the hints on shopping in the chapter The Enormous Store.

IXTEPETE
Approximately one mile east of Jocotepec the road meets Highway 15, the road to Mexico City. Turn right and you are back on the road to Guadalajara. The Periferico, the beltline highway which circles the city, is a few miles up the road. When you reach it, take the turnoff for Mazatlán and merge onto the Periferico. Immediately begin to look for a small sign pointing to Ixtepete. In a field near the highway is one of the few archaeological sites uncovered in this area. Little is known about the preconquest Indians who occupied this area, except for the information the conquistadores gleaned from the Aztecs who were generally unsuccessful in conquering the western groups. One crude, early attempt was made to reassemble the pyramid at Ixtepete some sixty years ago, but since then the site has been left in its natural state.

GREAT ESCAPES

PATZCUARO
If you want to combine a trip to Guadalajara with a few, quiet days

in the Mexican countryside, consider Pátzcuaro. Approximately 150 miles southwest of Guadalajara, Pátzcuaro offers a unique view of life in an ancient part of Mexico, now a protected colonial town. Pátzcuaro is one of Mexico's most beautiful communities, and the road from Guadalajara to this town in Michoacán winds through some of Mexico's most enchanting countryside. The area is rich in crafts, also. (For more details on Pátzcuaro, see the chapter **Mexico of the Colonials.**)

URUAPAN
Throughout Mexico, old haciendas have been restored as luxury hotels, often with very reasonable room rates. One of the best is located in Uruapan, near Pátzcuaro, about 150 miles from Guadalajara. Mansion del Cupatítzio is located on the edge of a national park and is surrounded by meadows filled with wildflowers. (For more information see the section "Hacienda Havens" in **The Unique and the Random.**)

PUERTO VALLARTA AND MANZANILLO
Both Puerto Vallarta and Manzanillo are within a day's drive of Guadalajara, or you can hop a plane and be there in less than an hour. If you are driving, consider touring the remote beaches around San Blas, north of Puerto Vallarta. The remote hotels here are seldom full. (For suggestions about where to stay on the Pacific coast and how to find hideaways there, see the chapter **The Astonishing Coastlines.**)

BOCADITOS

Guadalajara is a confusing city to navigate; invest in a good map of the city and study it. The city is divided into four sectors, Hidalgo in the northwest, Juárez in the southwest, Libertad in the northeast, and Reforma in the southeast. Maps are available at the Tourist Office that is located in the former Convent of Carmen at Av. Juárez 638 downtown. It helps to remember that Mexican streets often change their names after they intersect a major boulevard. Also, streets in Guadalajara used to be numbered rather than named, and as the phone book still uses the old numbered system, using it as a guide is a hopeless proposition. If you want to find out where a restaurant is located, call the number and ask what street it is on. (Use public phones. They only cost 20 centavos to use and are much cheaper than hotel calls.)

Homesickness Cures: If you get a little homesick, Guadalajara has plenty to remind you of the good ole US of A — Sears and Woolworth's both operate stores here, and you can use your Sears charge card. Kentucky Fried Chicken (Pollo Frito) and Denny's have several outlets around town. The American expatriate contingent has encouraged a flourishing ice cream trade in Guadalajara — Bing's, a favorite *neveria*, has ice cream parlors all over the city featuring its thirty or so flavors. All of Bing's dairy goods are pasteurized.

AROUND GUADALAJARA

VITAL STATISTICS

Climate. Springlike weather much of the year. Some hot summer days, cool nights. Occasional rain showers in summer.

Population. Three million.

Altitude. 5,000 feet.

State. Jalisco.

City phone code. 36.

HOTELS

Calinda Roma, Av. Juárez 170 (14-86-50). Part of the Quality Inn chain, a modern hotel, recently remodeled. Good location with a parking garage. C. Cr.

Camino Real, Av. Vallarta 5005 (21-72-17). Set in tropical gardens four miles from downtown. Quiet, but with all the facilities of a chain hotel. A. Cr.

El Tapatío, Hwy. 44 (35-60-50). This resort is located four miles to the south on a hill overlooking the city. Tennis, golf, horseback riding, jogging track, sauna, swimming, and disco. A. Cr.

Guadalajara Sheraton, Niños Héroes and 16 de Septiembre (14-72-72). A high-rise hotel with all the usual Sheraton amenities. Beautiful gardens and a large pool set in lush surroundings. Excellent rooftop restaurant, La Pergola. A. Cr.

Gran Hotel, Morelos 2244 (15-01-86). A grande dame with a face-lift. Popular with returning visitors. In the heart of the city. B. Cr.

Hotel de Mendoza, Venustiano Carranza 16 (13-46-40). This peaceful, colonial-style hotel is as charming as the city of Guadalajara. Courteous service. Quaint furnishings. C. Cr.

Posada Guadalajara, López Mateos 1280 (21-20-22). A colonial-style hotel built around a patio. Small, intimate, and popular. C. Cr.

RESTAURANTS

Albatross, Av. La Paz 1840 (25-99-96). Popular seafood restaurant in an old, restored home. Dining is outside under the stars. Moderate. Cr.

Benito's, three locations, Av. Americas 1184 (41-52-51), Francisco de Quevedo 44A (15-58-58), and Calzada Independencia Nte. 931 (17-66-65). Open noon to midnight for pizza, spaghetti, hamburgers, to eat there or to go. Moderate. Cr.

Bing's, various locations. The best ice cream in Mexico comes from this chain started by a former American consul in Guadalajara. Bing's also serves super hamburgers. Inexpensive.

Cazadores, several locations. Serving good regional food, including barbecued meats in *molé* and *adobado* sauce. The best location for lunch is in Tlaquepaque, the artists' colony, and in the Casa de los Perros, an old colonial house downtown near the square at Avenida Alcalde.

Chalet Suizo, Hidalgo 1983 (15-71-22). Popular American hangout. Housed in an old home that has been remodeled with a Swiss chalet in mind. The place is kept spotlessly clean by the Swiss proprietors. Try the Wiener schnitzel. Moderate. Cr.

El Ché, Av. Hidalgo 1798 (15-05-27). Argentine-style grilled steaks accompanied by Argentine gaucho music. Moderate. Cr.

Hacienda de la Flor, in the suburb of Zapopan. One of the most beautiful restaurants in the world. The decor is Mexican ranch style executed with flair and elegance. The alfresco effect is enhanced with magnificent flower arrangements and candlelight. The menu features excellent regional specialties. Expensive. Cr.

La Copa de Leche, Av. Juárez 414 (13-07-09). A dependable standby and the oldest restaurant in downtown Guadalajara. The sidewalk café downstairs is the place for a snack or a leisurely lunch. The dining room is upstairs. (The maître d' will probably try to seat you downstairs, but insist on going upstairs if you plan dinner.) Moderate. Cr.

Las Margaritas, Av. López Cotilla (16-89-06). Vegetarian dishes, milkshakes, and health foods for sale. Inexpensive. N.

Le Bistrot, Av. Vallarta (25-82-39). One of the city's top French restaurants. Intimate atmosphere. Expensive. Cr.

Recco, Libertad 1873 (25-07-24). Excellent Italian food served in posh Italian surroundings. The special cocktail is a Martini Oro, made with sherry. Expensive. Cr.

Suehiro, Av. La Paz 1701 (26-00-94). Authentic Japanese food prepared at the table. Moderate. Cr.

Tekare, Dies y Seis de Septiembre (14-97-91). One of the city's posh spots. A penthouse restaurant with a great view of the city. Continental food. Dancing. Expensive. Cr.

The restaurant with no name, Madero 80, Tlaquepaque (35-45-20). One of the most famous restaurants in Mexico, renowned for its Mexican specialties, Mexican haute cuisine. Expensive. Cr.

VIPs, various locations. This chain restaurant serves pancakes, burgers, sandwiches — all the "junk" food Americans miss. Inexpensive.

NIGHTLIFE

Dancing, cheek-to-cheek. The Sheraton's La Rondalla offers a nightly floor show and dancing a la Glenn Miller, Monday through Saturday 9–2. Located in the hotel at Niños Héroes and 16 de Septiembre (14-72-72).

Disco. Two popular "deesco" spots are The Blackout at the Camino Real Hotel, Av. Vallarta 5005 (21-72-17), and Delirium at the Sheraton Hotel, Niños Héroes and 16 de Septiembre (14-72-72).

Los Equipales, off Federalismo at Manuel Acuña. Ask the bellhop for directions to this, the best blues and jazz club south of Preservation Hall in New Orleans. Old home turned into a music lover's haunt. Mainly men. (Unescorted women are not admitted.)

Mariachis, Plaza de Mariachis, Av. Alcalde and Av. Juárez. Listen to mariachi serenades in the city where mariachi music was born. The fun begins about eight and goes on late into the night. Remember, you order a song, you pay for it.

Panchos, Maestranza near Priciliano Sanchez. Floor-to-ceiling (30 feet!) bullfight posters, collected by owner Paco Jauregui, dominate this café. Jauregui plays Viennese waltzes during the leisurely lunch hours. Serves *antojitos* (snacks) all day. Eat, sway to the music, and drink your siesta away here. Moderate. Cr.

SHOPPING

Antiguades Cosme, Hernán Cortés 4137. A good selection of Mexican antiques.

Bazar Capuchinas, Independencia 684. Located in an eighteenth-century convent (hence the name), this store features a fine selection of arts and crafts.

Casa de las Artesanías de Jalisco, Independencia near Parque Agua Azul. A government-owned exposition hall and gift shop where you can find some of the best regional crafts at fixed prices. Closed Sundays.

El Baratillo, Juan Zavala, east of Mercado Libertad. A Sunday flea market of junk, antiques, black market goods, and stolen property. Mexican flea markets are among the best. Hard to find, so ask your bellhop.

Glass factories, located at Catalan 324 and Medrano 281. The factories can make custom orders and arrange for delivery.

Helen Cerda, La Villa 2036, Colonia Chapalita (21-04-32). Located just one block north of the Hotel Posada Guadalajara, this store features custom orders for hand-embroidered casual clothes.

Instituto de las Artesanías, Av. Alcalde and Avila Camacho (14-86-70). A good selection of handicrafts from throughout the state of Jalisco. Open 10:00–7:30. Closed Sundays. Cr.

Mercado Libertad, near Juárez and Calzada Independencia. The city's huge market covers several blocks and caters to both tourists and everyday shoppers. Open daily.

Plaza del Sol, Av. López Mateos and Mariano Otero. There are over 200 new shops in the modern shopping plaza located in the southern part of the city.

Teles Plan, Hidalgo 1378. Handloomed cloth and linens for sale, many from local Indian craftswomen.

Tlaquepaque, suburb located southeast of the downtown area. Famed for its variety of stores and good restaurants. Plan to spend a day here. Maps available from the tourist office, Guillermo Prieto arcade, also in most stores.

Tonala, small village beyond Tlaquepaque. Thursdays and Sundays are market days in this village famed for its ceramics. Many "seconds" for sale here that don't make their way to the shops in Tlaquepaque.

POINTS OF INTEREST

Bullfighting, Plaza Monumental de Toros, Independencia. One of the largest plazas in the world stands in the center of Guadalajara, and some of the best toreros in the world perform there each Sunday from November to May. Check at your hotel desk for ticket information.

Calandrias. These open-air carriages can be found in the main plaza and Parque Agua Azul. A 40-minute ride costs about 180 pesos (subject to inflation and valuation).

Cathedral, main square. The exterior is a mélange of styles, everything from baroque to Gothic and in between. But inside are some of the best examples of ecclesiastical art in the New World, notably the altar dedicated to Our Lady of Roses. The sacristy is the home of Murillo's famed *The Assumption of the Virgin*. Climb the bell tower for a breathtaking view of the city.

Churches, various locations. The city boasts many fine examples of colonial architecture, notable examples include Church of Saint Francis of Assisi, Av. Corona (note its ornate facade); Church of Our Lady of Aranzazu; and the Church of Santa Mónica, Calle Santa Mónica and San Felipe.

Hospico Cabañas, Calle Hospicio, two blocks east of Independencia. This orphanage has been made famous by two murals, *Man of Fire* and *The Four Horsemen of the Apocalypse,* which adorn its walls. Both are by José Clemente Orozco, one of Mexico's three major muralists and native of Guadalajara. Open daily.

Palacio de Gobierno, west side of the main plaza. The Government Palace was built in the seventeenth and eighteenth centuries. Padre Hidalgo abolished slavery here in 1810. There are several notable murals by Orozco inside. Open Monday through Friday. Free.

Parque Agua Azul, Calzada Independencia Sur. A popular gathering place on Sundays for families. Band concerts, folkloric dances, strolling musicians, and vendors. A bird park, amphitheater, and flower market. Museums. Open daily.

Teatro Degollado, Plaza de la Liberación. This Belle Epoque theater is the home of the Guadalajara Symphony. Concerts are given throughout the year. Check at the tourist office for a schedule or visit the theater — the interior is magnificent.

MUSEUMS

El Museo Orozco, Aurelio Aceves 27. The workshop of José Clemente Orozco, one of Mexico's three major muralists, has been turned into a museum. On display are several of his sketches for larger works. Closed Mondays.

Museo de la Paleontológica, Hidalgo 290. This small museum houses the remains of a Stone-Age mammoth discovered in Guadalajara in 1962. Other exhibits include arrowheads and ancient skeletons found in the area. Closed Monday.

Museo Arqueológico de Occidente de Mexico, Plaza Juárez. Western Mexico's past has not been explored as much as that of other regions of the country, but what has been documented can be viewed here. Closed Sundays.

Museo del Estado, Av. Corona, one block north of Palacio de Gobierno on the main square. Housed in an eighteenth-century seminary, this museum features exhibits of colonial and pre-Hispanic art, including works by Murillo. Open daily.

SPORTS

Charreadas, Parque Agua Azul, Calzada Independencia Sur. *Charros,* Mexico's gentlemen cowboys, perform with great flair and precision at the *charro* ring in the park. Exhibitions by children and young women are held, also. Each Sunday, shortly before noon.

Golf, various locations. There are several clubs in the area. Two welcome visitors: Club de Golf Santa Anna — for reservations call long-distance 91-373-6-03-21 (the club is only 20 minutes from downtown, however) — and Bosques de San Isidro, a scenic valley course (call 21-11-48 for information).

Tennis, various locations. Three hotels have tennis facilties: Hotel El Tapatío (35-60-50), Camino Real (21-72-17); and Holiday Inn (21-21-00).

FIESTAS

Octoberfest, also known as Fiestas de Octobre, this is a collection of fiestas held in the city that usually center around a theme.

The Return of the Virgin of Zapopan, October 12. Check the date with the tourist office. The return of the statue to the church in Zapopan attracts a great number of spectators.

National holidays are celebrated on a grand scale in Guadalajara, particularly Cinco de Mayo and Deis y Seis de Septiembre.

TRANSPORTATION

Airport, located southeast of city. Thirty-minute drive to city. Served by both national and international carriers. Mexican Customs facilities. Taxi fares from the airport are approximately 600 pesos (subject to devaluation and inflation, prices may be less).

Buses. Guadalajara is a transportation hub, and luxury and first-class buses operate to and from here to many parts of the country. Local bus service is good and cheap.

Car rental. If you want to explore the area beyond downtown, this may be your best transportation bet, unless you can tackle the mysteries of the Mexican bus system. Rental agencies include Avis — at the international airport (35-81-90), at Hotel Fiesta Americana (25-34-34), at Niños Héroes 942-A (12-34-51), and at Avenida Vallarta and Calle Mazamitlá (15-48-25); Hertz — at the international airport (14-78-99), at the Guadalajara airport (domestic arrivals, 35-89-39), at Niños Héroes 9 and Calzada Independencia Sur (14-61-39), and at the Holiday Inn, López Mateos and Mariano Otero (21-24-00); and National — at the international airport (35-84-05) and at Av. Niños Héroes 938 Sur (14-71-75).

Taxis. The fares are low in Guadalajara and the cabs are metered; however, get an estimate before you get in.

Trains. Guadalajara is a major railroad crossroads. The station is at the southern end of Calzada Independencia Sur. (For general information about train service in Mexico, see the chapter **There and Back Again** or check at the local tourist office listed below.)

TOURIST SERVICES

American Express, Av. López Mateos Nte. 477 (30-02-00).

Divertel. Call 30-24-89 for a description in English of the cultural and artistic events planned for the coming week.

Hospital Mexico-Americano, Colomos 2110 (41-26-17). One of the best hospital facilities in Mexico with ties to the United States.

Tourist office (Delegación Federal de Turismo), Av. Juárez 638 (13-66-91 in town or 14-01-56 at the airport).

US Consulate (25-27-08).

Canadian Consulate (41-23-65).

COMMUNICATIONS

Newspapers. *The Guadalajara Weekly,* which is free, contains news of local American community and national news.

Post Office and Telegraph Office, Colon and Pedro Moreno.

7

MEXICO OF THE ANCIENTS

AN ARCHAEOLOGICAL TOUR

M exico's archaeological ruins, crumbling in the tropical rain forest or standing high against the clouds and blue sky on sheared mountaintops, are among the beautiful vistas in the world. They are the synthesis of art and science — Byronic inspirations for the romantic, satisfying challenges for the scientist. Each ruin has its own character, its own special aura. Teotihuacán is powerful, oppressive; Monte Albán, otherworldly, a city in the clouds; and Cobá, hidden in the jungle, is mysterious and compelling. Each provokes a different response. Some say Palenque is the most beautiful, others Uxmal, or Chichén Itzá, but each is different and time has worked on each with a different brush.

The ruins at Chichén Itzá are best viewed at sunrise, but the dawn passes quickly in the Yucatán peninsula, the sun rising fast and hot. At first light, the birds wake noisily in the jacaranda trees, and the heavy forest dew evaporates long before visiting city dwellers begin their mornings. It is not yet seven o'clock and already the humming-birds are at work in the heat. But this heat is not the man-made result of sun on metal and asphalt; this is the languid heat of the tropics. Inside the dank limestone temples, the packed earthen pathways are cool, damp tunnels in the forest.

For the modern romantic, the dreamer in search of some continuity or a message of security from the past, Chichén Itzá is a special place. It was to this Mayan city that Quetzalcoatl came.

Quetzalcoatl is the Plumed Serpent, a god of great power in the ancient pantheon; but he is also a man and a folk hero, the Toltec warrior who brought a cult of peace to the Yucatecan forests. Legend and history are hard to separate in any time; however, scholars generally agree that in the middle of the tenth century a child named Ce Acatl (One Arrow-reed) was born to a Toltec warrior name Mixcoatl and his wife, Chimalma. The child's uncle killed his brother, Mixcoatl, and his wife, Chimalma, and Ce Acatl was raised by his maternal grandparents. Ce Acatl became known as Ce Acatl Topiltzin (Our Prince) Quetzalcoatl — the last name probably to honor the god or to signify that Ce Acatl was an initiate in the cult of the Plumed Serpent.

When Ce Acatl came of age, he wrested power from his evil uncle and killed him. To honor his murdered father, he established the cult of Mixcoatl, symbolized by a deer. And to honor the Plumed Serpent, the young prince decreed at Tula, the Toltec capital, that the gods did not want human sacrifice; they would be satisfied with offerings of snakes, flowers, incense, tortillas, and butterflies. This decree so angered Tezcatlipoca, a leader of one of the warrior cults, that he plotted against Quetzalcoatl. Tezcatlipoca invited the young prince to a party and got him drunk on pulque; then he forced the prince's sister to lie next to her brother. When Quetzalcoatl awoke, he was ashamed of his drunken behavior and horrified when he believed he had slept with his sister. Tezcatlipoca was able to drive him from Tula. But as he left, Quetzalcoatl predicted that he would return on the anniversary of his birth in a One Reed year.

Legend says the young prince then made a raft of snakes and sailed east. In Yucatán, where Quetzalcoatl is believed to have landed, he is known as Kukulcán (Mayan for "plumed serpent"). Scholars say Chichén Itzá, a Mayan religious center, was taken over in the tenth century by Toltec warriors who superimposed Toltec structures on the site. In many ways Chichén Itzá is a replica, only on a grander scale, of Tula. El Caracol, the observatory, is similar to the observatory at Tula, and the Chac-mools, reclining humanlike statues, are found at both sites. The image of Kukulcán/Quetzalcoatl is seen at both sites, also.

But Quetzalcoatl's peaceful cult seems to have existed only in legend, for at Chichén Itzá there are grim reminders of human sacrifice — a bas-relief showing a ball player being beheaded; a platform with carvings of skulls, each representing individual victims; and carvings of eagles clutching human hearts. However, the legend persisted, particularly among the Aztecs, who revered Quetzalcoatl as a great hero. They believed he would return as he said he would, dressed in black with fair skin and a dark beard.

On April 21, 1519, a One Reed year, Hernán Cortés, dressed in black out of respect for Holy Week and bearded in the Spanish fashion, stepped ashore on the land where Quetzalcoatl had sworn to return.

When Cortés landed, many of the religious sites had already been abandoned; others, like the Aztec capital of Tenochtitlán, were flourishing centers of religion and commerce. The priests, some who arrived with Cortés and others who soon followed him, were invaluable in documenting the cultural and religious customs of the Indians. They were also quick to build temples of a different kind and to discourage, sometimes with the help of the Inquisition, the practicing of the old religion. The great religious centers quickly became hollow reminders of an overthrown empire. The Indian priests were conquered, and the gods were returned to the shamans, the ancient village conjurers and healers who had first brought them forth. And the people soon learned to genuflect before a different temple door.

Sitting in the grass on the overgrown plaza at Chichén Itzá, one may feel it fanciful to recall the legend of Quetzalcoatl and his promise to return. Little has changed for the Mayan people. The women still grind corn as they did, and the men still farm their milpas; though the Indian women no longer fear that their husbands and sons will be captured and sacrificed to appease the gods. Now the women buy bunches of flowers in the market and brush the Virgin's blue skirts with yellow gladiolus as they send their prayers heavenward.

ANCIENT MYSTERIES

No one knows how many temples lie in ruins in Mexico and Central America. The Indian may jealously guard the secrets of his ancestors — Bonampak with its famed Mayan murals was "discovered" in the 1940s, and Zaachila, the capital of the Zapotec kingdom, was unfriendly territory until recently — or he may regard the crumbling symbols of his ancient past as a good source of building materials for his home and animal pens. Only those who are not burdened by the present can afford the luxury of reconstructing the past.

New sites are being discovered constantly, and work on many of the well-known sites is far from complete. Of the existing sites, few have been spoiled by commercialization. Although several major sites, including Uxmal, Teotihuacán, and El Tajín, have sound and light shows at night, they are generally well done. All the ruins share the aura of mystery that surrounds the unfamiliar.

Among the first to marvel at the wonders of ancient Mexico was the American John Lloyd Stephens, and no serious visitor to Yucatán should go without first reading his books.

Controversy abounds in the literature on ancient Mexico; however, we've chosen the generally accepted dates and characteristics to distinguish among the various groups in Mesoamerican history. It may be easier to visit the sites without knowing a thing about them, but you can enhance your appreciation and sate your curiosity if you read as much as possible before you go. (Check the bibliography at the back of the book.)

Mesoamerican Civilization

All Mesoamerican groups shared certain distinguishing traits. Geographically, Mesoamerica stretched from a point just north of Tampico, across Mexico, dipping a little to a point south of the extreme tip of the Baja. In the south, the border crosses the middle of Honduras and Costa Rica. Humans occupied the Valley of Mexico as early as 10,000 B.C., and by the middle of the third millenium B.C. those traits identified as Mesoamerican (for example, the use of henequen fiber) had emerged. Mesoamerican civilization technically ended with the Spanish Conquest, although many cultural traits continue to exist.

One of the characteristics of Mesoamerican culture was the practice of superimposing structures on old buildings. Sites like Monte Albán in Oaxaca clearly illustrate this practice; and the stylistic motifs of each group are so distinctive that you can easily recognize them.

In addition to the superimposition of buildings, all Mesoamerican groups utilized subdivided markets (still in evidence today); Indian women cooked on a *comal* (many still do today); and their priests wrote in hieroglyphs and used a two-wheeled calendar to determine all worldly and spiritual affairs. Men and women harvested corn and used the henequen fibers of a certain agave to make rope. All the groups practiced human sacrifice and self-mutilation, and particularly the Maya practiced acts that artificially created physical deformities.

Another important common denominator was the shared pantheon of gods, which included a rain god, called Tláloc by the Aztecs, and their culture hero, Quetzalcoatl, known as Kukulcán among the Maya. The groups all believed in a multi-tiered heaven and underworld and held that the universe had four corners, each ruled by a god and a sacred color.

Although the groups shared many characteristics, they did not share a language. If fact, over a dozen language families have been identified, each further subdivided into specific languages and then dialects. Many of the Indian groups still speak the language of their ancient ancestors.

Another facet of Mesoamerican civilization has disappeared—the playing of a religious ball game on carefully constructed stone courts. Many stone reliefs, particularly those at Chichén Itzá and El Tajín, show the costumes and rituals associated with the game in great detail, but it has still not been determined if the captain of the winning or of the losing team was sacrificed at the end of the game.

At Chichén Itzá, a frieze that runs along the side of one of the ball court platforms shows two captains facing each other. One captain has been beheaded by the other, and as the blood pours out of his head it turns to corn, the sacred symbol of life. The ball court at Chichén Itzá is one of the largest and was probably used for ritual games; however, smaller courts may have been used for sport.

Mesoamerican people also shared a penchant for trade. Merchants, particularly under the Aztecs, were a special class, and throughout Mesoamerican history there seems to have been a flourishing trade system. Feathers, shells, styles of pottery, and precious and semiprecious stones were freely traded among the various groups.

For the tourist interested in the more accessible sites, Mesoamerican civilization can be divided into the following groups: the Maya, the Tarascan, the Aztec, the Zapotec, the Mixtec, the people of El Tajín, the Toltec, and the people of Teotihuacán. All the groups except the last three have identifiable descendants living today.

The Aztec

Of course, the best-known civilization is the Aztec, but the fierce Aztecs (also known as the Azteca, Mexica, or Tenocha) were late arrivals on the Mesoamerican scene. They were Chichimec, roughly translated as barbarians or the sons of dogs, who swept down from the north probably around the year A.D. 800, when Charlemagne was consolidating his European empire. By A.D. 1300 they were firmly established in the Valley of Mexico, and by 1427 their chief speaker or emperor, Itzcoatl (Obsidian Snake), had established a dynasty that included emperors with names like Moctezuma Ilhuicamina (Angry Lord Who Shoots the Sky) and Ahuitzotl (Water Monster) or Cuitlahuac (Keeper of the Kingdom) and Cuauhtémoc (Falling Eagle). Cuauhtémoc is something of a revered folk hero in Mexican legend — he led the last resistance against the Spaniards and was executed for his efforts.

The Aztecs ruled from their twin capitals of Tenochtitlán and Tlatelolco (now a suburb of Mexico City). Unfortunately, little remains of the Aztec kingdom. The canals that once served as the capital's thoroughfares were filled in by the Spaniards, and only the Floating Gardens of Xochimilco remain, a dismal remnant of what once must have been a marvelous network.

Most of the ruins visited by tourists in Mexico are not Aztec; however, the Aztecs did revere many of the sites they conquered and continued to use them. The original Aztec temples lie in ruins beneath Mexico City — the Zócalo, the main plaza, is built on the site of the Great Temple honoring Huitzilopochtli, the Aztec patron god of war. Remains of the Teocalli, the Great Temple, were uncovered in recent years when Mexico City's municipal government supervised construction of the subway.

The Aztecs believed it was their mission on earth to stop the cyclical destruction of the world. The earth had been destroyed four times, they believed, and to stop the fifth destruction, much human blood had to be spilled to appease the gods. Thus they practiced human sacrifice on a scale unmatched in Mesoamerican history and embarked on "wars of flowers" — ritual battles fought with their enemies in an attempt to capture prisoners for sacrifice.

Another obsession of the Aztec priests was the myth that Quetzalcoatl, the legendary Toltec warrior, would return in a One Reed year. Two One Reed years had passed, 1363 and 1467, without incident. The Aztec priests looked to the next One Reed year, 1519, for the warrior's return. Cortés landed in that year, and Moctezuma's subsequent indecision is legendary. Cortés's superiority in arms, if not in numbers, combined with the hatred of the Aztec's enemies allowed the conquistadors to conquer Mesoamerica quickly.

The Olmecs

If the Aztecs were the last Mesoamericans to rule an empire, who were the first? Some scholars say the Olmecs provided the "spark" that set off the creative fire in Mesoamerica. Although determining which group was first is a subject of great controversy, the most widely accepted theory is that between 1200 B.C. and 400 B.C. Olmec civilization arose near Veracruz on the eastern coast of Mexico. Sometimes called "the Magicians," the Olmecs had a powerful influence throughout Mesoamerica.

Olmec art is unlike other Mesoamerican styles; it is fluid, rounded, neither stylized nor static. The Olmec artistic signature is unique. Two good examples include the famous basalt heads of La Venta, located in a mangrove swamp south of Veracruz, and the Danzantes ("Dancers") bas-reliefs at Monte Albán in Oaxaca. The great basalt heads remain a mystery to scholars; the rock was transported from many miles away and carved in place. Each head has what scholars have described as "African" or "Negroid" features, and each appears to be wearing what looks like a football helmet. At Monte Albán, the Danzantes are contorted, sometimes physically deformed figures, which appear in various positions, some fetal.

The People of Teotihuacán

In Nahuatl, the language of the Aztecs, Teotihuacán means "place where men became gods." Located just 30 miles northeast of Mexico City at San Juan de Teotihuacán, the imposing site had been long abandoned when the Aztecs reached the Valley of Mexico.

In its prime, Teotihuacán ranged over eight square miles and was the largest of all Mesoamerican cities. (Some Mayan sites were larger; however, these were not true cities but religious centers.) Almost oppressive in its grandeur, Teotihuacán includes the remains of palaces and hovels, pyramids and temples. The site is dominated by two massive pyramids set at right angles to each other along a wide boulevard, the Miccoatli, popularly called "Avenue of the Dead." The

Pyramid of the Sun is the larger of the two, standing 207 feet high and measuring 720 feet by 440 feet at its base. Some historians believe the original symmetry of the pyramid was distorted by a botched restoration effort in the 1940s; however, it is the second largest structure to be built in Mexico during preconquest times.

Teotihuacán was begun in the second century B.C. and was abandoned sometime in the ninth century after Christ. In the fifth century the city's influence was felt throughout Mesoamerica, and pockets of Teotihuacán culture, as evidenced by pottery and architectural styles, have been found as far south as Guatemala. It has been estimated that the city boasted a population of 150,000 at its height.

Highlights of the ruins of Teotihuacán include the two pyramids — most hardy souls manage to climb one — and the so-called Citadel, not a fortress but part of a temple compound. At the eastern end of the plaza in front of the Citadel, which sits at the southern end of the Miccoatli, is the Temple of Quetzalcoatl. Plumed serpents with jaguar teeth and square images believed to be the rain god Tláloc decorate the facade.

Most of the ruins throughout Mesoamerica were once covered with stucco and painted in vivid colors; even the platforms that have now turned into grass-covered plazas were once painted with brilliant primary colors.

The key to recognizing the imprint of Teotihuacán design is to look for the *talud y tablero* style, basically a framed vertical panel supported by a sloping wall. Within the sphere of Teotihuacán's influence, one of the centers to retain its importance throughout Mesoamerican history was Xochicalco, 24 miles southwest of Cuernavaca. Scholars suggest Xochicalco survived because it is located on a hilltop in a good defensible position. The temple, with carvings of feathered serpents, is one of the most beautiful in Mesoamerica. The practiced eye can spot a variety of influences, even Mayan.

Another site thought to be linked to Teotihuacán is Cholula, near Puebla. This site had the largest structure in preconquest Mexico. Today the pyramid measures some fourteen hundred square feet and has a larger volume than the pyramid at Cheops in Egypt. The site covers 28 acres and may have been even larger in ancient times. At the instruction of the conquistadores, a church was built atop the pyramid, which is riddled inside with tunnels, the walls of which are decorated with frescoes.

Cholula has always been a significant religious center, and even after the mysterious fall of Teotihuacán it continued to be the site of religious services. In Toltec times, large numbers of humans were sacrificed at Cholula. The site has a long bloody history, which did not diminish with the coming of the conquerors — some three thousand Aztecs were killed there by Cortés and his men after La Malinche, his Indian mistress, warned that the Aztecs planned to murder them all.

Cholula and Xochicalco survived the disaster that destroyed Teotihuacán; the great city was abandoned and never occupied again. Some historians believe Teotihuacán was burned and sacked by the invading Toltecs circa A.D. 700.

The Zapotecs

While the people of Teotihuacán dominated the Valley of Mexico, the Zapotecs emerged as the dominant force to the south at the great center Monte Albán, overlooking the city of Oaxaca. Sometime in the third century B.C. the Zapotecs took over what had been, some believe, an Olmec outpost in the mountains. To create their city, they leveled a mountaintop, building one of the most impressive sites in Mesoamerica.

It is thought that the Zapotecs (President Benito Juárez was a modern-day descendant of this clan) were the first Mesoamericans to develop writing. The Danzantes at Monte Albán are marked with hieroglyphs that are believed to be the names of conquered and sacrificed warriors. Another interesting feature of Monte Albán is an arrow-shaped observatory, which is decorated on the outside with Olmec figures and Zapotec glyphs using the 52-year calendar. The dates are denoted by dots and bars — the system used later by the Maya.

Monte Albán was used as a religious center from Preclassic times to the tenth century after Christ, when Mixtec tribesmen, members of a Oaxacan hill tribe, invaded the Zapotec empire and turned Monte Albán into a funerary site. This inclination for elaborate funeral rites and burial customs is reminiscent of the early Egyptians. Tomb Number 7 has yielded one of the richest finds in the New World — gold masks, pearls, jade, silver, turquoise, jewelry, amulets, and even a pearl weighing 23 carats were found in the tomb where nine people were buried. The find is now displayed at the Regional Museum of Oaxaca.

Throughout the site stand several stelae, which are covered with hieroglyphs detailing victories by various chieftains. Throughout the site, a visitor can easily recognize the three elements of Olmec, Zapotec, and Mixtec cultures, the last group favoring symmetrical geometric designs often pieced together like a stone jigsaw puzzle. The best example of Mixtec design can be seen at nearby Mitla, a remarkable site that spills out over a hillside.

Other sites worth visiting, all within a one- or two-hour drive from Oaxaca, are Yagul, Zaachila, and Labiteyeco. The small roadside Mixtec site at Labiteyeco boasts two magnificent rain god masks and the images of a Mixtec man and woman buried there. Zaachila, the closely guarded capital of the Zapotec people, was only recently made accessible to archaeologists. Yagul is a small, rambling site with something of a Greek aura. The buildings lie in whitened ruins, and the site clings to a rocky promontory that points like a finger down to the Valley of Oaxaca. A hilltop tomb bears clear Mixtec markings.

The People of El Tajín

Much of what scholars know about the ancient ball game comes from the elaborate carved stone walls of the ball court at El Tajín, located south of the town of Tuxpan in the state of Veracruz. The site is now occupied by the Totonac Indians, but most scholars believe the site was originally occupied by the Huastec Indians, cousins to the Maya.

The people of El Tajín were a powerful influence throughout Meso-america in the Classic Period (A.D. 300–900), and they may have influenced the people of Teotihuacán. It is believed that they left El Tajín and went south into Chiapas several hundred years before the conquest.

The unique style of the city's architecture is most evident in the Temple of the Niches, a multiplatformed pyramid that has 365 niches on its tiers. The pyramid was dedicated to the wind and rain gods, two important deities at El Tajín, where agriculture, evidenced by the complex irrigation systems found there, was a major industry. Excavation work is still going on, and the uncovered site already exposes 140 of the original 2,300 acres. At least seven ball courts have been found.

The Maya

More is known about the Maya than any other Classic Mesoamerican civilization. In Mexico, the sites include Uxmal, Palenque, Chichén Itzá, Tulum, and Bonampak, the recently discovered, remote site in the southern highlands of Chiapas. In addition, there are dozens, maybe hundreds, of sites scattered throughout Yucatán alone. One knowledgeable guide suggests the visitor begin at Palenque, near Villa-hermosa, go north to Uxmal and the surrounding smaller sites, then on to Chichén Itzá, and finally to Tulum on the coast near Cancún.

Each of the sites rests in a unique natural setting—Palenque in the jungle, Chichén Itzá and Uxmal in the tropical forest, and Tulum on a rocky beachhead overlooking the Caribbean.

Classic Mesoamerican civilization reached a peak in the lands ruled by the Maya. It has been called one of the most brilliant civilizations, but unfortunately, romantic notions that the Mayans abhorred human sacrifice have been dispelled by scholars. At Chichén Itzá, ritual sacrifices were made at the great cenote (a limestone well); victims were tossed into the cold, deep waters of the well along with various valuable items. If a victim survived for a day, he or she was pulled out and honored; legend says one man did and lived to become a great chieftain.

In spite of the great "palaces" built at Palenque and other sites, scholars doubt that the Maya lived in what must have been dank, dark surroundings. It is thought that most of the buildings were used for rituals and worship. Limestone was the local material used to construct the temples, and the lintels of sapodilla wood — some survive — were erected over doorways. The Maya also constructed a network of "roads" (called *sacbeob*, plural; *sacbe*, singular) and canals that criss-crossed the Yucatán peninsula. (These can be seen from the top of the pyramids at Cobá.) However, they did not use the wheel. Trade in cotton, honey, and salt (important Mayan commodities) was carried out on the backs of Indians, a method still employed in rural Mexico.

The Mayans were skilled at using the two-wheeled calendar and also employed the Long Count system, a distinct dating method uniquely their own. By this complicated system, time was measured from an arbitrary point, a point long disputed by scholars. However, no Long Count date has been found past A.D. 900, the date used to mark the decline of Classic Maya, indeed Classic civilization in Mesoamerica. From this date, Mayan art becomes more baroque, and Chichén Itzá is taken over by Toltec warriors.

Of all the sites, Palenque is viewed as the best example of Classic Maya. A stream runs through the site, which is dominated by a terraced palace capped with a square tower. A large funerary crypt was discovered at the site in 1952. The crypt bore the remains of an unusually tall ruler, his bones covered with precious relics, including a mask of jade. No jade deposits have been found in Mexico; however, jade was valued highly by the Mesoamericans.

Another important element at Palenque is the Pyramid of the Sun, which contains the Temple of the Foliated Cross. The crucifix was a popular Indian symbol even before the conquest, which has led to some wild speculation about the possibility of wandering Irish priests or of reappearing apostles landing in Mexico.

The most distinctive characteristic of Classic Mayan art can be found at Palenque. The stone carvings and bas-reliefs have a unique, graceful liquidity, some with a suggestion of individuality and personality. They are the most realistic of Mayan carvings and are a product of the culmination of Classic Mayan civilization, five hundred years of Mayan ascendancy over the region. Their dominance began to decline circa A.D. 1000.

In contrast, Uxmal is more orderly, less ornate, and is representative of what is called Puuc Mayan, an architectural style named for a ridge of hills that crosses the peninsula. Stone mosaics and latticework characterize the site and the unusual main structures, the Pyramid of the Magician and the misnamed Nunnery. Uxmal was abandoned before the conquest, probably in the fifteenth century. Other nearby Puuc Mayan sites include Kabah (famous for its arch), Labná, and Sayil.

Chichén Itzá is a Mayan site that has been heavily influenced by Toltec designs. It is the legendary refuge of Quetzalcoatl, the Toltec warrior who fled Tula, in Central Mexico, and landed on the Yucatán peninsula. Chichén Itzá, which means simply "Itzá's well" (Itzá was a family name), was founded in A.D. 455 and was infiltrated by the Toltecs in the tenth century.

The site is dominated by the large pyramid El Castillo and the observatory El Caracol ("The Snail"), named for its interior spiral staircase. The Court of a Thousand Columns sits at the side of the Temple of Warriors, where a reclining Chac-mool figure looks out over the plaza.

Inside the pyramid is a small temple housing a jaguar throne, the cat's jade eyes shining in the darkness. (It's a steep, claustrophobic climb to the inner temple; watch out for slippery steps.) El Castillo is a superb example of Mayan architecture, and it is replete with symbolism. Four stairways face the points of the compass; each has 91 steps, making 364 in all; add the summit and you have the days of the year. The 52 panels on the sides symbolize the 52 years in the Mayan calendar; and the 18 sections or terraces on each side of the pyramid represent the 18-month religious calendar. Even more amazing is that twice a year, at the spring and fall equinox, the sun casts a serpent-shaped shadow on the northwest side of the pyramid.

The ball court at Chichén Itzá is probably the finest in Mesoamerica and is built on a grandiose scale; the court is larger, the platforms are taller, and the rings are higher than at any other site.

To the east lies Tulum, not an important site but one of the most spectacular in terms of location. Tulum is a walled city and was still populated at the time of the conquest. As that part of the peninsula becomes more populated (Cancún is nearby,) more ruins are being uncovered in the jungle. East of Tulum is the remote site Cobá. There the pyramids resemble those found to the south in Guatemala. Cobá has only recently been made accessible to the visitor, although the site is still remote and seeing all the ruins requires long walks through the jungle. Further south, near Chetumal on the Belize border, is a new site, Kohunlich, which promises to be fruitful.

One of the most remarkable modern discoveries is at Bonampak in the remote highlands of Chiapas. Here the Lacandon Indians kept the temple with its vivid paintings a secret for centuries until US scholars "discovered" them shortly after World War II. The vivid murals portray battles and hunts, women performing ritual self-mutilation, and victory celebration banquets. The site is remote and accessible by chartered light plane from Villahermosa or by jeep through the jungle.

The Toltecs

The Zapotecs in the south, the Maya in Yucatán, the people of El Tajín in the east, and the people of Teotihuacán in the Valley of Mexico represent the height of Mesoamerican Classic civilization. The invasions of the Mixtecs in Oaxaca, the sudden mysterious disruption of Mayan civilization in Yucatán and the highlands, the abandonment of Teotihuacán, and the migration of the people of El Tajín — all brought about the end of the Classic Period. These did not all occur at the same point in history, nor are the reasons for the disintegration of a group always known. However, by A.D. 1000, as Christians in Europe waited for the millenium to mark the end of the world, the Classic civilization of Mesoamerica began to crumble. In the south, the Mixtecs dominated; in the Valley of Mexico, it was the invading Toltecs — the Chichimec or "northern barbarians" — who swept down to conquer.

For a long time, scholars discounted the Toltecs, saying they were a mythical people who occupied a mythical capital, Tollan, as it was called by the Aztecs who revered Toltec memory. A hundred years ago archaeologists decided to investigate the town of Tula in Hidalgo. On the only hill in the valley, a man-made hill, they discovered Tula. There rest giant fourteen-foot warriors, pillars that once supported a temple roof. Scattered about the site are jaguars and Chac-mools. It was from here, legend says, that Quetzalcoatl was driven away, and this is where he promised to one day return.

The Toltecs were lost to history when they were conquered by the Aztecs, another Chichimec tribe that saw a brighter future for itself in the Valley of Mexico. Some scholars believe the Toltecs may have fled to Yucatán — they may have had ties already established there at Chichén Itzá — where they sparked the Mayan renaissance in the eleventh and twelfth centuries.

The Tarascans

The Mayans, the Mixtecs, and the Zapotecs all continued to exist as the Aztec empire grew. Paying tribute to the Aztec capital of Tenochtitlán was a necessary survival measure by the late thirteenth century. One group of Mesoamerican Indians, the Tarascans, resisted the Aztecs; they were the ancestors of those same peaceful, gentle fishermen and weavers who live on the shores of Lake Pátzcuaro between Mexico City and Guadalajara. There has been little exploration of archaeological sites in western Mexico, and not much is known about the people who lived there in ancient times; but in the small village of Tzintzuntzán, just outside Pátzcuaro, are the small, delicate ruins of the Tarascan kingdom. This was the "place of the hummingbird," and the delicacy of the Tarascan culture belies their fierce independence.

EXPLORING THE PAST

No two sites in Mexico are the same, and the visitor should discount the notion that "when you've seen one pyramid you've seen them all." There were common threads that bound the groups together; some of those threads still can be seen in the Indian markets and villages of rural Mexico, but the variety of culture and art forms becomes more apparent with each site that you visit.

An excellent starting point for any visitor interested in Mexico's ancient past is a visit to the National Museum of Anthropology in the heart of Mexico City. The museum ranks among the world's best. Following the section on the national museum is "Pyramid Schemes," our guide to the individual archaeological sites.

The National Museum of Anthropology

It is raining in Chapultepec Park, one of those heavy pewter-colored thunderstorms that hang over the pyramids of Teotihuacán and slowly roll southward to the city, where the wise unfurl their umbrellas and the whimsical dive into the warmth of a nearby café to while away the storm over a leisurely lunch. This is an ancient rain that falls every day in a ritual blessing, washing away the smog and clearing the air. It is the gift of Tláloc, the rain god, who sits in the heart of Chapultepec Park in the cold marble foyer of the world-renowned National Museum of Anthropology. Found in a village field, this ancient god was brought to the capital in 1964 after long negotiations with the villagers. As he entered the capital a sudden downpour ended a long drought that had left the *capitalinos* suffering in the heat and dust.

Now Tláloc sits in his place of honor at the museum, looking out on the slick rain-soaked steps, while behind him stands the giant stone mushroom waterfall, which dominates the museum courtyard, the rain mingling with the waterfall and spilling over the fountain's rim, pounding the floor with an ancient jungle rhythm. Deep inside this modern temple sit Xipe, the moon goddess; Chalchihuitlicue, the goddess with the jade skirts; Itzpapalotle, goddess of earth; and Quetzalcoatl, the Plumed Serpent. Here are the images wrought by the Olmecs and the Toltecs, the Maya and the Mixtecs, the mysterious men who built Teotihuacán, and the ancient potters of Tlatilco, who as long ago as 2000 B.C. created some intriguing female terra-cotta figurines. And here in the chill temple silence, wrapped in a cocoon of marble, are the gods themselves, lurking in the shadows, listening as the great Tláloc sends thunder resounding down the slopes of Mount Popocatépetl, and stalking the dark rooms like jaguars in the jungle.

The spirit of ancient Mexico has been distilled and preserved in this great museum. In a country where monuments dot the landscape like so many signposts to the past, the National Museum of Anthropology is an outstanding achievement. The paint may be peeling on the town hall mural, and the diesel fumes may have left a black shadow on the local hero's statue in the plaza; but in the midst of abundant social and political monuments to the past, the museum stands as an outstanding marble testament to Mexico's ancient heritage. No visitor to the capital should miss the museum, and no serious traveler, intent on visiting the country's archaeological zones, should begin his journey without first touring the museum. Here some of the country's most valued artifacts and treasures are carefully preserved and presented in a masterful setting. Track lighting allows each piece to be set in a halo and surrounded by a primeval darkness. The effect is chilling. A jaguar god crouches, ready to pounce; the skirt of snakes worn by an Aztec goddess seems to writhe in the darkness. The past is alive.

In addition, the upstairs salons are devoted to dioramas and exhibits depicting the customs and life-styles of modern-day Indians, providing a direct link from the past displayed below. These exhibits are not the most spectacular aspect of the museum, but they are interesting for anyone who does not plan to visit other regions of the country. The reproduction of a Mayan village, for example, accurately depicts present-day life in Yucatán.

If the museum has a shortcoming, it is that all the signs are in Spanish, and it is difficult for the non-Spanish-speaking visitor to fully enjoy the museum without a guide or a detailed guidebook. However, the museum does have an excellent shop, and tour guides are available for a modest fee.

The pivotal point of this magnificent museum is the raised platform in the farthest salon where the "Stone of the Sun," the so-called Aztec calendar, hangs. Discovered near the Mexico City Zócalo in 1790, the stone is thought to have been carved in 1479, just a few years before Cortés landed. When the Spanish destroyed Tenochtitlán, the Aztec capital, the stone was buried in the soft lake bed. Now it hangs above an invisible altar, drawing each visitor into the secrets of mystic rituals and cyclical destruction. It is a striking reminder of Mexico's past, a symbol of a conquered world in which human sacrifices were condemned by bloody conquerors, feathered crowns gave way to sombreros, and stone altars surrendered to gilt-covered *retablos*. The calendar, called the *tonalpohualli*, marked time in the ancient world. All things were governed by its spinning. A child's birth date became his name, and that date held his fate. Made up of two wheels, the calendar ruled everyday life and spiritual matters. Once every 52 years the wheels meshed and the ancient people of Mexico waited to see if the world would be destroyed. Pots were broken, fires put out, women and children hidden from the sight of the sun to prevent their souls from being captured and trapped in the bodies of animals. Every 52 years the Mesoamerican world held its breath and waited for the end. When the crisis was over and the wheels began to spin once more, its citizens rejoiced. New fires were kindled, more pots made, and life went on until the next time the great wheels would spin together.

In the Mesoamerican culture there was always this preoccupation with the nether side of life. Few of the artifacts show humor or humanity, although there are some exceptions — the "fat" gods of the island of Jaina, whose citizens ignored other deities and contented themselves with honoring their jovial rotund god. Most of the pieces in the museum are massive, almost overwhelming. There is a disturbing quality about the members of the Mesoamerican pantheon; the gods appear harsh and hungry. Even Tláloc, the benevolent rain god, has an austere countenance.

The museum's salons are divided among the various cultures, with Aztec dominating. In addition to the salons, small gardens opening from each side of the museum contain artifacts from sites throughout Mexico. One small garden displays an Olmec head carved from basalt.

In the past, many of Mexico's greatest archaeological treasures have been taken out of the country and placed in private and public collections abroad; however, enough have remained and more have been discovered to make the National Museum of Anthropology a repository of one of the world's greatest collections of Mesoamerican artifacts. Recent finds from the Mexico City dig near the Zócalo have included important artifacts. In 1977 a Mexico City utility crew uncovered a large carved stone disk depicting Coyolxauhqui, god of the moon. This led to new, exciting explorations in downtown Mexico City along Seminario Street, just a few blocks from the Zócalo. Before the conquest, the Zócalo was the main square in the Aztec capital of Tenochtitlán, and the National Cathedral was built, according to early Spanish chronicles, on the ruins of the Great Temple. However, recent finds seem to indicate a tall pyramid, perhaps two hundred feet high, is buried in the lake bed beneath Mexico City's streets. The Mesoamerican custom of superimposing structures combined with the rapidly sinking lake bed, makes it likely that an earlier temple, predating the conquest, stood on this site. The temple appears to have been dedicated to two gods, Tláloc, the rain god, and Huitzilopochtli, the Aztec patron god of war. Offerings to both gods have been found at the site, and many of them are on display in the museum or at the Palace of Fine Arts on nearby Avenida Juárez. To visit the site, take the Seminario Street exit off the Zócalo.

To visit the National Museum of Anthropology, located on the Paseo de la Reforma, take a cab (or the subway, exiting at the Chapultepec Park station — look for the grasshopper logo) or walk through the park. The museum is open daily except Monday from 9 A.M. until 7 P.M. Admission is 15 pesos, except on Sundays (open from 10 A.M. to 6 P.M.), when admission is three pesos. Many Mexicans work a six-day week, so this special rate makes it possible for the workingman to enjoy the museum with his family at a reasonable price. The museum is usually packed on Sundays. There is an excellent restaurant on the museum grounds, and you will find a good book shop in the main foyer.

PYRAMID SCHEMES

Mexico's archaeological zones are strictly monitored by the government. However, you will be left to wander on your own unless you hire a guide. The larger sites have guided tours available in several languages. Guides are available for a small fee, and they can usually be found around the entrance booth. (While most of the tour guides

Time Line

10,000 B.C. The Stone Age
Hunters roam in the Valley of Mexico.

5200–1500 B.C. The Archaic Period
Around 5000 B.C. chiles, corn, and pumpkins are being grown in plots. Circa 2400 B.C. small, usually female figurines are produced in the Valley of Mexico. Many have been found at Tlatilco.

2000 B.C.–A.D. 300 The Preclassic Period
Shamans, village witch doctors and healers, emerge as powerful members of society. The Indians begin to utilize two distinctive agricultural methods: slash-and-burn and *chinampas* (floating gardens where plants are grown on a raft covered with soil and afloat on a lake). Circa 800 B.C. the great mound, the precursor of the pyramid, at Cuicuilco, now a suburb of Mexico City, is covered by a lava bed. Also during this period, the Olmecs, thought by many to be the "spark" civilization, dominate the eastern coast 1200–400 B.C.

A.D. 300–900 The Classic Period
The Maya dominate the Guatemalan highlands and Yucatán; the people of Teotihuacán rule the Mexican highlands and wield influence throughout Mesoamerica; the Zapotecs, influenced by the Olmecs, conquer the Valley of Oaxaca; and the spiritual ancestors of today's Totonac Indians, possibly Huastecs, rule El Tajín on the eastern coast.

A.D. 900–1520 The Postclassic Period
Mexico is dominated by various militaristic groups, first by the Toltecs in the Valley of Mexico from their capital at Tula and then by the Chichimec, so-called barbarians from the north, including the Aztecs, who conquered the Valley of Mexico in the thirteenth century. In the tenth century there is evidence of a Toltec influence at Chichén Itzá in Yucatán. Also, the Zapotecs become subservient to the Mixtecs in the Valley of Oaxaca. In 1519 Cortés lands and various Indian groups join with him to conquer the all-powerful Aztecs.

are excellent and well versed in ancient history, a few embellish their stories with legend and popular myth. If you take your history seriously, consider taking along a well-illustrated, detailed text. You will find a bibliography at the back of this book.) Most sites are open daily, with shorter hours on Sunday, and there may be a small entrance charge. If you drive, you will be charged a nominal parking fee. There is no limit on how long you may ramble through the ruins; however, most sites close at or a little before sundown. Some of the larger sites reopen at night for special sound and light shows. Tickets are available for these shows at travel agencies in the nearest city or at the museum/ticket booth at each site. No flash photography is allowed at the sites. Not all the sites are easily accessible—Bonampak can be reached only by plane or by jeep through the jungle, and some Puuc Mayan sites are also deep in a forest and accessible only by jeep. But the major popular sites are easily reached.

You don't need to order your pyramid-climbing gear from African safari outfitters in London, but you should dress sensibly and consider taking along the following items:

Insect repellent—especially important in Yucatán.

A small plastic water flask—no nearby concession stands at most of the sites.

A hat—find one with a wide brim and tie a kerchief around the crown so that you can tighten the hat and stop it from blowing away.

Good climbing shoes—sandals, high heels, and thin-soled shoes can be dangerous. Take along a good pair of tennis shoes or hiking boots.

Munchies—a granola bar or two will give you a quick energy boost. A few of the larger sites have snack bars nearby, but generally they are not very good.

A watch—most of the sites close at six, and you don't want to be locked in with the ghosts of sacrificial victims.

Hiking shorts or loose jeans—you will spend a lot of time crawling down pyramids on all fours like a monkey; leave the white Calvin Kleins at the hotel.

A sweater—if you plan to make a day of it, take along a light sweater, something you can tie around your waist.

A raincoat—invariably, no matter what part of Mexico you visit, there will be a brief afternoon rain shower. Pack a small plastic poncho.

Money—small change. Most of the sites are very inexpensive, anywhere from 5 to 25 pesos.

A flashlight—a small penlight is good for examining dark, mysterious holes and finding your way along underground passages.

A knapsack—just a small one to pack all your gear in. This leaves your hands free for climbing.

Camera gear—if you have a 35mm interchangeable lens system, don't carry too much gear with you. A wide angle and a long lens should be sufficient. You might want to try a polarizing filter to bring out those inevitable clouds. Most sites forbid flash or tripod photography without a special permit, so take fast film. Although the sites have little color, except where the remains of frescoes can be seen, color film will capture the sky and mountains well. Black and white film is good for detail shots.

First aid — drop a few Band-Aids in your pocket, and don't forget to wear some sun protection if you burn easily.

Below, the archaeological sites are divided into regions. Sites in each region are listed alphabetically. (Most of the sites within a region are geographically close. One exception is El Tajín, which is included in the Central Mexico section. El Tajín should not be considered a day trip from Mexico City, unlike the other sites in that region. An overnight stay is recommended.)

PYRAMID SCHEMES/CENTRAL MEXICO
CHOLULA

Location: On the outskirts of Puebla, 80 miles from Mexico City.

Getting there: Rental car; bus or train to Puebla, followed by bus or taxi to Cholula. By car, take Hwy. 190D, a toll road, out of Mexico City west toward Puebla. Cholula is approximately eight miles west of Puebla.

Sight-seeing time: An afternoon. Cholula is a pleasant village with many interesting churches. You might consider an overnight stay.

Brief history: The Tepenapa pyramid was constructed circa 400 B.C. and had ties to Teotihuacán. Cholula was an important religious center and survived whatever disaster overtook Teotihuacán. It was a thriving religious center at the time of the conquest with an estimated population of 100,000. Approximately 3,000 Indians were massacred there by Cortés who feared he was about to be killed. The Spaniards razed the temples and built a church atop the ancient mound to express their dominance over the Indians. Many of the neighboring mounds also have churches on what was once a temple platform. There are estimated to be 365 churches in Cholula, and the landscape is dotted with mounds.

Features: The pyramid was once the largest in volume in the New World. Diminished, it is still an impressive site, topped, as it is, by a church. The surrounding plain is covered with possible temple sites that have not been excavated. Tunnels riddle the pyramid and are open to the public. Excavations to the west of the pyramid are of some interest, although some restoration has been poorly executed.

Facilities: Hotels in nearby Puebla; restaurants in both Puebla and Cholula. Club Med operates one of its excellent Villas Arqueologicas at the site, virtually at the base of the pyramid. The hotel also boasts a French restaurant and a beautiful view of nearby snowcapped volcanoes. (For reservations dial 7-15-08 in Cholula, 533-4800 in Mexico City, or 1-800-528-3100 in the United States.)

Bocaditos: There's a special fiesta September 8, Día de la Virgen de los Remedios, which celebrates the return of the Virgin to the church atop the pyramid after the statue has toured the neighboring churches.

EL TAJIN

Location: Approximately five miles from Papantla in the state of Veracruz; ten miles south of Poza Rica, an important oil town.

Getting there: Rental car; taxi from Veracruz. Take Hwy. 85 from Mexico City to Pachuca, Hwy. 130 to Poza Rica, and then go south to the site. Approximately 180 miles.

Sight-seeing time: A day. Take along a packed lunch.

Brief history: El Tajín was occupied probably by the Huastecs at the same time as Teotihuacán. It was abandoned around A.D. 900. At the time of the conquest, the Totonacs ruled the region and used the site for religious purposes.

Features: The large site, some 2,300 acres, is still being worked. The dominant feature is the Pyramid of the Niches, dedicated to the rain and wind gods. There is a niche for each day of the year. In the plaza in front of the pyramid is a tall pole used in the Danza de los Voladores (the flying Indians). Four dancers and a musician ascend the pole, the musician begins to play, and the four dancers leap off the top of the pole, saved only by ropes that they have tied to their ankles. As they descend, they whirl around the pole. The dancers perform the ritual during a ten-day Corpus Christi festival in May. The dance has its origins deep in Mesoamerican culture and may have Huastec or Olmec origins.

Two other prominent features of the site are the ball court and the Building of the Columns. El Tajín appears to have played an important role in the evolution of the ball game, a ritual which is repeated in all Mesoamerican cultures. The ball court here is a particularly fine example.

Facilities: There are no hotels at the site. Drive in from Veracruz or stay in one of the nearby towns. (Poza Rica is not a pleasant town to stay in owing to the oil boom.) In Papantla there are several hotels — the Hotel Pulido and the Hotel Papantla, both on the zócalo, and the Hotel Tajín on Calle Dr. Nunez. Reservations are not likely to be necessary except at fiesta time. Tecolutla, a coastal village, has two hotels on the beach — the Tecolutla and the Marsol — and two on Avenida Carlos Prieto — the Posada Guadalupe and the Casa de Huespedes Malena.

Bocaditos: Don't forget to buy little baskets made from the locally grown vanilla. Placed in sugar jar they will flavor the sugar.

MALINALCO

Location: Forty miles west of Mexico City.

Getting there: Take Hwy. 15 to Toluca, go south on Hwy. 55 for nine miles, and then travel 17 miles east on the highway marked with signs to Malinalco. Approximately 70 miles.

Sight-seeing time: Two hours.

Brief history: Malinalco means "place where the herb malinalii grows" in Nahuatl, the Aztec tongue. The site was founded between A.D. 200 and A.D. 400 and was influenced by the Toltec culture. The Aztecs were still building there as late as 1521, after the conquest. The site had a great deal of religious significance for the Indians, and so the Augustinians established convents and churches in the area.

Features: The temples were hewn out of the rock face. The visitor approaches the House of the Eagle by a rock staircase carved with jaguar heads. Inside the temple, there are three figures of sacred animals — two eagles and a jaguar. Another carved rock form in the center represents an eagle skin. In Building III there are the remains of frescoes illustrating the Aztec belief that the dead souls of warriors ascend to heaven and become stars.

Facilities: There are hotels in nearby Toluca and at the spa Ixtapan de la Sal.

Bocaditos: Tenancingo, a small village famed for its furniture and rebozos, is just seven miles west of the site. East of the site is Calma, a town to which Indians still make annual pilgrimages. Before the conquest a statue of Otzeoteotl, the god of war, was revered and kept in a cave.

TEOTIHUACAN

Location: Approximately 30 miles northeast of Mexico City.

Getting there: Rental car; guided tour; bus from the Terminal del Norte in Mexico City. If you are driving, take Insurgentes Norte out of the city; pick up the Pan American Highway (Hwy. 85) northbound, a toll road; and follow the signs to San Juan de Teotihuacán, the nearby town.

Sight-seeing time: If you are not an archaeology buff or you tire easily (remember the altitude), you can see the major features in a long afternoon. Otherwise, spend the day or a couple of days and visit the outlying sites.

Brief history: The city of Teotihuacán reached its peak between A.D. 300 and A.D. 600. It was burned, probably by invading Toltecs circa A.D. 700 and then abandoned. The Aztecs revered the site and called it "place where men became gods." It was not occupied at the time of the conquest. At its height, Teotihuacán was a city of some 150,000 people, and its influence was felt throughout Mesoamerica. Pottery and architecture bearing the Teotihuacán mark or design have been found in Guatemala.

Features: The highest pyramid in the New World, the Pyramid of the Sun, stands at right angles to the main street — 207 feet high and 720 feet by 440 feet at its base. The pyramid dominates the valley as it must have dominated the city that covered nine square miles. The main street, the Miccoatli, commonly referred to as the "Avenue of the Dead," is the heart of the ceremonial center of the city. At the northern end is the Pyramid of the Moon, an arbitrary name given by archaeologists to the structure. (Modern-day archaeologists have abandoned the romantic whims of the past and now name buildings by number or Roman numeral.) At the southern end of the street is the Citadel and the Temple of Quetzalcoatl. It is not known what the function of the so-called Citadel was. It was probably a priestly building, not a fortress. But the Temple of Quetzalcoatl obviously had some connection with the cult of the Plumed Serpent. The exterior is covered with "feathered" snakes and masks of the rain god. There is an impressive, dramatic sound and light show given at the site each evening from October through May at 7:00 P.M. in English and at 8:15 P.M. in Spanish.

Facilities: You'll find a good museum shop at the entrance, a decent restaurant, and a bar. Try Posada Piramides or La Grotta, two restaurants in the nearby town of San Juan de Teotihuacán. You will be approached by vendors at the site who sell fake artifacts and cheap jewelry. Club Med operates one of its Villas Arqueologicas at the site. The hotel has a library and offers lectures on the sites. By staying overnight, you will be able to visit some of the outlying temples, like Atetelco and Tetitla, where frescoes depict jaguars, priests, coyotes, and feathered serpents. For reservations, call 6-02-44 in Teotihuacán, 533-4800 in Mexico City, and 1-800-528-3100 in the United States.

Bocaditos: Six miles south of the site is the Convent of Acolman de Netzahualcóyotl, noted for its Plateresque style and collection of religious art.

TULA

Location: Approximately a 90-minute drive from Mexico City. Tula is located near the village of the same name, close to Pachuca, the capital of the state of Hidalgo.

Getting there: Rental car; bus. Take the Pan American Highway (Hwy. 85) toll road to the Tepeji del Río exit. Take Hwy. 57 northwest and then the Actopan exit; pick up Hidalgo State Highway (Hwy. 126) to Tula.

Sight-seeing time: An afternoon.

Brief history: In the 1930s Tula was finally established as Tollan, the capital of the Toltecs, the northern tribe that came down into Mesoamerica circa A.D. 700. Previously, historians had believed Tollan was a mythical city. The Toltecs dominated the region until they were defeated by the Aztecs in the eleventh and twelfth centuries A.D. Tollan was the legendary home of Ce Acatl, the Toltec prince who fled to the Yucatán and is thought to have founded Chichén Itzá. Ce Acatl was the Quetzalcoatl of legend—the priest of the feathered serpent cult who vowed to return. Cortés was believed by some to be Ce Acatl returning.

Features: The dominant feature of the Tula site is the pyramid topped by the so-called Atlas figures. These huge, 15-foot stone warriors wear the symbol of Quetzalcoatl, the butterfly, on their breastplates. The site at Tula bears many similarities to Chichén Itzá in Yucatán, and several Chac-mools, the reclining gods whose stomachs cradled the hearts of sacrificial victims, are found at Tula.

Facilities: Limited. Take along a picnic lunch.

Bocaditos: Combine a trip to Tula with a visit to El Cielito, a hilltop site located four miles southeast. There you will find the ruins of an Aztec palace once owned by Pedro Moctezuma, the son of the ill-fated Aztec monarch. He was named "cacique" or chief of the region by the Spaniards.

On the way back to Mexico City, stop at the Church of San Francisco de Javier in Tepotzotlán on Hwy. 57. Now a national museum, the old monastery houses a handicraft shop.

XOCHICALCO

Location: Twenty-four miles southwest of Cuernavaca.

Getting there: Rental car; bus tour from Cuernavaca; taxi. Go 17 miles south on Hwy. 95D to Alpuyeca, and then go five miles west to Xochicalco.

Sight-seeing time: An afternoon.

Brief history: Contemporary with Teotihuacán, but like Cholula it somehow survived the disaster that struck the large city. It was still in use in Aztec times and served as a major trading and teaching center. Ce Acatl (later the cult hero who assumed the god's name Quetzalcoatl) was educated here, according to legend.

Features: One of the most beautiful buildings was dedicated to Quetzalcoatl, the feathered serpent god. Mysteriously, many of the design details appear to be Mayan. Other influences can also be recognized, possibly because this was a trading post. The site covers some four square miles, but most buildings of interest are concentrated in the center. There are Mayan glyphs on stelae found at the site. The ball court is well preserved.

Facilities: Excellent in nearby Cuernavaca.

Bocaditos: Combine a visit to the site with a side trip to the Grutas de Cacahuamilpa, said to be the largest caves in the world. Drive back to Alpuyeca and follow the signs to the caves.

PYRAMID SCHEMES/SOUTHERN MEXICO

BONAMPAK

Location: Far eastern Chiapas, near the Guatemalan border.

Getting there: Accessible by air taxi from Palenque, Villahermosa, and

San Cristóbal de las Casas; or from Palenque by jungle road, passable only by jeep at certain times of the year.

Sight-seeing time: A day.

Brief history: Bonampak reached its peak between A.D. 650 and A.D. 850. It was not an important Mayan site and was probably a subject community of Yaxchilán. It is the site's remarkable frescoes that have brought world attention to it. Hidden deep in the jungle, it attracted little scientific interest until 1946 when scholars discovered the frescoes. (Local Indians had, of course, known about the frescoes all the time.) The paintings had been protected by a natural climatic lime coating, and the colors were still clear. Several have been moved to Mexico City, most have been copied, and those that remain are still remarkable, although in danger of fading.

Features: There are several stelae at the site from the eighth century. The Temple of Frescoes (circa A.D. 800) has a series of frescoes on its walls depicting musicians, warriors, festivals, and human sacrifices. Copies can be seen in the National Museum of Anthropology in Mexico City.

Facilities: None.

Bocaditos: Nearby is the village of Lacan-Lá, home of the Lacandon Mayas. These modern-day descendants of the Mayas were not influenced by the conquest and until very recently followed their own religious rites and hunted in Stone-Age fashion with bows and arrows. Of course, scientists and tourists have had their effect on the Indians.

CHINCULTIC

Location: Far south Chiapas.

Getting there: Take Hwy. 190 out of San Cristóbal de las Casas for 64 miles to La Trinitaria; head east and follow the signs to the Lagunas de Montebello National Park.

Sight-seeing time: A day.

Brief history: Chincultic is a Classic Mayan site. It was occupied from about A.D. 100 to A.D. 1200. Its heyday was from A.D. 300 to A.D. 900.

Features: The site commands a hillside overlooking the lakes that are located within the national park. The ball court is exceptional, and there are several stelae scattered about the site with Mayan date glyphs. There is also a large cenote (sacrificial well) on the site. Recovery of sacrificial objects has been difficult, and the cenote has yet to yield up all its treasures.

Facilities: There is a campsite at the park.

Bocaditos: This is a remote region of Mexico and is recommended for hardy travelers only. A guide is necessary if you plan any excursions into the jungle.

LA VENTA

Location: At the mouth of the Tonalá River in the swamps, near Villahermosa, Tabasco.

Getting there: The site is very difficult to reach and is now in the middle of a booming Tabascan oilfield. Most of the artifacts have been removed and the larger pieces taken to a special park in Villahermosa, Parque Museo de la Venta. Villahermosa has an airport, and flights are available from Mexico City. Or Hwy. 180 may be taken into the city. The park is on the outskirts of the town.

Sight-seeing time: A tour of the park takes an afternoon.

Brief history: La Venta was an Olmec ceremonial city. The Olmecs, sometimes called "the Magicians," were among the first Mesoamericans to rise out of the Neanderthal gloom. Scientists date La Venta's origins at 1200 B.C. The city was in its heyday until 400 B.C. Some historians believe the Olmecs were the "spark" that ignited the creative blossoming of several groups in Mesoamerica. Their influence was widespread, and their distinct artistic style can be easily spotted at other sites. Perhaps the most widely recognized Olmec artifacts are the huge basalt heads that appear to have Negroid features and be wearing what some have described as football helmets.

Features: The Olmecs possessed a unique artistic style. Basalt heads, now on view in the park, have round, full features. The basalt was somehow transported a great distance to the river swamps. Other Olmec influences can be seen in the famous Danzantes figures at Monte Albán in Oaxaca.

Facilities: Few at the original site; an abundance of hotels in Villahermosa. The park is open daily, but closed on certain national holidays. There is a small admission fee.

Bocaditos: Villahermosa is an oil boom town and is not a particularly picturesque town. Stay at nearby Palenque and combine a visit to that beautiful site with a visit to the archaeological park.

PALENQUE

Location: Approximately 75 miles east of Villahermosa.

Getting there: Rental car; tour bus from Villahermosa; bus from Villahermosa; train from Mexico City or Mérida.

Sight-seeing time: At least a day. This is one of the most beautiful sites in Mexico, and the nearby hotels make a two-day stay worthwhile.

Brief history: Palenque was capital for a Mayan dynasty whose history is recorded on the walls of the city. Archaeologists don't believe the "city" was occupied, but it was the ceremonial center of a great family. It is an expression of Classic Mayan civilization. Its heyday was between A.D. 300 and A.D. 600. Archaeologists, studying the glyphs at the site, have been able to establish the royal genealogy from Chaacal I in A.D. 501 to Kuk in A.D. 783. The capital was abandoned, like other Mayan sites, in the ninth century. The most recent glyphs at the site date to A.D. 799.

Features: Some say Palenque is the most beautiful of all Mayan sites, if not all Mesoamerican sites. It certainly ranks as one of the most aesthetically pleasing. Mayan art reached its peak here as evidenced by the bas-reliefs found on the temple walls and in the stucco busts recovered from the site. Their lines are elongated and classical, with movement and emotions expressed in stone, as opposed to the stiffness of other sculptures found in Mesoamerica.

One of the most sensational archaeological finds in modern times took place at Palenque in 1946 when scientists discovered a burial crypt under one of the temples — the first time evidence of burial in a pyramid, similar to Egyptian burials, had been found. The skeleton of an unusually tall man was found buried in the crypt, his face covered with a jade funerary mask. Other artifacts, including two beautiful stucco heads, were found in the tomb. The artifacts can be seen in the National Museum of Anthropology in Mexico City.

A small river runs through the site and the temples lie on each side of it, surrounded by the jungle. Each temple is decorated with scenes depicting the royal succession and ceremonial life at Palenque. An extensive text is essential in studying the site. *A Guide to Ancient Maya Ruins*, written by C. Bruce Hunter and published by the University of Oklahoma Press, is a good guide for serious visitors.

Facilities: There are several hotels near the site, including the Chan Kah, Apartado Postal 26, Palenque. There are several hotels in the nearby town of Palenque, and reservations are usually not necessary.

Bocaditos: The best way to get to Palenque is by train from Mexico City or Mérida. It's an overnight trip either way, so reserve a pullman. Train fares in Mexico are incredibly cheap.

YAXCHILAN

Location: Far east Chiapas on the Guatemalan border, in a loop of the Rio Usumacinta.

Getting there: By air taxi from Palenque or San Cristóbal de las Casas; also by air to Agua Azul and down the river by boat.

Sight-seeing time: A day for the main sites.

Brief history: Yaxchilan was a major Mayan city with its greatest vigor A.D. 600 through A.D. 900. As was true with other great Mayan centers like Palenque and Tikal in Guatemala, Yaxchilan was abandoned in the ninth century. There are numerous theories about the catastrophe that caused these abandonments — pestilence, earthquake, flood — but none have been proved.

Features: Only a few structures have been excavated in this large remote site. Several palaces have distinctive Mayan roof-combs, and there are numerous stelae at the site. Mayan heiroglyphs remain a mystery, although dates and some names have been transcribed.

Facilities: None.

Bocaditos: This is a trek for the hardy only. The trip to the remote jungle sites in Chiapas can be very rewarding for history buffs eager to thrill to the feeling of discovery. Yaxchilan's proximity to the troubled country of Guatemala should be noted. Ask the tourist authorities and US Embassy officials for their advice before embarking on a journey to this remote area of Mexico.

PYRAMID SCHEMES/OAXACA

MITLA

Location: A small village 27 miles southeast of Oaxaca.

Getting there: Rental car; taxi; local bus; private automobile. Take the Pan American Highway (Hwy. 190) south out of Oaxaca. After approximately 24 miles, take right fork to Mitla, following the signs.

Sight-seeing time: Two or three hours. You will pass several sites on the way—Yagul, Labiteyeco, Dainzu—small and easily visited in an hour or less. You may want to combine these sites into a day of visiting tombs.

Brief history: Mitla is a Mixtec site with some Zapotec influences. The Mixtecs were latecomers to the Valley of Oaxaca, circa A.D. 800. They dominated the Zapotecs, but the two people lived side by side. In the fifteenth century the Valley came under Aztec dominance and was a subject nation at the time of the conquest.

Features: Mitla, like Cholula in the state of Puebla, is one of those anachronistic historical experiences in which time is condensed and symbols of different eras sit side by side. Located literally in the middle of a flourishing village, the ruins at Mitla are strewn about backyards and courtyards like pebbles on a hillside. Goats graze on a temple patio; washing hangs next door to an ancient wall. Atop one temple is a church built by the conquistadores. (Many of the churches in Oaxaca were built from temple stones and pieces of friezes can be spotted in the church walls.)

Mitla is noted for its beautiful stone mosaic friezes. No animal or human forms are represented at Mitla, only geometric patterns worked in stone like giant jigsaw puzzles. They are thought to be abstract representations of the soul. Many of the designs can still be seen in the blankets and serapes woven by local Indians.

Facilities: The University of the Americas operates a small museum/hotel/restaurant at the entrance to the village. The museum is worth a visit, and the hotel patio is a good place to rest on a hot day. For information about reservations, write to the university in Mitla, Oaxaca. If you plan to spend the day at the sites in this area, ask your hotel to pack a lunch or assemble a picnic basket.

Bocaditos: There are several mescal bottling factories—small family businesses—on the road to Mitla. Free samples are available. Drink a toast to Mayahuel, the goddess of pulque.

MONTE ALBAN

Location: Six miles west of Oaxaca overlooking the city.

Getting there: Rental car; bus tours; taxis. Signs in the city point the way. Air tours available at the Oaxaca airport.

Sight-seeing time: It's possible to spend a day at the site; however, an afternoon will suffice for most visitors.

Brief history: One of the most impressive sites in Mexico, Monte Albán is built on a flattened mountaintop. The deep blue skies and the constant small, white clouds that dot them make this site very beautiful. The site has Olmec origins in the fourth or fifth century B.C. Later, Zapotecs took over and still later the Mixtecs. By the time the Aztecs extended their influence over the area in the fifteenth century, Monte Albán was primarily a funerary site.

Features: Well-read visitors can have fun trying to spot the various influences on style made by different Mesoamerican groups at Monte Albán. The ball court and various stelae suggest Mayan influences; the so-called Danzantes, bizarrely twisted bodies depicted in stone basreliefs, have Olmec origins; the *talud y tablero* style of architecture (a stone panel and slanted wall) can be attributed to origins at Teotihuacán; and the friezes show Mixtec style.

Before visiting the site, spend an afternoon at the Regional Museum of Oaxaca, next to the Church of Santo Domingo at Constitución and Cinco de Mayo, and the Rufino Tamayo Museum of Pre-Hispanic Art at Avenida Morelos 503. The regional museum is home to the priceless collection of funerary jewels found at Tomb Number 7 at Monte Albán.

Facilities: There's a small museum shop and a poor restaurant at the entrance to the site. Take along a packed lunch or eat a hearty breakfast in nearby Oaxaca.

Bocaditos: After a day at Monte Albán, come down the mountain and follow the signs to Cuilapán. The abandoned convent here contains the tomb of the last Zapotec princess, Juana Donaje (her Christian name), who was the daughter of the Zapotec chief Cocijo-eza. Just beyond is the village of Zaachila. The ruins here were jealously guarded by local Indians until very recently.

YAGUL

Location: Twenty miles southeast of Oaxaca on Hwy. 190.

Getting there: Rental car; bus; taxi.

Sight-seeing time: Two hours.

Brief history: Yagul has ancient origins in the ninth century B.C. The site reached its peak of prosperity between A.D. 900 and A.D. 1200.

Features: The rocky hillside site commands a view down the long Valley of Oaxaca. It is remotely Greek in appearance because most of the walls are gone and only the outlines of buildings can be seen. In the center of one plaza at the front of the site a stone frog crouches. There is a large ball court and on the Citadel, the hill above the site, are many tombs bearing Mixtec friezes.

Facilities: None.

Bocaditos: Combine a trip to Yagul with visits to Dainzu, Labiteyeco (on Hwy. 190), and nearby Mitla.

PYRAMID SCHEMES/YUCATAN

CHICHEN ITZA

Location: Approximately 75 miles east of Mérida on Hwy. 180; 130 miles west of Cancún on Hwy. 180.

Getting there: Rental car; taxi from Mérida; bus from Cancún or Mérida (the local stop is at Piste); bus tours from Cancún or Mérida; also air taxi from Cancún and Mérida.

Sight-seeing time: It's possible to see Chichén Itzá in a day, but it's worth spending a couple of days here – there are excellent hotels set in the peaceful Mayan jungle. (Most bus tours spend about an hour.)

Brief history: The name means "Itzá's well," and there is a large cenote north of the site – sacrificial victims and objects were deposited there. Chichén Itzá was a minor Mayan site that was taken over by Toltec invaders in the tenth century. Legend has it that Quetzalcoatl, the Toltec prince, led the invasion. Toltec influences, such as the Tzompantli ("Wall of Skulls") and the feathered serpent motif, are combined with Mayan architecture.

Features: Chichén Itzá's magnificent pyramid has a mysterious inner chamber (claustrophobics beware!) that houses a jaguar god statue; the observatory, the most familiar sight, is especially beautiful when viewed at dawn; the ball court is one of the most well preserved; and the Chac-mool has become a popular symbol of the Yucatán in travel posters and ads. There are several small temples in ruins along the forest trails, and the cenote is an awesome sight set in the middle of the jungle.

Facilities: Two of the best hotels in Mexico are located at Chichén Itzá – the Hotel Mayaland (Box 90, Mérida) and the Villas Arqueologicas run by Club Med (533-4800 in Mexico City, 1-800-528-3100 in the United States). Both are set in tropical gardens, and the hummingbirds will not disturb you if you don't disturb them. Both have good restaurants and quiet bars. You can call the hotels by asking the operator for them by name.

Bocaditos: Get up just before dawn and watch the sun rise as you sit on the ramparts of El Caracol, the observatory. (Hwy. 180 bisects the site. The northern portion is closed in the early morning – there's a chain across the entrance – but the southern portion is open, and local Indians pass freely through the site on their way to work.) Take a siesta in the late afternoon when the tour buses arrive.

COBA

Location: Approximately 25 miles northwest of Tulum; 30 miles south of Valladolid on Hwy. 180 by a rough dirt road.

Getting there: The best way to approach the site is by driving south from Cancún to Tulum (approximately 80 miles) and then taking the paved road inland, northwest, to Cobá (approximately 25 miles). Rental car; first-class bus service to Tulum, limited second-class service to Cobá.

Sight-seeing time: The ruins at Cobá are spread out over an 18-square-mile site. The major ruins can be seen in a day; however, two or three days of jungle rambling can be fun for amateur archaeologists or anyone eager to leave the modern world behind for a couple of days. (There are no telephones at Cobá.)

Brief history: Cobá in Mayan means "wind-ruffled waters," and this exotic name describes the location. Set among several lakes, the site stretches out through the forest, and excavations are far from complete. It is a Classic Mayan site, and some of the pyramids are reminiscent of those found south in Guatemala. The Spaniards never discovered it, and it remained untouched until this century.

Features: Cobá is the center of a series of *sacbeob* ("ceremonial roads") constructed in the jungle out of limestone. From the top of El Castillo, 138 feet high, they can be seen running across the peninsula in several directions. Since the Mesoamericans did not utilize the wheel, except for toys, the roads were probably used for ceremonial purposes. (Some far-out theorists say they were landing strips for spacemen.) Throughout the jungle, persevering tourists will find numerous stelae and, equipped with a good text on Mayan history, they may be able to decipher the date glyphs — a system of bars and dots that is very easy to learn. (See *The Maya* written by Michael D. Coe and published by Thames and Hudson Press.)

Facilities: Club Med runs one of its Villas Arqueologicas at the site — it's the only hotel. Call 533-4800 in Mexico City or 1-800-528-3100 in the United States for reservations. The hotel has a library, a restaurant, a bar, and a small shop. The chef does wonderful things considering he is miles from civilization. Cobá is the ultimate getaway.

Bocaditos: Take along a copy of J. Eric S. Thompson's *Maya Archaeologist*, published by the University of Oklahoma Press. Thompson recounts his archaeological ramblings of the thirties.

DZIBILCHALTUN

Location: Approximately 11 miles north of Mérida on the road to Progreso.

Getting there: Rental car; taxi; bus.

Sight-seeing time: An afternoon.

Brief history: The city covered some 20 square miles at its height. The name in Mayan means "flat stones that bear writing." It was an important religious center with roots possibly as far back as 1500 B.C. The city was still occupied at the time of the conquest.

Features: Many sacbeob converge on this important center and can be seen from atop the buildings. Building I sub, more romantically known

as the Temple of the Seven Dolls, contains the first windows found on a Mayan building. Nearby is the large cenote of Xlacán from which over 30,000 offerings have been recovered.
Facilities: None.
Bocaditos: Combine a trip to Dzibilchaltún with an afternoon in Progreso on the coast.

EDZNA

Location: One hundred twenty-five miles south of Mérida; 70 miles south of Uxmal; 60 miles east of Campeche on the coast.
Getting there: From Mérida, take Hwy. 180 south to Chencoyi (approximately 115 miles); go east on Hwy. 261 for approximately five miles; and then go south, following the signs to Edzná. From Uxmal, head south on Hwy. 261 approximately 60 miles. After passing through Hopelchén, watch for signs to Edzná, and take a side road heading south. Rental car; bus service; jeep rental at Uxmal.
Sight-seeing time: An afternoon.
Brief history: Edzná is a Classic Mayan site with the somewhat disconcerting name of "House of Grimaces." Its heyday was A.D. 600–800.
Features: There are many outlying ruins in this three-square-mile site; however, many of them are overgrown. The main plaza is surrounded on the east side by the 102-foot Five Story Temple, on the west side by the House of the Moon, and on the north and south sides by other structures. In the northwest corner is an ancient Mayan *tezmacalli*, a sweat bath. Underground, archaeologists have found channels and reservoirs used to collect ground water that would flood the site owing to its location below sea level.
Facilities: None.
Bocaditos: From Edzná, it's only 60 miles to Campeche, a large seaport that is worth a sidetrip. Campeche was founded on the site of a Mayan settlement called Ah-kin-pech, which meant the place of the tick and the flea — but don't let that discourage you.

IZAMAL

Location: Approximately 40 miles from Chichén Itzá; 40 miles from Mérida; 170 miles west of Cancún.
Getting there: Rental car; taxi; bus service. The small town is located just north of Hwy. 180, midway between Chichén Itzá (Piste) and Mérida.
Sight-seeing time: An afternoon.
Brief history: The site is Classic Mayan (A.D. 300–900), and much of it was destroyed by the Spanish. Abandoned three hundred years before the conquest, it was founded, according to legend, by Itzamná ("Dew from Heaven") who later became a god in the Mayan pantheon.
Features: This little-visited site has one of the largest pyramids in Mexico, Kunich-Kakmo, which offers a view of the jungle after a steep climb. There are 12 pyramids left in the ceremonial city. The Spaniards

built a magnificent convent here on a large plaza. The Convent of San Antonio de Juan de Mérida was begun in 1553 and finished in 1561.
Facilities: None. There is a snack bar in the village.
Bocaditos: On August 15 a large fiesta honoring the Virgin of Izamal is held here.

KABAH

Location: Approximately 70 miles south of Mérida; 12 miles south of Uxmal.
Getting there: Rental car; bus; rental jeep. Take Hwy. 261 south, follow the signs to Kabah, which is located on the west side of the highway and set back in the jungle.
Sight-seeing time: An afternoon.
Brief history: Kabah is connected to Uxmal by a *sacbe.* This Classic Mayan site is noted as a good example of Puuc Mayan by archaeologists. (Puuc refers to a low range of hills on the peninsula.) Little is known about the specific history of Kabah. It is one of the sites visited by J. L. Stephens and Frederick Catherwood in the last century. (See *Incidents of Travel in Central America, Chiapas and Yucatan* by John L. Stephens.)
Features: The Palace of the Masks is named so because it holds numerous masks of the Mayan mythological rain god Chac, whose trunklike nose is a distinctive feature in Mayan decoration. The Arch of Kabah is a typical Mayan corbeled arch — stones are laid in inverted pyramid fashion until the two sides meet.
Facilities: None.
Bocaditos: The site makes a pleasant place to browse through Stephens' memoirs. The Dover Press edition has original drawings by Catherwood.

KOHUNLICH

Location: Approximately 25 miles southwest of Chetumal, near the border with Belize.
Getting there: Rental car; bus service. Take Hwy. 186 west out of Chetumal.
Sight-seeing time: A day.
Brief history: Kohunlich lay forgotten until 1968 when thieves were caught trying to steal several sun god masks at the site. Since then activity has increased, and the sun gods are back in place. A Classic Mayan site (A.D. 300–900), Kohunlich was abandoned, like other sites, around 1200.
Features: Set in a beautiful jungle location, Kohunlich has the same aura of mystery as Cobá — visitors feel they are looking at the ruins after centuries of secrecy. The Pyramid of the Masks is notable, as is the ball court. Many stelae dot the site.
Facilities: None. Nearby Chetumal, a free port and therefore attractive to Mexican visitors who shop for appliances there, now has several

hotels. Check at the tourist office, Avenida Obregon 457 (2-09-42), for information on what to see and do in Chetumal.

Bocaditos: There are several little-visited sites hidden in the jungle around Chetumal—Becán, Chicaná, and Xpuhil. Ask for a map of the region at the tourist office.

LABNA

Location: Six miles south of Oxkutzcab on Hwy. 184 south of Mérida.

Getting there: From Mérida, take Hwy. 261 south for approximately 60 miles, turn left at Maní, and drive southeast approximately 25 miles on Hwy. 184 to Oxkutzcab. Follow signs to the site. From Uxmal, head north on Hwy 261 for 16 miles, turn east at Maní onto Hwy. 184 to Oxkutzcab, and follow signs to the site.

Sight-seeing time: An afternoon.

Brief history: Late Classic Puuc Mayan site, prominent in the ninth century A.D. and visited by J. L. Stephens and Frederick Catherwood in the last century. Catherwood's famous drawing of the Arch of Labná was sketched here.

Features: The corbeled arch made famous in Catherwood's sketch still stands, and its beauty is compelling. The Palace is covered with rain god (Chac) masks found at other Puuc sites.

Facilities: None.

Bocaditos: Muna, a little town on the road to Labná, was a major Mayan city at the time of the conquest. It was established in 1450 after the great city of Mayapán was destroyed. Ironically, Muna means "it has ended" in Mayan. And it did end in 1542 when the last ruler of the Maya surrendered to Francisco de Montejo. Twenty years later, the Bishop Diego de Landa burned all but three of the Maya codices in the town square at Maní. Some scholars believe the codices might have enabled them to transcribe the Mayan glyphs that appear on stelae throughout the peninsula.

SAYIL

Location: Ten miles south of Uxmal, off Hwy. 261; 71 miles south of Mérida.

Getting there: Rental car; bus; jeep rental at Uxmal.

Sight-seeing time: Two to three hours.

Brief history: Construction of new buildings at this Late Classic site (circa A.D. 900) ceased after the year 1000.

Features: The Palace is decorated in typical Puuc Mayan style with Chac masks, which have a curved trunk as the dominant feature. Clusters of columns, carved to represent the wooden posts used in the construction of the Maya *palapas* ("huts") decorate the front of the palace. The *palapas* that proliferate in the countryside are probably very similar to the huts occupied by the preconquest Mayans. Historians believe that most stone buildings were used only for ceremonial purposes.

Facilities: None.
Bocaditos: It's possible to drive by dirt road from Labná to Sayil. On the way, you will pass a small site called Xlapak.

TULUM

Location: Approximately 70 miles south of Cancún on Hwy. 307.
Getting there: Rental car; bus service from Cancún; bus tours; air taxi from Cancún and Cozumel.
Sight-seeing time: An afternoon.
Brief history: Tulum is a walled city built in the late thirteenth century. Buildings were being added 50 years before the conquest, and it is thought to have been occupied at the time of the conquest. After the fall and disintegration of Classic Maya society in A.D. 900, the Toltecs exerted greater influence on the peninsula. This, followed by rivalries among families, led to the development of walled cities.
Features: Tulum is not noted for its artistic merit, although it is extremely popular with tour groups. It is an example of late decadent Maya-Toltec architecture. The temples are heavy and somehow crude. The site is worth visiting because of its beautiful location on the cliffs above the blue waters of the Caribbean.
Facilities: There are two small, clean restaurants at the entrance to the site on the main highway that serve local specialties and cold beer. There is a collection of tourist shops in front of the site, selling mostly souvenirs; however, just across from the ticket booth, there's a small hut where a Mayan Indian and his family weave baskets out of green palm leaves. The baskets are a vivid green, the leaves edged in yellow; unfortunately, they lose their color after a few days.
Bocaditos: Bring along your swimsuit, perhaps a picnic lunch. The small cove at the Tulum site has white sand, palm trees, and clear blue water.

UXMAL

Location: Approximately 60 miles south of Mérida on Hwy. 261.
Getting there: Rental car; bus tours; bus service from Mérida.
Sight-seeing time: History buffs will want to spend several days in this area, and Uxmal makes a good base; the casual visitor can see the site in a day. Many tour companies run buses down to Uxmal for the afternoon and include dinner and the sound and light show in their tour package, heading back to Mérida late in the evening.
Brief history: Uxmal is the definitive Puuc Mayan site. At its height, Puuc Mayan was one of the most beautiful architectural styles in the ancient world. The name *Uxmal* means "built three times," and it may have been first built by the Petén Maya in A.D. 600. (The Peten came from what is now Guatemala.) Architecturally, the zenith was reached at Uxmal in the ninth century. The area was later occupied by Indians from the Mexican highlands.
Features: One of the most unusual buildings at the site is the Pyramid

163

of the Magician. This 125-foot pyramid has an unusual oval base. The Nunnery, so-called because of the small cell-like rooms inside, has one wall covered with red hand prints. On the west side of the plaza in front of the Nunnery is a building (called "West Building") that has an elaborate Puuc Mayan frieze.

Facilities: Many visitors stay in Mérida; others, intent on exploring the many sites in this area, stay at the hotels situated near the site. La Palapa (Box 797, Mérida), Hacienda Uxmal (Box 407, Mérida), and Villas Arqueologicas (Club Med, 533-4800 in Mexico City or 1-800-528-3100 in the United States) all offer excellent facilities. Visitors may rent jeeps at the hotels, also. To reach the hotels by phone, call the operator and ask for the hotel by name.

Bocaditos: There's not much to do after dark at Uxmal, except watch the stars as the Mayans must have. For a bedtime story, read the *Popol Voh*, the sacred book of the Quiché Maya. The myth comes alive in a new translation by Ralph Nelson that was published by Houghton Mifflin Company.

8

MEXICO OF THE COLONIALS

A TOUR OF PAST SPLENDORS

Mexico's colonial past hangs like a veil over the country. The history of some cities and towns is as richly detailed as an ornate tapestry, evoking memories of Spanish grandees and their fine-boned, high-collared ladies, while casting a shadow on the country's Indian past; elsewhere, the veil is light, almost transparent, and colonial trappings are merely a lacy embellishment of the distant past.

Few places in Mexico escaped colonial influence; what the conquistadores did not conquer, the Church did. No matter how small the village, how Indian its origins and customs, the focal point of each community is the parish church—more magnificent than any other building, gilded and painted, cared for and visited. The colonial church on the plaza remains a constant even in the life of modern Mexico.

The intermarriage of Spaniard and Indian had varying results across Mexico, so that just as there was a multiplicity of Indians before the Spanish Conquest, there is a diversity among the people of the regions today. The conquerors, though most came from the same region of Spain, represented a mixed bag of adventurers from different classes and backgrounds, and with varying sensibilities and goals. The two cultures, Indian and Spanish, were both similar and dissimilar: the priesthood played a powerful role in both; Spaniard and Indian each usually held a fixed place in a rigid class structure; and, in perhaps the most obvious parallel, both Spanish and pre-Hispanic cities were centered around great plazas, dominated by palaces and temples. Such architectural similarities enabled the Spanish to impose a colonial facade on a preexisting structure so that many of Mexico's "colonial cities" rest on the ruins of Indian cities and towns. Most notable among such makeovers is Mexico City, which sits on the ruins of Tenochtitlán. Other cities were built as colonial outposts to house miners or intercept business on crucial trade routes.

Of course, the colonial impact goes beyond architecture, though buildings are the most obvious evidence of Spanish influence. The religion and language of Spain also permeated the country, although both made concessions to what went before. Many Mexican words and names are Spanish versions of Indian words, and the Church was quick to assimilate local fiestas and customs into the liturgy. In fact, many aspects of life in Mexico — poetry, art, literature, music, social customs, and crafts — result from the mixing of the two cultures. What has emerged is Mexican in character, a mix of Indian and Creole that varies in subtle ways throughout the country. To separate the two elements is often impossible. Superimposition of one pyramid on another was a common architectural custom in pre-Hispanic times, and the imposition of the Spanish culture on that of the Indian adds yet another layer to Mexico's mysterious history.

The intermingling of the two cultures took place over a relatively short period. Three hundred years after the conquest, the majority of Mexico's population was of mixed Indian and Spanish blood (today approximately 85 percent of the population is mestizo). But that intermingling produced different results in various regions of the country. We have chosen nine colonial towns, each with a distinct character and mood, the result of mixing Indian and Spanish cultures with the customs peculiar to that region. Each colonial city wears the mantle of the conquest in a unique manner. If the cities and towns share any one characteristic, it is that sense of history that is missing in so many modern cities.

OAXACA

Lying hidden in the lush, green mountains of the Southern Highlands, Oaxaca is a city masquerading as a town, a city of open plazas and narrow streets, inhabited by men and women of small stature and ancient Indian blood. Over 100,000 people live in Oaxaca, the capital of the state with the same name, but the city seems more intimate than the statistics might reflect. Located in the heart of one of the richest archaeological zones in all Mexico, Oaxaca is a popular tourist center; yet its location (250 miles south of Mexico City) allows it to remain an out-of-the-way spot, untouched by the commercialism associated with the more accessible cities.

The city is crowded onto a small plateau that sits at five thousand feet above sea level. At nine thousand feet, atop the surrounding mountains, great pyramids and temples built by men with Stone-Age tools dwarf the city below. This is the land of the Zapotec Indians, the Cloud People, and in the Valley of Oaxaca the visitor is surrounded by a feast of vistas. Here the colonial influence is a mere chapter in the history of an ancient land. A fitting symbol of the colonial past might be the abandoned Convent of Cuilapán, located on a hillside outside Oaxaca. It is a crumbling twin-towered monastery with thick-walled cells and overgrown gardens, so Spanish in appearance that it evokes the harsh plains of Spain, and yet so Mexican as it sits roofless under the cloud-filled sky.

The conquistadores found little in the Valley of Oaxaca to keep them here. (Had they known about the treasures buried in the tombs at nearby Monte Albán, they might have lingered.) At the time of the Spanish Conquest the town was an Aztec outpost — the Zapotecs, the original inhabitants, and the Mixtecs, their conquerors, lived, for the most part, in peace with the Aztecs. Hernán Cortés was charmed by the valley and took for himself the title *marqués* del Valle de Oaxaca, although he spent little time here as his problems with the viceroys and the bureaucracy that followed his conquest increased. The priests did remain in the area and the Dominicans, the builders of Cuilapán, were ordered to move their monastery to the city; consequently, Cuilapán was abandoned and the beautiful ornate Church of Santo Domingo was built in the city. ˙

Oaxaca is the birthplace of two of Mexico's most influential leaders: Benito Juárez and Porfirio Díaz. Juárez, a Zapotec Indian, was raised and educated in Oaxaca, and his home is now a museum. Díaz, a Mixtec Indian, was the dictator who ruled Mexico during the latter part of the last century and whose actions led to the Mexican Revolution. He is generally held in disfavor throughout Mexico, although his hometown has named a street after him.

Another famous native son is the artist Rufino Tamayo, who has provided the city with one of the best collections of pre-Hispanic art to be found anywhere in the world. The collection is on view at the Rufino Tamayo Museum of Pre-Hispanic Art on Avenida Morelos.

In the marketplace the women of the valley, the Zapotecs and the Mixtecs, still sell their *atole* as they have always done, pouring the gruel into colorful hand-carved gourds as they chatter in their native Indian dialects. It would appear that only the Church has left a lasting impression on the valley. In Tlacochahuaya, just outside Oaxaca on the Pan American Highway, every remarkable inch of the village church is decorated with flowers and birds, saints and supplicants, all painted in naive style and in the colorful hues favored by the Indian artists. In Tlacolula, the church overflows when the priest offers mass on market day, and tiny Indian women kneeling before the image of Christ mutter their prayers in dialect. And in Mitla, site of a Mixtec city, a platform that once supported a temple is now the foundation of a Catholic church. Essentially, the heart of the city of Oaxaca is colonial in design but Indian in nature, and in the surrounding villages the juxtaposition of the two cultures is more defined. Much of what goes on in the daily lives of the people of Oaxaca is part of a pattern that dates back to the time of Cortés.

Oaxaca is also one of the last hangouts of the "jippies" — the term the Mexicans use to describe the wandering young gringos who enjoy the cheap prices and relaxed atmosphere. Many of them come from Europe, and the majority look like they may have been south of the border too long; too many magic mushrooms have passed their way. There is a certain amount of illegal drug dealing in the area. The wise tourist will avoid buying from or dealing with anyone in Oaxaca.

Oaxaca is a good place to go shopping for mementos of Mexico. Going to market can become a daily affair, especially if you have a car and can reach the outlying villages. Sunday is market day in Tlacolula, east of the city; Monday, Miahuatlán, southeast of the city on the highway to Puerto Angel, holds its market featuring the local mescal; Wednesday is market day in Zimatlán and Etla; Thursday the former Zapotec capital, Zaachila, holds a market, and, farther east, Ejutlá also claims Thursday as its market day; Friday, off to Ocotlán; and then Saturday, stay in town for the Oaxaca market. (Most of the hotels supply a map of the area showing the various sites and market days, and the tourist office at the northwest corner of the zócalo has a selection of free material.)

Oaxaca is a crafts shopper's paradise. If some of the items you lust after are too large to carry back on a plane, find out if the shop will ship, or check with your hotel; it may pack and ship for you. Leave space in your suitcase for a blanket or serape or both; prices are very reasonable. Each night, vendors selling a variety of blankets, rebozos, shawls, and serapes wander through the sidewalk cafés. The prices are low, but bargain because quality varies. Most of the blankets are made in the nearby village of Teotitlán del Valle, and it's worth a trip by cab or car to the village to inspect the *tallers* ("workshops") and buy at the source. Much of the work is done on the Spanish loom using natural fibers and dyes — the workers are quick to tell you what is natural and what is not. You can order custom-made blankets at some of the *tallers*.

To the south of the city is the village of San Bártolo Coyotepec, where the famous black pottery is made. The potter Doña Rosa died in the spring of 1980; however, some of her signed work may be found at the *taller* now run by her son. Other *tallers* in the village also produce excellent examples of this unglazed ware. After stopping to buy pots, drive on to Santo Tomás to buy *fajas* ("woven belts") — you won't even have to get out of your car because you will be besieged by small children carrying brightly woven bundles in varying widths and lengths.

Many of the crafts have creative roots in Mexico's Indian past. The ancient shapes of the black pottery, the geometric designs reminiscent of Mixtec friezes now found on blankets, and the cotton *huipiles* worn by the women, all echo Oaxaca's rich Indian culture, a culture still very much alive. Oaxacan craftsmen and builders do not hesitate to find inspiration in the past, a past that surrounds them.

Oaxaca is the heart of the southern archaeological zone and boasts some of Mexico's most beautiful and imposing sites. Just outside the city is Monte Albán, the Zapotec city that the Mixtecs turned into a funerary site — it's a short cab ride from the city. To the south are the ruins at Zaachila, while to the east lie Mitla, Yagul, Dainzu, and other smaller sites. (For a detailed description of the sites, see the chapter **Mexico of the Ancients.**)

When a team of archaeologists uncovered the treasure of Tomb Number 7 at Monte Albán, efforts were made to move the treasure to the capital; however, the Oaxaqueños won the battle, and the treasure remained in their city. It is now housed in the Regional Museum in Oaxaca and includes some of the most valuable jewels ever found in the Americas. The museum is a good place to begin a tour of the local sites. The Frissell Museum of Zapotec Art in the small town of Mitla also has a notable collection of artifacts discovered locally.

One of the best times to visit Oaxaca is mid-July, when the Fiesta Lunes del Cerro (Guelaguetza) is held. Essentially a dance festival, the fiesta is held in the Cerro del Fortín, a large open-air arena on a hill outside the city. Thousands, both poor and rich, flock to the arena to watch as village dance troupes from throughout the region perform their native dances in colorful costumes. The women wear the embroidered *huipiles* indigenous to the region, and everyone carries gifts of handicrafts and produce from his village or town. These are presented to the government guests at the fiesta, and samples are thrown into the crowd. If you are lucky enough to sit in the front sections of the semicircular arena, you may be struck by a flying pineapple, a piece of sugarcane, a small piece of pottery, or a miniature bottle of mescal. Make hotel reservations well in advance of July if you plan to attend — most hotels reserve a block of good seats for their guests, and you can buy these tickets when you arrive.

There is much to see and do during the daytime in Oaxaca, and the evenings are usually spent relaxing after a day of shopping or climbing ruins. The market closes at dusk in an unnatural show of haste as the vendors rush to close up their stalls before the mandatory evening blackout. In the zócalo, waiters bring out candles, shopkeepers in the tourist crafts shops light gas lamps, and patrons read menus and price tags by match light. If a local politician is making a speech from the bandstand, the plug is pulled and he is left to shout his message. Within an hour, the blackout is lifted, and the zócalo begins to come alive in a nightly ritual, which is enhanced by the music of brass or marimba bands on Tuesdays, Thursdays, and Sundays. By ten or eleven, the square is quiet and tourists wander back to their hotels, wrapped against the chill night air in a newly purchased blanket.

The weather in Oaxaca is usually mild, but sometimes hot in the daytime and chilly at night. It's best to take along a raincoat if you are sight-seeing outside the city.

Besides the Lunes del Cerro mid-July, special fiestas include the famous Noche de los Rábanos, Night of the Radishes, December 23, when farmers bring large carved radishes to a special contest held in the zócalo. All Oaxaca's Christmas celebrations are popular, and reservations should be made well in advance.

BOCADITOS

It's about an eight-hour drive from Mexico City to Oaxaca through some of the most beautiful, but torturous mountains in Mexico. An alternate way to reach Oaxaca is to fly from the capital — the flight takes about 45 minutes. If you make your reservations through an international carrier in the United States and fly to Mexico City, you will get a break on the round trip fare on Mexican airlines.

There's so much to see in Oaxaca that it's worthwhile spending at least a week there and renting a car. Although the region is relatively unspoiled, Oaxaqueños cater to the tourist trade, and most of the hotels provide maps listing all the local market days and festivals. Be sure to stop by the tourist office at the corner of Independencia and Vigil, near the cathedral.

Don't miss the Sunday market at Tlacolula, and try to visit the village of Teotitlán del Valle where serapes and blankets are woven. If you do get out to the country markets, you will see many things to buy, so pack lightly and include an extra collapsible bag. You won't need many clothes in Oaxaca, jeans are *de rigeur*. Don't take a coat; buy a serape.

Take a small flashlight along — it's handy at the ruins and also in the cafés on the zócalo during the nightly blackout.

AROUND OAXACA

VITAL STATISTICS

Climate. Balmy, springlike year-round. Cool nights. Occasional rain showers in the afternoon. Beware of sunburn at this altitude and latitude.

Population. 130,000 but with a small-town atmosphere.

Altitude. 5,000 feet.

State. Oaxaca.

City phone code. 51.

HOTELS

El Presidente, Cinco de Mayo and Abasolo (6-06-11). The best in town. Not at all like other hotels in this chain, it is built in a former convent, decorated with antiques and colonial reproductions. High walls keep out the street noise. Just a short walk from the zócalo. Heated pool. Good restaurant featuring continental and local dishes. A. Cr.

Hotel Misión de los Angeles, Calzada Porfirio Díaz (6-15-00). Known to generations of gringos as the Oaxaca Courts, the new name hasn't changed the peaceful ambience of the place. Owned by the Aristos chain. Comfortable, quiet, colonial rooms set amid tropical gardens. Dining room, bar, tennis, and pool. A. Cr.

Hotel Victoria, Apartado Postal 248, off Hwy. 190, overlooking city (6-26-33). Popular luxury hotel set in tropical gardens with a view of the city. Pool, tennis courts. Tour groups often booked here. A. Cr.

Marqués del Valle, Puerta de Claveria (6-34-77). This old standby is on the main plaza. The lobby is a popular meeting place, and the rooms facing the square, although pleasant, can be noisy on those few nights when Oaxaca stays up late. C. Cr.

Señorial, Portal de las Flores (6-39-33). Located in the heart of the city, a good place to stay if you don't have a rental car. Roof garden and pool. B. Cr.

RESTAURANTS

Most of the better restaurants are located in larger hotels. Try the dining rooms at El Presidente, Misión de los Angeles, and Hotel Victoria. Most hotel dining rooms close early, around 10 p.m.

Café del Portal, Portal de Mercaderas, east corner of the zócalo. Good view of the square, and rug vendors wander among the tables. Try the Oaxacan tamales with *mole negro*. Don't miss a trip to the john—it's upstairs, through the kitchen, and up a winding, circular, free-standing staircase. Moderate. Cr.

Doña Elpidia, Miguel Cabrera 413. This boardinghouse is another Oaxacan tradition. Homemade local specialties served in a family-style dining room. If you want to eat like the natives, this is the place. Lunch only 1-5 p.m. Inexpensive. N.

El Asador Vasco, west side of the zócalo, above El Jardin. Extensive menu featuring grilled meats, local Oaxacan dishes, and some continental entrées. You can eat cheaper elsewhere, but the view is part of the price—half a dozen candlelit tables along the edge of the veranda overlook the square. Cr.

El Jardín, west side of the zócalo. Businessmen, "jippies," and tourists gather here at sundown around metal café tables squeezed under the archways. The squeeze gets even tighter when it rains and the sidewalk tables are moved in. Cheap drinks, beer, snacks, and meals. Sit here long enough and all Oaxaca will walk by. Inexpensive. Cr.

Guelatao, Portal de Mercaderas (6-23-11). Sidewalk café on the zócalo. Good *comida corrida*, plus local specialties and stuffed rolls. Inexpensive. Cr.

NIGHTLIFE

As in many of Mexico's small cities and towns, nightlife in Oaxaca is limited to a stroll around the main square, a quiet nightcap in a café, or a late dinner. Some of the hotels have bars, occasionally with entertainment, but the lights go out early in this colonial mountain town.

SHOPPING

It's possible to go to market every day in Oaxaca. Surrounding towns and villages are famed for their *tianguis*, Indian markets. Most hotels give away maps showing the villages and their market days—Etla on Wednesday, Zaachila on Thursday, Zimatlán on Wednesday, Miahuatlán on Monday, Ejutlá on Thursday, and Ocotlán on Friday.

Oaxaca Market, 20 de Noviembre, two blocks south of the zócalo. Good buys on clothes, pottery, hats, knives, leatherwork. Busiest day is Saturday. There's a new market west of town near the railroad station but most Oaxaqueños still shop at the old market.

San Bártolo de Coyotepec, five miles south, past the airport on Hwy. 175. A short ride by cab or rental car will get you to this small village famed for its black pottery. There are two San Bártolos on the road—you need the second. Doña Rosa, the most famous potter, had a large sign pointing the way to her *taller*, now run by her son. Other *tallers* are worth visiting, also.

Santo Tomás, three miles beyond San Bártolo de Coyotepec on Hwy. 175. This small village is famous for its woven belts, or *fajas*. Shop from your car; you will be besieged by children carrying bundles of colorful belts.

Teotitlán del Valle, about 14 miles southwest on Pan American Highway (Hwy. 190), take dirt road for another ten miles. This is the place to go for good, handmade blankets or serapes. The weavers' workshops line the dirt streets—just walk in, look around, and bargain. Most blankets are woolen and dyed with natural pigments. Custom work done. There's a small *tienda* near the church where you can buy a soft drink or a beer.

Tlacolula, 15 miles southwest on Pan American Highway (Hwy. 190). One of the best Indian markets in Mexico. Held every Sunday in the middle of this dusty, dilapidated town. Good place to buy baskets, pottery, and leatherwork.

POINTS OF INTEREST

Oaxaca is rich in archaeological ruins. We've listed the major sites; for more information, read the chapter **Mexico of the Ancients.**

Dainzu, southwest on Pan American Highway (Hwy. 190) toward Mitla. The road to Mitla and Yagul is dotted with smaller sites like Dainzu. Watch for signs. Dainzu is a recent dig, located in a hillside. Open seven days.

Labiteyeco, southwest on the road to Mitla, Hwy. 190. A small site with a friendly caretaker who will show you the tombs of a prominent Zapotec lord and his lady. The tombs are decorated with masks of the rain god known as Cocijo. Tip the caretaker. Open seven days.

Mitla, 24 miles southwest on Pan American Highway (Hwy. 190). Take left-hand fork to Mitla at 20-mile point. This was a flourishing Mixtec city when Cortés conquered Mexico. Mitla is still a large village, much of it set on top of the ruins. A large church sits on one temple platform and is built from the ruins of a preceding temple. The geometric designs of Mixtec friezes can still be seen on some buildings. Open seven days.

Monte Albán, on the mountain plateau west of Oaxaca. A 15-minute ride by cab or car. The most famous site in southern Mexico is this level mountaintop amid the clouds. Features a reconstructed ball court, a large pyramid, several tomb sites, and an observatory. Inhabited first by Zapotecs in 800 B.C., it was turned into a funerary city by the Mixtecs in A.D. 900. Note the Olmec influence in the building of the Danzantes, north side of the Great Plaza. Open seven days.

Yagul, about 19 miles southwest on Pan American Highway (Hwy. 190). Follow the signs down a short side road to these crumbling ruins built on a small plateau in the center of the valley. Well-restored ball court. A Mixtec tomb is located at the top of the hill. Open seven days.

Zaachila, nine miles south, beyond Cuilapán and the village of Xoxo. Once the capital of the Zapotec nation, these ruins were until very recently off-limits to prying tourists and archaeologists. Open seven days.

Church of San Juan de Dios, Aldama and 20 de Noviembre, near the market. This church is the home of a revered Virgin. A visit to the church is a part of the daily market ritual for many Indian women.

Cuilapán, about five miles southwest on the road to Zaachila. This is the unfinished Convent of Santiago the Apostle, originally the home of Dominican friars who were ordered to abandon their building and move into the city of Oaxaca. The monastery with its twin towers has a Spanish look. Vincente Guerrero was executed by a firing squad here in 1831. A statue of the former president of Mexico stands in the courtyard. Inside are Guerrero's cell and the remains of murals painted by the friars. Princess Juana Donaji, daughter of the last Zapotec king, is buried here, also. Open seven days.

Church of Santo Domingo, Constitution and Cinco de Mayo. This large sixteenth-century church is a masterpiece of gilding and ornate decoration.

Tlacochahuaya, the next village beyond Santa Maria del Tule on Pan American Highway (Hwy. 190), approximately six miles east of the city. Take the dusty side road into the village and ask to see the inside of the parish church. Magnificently decorated in a blaze of primary colors and primitive designs. Tip the caretaker.

Tule Tree, five miles east on Pan American Highway (Hwy. 190). In the small hamlet of Santa María del Tule stands a 2,000-year-old *ahuehuete* tree, a Moctezuma cypress. A smaller, younger, and yet still massive tree stands nearby. Visitors stand before the trees like ants to have their pictures taken. While you watch, buy a mango on a stick from the Indian girls.

MUSEUMS

House of Benito Juárez, Calle Garcia Virgil, one block north and west of the Church of Santo Domingo. This was the home where young Benito Juárez was taken under the protection of a wealthy man and educated. Juárez became president of Mexico in 1857. The museum contains personal papers and memorabilia. Open seven days.

Regional Museum of Oaxaca, Calle M. Alcala, next door to the Church of Santo Domingo. The old convent has been converted into a museum that holds some of the most valuable pre-Columbian artifacts yet discovered, including the jewels from Tomb Number 7 at Monte Albán. Closed Monday.

Rufino Tamayo Museum of Pre-Hispanic Art, Av. Morelos 503. Artist Rufino Tamayo has given his fellow Oaxaqueños one of the most beautiful collections of pre-Hispanic art in the world. Includes works of historical and aesthetic value. Open seven days. Small admission fee. Free on Sundays.

FIESTAS

Cerro del Fortín (Guelaguetza), the two Mondays after July 16. *Guelaguetza* means "offering" in Zapotec, and these popular fiestas are held for two Mondays at the Cerro (Hill) del Fortín outside the city. The various villages and towns in the region present dances and then toss gifts at the audience. Popular with visitors.

Fiesta de los Rábanos (Festival of the Radishes), December 23. Farmers carve radishes into fantastic shapes, and they are exhibited in the marketplace and the zócalo.

TRANSPORTATION

Airport. National carriers serve the airport, which has an approach route over the ruins of Monte Albán.

Buses. There's first-class bus service from Mexico City, and there is second-class service to many of the neighboring towns and villages.

Car rental. Agencies include Avis — international airport (no phone), Alameda de León 1 (6-50-30), and Hidalgo 313 (6-64-22); Hertz — international airport (no phone) and C. M. Bustamante 620 (6-19-91).

Taxis. Reasonable rates. Check before you get in. Taxis may be rented by the day for trips to the ruins or village markets.

Trains. There's daily service from Mexico City to Oaxaca. Be sure to carry a packed lunch because the dining car is not always available. (For general information about train service in Mexico, see the chapter **There and Back Again** or check at the local tourist office listed below.)

TOURIST SERVICES

Tourist Office (Delegación Federal de Turismo), Av. Independencia and García Vigil, Palacio Municipal (downstairs) (6-38-10).

COMMUNICATIONS

Post Office, Av. Independencia and 20 de Noviembre.

GUANAJUATO

A hillside city, Guanajuato is crowded in and around a deep gorge cut out of the mountains by fierce floods. Reminiscent of northern Spain or a village in Tuscany, Guanajuato is the most Spanish of Mexico's colonial cities. Founded and nurtured by conquistadores, the city has shrunk by half since the days when 100,000 people lived here, their lives bound to the king's silver mines. What has remained, among the abandoned mines and the crumbling haciendas, is the essence of Spanish culture in Mexico.

Guanajuato is a conservative and Catholic city where aesthetic values are nourished. Its narrow cobbled streets and the dark buildings hovering over them evoke a past where hidalgos were forced to woo their ladies in the company of a duenna. This is the home of the Sinarquista movement, the right-wing, profoundly Catholic political group that has resisted revolution in Mexico; and yet this is also the birthplace of Diego Rivera, the revolutionary muralist, who was an avowed Marxist. Such contradiction is not new to Guanajuato; it has long been a center for dissent, a breeding ground for radical thinkers of the left and right, and a rallying point for revolutionaries. It was to this city that Padre Hidalgo came to lead his followers in the 1810 uprising against Spain. Guanajuato's loyalists took refuge in the granary, the

Alhóndiga, where most of them died at the hands of Hidalgo's men. A statue of a miner nicknamed "El Pípila" stands above the city on a hilltop in honor of the man who strapped a granary stone to his back and led the revolutionaries to the doorway of the Alhóndiga. And it was to Guanajuato that Hidalgo was returned—his head hung on the ramparts of the granary for several years after his execution. Now, in more peaceful times, the old granary is the home of one of the best small museums in Mexico; inside is a rich collection of colonial pottery and painting. (The colonial potters of Guanajuato were famed for their *faience* ware, similar to the pottery produced in Italy. A few local artists have revived the art, and the pottery can be bought in their studios; however, some of the best can be found in the government crafts shops on Avenida Juárez in the capital.)

The main road through the city is a subterranean passage, which once served as a tunnel for the floodwaters that often burst through the dam above the city. In the early part of this century, thousands died in such a flood; however, the dam is now secure. Maps of the city are available from the tourist office at Juárez and Cinco de Mayo or at the local hotels, but these are not much help unless you went to West Point and got top marks in cartography. Guanajuato is a maze of cobbled streets that wind back and forth along the gorge and up the hillside. Fortunately, the city is small and you can get your bearings after a few hours of strolling about. Walking is the best way to see the city, and nearby sights can be reached by cab for a small fee. Only adventure into the countryside demands a car. However, getting to the city can be difficult without a car, though buses from the capital, some 250 miles away, stop at Guanajuato. The train from Nuevo Laredo stops in nearby San Miguel de Allende, and buses connect the two towns.

The city's small plazas are the scene of a cultural happening in late April and early May, when the Entreméses, short period plays mostly in pantomime are performed by costumed players from the University of Guanajuato. The Entreméses, some written by Cervantes, take place in conjunction with Guanajuato's International Cervantes Festival, which attracts artists in theater and music from throughout the world. Beverly Sills, members of the Old Vic, Ray Charles, Leonard Bernstein, and other prominent artists have participated in the festival. (Make hotel reservations months in advance.) Many of the festival concerts are performed in the Teatro Juárez, a magnificent theater with an exterior built in the style of La Belle Epoque and an interior executed in the Moorish fashion. Teatro Juárez sits on one of the main squares, Jardín de la Unión. Next door to Teatro Juárez is the Franciscan Church of San Diego and the parish church, La Parroquia, is located a few steps away on the Plaza de la Paz. A narrow street leads from the plaza to the university area, where one of Guanajuato's most beautiful churches, La Compañía, stands. However, two of the most beautiful churches are found outside the city. The first is a crumbling ruin set in an overgrown meadow in the suburb of Marfil ("ivory").

Located along a stream bed west of the city, this district was once a flourishing center of the silver trade. Mule trains gathered here to unload their precious burdens, and the wealthy built walled haciendas on the hillside. The church of Marfil is empty, but a few of the haciendas have been restored by artists and writers from the capital.

The second church stands high on the hill above the city in the mining community of Valenciana. Many consider La Valenciana one of the most beautiful churches in Mexico. It is slowly deteriorating, like so many of the country's old churches and convents, but the delicacy of its decoration and the magnificence of the architecture can still be appreciated. The church is still in use, and old women sell wooden rosaries in the small plaza outside.

Across the mountain road from the church is the old mine of Valenciana, and though it is not the booming mine it once was, it is one of the few that are still active. Miners sell rock formations, many of them quartz crystals, in the mine yard. The view of Guanajuato from La Valenciana is worth the climb, although the trip can also be made by cab.

Perhaps the mummies (*momias*) are Guanajuato's most celebrated tourist attraction. The mountain air has somehow worked to preserve certain corpses buried in the town cemetery, and these are on view at the catacombs, north of the city. It is not a sight for the squeamish. Spun-sugar mummies are sold in the town's market, which is housed in a Victorian glass and iron building in the center of the city.

Guanajuato is not one of Mexico's best crafts centers, although the market has several stalls that sell the everyday brown pottery made in nearby Dolores Hidalgo. There is a government crafts store at the south end of the city on Avenida Juárez. However, the city is a good point of departure for exploring the various towns of the Bajío region. Irapuato, the strawberry capital, is nearby, and although the town is not particularly attractive, the market there has excellent basket ware stalls. If you plan to visit nearby San Miguel de Allende, be sure to stop at the convent at Atotonílco on your way. Dolores Hidalgo, named in honor of its famous padre, is also on the road to San Miguel — check out the tile shops. You might want to plan a few days in Guanajuato and then go to San Miguel for a day or two.

Querétaro, a booming industrial town, can be reached in a few hours from Guanajuato and is worth visiting because it has a variety of churches and plazas built in the colonial manner. The Hill of Bells outside the city is the site of Emperor Maximilian's execution. Nearby Celaya is famous for the Church of El Carmen, which was designed and built by Francisco Eduardo Tresguerras, popularly known as the "Michelangelo of Mexico." You might want to compare his church with the parish church on San Miguel's main square, which, according to popular legend, was built by an Indian mason who had admired a postcard of Chartres Cathedral.

In Querétaro, you will be approached by opal vendors, but it's best to buy from local shops, where you will be given a written guarantee. The local specialty in Celaya is *cajeta*, candy made from goat's milk.

If you are traveling the Pan American Highway on your way back to the capital after a stay in the Bajío, stop for lunch at La Mansión, a posada just south of San Juan del Río (a good place to buy baskets and rebozos). La Mansión, an old granary that has been converted to a gracious hostel, is one of the best posadas in Mexico. (For more information, see Querétaro under "Roadhouses" in the chapter **Mexico and the Wheel.**) You might consider spending a day or two here and making a side trip to Tequisquiapán, where local wines are bottled under the Hidalgo label — there are some for sale at the small shop at La Mansión's Pemex station.

This region is the heart of colonial Mexico and offers limitless possibilities. Some of the country's best hotels and restaurants are located in the Bajío, and the region is easily accessible to Texans. It's a one-day drive from the border to San Luis Potosí or to San Miguel de Allende if you start early, and the Aztec Eagle makes daily stops on its way south to Mexico City.

The climate is pleasant year-round, but a little cooler than the capital, so take along a sweater.

BOCADITOS

Guanajuato is an excellent home base for exploring the Bajío. Either drive from Texas to San Miguel de Allende and then on to Guanajuato, or fly to Guadalajara or Mexico City and rent a car. You won't use the car much in Guanajuato (the streets are impossibly narrow), but you will want to make forays into the countryside — to Irapuato for baskets and strawberry jam, to Dolores Hidalgo for cookware, and to Celaya for candy.

The city has several excellent hotels, including the new El Presidente housed in an old hacienda, and several eccentric hostelries — try the Santa Cecilia, a castlelike construction. One of the best buys in town is the Motel Guanajuato. (See city listings that follow.)

Don't miss muralist Diego Rivera's home at Calle Pocitos 47. The artist was born here and lived here until he was six years old. The rooms are hung with his early works, including some illustrations for the *Popol Vuh*, the Mayan book of legend.

The famed *faience* ware is hard to find in Guanajuato, but with perseverance you may be able to find the *taller* of the master Gorky Gonzalez who signs his work with a distinguishable *A* and *T* for the name of his studio, Alfareria Tradicional. The *taller* is located on the hillside above the city on Calle Pastita.

AROUND GUANAJUATO

VITAL STATISTICS

Climate. Mild, moderate weather; cool evenings. Summer afternoon rain showers.

Population. 46,000.

Altitude. 6,700 feet.

State. Guanajuato.

City phone code. 473.

HOTELS

Castillo de Santa Cecilia, Box 44, Old Castle, Dolores Hidalgo Highway (Hwy. 110) (2-04-85). This hotel has a castle motif that seems to fit its setting of rugged hills. A pool; some rooms with fireplaces. Located above and northeast of the city. Terrific view in luxurious surroundings. A. Cr.

Hosteria del Frayle, Sopena 3 (2-11-79). The del Frayle is located in a seventeenth-century silver-coin factory across from the Teatro Juárez. Pleasant, colonial ambience. Parking a block away. C. Cr.

Hotel El Presidente Guanajuato, Marfil (1-800-854-2026). Located in an old mansion, the Hacienda de San Gabriel, in Guanajuato's historic suburb of Marfil. One of the most beautiful hotels in Mexico, unlike most of the modern El Presidente hotels. A. Cr.

Motel Guanajuato, Cerro San Antonio, Dolores Hidalgo Highway (Hwy. 110) (2-06-89). A new motel built in the colonial style with domed brick ceilings and tiled bathrooms. Great view of the city. Dining room and small bar. C. Cr.

Parador de San Javier, Box 66, Dolores Hidalgo Highway (Hwy. 110) (2-06-26). Old, charming colonial building with about 16 units, some with fireplaces. Located northeast of Guanajuato with a good view of the town. Suites available. A. Cr.

Real de Minas, Nejayote 17 (2-14-60). Large hotel built in the colonial style. Sits at the northern entrance to the *subterrano*, a subterranean highway that weaves through the city. Rooms are well appointed, some with fireplaces. Cars and scooters for rent. Swimming pool and dining room. One of the town's few nightspots, the Cantarranas Bar, is located in the hotel. A. Cr.

San Diego, Jardín de la Unión (2-13-00). This hotel is housed in a seventeenth-century convent in the heart of the city, the popular Jardín de la Unión. Rooms have balconies overlooking the narrow streets. Parking garage a block away. B. Cr.

RESTAURANTS

The best are located in the luxury hotels.

El Retiro, Sopena 12 (2-06-22). A popular café near the Teatro Juárez. Good place for a buffet-style lunch of local specialties.

La Antorcha, near El Pípila's statue on Hwy. 110, above the city (2-23-08). International cuisine served in quiet surroundings. Terrific view of the city below. Moderate. Cr.

Las Embajadoras, corner of Paseo Mandero and Embajadoras (2-00-81). In a motel at the end of the *subterrano*, this restaurant features good regional specialties at moderate prices.

Parador de San Javier (2-06-26); El Companero in the Real de Minas (2-14-60); and Castillo de Santa Cecilia (2-04-85).

NIGHTLIFE

Guanajuato is not known for its lively nightspots. This scholarly, conservative city does have some sidewalk cafés where students and professors meet. Try those near the university, and El Jardín de la Unión. The hotel bars are quite intimate and cozy on cool mountain nights.

During the Cervantes Festival (see Fiestas) there is a great deal of activity at the theater and local concert halls.

SHOPPING

Casas de las Artesanias, Av. Juárez. There are two government-owned craft shops in town, one near the Teatro Juárez and the other on Plaza de la Paz. Fixed prices. Open seven days.

Mercado Hidalgo, Av. Juárez, center of the city. Looks like a Victorian railway station with its vaulted roof and wrought iron decorations. Find good buys upstairs, food downstairs (look for the candy mummies); pottery and antiques on the second level.

POINTS OF INTEREST

Cerro del Cubilete, ten miles west on Hwy. 110. This 9,442-foot peak is topped with a large statue of Christ the King and affords a view of the entire region.

Church of San Diego, Jardín de la Unión. Much visited by the locals, this church is not very attractive on the outside but has an ornate interior. Built in 1663. A good place to watch or join the daily devotions of the citizens.

El Pípila's statue, Scenic Highway (Hwy. 110). Located on the winding highway above the city, this large statue of the local hero, a miner who broke down the doors of the Alhóndiga during the battle for independence, looms above the city. Can be reached by an exhausting climb up steep steps from the center of the city — or by cab.

La Parroquia, Plaza de la Paz, center of the city. This parish church holds what is claimed to be the oldest piece of Christian art in Mexico. The statue, known as Our Lady of Guanajuato, was given to the city by Philip II of Spain in 1557.

Marfil, five miles south on Hwy. 110. A suburb with crumbling and restored haciendas and an old, deteriorating church. Take a walk along the stream bed.

Mummies, Calzada de Panteón. *Las momias,* corpses preserved by a freakish reaction in the soil, are one of the main attractions in Guanajuato. Not for the weak of stomach. The bodies, dressed in burying clothes, are displayed in glass cases inside a large cavern near the cemetery. Open seven days 10–noon and 4–6. Small admission fee.

Plazuela de Baratillo, Jardín de la Unión. This small but popular square (*plazuela* means "little plaza") in the heart of the city is the site of a beautiful fountain given to the city by Emperor Maximilian.

Parque de las Acacias, southern end of the city, next to the Presa de la Olla, the large city dam. This is a favorite Sunday haunt of the locals. Rent a small boat and row on the artificial lake, or take a walk in the flower gardens.

Plazuela de los Angelos, Callejón del Beso. *Beso* means "kiss" in Spanish, and this small side street off the plaza is named "Street of the Kiss" because it is only two feet three inches wide.

Teatro Juárez. Dating from the turn of the century, this opulent building in Belle Epoque style is a magnificent conglomeration of marble, gilt, red velvet, carvings, and wrought iron. Open seven days. Small admission fee.

Valenciana, three miles northwest on Dolores Hidalgo Highway (Hwy. 110). The Church of San Cayetano was built in the sixteenth century by the County of Valencia in honor of the Virgin of the Immaculate Conception. This beautiful church stands above the city and is attended by miners who work the Valenciana Mine across the street, one of the few still operating. Visit the mine, also.

MUSEUMS

Alhóndiga de Granaditas, Calle Pocitos and Cinco de Mayo, north end of the city. Housed in an old granary, this is among the best small museums in Mexico. Ancient artifacts, colonial pottery, clothing, artworks, murals by Chavez Morado, and a good book shop. Closed Mondays. Small admission fee.

Diego Rivera Museum, Calle Pocitos 47. This small museum is housed in the home where the famous muralist was born and lived for much of his youth. Examples of his work and personal effects are displayed. Open seven days. Free.

FIESTAS

Cervantes Festival. Held annually during the last of April and the first of May. Internationally famous performers like Beverly Sills, Ella Fitzgerald, the Royal Shakespeare Company, the National Ballet of Cuba, and the famed marionette troupe from Czechoslovakia perform at the town's two principal theaters and several outdoor plazas. Seminars, lectures, and art exhibits are also performed in conjunction with the festival.

Entreméses, Plaza San Roque. These one-act plays, mostly farces by Cervantes, are usually performed in conjunction with the Cervantes Festival.

Fiestas de Purísima, La Valenciana, December 8. Held in the plaza in front of the hillside church, this festival is very popular among local villagers.

Fiesta de Virgen de Guanajuato, late May. The revered statue in the basilica is carried about the city in this ancient ritual.

TRANSPORTATION

Automobiles. Private cars are convenient for exploring the region; however, the streets are extremely narrow and confusing. Large motor homes or vans may find the city streets too narrow.

Buses. First-class service from San Miguel de Allende and Irapuato; connections to other cities in area.

Taxis. Reasonable. Settle fare before you get in.

Trains. There's train service to nearby San Miguel de Allende and Irapuato. (For general information about train service in Mexico, see the chapter **There and Back Again** or check at the local tourist office listed below.)

TOURIST SERVICES

Tourist Office (Delegación Federal de Turismo) Av. Juárez and Cinco de Mayo (2-00-86).

COMMUNICATIONS

Post Office, across from the main university building at Aguilar and Poutos.

PATZCUARO

There is an oriental delicacy to the mountains surrounding Pátzcuaro, whose name means "place of delights." Mountain clouds hanging low over blue pines and islands hiding in the morning mists give this region of Mexico a quality reminiscent of Japanese watercolors. This is the homeland of the Tarascan Indians, renowned in Moctezuma's time for their resistance to Aztec militarism, their fierceness in battle, and yet their sensuality and poetic nature. Pátzcuaro reflects its artistic heritage: this is one of the richest crafts regions of Mexico, and Pátzcuaro is the town to stay in if you want to enjoy the true ambience of colonial Mexico.

Located on the banks of the lake of the same name, Pátzcuaro (in the Tarascan dialect, the emphasis is on the first syllable) lies midway between the country's two largest cities — two hundred miles or so from Guadalajara and Mexico City. It is an unspoiled vacation spot, particularly popular with affluent Mexicans, who come here on weekends to relax or ride; many of them keep stables in the area. The town itself, like San Miguel de Allende and Taxco, is a protected colonial monument, and nothing can be built that would disturb the harmony.

Like many Mexican towns, Pátzcuaro is a place for walking, although a rental car is advisable if you plan to explore nearby villages and craft centers. However, much of what is made in the region finds its way to the Pátzcuaro marketplace. The town is not on the tour bus route, and most foreigners find their way here as they roam from Guadalajara to Mexico City. The promise of an international airport in nearby Morelia may bring more tourists to the area, but for now most who visit the region are drawn by the leisurely pace, excellent cuisine, and a chance to buy first-rate crafts.

The climate in Pátzcuaro is invigorating, and nights can be quite cold, but most of the hotels boast large fireplaces in the lobby or on the patios. Some rooms have fireplaces, but be warned: take along your pajamas with feet; even those thick blankets are sometimes not enough. The days can be quite warm, however, during the summer.

The town has several excellent hotels, and one of the best is the Posada de Don Vasco, an antique-filled colonial inn that reflects the gentility of the Mexican good life. On Wednesdays and Saturdays the patio at the Don Vasco is the scene for a popular regional dance, Los Viejitos, the Dance of the Old Men. Young men, wearing masks that make them look old and wrinkled, hobble about on canes, gradually dancing to the music and finally leaping into the air, tossing their canes away. On other evenings musicians perform on the patio, as guests sip a little warming glass of sherry. Dinner, featuring *pescado blanco*, a sweet whitefish sautéed in butter, is not to be missed. Fish is offered at every meal in every restaurant in the city, and it is always fresh from the ice-cold lake.

It is worth rising at dawn to catch a glimpse of the local fishermen at work. Traditionally, the Tarascans have used butterfly-shaped nets to catch the little fish, and a lucky early riser may see them in action. Watching the Tarascan fishermen at work in the early morning mist, you will witness a scene of unmatched peace.

In the middle of the lake stands the island fishing village of Janitzio, which is accessible by boat from the *embarcadero*, the dock at the bottom of the hill in Pátzcuaro. Rising out of the red-tiled roofs in the middle of the island is a huge hollow statue of José María y Pavón Morelos, the patriot-priest who was born in the state of Michoacán. Here, as at the Statue of Liberty, visitors can climb inside the statue for a view of the area. Janitzio has no hotels, however, and visitors must stay in nearby Pátzcuaro.

After returning from the island, stop in at one of the dockside restaurants for more *pescado blanco* (it's addicting), or try *charales*, dried and salted whitefish. (Unfortunately, there is a reported shortage of *pescado blanco*. The government is restocking the lake.) Another specialty of the region is Tarascan soup, a rich chicken and tomato broth topped with crumbled cheese.

Two main plazas and several smaller squares dot the many narrow streets. In the Plaza de San Agustín stands a large statue of the local heroine Gertrudis de Bocanegra in memory of her patriotism during the 1810 Revolution. Gertrudis, the daughter of a Spanish father and a Tarascan mother, was executed in 1817 for her support of the revolution. Another local hero is Bishop Vasco de Quiroga, who saved many of the Tarascan Indians from the clutches of the bloodthirsty conquistador Beltran Nuño de Guzmán.

The town has several beautifully appointed churches, and the largest, the Colegiata, houses an image of the Virgin Mary made from cornstalks — corn, of course, was a potent religious symbol in pre-Hispanic times. One of the most interesting sights in Pátzcuaro is the House of Eleven Patios, formerly a convent, now a collection of craft shops. Beautiful handwoven serapes are made here by an Indian woman using an ancient backstrap loom. In another area, a large Spanish loom is used to make multicolored linens. Prices are reasonable, but a little higher than in the marketplaces or the villages nearby.

About four miles outside Pátzcuaro, on the road to Quiroga, is the small village of Tzintzuntzán, the ancient capital of the Tarascan nation. The name means "place of the hummingbirds," and in the clear, bright mountain air it seems appropriately named. Scattered in the village are small Tarascan ruins, which are a delight to explore, but the main attraction here is the pottery. The wife of artist Juan O'Gorman encouraged the local potters to make dishes, cups, and saucers that would be useful in the modern home, but to make them in the traditional manner. There are three types of pottery sold here: a brown-glazed ware decorated with green designs, a cream-colored ware decorated with brown, and a brown-colored ware decorated in cream. All are decorated with scenes from the life of the lake — swans, fishes, fishermen with their butterfly nets—and are painted in a simple, naive manner. And all sell for incredibly cheap prices. The local weavers also sell mats, mobiles, and decorations made from lake reeds. (If you don't have a car, take a cab.)

Another nearby town worth a visit is called Villa Escalante by the government but Santa Clara del Cobre by the local people. Since ancient times, the artisans here have worked in copper, one of the few metals utilized by the ancient Indians. Hammered by hand and burnished with burro dung, these piecies are sold elsewhere in the country at double or triple their price here. Platters, candlesticks, and large bowls can be found in the workshops or in the market at Pátzcuaro. Santa Clara is south of Pátzcuaro, and signs in the town point the way.

Some fifty miles west of Pátzcuaro is Uruapan, famed for its lacquerware. Handmade guitars are made in nearby Paracho. However, most of these items find their way to the local market.

The countryside around Pátzcuaro is very different from other regions; tall pine trees cover the mountainsides, and the villages are filled with pale-faced, green-eyed children, many of them descendants of the French soldiers who settled here. If you are planning a trip to Guadalajara or Mexico City, Pátzcuaro makes an ideal side trip, or it can be a good stopping-off point on a journey between the two cities. Janitzio is renowned for its colorful All Souls' Day and Day of the Dead celebrations, November 1 and 2, although many city dwellers also come to Pátzcuaro to celebrate Diez y Seis, September 16.

BOCADITOS

This lakeside colonial town is off the beaten tourist track, but Mexicans know it well. Consequently, it's vital that you make reservations if you want to stay at one of the larger hotels. If you do arrive in town without a reservation, try the hotels on the plaza, or stop at the motel with no name on the Tarascan Circle, just south of the Don Vasco.

Spend at least three days in Pátzcuaro, more if you have a rental car. The pace here is relaxing and the region rich in crafts.

When you visit the local Indian markets, take along plenty of small change. In Tzintzuntzán, the Indian women keep their money hidden in small bundles all over their stalls and shops, and they may not have enough change for a large bill.

Pátzcuaro is the sort of place where you will regret not bringing the family car—there are many things you will want to buy that are impractical to take back on a plane. For example, just outside Tzintzuntzán, vendors sell animals and fountains carved from the local porous rock for unbelievably low prices. And for less than $20, you can stock an entire kitchen cupboard with the fragile pottery sold at Tzintzuntzán.

If you are flying home, buy copper pieces; the black rebozos sold in the market; and rugs, serapes, and linens.

AROUND PATZCUARO

VITAL STATISTICS

Climate. Clear mountain air; springlike temperatures; cool nights. Occasional rain showers.

Population. 40,000.

Altitude. 7,000 feet.

State. Michoacán.

City phone code. No direct dialing code.

HOTELS

Mesón de Cortijo, Apartado Postal 202 (2-95). Located just off the main highway, Calzada de las Américas, leading into the town, near the Tarascan Indian Monument. Originally the stable of an old hacienda, this small hotel has been redecorated in colonial style. Some rooms with fireplaces. B. Cr.

Posada de Don Vasco, Apartado Postal 15 (2-27 or 525-9081 in Mexico City). The best in town; a beautiful, colonial-style hotel and motel filled with antiques. Offers tennis, riding, bowling, and a good restaurant. Part of the Hostales de Mexico chain. Located on the main boulevard into Pátzcuaro, the Calzada de las Américas. Good view of the lake from some rooms. Folk dancing on the patio each Wednesday. A. Cr.

Posada de la Basílica, Aruga 6 (1-08). The most charming hotel in town. Small, cozy, cheap. Fireplaces in most rooms. Small bar. B. Cr.

Posada de San Rafael, Portal Aldama. A new, comfortable colonial-style hotel on the main plaza. Parking garage, restaurant. C. Cr.

RESTAURANTS

Fonda del Sol, Calzada de las Américas. Regional specialties. Moderate. Cr.

Hostería de San Felipe, Calzada de las Américas, next door to Rafael's furniture shop. Sandwiches, soups, regional dishes. Moderate. Cr.

Las Redes, Lazaro Cardenas 6. Offers a good view of the lake. Try the soups. Inexpensive. N.

Retaurante Flotante, at the *embarcadero* ("the dock") bottom of Calzada de las Américas. A good, cheap place to try the local fish and soups. (There have been some shortages of *pescado blanco*, the delicate whitefish that is a local specialty. The government is restocking the waters.) Inexpensive. Cr.

Restaurant San Felipe, Calzada de las Américas. On the south side of the calzada just past the Posada de Don Vasco. Grilled steaks, local specialties. Moderate. Cr.

NIGHTLIFE

Unless there's a fiesta, nightlife is nonexistent in Pátzcuaro. The mountain air will make you sleep better, especially after a postdinner stroll around the square.

The Posada de Don Vasco offers one specialty that might qualify as "nightlife" — its nightly performances by local artists, guitar or harp players, or Los Viejitos, the dancers who wear masks so that they appear old. As they dance, they gradually throw away their canes and leap like young men. All this usually takes place before dinner on the hotel patio.

SHOPPING

Casa de las Artesanías, next door to the Basílica, two blocks east of the main plaza. Government-owned store and exhibition hall, showing and selling best examples of regional crafts. Open seven days. Fixed prices.

Casa de los Once Patios, one half block south of the main plaza. A convent converted into a crafts center. Indian women using backstrap looms demonstrate their art here. A large, wooden Spanish loom is also in use. Good place to buy local crafts, although prices are higher than at the market. Fixed prices.

Market, two blocks north of main plaza. Pátzcuaro's market is a good place to buy copper, rebozos, pottery, and blankets. Friday is the busiest day. Bargain.

Santa Clara del Cobre (Villa Escalante), 13 miles south on Hwy. 120. Much of the copper ware made here makes its way to the market in Pátzcuaro; however, prices are cheaper in the *tallers.*

Tzintzuntzán, eight miles north along the lake road. This is the place to go for pottery and straw mats or wall hangings. Be sure to take small denominations of currency.

POINTS OF INTEREST

Basílica, located on a hill two blocks east of the main plaza. A revered statue of the Virgin made from cornstalks and orchid mucilage is kept here.

CREFAL (Centro Regional de Educación Fundamental para América Latina), southern bank of the lake. This school, operated under the auspices of UNESCO, trains schoolteachers for work in rural Latin America. Visitors are welcome. Open Monday through Friday 9-1 and 3-7.

187

Cerro del Estribo ("Stirrup Hill"), above the city. Follow the signs from downtown. This extinct volcano, topped by a pavilion, is an ideal picnic site and offers a lovely view of the lake. From here follow the signs to Tacambaro for a scenic afternoon drive.

Janitzio Island, small island in the middle of Lake Pátzcuaro. Take a boat ride from the *embarcadero* at the bottom of the calzada to the island village. You can climb inside the statue of Morelos that dominates the island. There are no hotels on the island.

Plaza Bocanegra, two blocks north of the main plaza. (Also known as Plaza Chica and Plaza de San Agustín.) Gertrude Bocanegra was Pátzcuaro's heroine during the 1810 War of Independence. She lost a son and her husband to the cause. The library, which stands on the square, is named in her honor and contains murals by Juan O'Gorman showing the history of this region.

Quiroga, 16 miles on the north side of the lake. This small town, named after the much-loved Bishop of Quiroga who saved many of the local Tarascan Indians from death, is the site of a beautiful Franciscan convent. Indians also sell crafts and folk art here. The Tarascans are noted for their love of beauty.

Uruapan, 30 miles west of Pátzcuaro. This city is not visited by many tourists. It is famed for its lacquerware and the toys, guitars, and furniture made in nearby villages. A large handicraft fair is held November 18–28. There's a beautiful national park on the outskirts of the city, Barranca de Cupatítzio. The famous Mansión del Cupatítzio, one of Mexico's best hacienda hotels, is located in the park (3-21-00 for reservations). If you can't stay overnight, drop by for a late lunch. West of the city is the famous village of Paricutín, located at 8,449 feet. A volcano thought to be extinct erupted here in a cornfield in 1943 and buried the village. You can examine the lava fields on horseback (horses available at the nearby town of Argahuan).

MUSEUMS

Museum of Popular Arts, Colegio de San Nicolas de Obispo, Calle Ensenanza, north of the plaza. Local handicrafts and folk art are displayed in this building that was the site of the oldest university in the New World, founded in 1540 and moved 40 years later to nearby Morelia. Open daily, but closed for siesta 1–3.

FIESTAS

Día de la Preciosa Sange de Cristo, first Sunday in July, Quiroga.

Copper fair, August 15, Santa Clara del Cobre (Villa Escalante).

All Souls' Day and Day of the Dead, November 1 and 2, Janitzio Island.

Día de Nuestra Señora de la Salud, December 8, fiesta honoring the revered cornstalk virgin of Pátzcuaro.

TRANSPORTATION

Buses. First-class bus service from nearby cities, including Morelia, Uruapan, Guadalajara.

Taxis. Local taxis are few but cheap.

Trains. Train service by a branch line of the Mexico City to Guadalajara line. (For general information about train service in Mexico, see the chapter **There and Back Again** or check at the local tourist office listed below.)

TOURIST SERVICES

Tourist Office (Subdelegación Federal de Turismo), Casa de los Once Patios (9-14-54 and 2-12-14).

MERIDA

Mérida was once known as the "Paris of the West," and strolling down the wide boulevards, peeking through the open doorways of the baroque mansions, anyone can easily see why. Whoever penned the name was probably so surprised to find an oasis of culture in the middle of the remote Yucatán peninsula that he allowed his rapture to get the better of him. Mérida is not a Spanish city. The houses are not hidden behind tall blank walls; windows are left open, and there is a languid air about the town. Given the tropical heat, there's no rushing around. The heat is a fixture. It was hot when the Mayan city T'ho stood there, and it's hot today, despite the blessings of air conditioning and ceiling fans.

The whitewashed, French-windowed mansions that line the wide, tree-shaded boulevards give the city a Creole air. Indeed, some of the flavor of New Orleans's French Quarter can be found in Mérida. Horse-drawn carriages ply their trade along the boulevards, and instead of the formal iron benches found in most Mexican towns, S-shaped Victorian love seats dot the plazas. This is a city settled by men of Latin temperament who, like their cousins in New Orleans, Martinique, and Cuba, soon found that the tropics discouraged the ascetic side of the Spanish nature and encouraged any predisposition to elegance and ease. With ingenuity, the vast Indian labor force, and an unlimited jungle, the men became sisal planters and, for many, wealth soon followed. Adventurers from France and other European countries joined the planters and together they forged a cosmopolitan city with more ties to the port city of New Orleans than to Mexico City.

When the "Paris" title wore a little thin, Mérida was redubbed the "white city"—a more apt description. The houses are grand; even the new modern mansions have an Old World charm, and the streets and plazas are immaculate.

But the real miracle of Mérida is that the trees and flowers that bloom throughout the city — each mansion stands in a tropical garden — grow in only one-half inch of natural topsoil. This thin layer covers a limestone shelf, which extends deep into the earth. And yet, flamboyant trees, jacarandas, orchids, hibiscus, orange trees, and avocado plants grow everywhere. The effect of all this tropical greenery is one of a greenhouse set down in the middle of endless maguey fields.

Surprisingly, this region, which is so poor in soil, is rich in natural products — sisal from the maguey and honey, salt, coconuts, cotton, sugarcane, and tobacco. And these are not recent innovations; many of these products were sold by the Maya in pre-Hispanic times. Also unique to the region are the savannahs and jungle, which are rich in game and serve as havens for the birds of North America that migrate here each year. Indeed, Mérida has become a base of operations for hunters and bird-watchers.

The city also serves as home for those interested in exploring the Mayan ruins, which dot the jungle across the peninsula. The ruins at Chichén Itzá and Uxmal are within a day's drive — many visitors fly into Mérida, stay a few days, drive on to Uxmal to visit the several sites in that area, and then move on to Chichén Itzá. (There is excellent bus service between Mérida and the coast, with a stop at Chichén Itzá on the way.) Mérida offers a change of pace from Cancún or Cozumel, and some travelers combine a week at the beach with a week of visiting the ruins found inland. It is possible to drive to Mérida from Mexico City, but it is an arduous trip. For much of this century, no roads linked the peninsula with the capital, and Yucatecans liked to boast of their independence — at one time there was talk of Yucatán joining the United States. There has long been a link between the United States and Yucatán since many Yucatecans are educated in the United States and have ties, either through business or family, with the Creoles of New Orleans.

Mérida is an easy city to navigate, once you have mastered the street numbering system. East-west streets are odd-numbered; north-south streets are even-numbered. Consequently, Calle 51 is followed by Calle 53, not Calle 52. The main boulevard, which runs through the middle of the city, is the Paseo de Montejo, named after Francisco de Montejo, a conquistador who settled here. His palace, still occupied by his descendants, is on the main plaza and open to visitors each afternoon from two to four. The facade of the palace, built in 1549, shows members of the Montejo family standing on the heads of the conquered Mayans.

On the east side of the zócalo is a cathedral designed by Juan Miguel de Aguero, an architect whose work can also be seen in Cuba. A statue of Christ, reputed to be carved out of a piece of wood that escaped a fire unscathed, is on display in one of the chapels and is known as the "Christ of the Blisters." As is the custom in Mexico, the government buildings front on the zócalo; Mérida's Palacio del Gobierno, on the north side of the plaza, contains some excellent murals by Pacheco.

The main zócalo was once the site of a large pyramid, and although the Indian center was razed, the Mayan men and women sitting in the square still speak in their ancient tongue. The Mayan language is taught at the Archaeological Museum on the Paseo de Montejo and Calle 43, just north of the zócalo. The museum houses an excellent exhibit of Mayan artifacts.

The main market is two blocks south and east of the plaza near Calles 60 and 61. This area is dominated by *guayabera* factories and is the best place to find the sensible, open-collared, loose-fitting shirts worn everywhere in Yucatán. Shops in the market area sell real Panama hats, the indestructible version essential for pyramid climbing. Yucatecan hammocks are another local specialty, and you won't find them any cheaper. Look for hammocks made with strong fibers with three or four strands running through each loop. Sizes vary, *matrimonial* being the largest.

Also worth visiting is the Church of the Third Order, a popular Franciscan church where many weddings are held (located on Calle 60, between Calles 59 and 57). And the church of La Ermita de Santa Isabel has a delightful garden filled with Mayan statuary (Calle 64, a few blocks from the main zócalo).

Mérida does not have the profusion of statues found in most Mexican cities, but a monument of some local pride is the Monument to the Fatherland, located in the middle of the Paseo. Carved from local limestone in the social-realistic style favored by public artists in Mexico, the monument depicts the history of the country.

For an interesting side trip, rent a car or take a cab to Dzibilchaltun, a Mayan city that once stretched for miles over the jungle. Located about six miles north of the city, it is the Mayan ruin closest to Mérida. Some twenty miles away is the seaport of Progreso; a trip to the small town makes a pleasant afternoon outing. Along the way, stop at one of the government sisal factories, where workers will show you how the maguey is fed into a machine and squeezed to remove the pulp and separate the fibers, which are then made into rope. Many of the plants sell bags and rugs made from sisal.

Nightlife in Mérida is a little better than in most colonial cities in Mexico because several of the hotels have lively nightclubs. Given the warm climate in Mérida, most people dine late in the cool of the evening. There are mariachis and musicians at Santa Lucia Park on Thursday nights.

Like its cousin New Orleans, Mérida celebrates Mardi Gras in style. Beginning the Friday before Ash Wednesday, the fiesta features bullfights, parades, cockfights, dances, and the inevitable fireworks.

BOCADITOS

Yucatecan food is unlike any other regional food in Mexico. The seafood is excellent; try the "Return to the Good Life" cocktail at Soberanis. (See city listings for Mérida that follow.) And for breakfast, don't miss the local specialty, *huevos motuleños*, fried eggs atop tortillas and black beans, sprinkled with ham, cheese, and peas.

Be sure to bring back two Yucatecan specialties—honey and *chile habanero* sauce.

Most of the women in the Yucatán still wear the beautifully embroidered *huipiles*—you can buy them in the market, but try them on first. Mayan women are very tiny.

AROUND MERIDA

VITAL STATISTICS

Climate. Tropical year-round. Extremely hot and humid mid-summer. Warm and pleasant in winter. Occasional tropical storms and hurricanes. Although Mérida is not on the coast, evacuation is recommended if a hurricane threatens. (If it's impossible to get a reservation on an international flight, fly west on a national airline. Mérida is not protected by mountains from coastal winds and tidal waves.)

Population. 360,000.

Altitude. 26 feet.

State. Yucatán.

City phone code. 992.

HOTELS

Caribe, Rincón del Parque Hidalgo 1 (1-19-23). This small hotel is built in an old convent and capitalizes on that familiar, peaceful air that is a trademark of Mexico's smaller inns. C. Cr.

Casa del Balam, Calles 57 and 60 (1-94-74). Colonial decor. Located just two blocks from the main plaza. Tropical atmosphere and white-jacketed waiters in the pleasant dining room. Rooftop terrace. C. Cr.

Misión Mérida, Calle 60 No. 491 (1-75-00). One of the city's oldest hotels. Colonial style with a good bar. Patio gardens where mariachis play. C. Cr.

Montejo Palace, Paseo Montejo 483 (1-16-41). On the city's main boulevard, this modern hotel has a popular rooftop nightclub. Good location for Carnival. C. Cr.

RESTAURANTS

Alberto's Continental Patio, Calles 64 and 57 (1-22-98). One of the best restaurants in Mexico serving Mexican haute cuisine, regional specialties. Alberto's also offers Arab and continental dishes in a romantic setting amidst the patios and arcades of an old mansion. Expensive. Cr.

El Pórtico de Peregrino, Calle 60 (1-67-44). Located behind the Hotel Mérida, the restaurant serves dinner alfresco under the arches. Local and continental dishes. Expensive. Cr.

Las Palomas, Calle 55, between Calles 56 and 58 (3-15-45). Romantic dining in a colonial mansion. Yucatecan specialties. Expensive. Cr.

Real Montejo, Calle 80 No. 332 (1-27-93). Dining and entertainment in this popular hotel. Mayan specialties; continental fare. Moderate. Cr.

Soberanis, Plaza de la Independencia and Montejo. This chain restaurant features the best local seafood and Yucatecan specialties. Several locations throughout the peninsula. Always good food. Inexpensive. Cr.

NIGHTLIFE

There's not much going on after dark in Mérida. Most locals dine late in the cool of the evening. There are several excellent restaurants where a leisurely dinner can be enjoyed. Finish with a glass of Ixtabentun, the local liqueur. Most hotel bars offer a quiet drink late in the evening. Try Parque Santa Lucia on Thursday nights as local Romeos serenade (or pay someone to serenade) their sweethearts.

The Hotel Mérida, Calle 60 No. 491 (1-75-00) offers occasional folkloric evenings. Check at the hotel desk. Or you can join a tour group for dinner and the light and sound show at the ruins in Uxmal. Check your bell captain or hotel desk for information on tours.

SHOPPING

Mercado, Calles 60 and 61. The market is the heart of a flourishing, bargain-filled shopping district where you can buy Mayan *huipiles, guayaberas,* hammocks, leather, and straw baskets.

POINTS OF INTEREST

Archaeological sites. Various locations throughout the area. Mérida is located at the hub of a number of roads to some of the greatest Mayan sites. Chichén Itzá is 80 miles west of the city; Dzibilchaltun is six miles north; Uxmal, with its neighbors Labná, Edzna, and Sayil, is 35 miles south of the city; and Izamal with its magnificent convent and ruins, little visited by tourists, is 40 miles west of the city. Read the chapter **Mexico of the Ancients** before planning your forays into the countryside.

Calesas, Parque Cepeda Peraza. These horse-drawn carriages gather in the small park, one block north of the main plaza. A carriage ride is a fitting way to tour this graceful city.

Cathedral, east side of the main plaza. There's an old legend that the plans for Mérida's cathedral, designed by a Cuban architect, were sent mistakenly to La Paz, Bolivia, and vice versa. And so Mérida ended up with the big church and La Paz, the smaller. Inside is a wooden crucifix that is revered by local residents as having miraculous powers.

Church of the Third Order, Parque Cepeda Peraza, one block north of the main plaza. This church has a magnificent Plateresque altarpiece.

La Ermita de Santa Isabel, Calle 64. A charming old church. Once a hermitage, now a retreat where visitors can sit in the gardens, admire the Mayan statuary, and listen to piped-in Mayan music.

Palacio del Gobierno, northeast corner of the main plaza. Notable for its modern murals by Fernando Castro Pacheco depicting Mayan history. Open Monday through Friday.

Palacio Montejo, south side of the main plaza. The Montejo family still lives in the palace built by its conquistador ancestor. The facade depicts the Spaniards conquering the Maya. Open daily in the early afternoons. Small admission fee.

Progreso, 22 miles north on the coast. This is Yucatán's principal port. To the west are the small resort villages of Yucalpetén and Chelem; to the east Chicxulub where city dwellers go to fish and sunbathe.

MUSEUMS

Archaeological Museum, Paseo de Montejo and Calle 43. Many Mayan artifacts unearthed locally are housed here. A good preview before visiting the sites. Closed Monday.

SPORTS

Hunting. Mérida is a base camp for many hunters and guides. Duck and quail hunting is popular November through March. Boar and prized, small Yucatecan deer also roam the jungles.

FIESTAS

Carnival, week before Lent. Popular fiesta with parades, fireworks, and dances.

Fiesta del Cristo de las Ampollas, September 28 through October 13.

Día de la Nuestra Señora de Guadalupe, December 12.

TRANSPORTATION

Airport. The airport is located a few miles outside the southern edge of the city. International and national carriers serve Mérida.

Buses. First-class bus service to and from Cancún, Villahermosa, and other cities. Local buses primarily serve outlying villages.

Car rental. Agencies include Avis — at Calle 59 No. 448 (1-45-99), at Hotel Montejo (3-61-91), and at the international airport (3-78-49); Hertz — at Calle 55 No. 479 (1-80-20), Calle 60 in front of the Hotel Mérida (1-96-88), Calle 59 in the lobby of the Hotel Panamerica (1-79-60), and at the international airport (1-38-28); National — at Calle 62 No. 483 (4-17-64) and at the international airport (no phone).

Taxis. Cabs are reasonable. Check rates before you get in. It's possible to rent cabs by the day at reasonable rates to visit archaeological sites.

Trains. Travel by car or bus to Mérida from points south is difficult. Mérida, until very recently, was very isolated, and communication with New Orleans was easier than with Mexico City. However, train travel is one of the best ways to reach Mérida from Central and South Mexico. Rates are extremely cheap. There's also train service from Mérida to Palenque, a major Mayan site.

TOURIST SERVICES

Tourist Office (Delegación Federal de Turismo), Itzaes 590 (corner of Calle 59) (1-59-89 or 3-00-95).

COMMUNICATIONS

Post Office, Calle 65 and Calle 56, just north of the market.

Telephones. Be prepared for difficulty in placing long-distance calls to the United States or Mexico City.

SAN MIGUEL DE ALLENDE

Like its neighbor Guanajuato, San Miguel de Allende wears a Spanish mantle. Founded by Fray Juan de San Miguel in 1542, this city has a northern Spanish air. The Creoles used their vast fortunes, made in silver and land, to build a town of mansions and churches from the gray stone of the region. It was a town where wealth encouraged culture. This tradition has survivied for over four hundred years in San Miguel. While Guanajuato owes much of its cultural air to Mexican scholars and artists, San Miguel has become a haven for American writers and artists who enjoy the city's climate and ambience.

The town's history is filled with stories of artists who have found inspiration among the gray cobblestones. Perhaps one of the most remarkable tales is that of the parish church, located on the south side of the main square, Plaza Allende. The architect Ceferino Gutiérrez was a self-taught craftsman of Indian descent. Supposedly, Gutiérrez saw a picture postcard of France's famed Chartres Cathedral. Inspired, he created La Parroquia, drawing his designs in the sand so that the native artisans could reproduce the beauty of Chartres in the mountains of Mexico. The result is an exquisite, small Chartres with a large rosarian window and two mismatched Gothic towers, a church quite unlike any other in Mexico.

The Plaza Allende, in the heart of town at the bottom of a steep hill, is surrounded by stone arcades, similar to those found in other colonial towns; however, like the square in Morelia, the square itself is reminiscent of a plaza in Spain or Italy. The manicured trees, and wrought-iron and stone benches give it a formal air.

Following Spanish tradition of Moorish architectural style, most of the homes in San Miguel are built around courtyards and behind walls; consequently, the visitor is constantly surprised at the beauty hidden behind high walls. This privacy makes the town a favorite retreat for Americans, both retirees and artists. But San Miguel is also a pleasant town just to visit, with several excellent hotels. Given the town's busy café society, you can easily strike up a conversation with an American resident who will help you find the best restaurants and bars in town. (Many Americans lease homes or run small hotels, which makes San Miguel a good place for an extended stay.)

The town was originally known as San Miguel la Grande, in deference to its size among the lesser San Miguels, but following the Revolution of 1810 led by Padre Hidalgo, the city fathers renamed the town in honor of local hero Ignacio Allende, who had joined the Revolution. The young Creole officer had echoed the padre's fears for Mexico should the Bonapartists continue to rule Spain. Along with Hidalgo, he lost his life in the fight. The area is rich in Mexican colonial history. To the northwest on the road to Dolores Hidalgo is the Convent of Atotonílco, a crumbling but beautiful example of colonial sacred architecture. Every inch of the convent's inner walls and doors are covered with religious paintings. Since the disestablishment of the Church, the convent has suffered. The paintings are peeling from the walls, but it is still a revered shrine to which thousands of Indians make pilgrimages each year. The convent is located about eight miles northwest of San Miguel; look for a small sign pointing left that reads Atotonílco. It was here that Padre Hidalgo wrested the banner of the Virgin of Guadalupe from the altar and used it as his army's flag of liberation.

The ill-fated Padre Hidalgo was inspired to revolution in a sleepy town where he served as parish priest. That town, now named Dolores Hidalgo in his honor, is 25 miles northwest of San Miguel de Allende. A rather unprepossessing little town with a bare plaza and a plain parish church where Hidalgo issued his *grito*, his cry for freedom, Dolores Hidalgo is rarely visited by tourists except those looking for the town's famous brown clay cookware and glazed tiles. The student of history will enjoy a visit to the plaza, and there are several interesting burial vaults in the church walls. Sunday is the best day to go to the market.

The market in San Miguel caters to the townspeople, but there are some good buys including wooden bowls and serapes. The market is located just east of the Church of San Francisco at Calle San Francisco and Calle Juárez. The vendors are accustomed to having photographers and artists record their daily tasks.

Many Americans take classes at the Instituto Allende. Housed in a converted hacienda located at San Antonio 20, the school offers a variety of classes in the arts and humanities. (For information, write to Instituto Allende, San Antonio 20, San Miguel de Allende, Guanajuato, Mexico.) Classes are also given at the Centro Cultural Ignacio Ramirez, and there's a small museum and restaurant as well as a news bulletin board for Americans in this restored convent located at Hernández Macías 75.

The abundance of artists and craftsmen makes San Miguel a boom town for boutiques and galleries. Prices may be higher than at the source, but most San Miguel residents are hard to fool, so the selections are very good. You will pay less in San Miguel for high-quality crafts than at many import shops in the United States.

The main activity in San Miguel, for those not occupied by pottery classes or writing another bestseller, is café sitting. For the athletically inclined there are several stables that rent horses by the hour. The Spanish riding traditions are held high here. The Escuela Ecuestre riding school and resort ranks as one of the best in the world. The resort has a swimming pool, tennis courts, a jai alai fronton, and an airstrip.

A popular Sunday pastime in San Miguel is the home tour. Check at your hotel for information, or at the public library, Biblioteca Publica, Calle de los Insurgentes 9. One glimpse of the interior of a colonial mansion will make you want to write a bestseller and move south. If you must settle for a hotel room, don't be disappointed; several hotels in San Miguel are located in restored mansions and convents. Cantinflas, Mexico's Charlie Chaplin, is one of the owners of Posada La Ermita, a luxury hotel located above the city on Calle Real, a hillside street. On Plaza Allende, the Posada de San Francisco features huge, high-ceilinged rooms, some with fireplaces, all built around a pretty courtyard.

The nights can be chilly in San Miguel, which is 6,000 feet above sea level. Daytime temperatures range from the mid 50s to the high 60s, with cool nights throughout the year. The rainy season is from late June to September.

Nightlife in San Miguel, unlike that of other colonial towns, is lively. Several bars stay open as long as there are paying customers. Discos and nightclubs, even hamburger restaurants, are hidden behind colonial walls. The town allows no modern construction.

There are several spectacular fiestas in San Miguel; the American influx has failed to dampen the Mexican enthusiasm for fiesta. The feast day of San Miguel on September 29 is celebrated with fervor, and the fiesta lasts for two days. During the fiesta, there's a "running of the bulls" similar to the one held in Pamplona, Spain. Chasing wild bulls down narrow, cobbled streets is fun only for those with Hemingway hang-ups. All national holidays are celebrated in a grand manner in San Miguel, and January 20 is set aside to honor Ignacio Allende.

BOCADITOS

The best way to get to San Miguel is to drive from the Texas-Mexico border. It's a leisurely two-day drive with a stopover in Monterrey or Saltillo or a hurried one-day drive. If you try to make it in one day, cross over the night before and go through customs. Stay on the Mexican side and set out early — many Mexican hotels will supply a boxed lunch on request. The road south is patrolled by the Green Angels, Mexico's mechanics of mercy. (See **Mexico and the Wheel.**)

Another way to reach San Miguel is via the Aztec Eagle, which leaves Nuevo Laredo daily in the evening. Train fares are very cheap, but be sure to take along some snacks in case the dining car is not attached or there's a problem along the way. For information on train schedules and fares call the nearest Mexican National Tourist Office (see list at the back of the book).

Make hotel reservations in San Miguel in advance if possible, especially during fiesta time.

There are no car rental agencies in San Miguel.

AROUND SAN MIGUEL DE ALLENDE

VITAL STATISTICS

Climate. Springlike weather much of the year. Cool, sometimes cold, nights in the winter. Occasional rain showers.

Population. 34,000. (It only *seems* like half of them are Americans.)

Altitude. 6,300 feet.

State. Guanajuato.

City phone code. 465.

HOTELS

Casa Carmen, Correo 31 (2-08-44). Located diagonally across the street from the post office in the center of town, this is one of the least expensive and most charming pensions in San Miguel de Allende. Casa Carmen has a pleasant patio and spacious rooms (some with balconies) that are nicely furnished with colorfully painted wood furniture. C. Cr.

Hotel Sauto, Dr. Hernández Macías 59 (2-00-51). Down the street from the Bellas Artes, Hotel Sauto has acres of grounds and two pools, which make it a great place for children. The rooms are somewhat primitive but clean, with a lot of Old World charm. D. Cr.

Huespedes Feliz, next door to Instituto Allende. A clean sunny room with breakfast and lunch at bargain basement rates. Each room has a hot-water heater, stoked with corn cobs, that you light before you shower. D. Cr.

Mansión del Bosque, Aldama 65 (2-02-77). This picturesque favorite of long-term residents is run by an American. The prices are somewhat steep for what they have to offer. C. Cr.

Posada La Ermita, Hwy. 51, outskirts of town (2-07-77). This hilltop retreat is owned by the world-famous comedian Cantinflas (*Around the World in 80 Days*). Named after a small church on the grounds. Beautiful suites with fireplaces. Overlooks the town. A. Cr.

Posada Aristos San Miguel, on the grounds of the Instituto de Allende (2-01-49). Colonial inn. Some rooms with kitchens. Rental available by week or month. C. Cr.

Posado Aristos San Miguel, on the grounds of the Instituto (2-01-49). Colonial inn. Some rooms with kitchens available for weekly rental. C. Cr.

Posada de las Monjas, Canal 37 (2-01-71). Some rooms offer fireplaces and views, though the decor is plain. Special rates for long stays. D. Cr.

Posada San Francisco, faces the main plaza (2-00-72). Pleasant patio and dining room overlook the garden. The food is fair, and prices are fairly expensive for San Miguel. B. Cr.

Quinta Loreto, Loreto 13 (2-00-42). Rents rooms on a daily basis and also has apartments available for longer rentals. The spacious grounds include a large pool, but the location, behind the market, is not the best. A lot of Americans living on pensions make Quinta Loreto their home. Meals are served to nonguests and the food is excellent.

Villa Santa Monica, Baéza 22 (2-09-14), across from Juárez Park. An eighteenth-century hacienda once owned by opera singer José Mojica. The current owner, Betty Kempe, has created a small posada by restoring rooms around a gorgeous central patio. These rooms may be rented for a minimum of two weeks. The food is superb. Kempe attended hotel school in Switzerland and passed her culinary expertise on to her capable staff. The grounds and gardens are extensive, and there's a small heated pool. The location is within walking distance of both town and the Instituto. And Betty Kempe will arrange a party, keep you apprised of local customs, gossip, and current events, or enliven a gathering. She also has two apartments on the premises for long-range (six months) rentals.

Villa Jacaranda, Aldama 53 (2-10-15). Well known for its good food and its gracious hospitality, this hotel has one of the best restaurants in town. B. Cr.

RESTAURANTS

Because San Miguel is a haven for Americans, many new spots open up each tourist season. Check with the hotel desk or ask the Americans you meet for the latest fashionable spot.

Carousel, Canal opposite Casa Maxwell. This is the place for burgers and American soda fountain specialties. A small disco in the rear provides nightly bumping and grinding. Inexpensive. Cr.

Genio's, Zacateros near Umaran. Another favorite of San Miguel residents. A Swiss chef specializes in Swiss–German cuisine. Curiously, almost all of the entrées are served with pasta, and the most popular item on the menu is African froufrou, a curry dish. Pepper steak is especially tasty. The atmosphere is on the cute side, done in a country-colonial style. Moderate. Cr.

El Cartuja, on Calle Hernandez. A real sleeper. There are eight tables and no bar, but the menu, composed largely of Spanish dishes, is unusual and uniformly excellent. Inexpensive. N.

El Patio, Correo 12. Famous for *enchiladas suizas*, El Patio is an old favorite — one of the oldest restaurants in town. Its disco is popular on weekends. Prices are very reasonable. Cr.

La Bodega de Marqués, Correo 34 (2-14-81). "If you're hungry, go to Connie's," say the natives. Portions are mammoth. Hamburgers are the best in town — large enough to satisfy King Kong — and the excellent guacamole easily serves two. The menu lists everything from seafood to Chinese dinners, but stick to the Mexican or meat dishes and steer clear of the Italian and Chinese food. The wine-cellar decor is pleasant. Located in a colonial building on Correo a few blocks from the post office. Moderate. Cr.

La Princesa, Recreo 5 (2-14-03). Located on a side street and not to be confused with the snack bar of the same name on San Francisco. This is a first-class restaurant, on the expensive side, but worth the price. The portions are large, but the doggy bags are worth asking for — beautifully sculpted foil replicas of birds and baskets. Especially good, but hot, is the chicken *mole.* All of the Mexican dishes are recommended, along with the shrimp brochette. Expensive. Cr.

Mamá Mia's, Umaran 8. Although the pizza is only so-so, Mamá Mia's is the place for after-hours sipping and socializing. Good jazz, candles, checkered tablecloths. Josefa, the locally famous *ranchero* singer who was the big attraction at the now-closed Hostería del Parque, sings here from 8 P.M. until the jazz starts up. Moderate. Cr.

Pan y Vino, Reloj 5. Upstairs restaurant on Reloj, across from Casa Cohen. Specializes in crepes, including some interesting Mexican varieties. Very good salads, omelets, and sandwiches. All quite inexpensive. Cr.

Pepe's Pizza, Hidalgo 15 (2-18-32). If you're really homesick for pizza, Pepe's is a slice above Mamá Mia's and slightly less expensive. Takeout service available. Inexpensive. N.

Señor Plato's, Jesus 7. Difficult to find since the sign outside says

"Bazar 7" in large letters, and "Señor Plato's" in small print. Part of the Carlos Anderson chain, with the same menu, more or less. The food is fair, but service is excellent and the atmosphere on the patio is very inviting. Best margaritas in town. Moderate. Cr.

Sierra Nevada, Hospicio 35 (2-04-15). Consistently good food and service make this restaurant a favorite of tourists and natives alike. Atmosphere is elegant and European. The beef Stroganoff and filet brochette are both good. The owner, an American, is a very gracious hostess. Additional well-appointed dining rooms are available in an adjacent converted home. Expensive, but no more than the other first-class restaurants in San Miguel; and you can depend on excellent food and service. Expensive. Cr.

NIGHTLIFE

Like restaurants, San Miguel's "in" night spots change with each season. Ask around.

El Patio, Correo 12 (2-00-17). The original disco. Less glamorous than the Ring (see below), but plenty of weekend action.

Laberintos, across the street from the Instituto. Attracts the young and affluent crowd. On Friday and Sunday from 5 till 9 Laberintos closes to adults and lets the tennyboppers have at it. No drinks served then.

La Fragua, Cuna de Allende 3 (2-01-09). Mexican music, bad food, but always a good crowd—both town regulars and tourists. Very lively.

The Ring, Hidalgo 15 (2-19-98). This glamorous disco attracts the jet-setters from Mexico City. Cover and drinks are expensive, but if you're looking for a place that's hopping, this is it. Cover.

SHOPPING

Boutiques. There are several arts and crafts boutiques, handicrafts showcases, and clothing stores dotted about the town. The selections are very good, high quality, and the prices, although higher than at the source, are not out of line.

Market. Plaza in front of Church of Nuestra Señora de la Salud. Market days are Sunday and Tuesday. Good buys in basketry, kitchenware, and blankets.

Supermarkets, Calle San Francisco, east of the plaza. There are a couple of small supermarkets—expanded grocery stores, really—that cater to the American residents.

POINTS OF INTEREST

Atotonílco, seven and a half miles from San Miguel. Perhaps the most interesting church in the area. The walls and ceilings are covered with native-style frescoes. The church is a religious center of great importance to the Indians, who (along with vendors of soft drinks and religious trinkets) flock there on religious holidays. Rites of flagellation are sometimes observed, and Indian women wearing crowns of thorns can be seen attending the services.

Benito Juárez Park, or French Park. A beautiful spot with tall trees, fields of flowers, paths, and grassy areas. On Sunday vendors sell food from carts. One man has the equivalent of a floating game of chance — a crude roulette wheel that spins around a ring of nails. Guess the number, you win a pastry.

Dolores Hidalgo, 25 miles west of town. Perhaps the most famous spot in all Mexico. In this drab little village, Padre Hidalgo issued the call for independence. His church still stands, and there is a small museum next door. The town is also famous for its ceramics.

La Salud Church and Oratorio de San Felipe Neri. Both house a series of paintings attributed to Miguel Cabrera, a Zapotec Indian who was one of the leading artists of the colonial period.

Los Pocitos, Santo Domingo 28. The home of Stirling Dickinson, director of the Instituto Allende, has an extensive garden and orchid collection, which Dickinson allows tourists to visit. Orchid fanciers shouldn't miss it.

Parish Church, on the square. A wonder of pseudo-Gothic architecture, constructed in 1880 by an Indian stonemason who was inspired by postcards of French Gothic churches.

San Francisco Church, one block from the main plaza. Noted for its Churrigueresque portal.

Schools. San Miguel is home to two renowned schools. Instituto Allende teaches many classes in art and history; for more information write to the institute or call 2-01-90. The Academia Hispana Americana, Calle Insurgentes 21 (2-03-49), offers excellent courses in Spanish culture and language.

SPORTS

Horse riding. There is a well-known equestrian school in San Miguel located behind the Hotel Atascadero on the road to Querétaro. Horses may not be rented; however, serious riders should direct their requests for information on the school to Escuela Ecuestre, Apartado Postal 185, San Miguel de Allende, or call 2-02-55.

FIESTAS

Día de San Miguel Arcangel, September 29. The town's patron saint is honored with a two-week fiesta beginning around September 15 and culminating on September 29. During that time, an event similar to the running of the bulls in Pamplona, Spain, is held.

The birthday of Ignacio Allende, hometown hero, is celebrated January 20.

TRANSPORTATION

Buses. First-class bus service from neighboring towns.

Taxis. Few, but reasonable.

Trains. The Aztec Eagle from Nuevo Laredo makes a daily stop in San Miguel. (For general information about train service, see the chapter **There and Back Again** or check at the local tourist office listed below.)

TOURIST SERVICES

Tourist Office (Subdelegación Federal de Turismo), Edificio de Gobierno del Estado, Calle San Francisco 33 (2-12-88).

COMMUNICATIONS

Post Office. Across from La Parroquia, the parish church, Calle Correo.

Radio station. Local radio station XESQ, 12.80 on the AM dial, broadcasts the news in English.

Newspapers. *The News*, Mexico's free English newspaper, is distributed, as well as several local gossip sheets.

CUERNAVACA

People have been coming to Cuernavaca to get away from it all for over six hundred years: the Aztecs built summer palaces here, Cortés enjoyed the balmy weather, Empress Carlota walked in Cuernavaca's gardens, and for the last twenty years everybody from Helen Hayes to the Shah of Iran has established a little or a generous *pied-à-terre* among the bougainvilleas. Cuernavaca is popularly called the City of Eternal Spring, and though the city's growth has wilted the blooms a little, Cuernavaca remains one of those places rightfully called an international playground. The city has an air of luxury about it, mysterious luxury since most of the playgrounds are hidden behind high walls.

Cuernavaca was once surrounded by huge sugar plantations called haciendas. A local boy, Emiliano Zapata, put a stop to that by rallying the vast majority of poor Mexicans around the flag of land reform. The land holdings were split up, but the big houses remained, and now many haciendas have been turned into luxury hotels where opulence is for sale. (There are several of these hotels surrounding Cuernavaca. See "Hacienda Havens" in the chapter **The Unique and the Random.**) Not all the hotels in Cuernavaca are expensive, and it is possible to stay in nineteenth-century luxury for a reasonable amount of money.

But the whole idea of going to Cuernavaca is to get away from it all, throw caution and parsimony to the winds, and wallow. Cuernavaca is like Puerto Vallarta, a place to go to spoil yourself. You say, "I've been good. I deserve this." Sit back, sip your piña colada, and watch the bougainvilleas grow.

Much of what makes Cuernavaca a popular resort is hidden behind walls. Two of the best luxury hotels are the Posada Jacaranda with its honeymoon treehouse and Las Mañanitas, a 15-room country inn surrounded by tropical gardens where flamingos and peacocks stroll. The restaurant at Las Mañanitas is among the best in Mexico.

Getting to Cuernavaca is no problem. A fast, four-lane super highway carries escaping Mexico City dwellers south 40 miles to the city in the mountains. The road climbs from 7,200 feet in the capital to 10,000 feet and misty pine-topped mountains and then down to the land of eternal spring at 5,000 feet. This altitude guarantees a year-round balmy climate where tropical plants flourish. Temperatures are usually in the high 60s to mid-70s in the daytime, and only occasionally, in winter, is a jacket needed. With such balmy weather, the hardy may want to take on the city on foot, but a rental car or cab is really the best way to get around (cabs are extremely cheap in Cuernavaca) because many of the sights are scattered throughout the city.

Architecturally, Cuernavaca is a mixture of colonial, sumptuous nineteenth-century pseudocolonial, and modern. There's an archaeological site, the Pyramid of Teopanzolco, near the railroad station, and some of the colonial structures were built atop Aztec ruins. The gardens here were first cultivated by the Aztecs. The heart of the city is the zócalo with its twin gardens. Surprisingly, there is no church on the main square. There are several sidewalk cafés where the vendors and mariachis entertain in the late afternoon and evening as everyone gathers at his favorite bistro. Nearby, at the corner of Hidalgo and Morelos is the Cathedral of San Francisco, founded by Cortés in 1529. The church is famous for its Sunday mariachi mass and Indian murals. One of the few monasteries still in existence in Mexico following the anticlerical movement earlier in this century is the Emaus Monastery at Calle Laurel. The monks sell Chartreuse-flavored candy and silver work.

Over the centuries city planners have made good use of the area's fertile land by creating several parks throughout the city. Chapultepec Park, located west of downtown, is named after the large park in the capital. Like its namesake, it boasts gardens, a zoo, a children's amusement park, a boating lake, and picnic areas. In the vicicnity is El Salto de San Antonio, a beautiful waterfall. According to popular legend, Empress Carlota, the ill-fated archduchess whose Austrian husband laid claim to the throne of Mexico, spent a great deal of her time walking in the gardens of the Borda mansion in Cuernavaca. Here, she agonized over the difficulties that beset the couple; later she went insane, and though she lived well into the twentieth century, never realized that her husband had been executed in Mexico. The Borda Gardens are somewhat neglected now, but they are still a haunting place to visit. The grounds and mansion, built by Manuel de la Borda, son of the Taxco silver mine owner, are located on Calle Morelos, across from the cathedral.

The city was named Cuauhnahuac by the Indians — literary buffs will recognize this as the name of the town in Frank Lowry's *Under the Volcano*, a good book to read as you relax in Cuernavaca. The Spanish who had difficulty with the Mexican names changed this to Cuernavaca, which translates as "cow's horn" and has no significance whatsoever.

Cortés spent a great deal of time here with his mistress La Malinche, and the city was given to him by the Crown. (His lineage died out in the seventeenth century.) His residence here is known as Cortés's Palace, but it's an oppressive, fortresslike structure that suggests Cortés's purpose. It is now a museum, and there's a good view of the city from the ramparts. Following a conquistadorean habit, the fortress was built atop an Aztec temple, the Tlauican pyramid, which can seen at the base of the structure. One of the highlights of the museum is its collection of murals by Diego Rivera, one of Mexico's three principal muralists. The works depict the conquest. There are also exhibits portraying the history of Mexico.

Cuernavaca has attracted its share of artists and writers; muralist David Siqueiros executed several works that can be viewed by the public at the heliport hangar at the Hotel Casino de la Selva. The hotel is located at Leandro Valle 1001. Siqueiros's workshop is also open to the public 10-2 and 4-6 at Calle Verdes No. 2 daily except Monday.

Although Cuernavaca is a popular holiday spot, shopping is limited here. The market is geared toward the locals; however, there are some good buys in huaraches, hats, and kitchenware. To reach the market, take Guerrero north from the zócalo, cross the footbridge over the ravine, turn right, and ahead is the market. Several of the hotels have boutiques featuring crafts and designer clothes, and there are a few arts and crafts shops around the zócalo.

There are several special fiestas in Cuernavaca, and the Mardi Gras celebration, held just before Lent, grows more popular every year. An unusual carnival celebration that has both Christian and pre-Columbian origins is held at the Pyramid of Tepozteco in nearby Tepoztlán. The pyramid was dedicated to Tepoztecatl, the god of pulque, and the carnival celebrations here involve a great deal of pulque drinking and Indian dancing. Tepoztlán is also famous for the annual fair held in the Ixtepec barrio of the town. The fair usually begins on May 8 and lasts for a week. (Don't confuse Tepoztlán with Tepotzotlán, the monastery north of Mexico City.) Sunday is market day in Tepoztlán, and it is an authentic *tianguis* ("Indian market"). There's a small museum and artisans' shop in the convent behind the parish church on the zócalo.

Beyond Tepoztlán is Hacienda Cocoyoc, a restored hacienda that serves as a luxury resort. You can enjoy lunch or a quiet drink in the hacienda after a day of sight-seeing in Tepoztlán.

There's not much to do in Cuernavaca after dark — there are a few discos and bars (see city listings that follow), but most visitors opt for a leisurely dinner at one of the excellent hotel dining rooms in town and retire after dinner to their hotel patio for a final glass of brandy under the stars.

BOCADITOS

Make your reservations well in advance if you plan to stay in one of Cuernavaca's luxury hotels. Dinner reservations are recommended, also.

Since Cuernavaca is easily accessible from the capital, a rental car is a good investment. The worst part of the journey will be from Mexico City's international airport to the city limits; however, the numerous sights around Cuernavaca make a rental car worthwhile. Xochicalco, the archaeological site, is located south of Cuernavaca — take the Alpuyeca turnoff from the toll road, then head northwest, following the signs. The site is a baffling mix of pre-Colombian styles and includes a beautiful pyramid dedicated to Quetzalcoatl, the plumed serpent.

Hacienda Vista Hermosa is located on the road to Xochicalco. (See "Hacienda Havens" in the chapter **The Unique and the Random.**)

Forty miles east of Cuernavaca is the public resort of Oaxtepec, a mecca for Mexico City's working people on the weekends. Once the site of Moctezuma's botanical gardens, here a hospital was built in the seventeenth century so that people could take the waters. Now, Oaxtepec is one of Mexico's most popular bathing spots (see "Spas" in the chapter **The Unique and the Random**), and the park has soccer fields, swimming pools, restaurants, arts and crafts shows, picnic facilities, and children's playgrounds.

AROUND CUERNAVACA

VITAL STATISTICS

Climate. Eternal spring. That's what it says in all the brochures and that's what it is like most of the year. Occasional afternoon showers. Cool, if not chilly, nights.

Population. 200,000, but looks smaller.

Altitude. 5,000 feet.

State. Morelos.

City phone code: 731.

HOTELS

Cuernavaca Racquet Club (3-03-00). Originally the home of a Swedish industrialist, this luxurious resort is set in 23 acres of gardens. Famed for its tennis facilities (white is obligatory on the courts) and renowned for its genteel service. Many of the rooms have private patios, king-sized beds, and fireplaces. For reservations write Robert F. Warner, Inc., 711 Third Ave., New York, NY 10017, or call 1-800-223-6625. A. Cr.

Hotel Hacienda Cocoyoc (2-20-20). A magnificently restored seventeenth-century hacienda near Cuautla, 20 miles east of Cuernavaca. The manicured grounds enjoy a fine view of Popo and include two large swimming pools, an 18-hole golf course, two tennis courts, and trails for riding. The hotel itself has 325 rooms and suites (some with private pools), nine restaurants, five bars, a disco, piano bar, nightclub, and several boutiques. In spite of its enormous size, the hotel is arranged around a series of plazas and fountains that give the rooms added privacy. The setting, architecture, and decor made Cocoyoc one of the most beautiful resorts in all of Mexico. Unfortunately, the food and service are not on par. For reservations write Amazones 85, Mexico 5, DF, or call 514-1428, 511-4460, or 514-9706 in Mexico City. B. Cr.

Hacienda Vista Hermosa, Tequesquitengo, Morelos, Mexico (2-03-00, locally or 546-4540 in Mexico City). This once grand hacienda was the center of a sugar plantation in the seventeenth century. Stop by for a drink and you may see a movie being filmed. The hotel's picturesque setting and the spectacular countryside are popular among filmmakers. B. Cr.

Hosteria Las Quintas, Las Quintas 107 (2-88-00). One of the best in town. A small, colonial-style inn with beautiful gardens. Cr.

Las Mañanitas, Ricardo Linares 107 (2-46-46). One of the best, most elegant small hotels in the world. Filled with artworks, antiques, and gardens inhabited by exotic birds. Famous for its cuisine. Fifteen suites available. A. Cr.

Posada Jacaranda, Cuauhtémoc 805 (2-46-40). Beautifully landscaped resort with a treehouse for honeymooners, an excellent restaurant, and a waterfall in the pool. B. Cr.

Posada de Xochiquetzal, Leyva 200 (2-02-20). Don't let the drab exterior fool you; inside is an exquisite garden surrounded by colonial-style rooms. Cortés's mistress, La Malinche, lived here. C. Cr.

RESTAURANTS

Harry's Bar, on the zócalo (2-76-79). Locally popular and owned by the ubiquitous Carlos Anderson. Good food, good company, good spirits. Closed Monday. Moderate. Cr.

La Casa de Piedra, Plan de Ayala 629, east of the zócalo. Features soufflés and mousses that will melt in your mouth. Moderate. Cr.

Las Mañanitas, at Ricardo Linares 107 (2-46-46). This Cuernavaca landmark has managed to retain the good food, service, and pleasant ambience that is responsible for its well-deserved reputation. Weekend crowds don't diminish the attentive service. The menu features several unusual dishes, such as calf brains, but the Mexican dishes are the best buys. As in many of Cuernavaca's restaurants, the *botanas* are generous for those who just drop by for a drink. The grounds are lush and lovely, with a large, well-landscaped pool reserved for hotel guests. Expensive. Cr.

Lancer's, Av. Dwight Morrow. Hard to miss, since signs with arrows appear on virtually every street corner to lead you here. Located in a colonial mansion, it has a delightful garden and tastefully decorated dining areas. The pastries are especially good. Lancer's is a good place to stop for drinks, since the *botanas* (featuring tiny tacos filled with mushrooms and cheese) are plentiful and good. Moderate. Cr.

Vienes, Lerdo de Tejada 4 (2-02-17). Native Cuernavacans recommend this Austrian restaurant, not to be confused with Viena, which is a coffee and pastry shop where Americans hang out. Features home cooking, Viennese style. Moderate. Cr.

Zapata's Grille, on the road to Mexico City. A rustic restaurant, from the outside it looks like a pottery, with piles of pots and vases stacked on both sides of the entrance. Inside the decor is country casual, with strings of peppers and garlic hanging from beams and light fixtures designed from straw sombreros. Specialties are steaks, charcoal grilled chicken, and pork chops. You may select your cut of meat before it is grilled. Portions are large and are served with vegetables, rice, and an excellent herb butter to spread on your tortillas. The tortilla soup is recommended, as is the watercress salad with house dressing. Steaks are expensive, but the chicken is a bargain.

NIGHTLIFE

Cuernavaca dines late, and most folks sleep deeply in the mountain air; however, the disco crowd hangs out at Tabasco Charlie's, Av. del Parque 104, and Le Club at Las Palmas Centro.

SHOPPING

Boutiques, various locations. Cuernavaca attracts the wealthy and so boutiques abound. Some of the best include Casa Beltran, Guerrero 14, leatherwork; Galeria Akari, Jardines Tlaltenango 49, artwork; Olinala, cathedral courtyard, handicrafts; Van Gelder Art Gallery, Galeana 102; Cerámica Santa María, Av. Zapata 900; and Las Casa de los Campanas, adjacent to the cathedral in the main plaza.

El Mercado, five blocks north of the zócalo. Cuernavaca is not known for its crafts, but huaraches are a good buy in the market. Try on both shoes before you buy.

FONART, Cortés's Palace in the zócalo. The government arts and crafts exhibition hall is also a salesroom. Fixed prices; good selection of regional crafts. Open daily.

Tepotztlán, 15 miles east on Hwy. 95D (toll road) then six miles east on Hwy. 115D (toll road). This 'ndian village holds a *tianguis* (Indian market) every Sunday.

POINTS OF INTEREST

Borda Gardens, across from the cathedral. Built by the silver king José de la Borda, these gardens were a favorite haunt of Empress Carlota. They are somewhat rundown now but still worth a visit.

Casa de Maximiliano, Calle Galeano. This is where Emperor Maximilian and his wife, Carlota, sought refuge from their problems in Mexico City.

Chapultepec Park, Blvd. Plan de Ayala. Located in a ravine west of the city, this park boasts a children's amusement park and a small zoo. Boats can be rented for sailing on the canals. The remains of an aqueduct built by Cortés span the park. Closed Monday. Open Tuesday through Friday 10–6; Saturday and Sunday 10–7. Small admission.

Cathedral, Calle Morelos. Begun by Cortés, the cathedral contains some intriguing murals that show Spanish friars on missions in Japan. Mariachi mass every Sunday at 11 A.M.

Grutas de Cacahuamilpa, 30 miles southwest of town. Take Hwy. 95 or toll road Hwy. 95D south to Alpuyeca, turn west onto Hwy. 55, and follow signs. Still partially unexplored, these caverns are said to be the largest in the world. The areas open to the public are not as extensive as Carlsbad Caverns, but the formations are equally impressive and dramatic. The two-hour tour on well-lighted and paved paths is not strenuous. Tour conducted in Spanish. Small charge.

Oaxtepec, 21 miles north of Cuernavaca off the toll road to Mexico City (Hwy. 95D). A huge and immaculate public park with picnic tables, ten large swimming pools and wading pools, two special pools, snack stands, gardens, and luxurious cottages and a campground for overnight stops. Unfortunately, the campground is located in the most dismal area of the park, where there are practically no trees, and the campsites are too close together. Oaxtepec is extremely popular with Mexican families and has a Coney Island atmosphere on weekends. However, it is well worth visiting and is a perfect place for a day's picnic outing. The large groups and numerous pools can accommodate an enormous number of people. Small admission fee.

Pyramid of Teopanzolco, east of the railroad station at Av. del Balsas and Miguel Aleman. The name means "abandoned temple," and it was not discovered until this century. Predominantly Aztec style, it was used from about the thirteenth century to the conquest.

Tepoztlán, 15 miles east of Cuernavaca. Take Hwy. 95D north six miles, then go east on Hwy. 115D (toll road) five miles. This Indian village is picturesquely situated at the foot of a mountain, and in spite of its inclusion in all the guidebooks and its proximity to Cuernavaca and Mexico City, it remains largely untouched. The most interesting sight in town is a former convent that commands a view of the mountains and the valley below. There are also a small archaeological museum, a colorful market, and at least one luxury restaurant: the Bistro del Convento. The latter is artfully decorated and has an interesting menu (expensive). An Indian shrine to Tepoztecatl, the god of pulque, can be reached by a precipitous climb up the mountain. The town's Indian heritage is celebrated at several fiestas and fairs throughout the year.

San Antonio Falls, on the western edge of town. Lush, tropical vegetation surrounds the falls, which cascade 100 feet into a clear pool. Steps set in the cliff lead to a walkway behind the falls, and there are picnic tables at the edge of the water. To arrive at the falls, go through the pottery village of San Antonio, a cluster of buildings set around a plaza that also serves as a parking lot for visitors. One of the restaurants around the plaza advertises iguana as the specialty of the day. The pottery shops have an interesting selection of ceramics at reasonable prices. To find the village, follow the signs that say Salto or Salto San Antonio. Free.

Xochicalco. Take Hwy. 95D (toll road) southwest for 22 miles, turn west at Alpuyeca and go 17 miles, finally traveling five miles on Hwy. 421 and following signs to Xochicalco. This is one of the most beautiful sites in Mexico, particularly the Pyramid of the Feathered Serpents dedicated to Quetzalcoatl. There is a mixture of styles here that the practiced eye can recognize—Mayan, Zapotec, Mixtec, and Toltec. This was a teaching center in Toltec times, and it is thought that Ce Acatl, the prince who fled to the Yucatán and became revered as Quetzalcoatl, was educated here.

MUSEUMS

Cortés's Palace, southeast corner of the zócalo. Conquistador Hernándo Cortés was following Aztec tradition when he had his summer home built here in 1530. The murals, a gift of US Ambassador Dwight Morrow, are by Diego Rivera and portray the conquest of the Indians.

FIESTAS

Mardi Gras, week before Lent, celebrated in Cuernavaca and at nearby Tepotzlán.

Fiesta de los Flores, May 2, a festival of flowers in the Borda Gardens.
Ixtepec Annual Fair, early May, the barrio of Ixtepec in nearby
Tepotzlán celebrates with a fair and fiestas.
Festival Miquiztli, Day of the Dead, November 2.

TRANSPORTATION

Buses. Luxury and first-class bus service from the capital and other
nearby cities.
Car rental. Agencies include Hertz at Plan de Ayala 300 (4-38-00) and
National at Plan de Ayala 1304 (5-00-08).
Taxis. Always settle on price before getting in.
Trains. Train service through the capital. (For information about train
service in Mexico, see the chapter There and Back Again or check at
the local tourist office listed below.)

TOURIST SERVICES

Tourist Office (Delegación Federal de Turismo), Av. Morelos 205A
(2-34-95 or 2-18-15).

COMMUNICATIONS

Newspapers. *The News,* Mexico's free English language daily is distributed with a column on Cuernavaca social happenings.
Post Office, Hidalgo and Matamoros, north of the cathedral.

MORELIA

A city worker, wearing a rumpled straw hat and dressed in baggy
khaki pants and worn huaraches, is sweeping the square with a long,
dried palm frond. Meanwhile, businessmen sit at metal tables and sip
espresso in the afternoon shade of *los arcos,* the vaguely Moorish
arcades that line the square. Their nails are manicured, their hair bar-
bered, and their shoes are being shined by a collection of young boys
carrying brass-covered boxes. This fastidiousness, reflected in the
work of the street sweeper and the shined shoes of the businessmen,
is typical of Morelia, a colonial city with a clean, light air, almost
reminiscent of the plazas of Venice.
Morelia is little visited by tourists, and yet it is the capital of one of
Mexico's most beautiful states, Michoacán. Unlike most Mexican
cities, Morelia is a city painted in pastel tints, a city of sculptured
gardens and pink and light-gray stone buildings. There are even prices
on the vegetable stands, an unheard of thing in Mexico. While there
are several excellent hotels in the area, including Villa Montaña above
the city, which was to be Tyrone Power's home, there is little of the
flash and glare associated with the tourist trade. The city is a good

place to unwind on the road between Mexico City and Guadalajara or to use as a base for exploring the surrounding craft-rich region.

The language of Cervantes is a poetic one, and Mexicans with their dual artistic heritage are not given to skimping on metaphors; consequently, Morelia is "the queen of cities." Originally named Valladolid after the Spanish city of that name, the town was founded by Viceroy Antonio de Mendoza, one of the more enlightened viceroys. The area was, and still is, populated by the Tarascans, an Indian clan known for their sensuality and artistic ability. Mexicans still consider a man with Tarascan blood an artist. The Aztecs never managed to conquer these people; it took the cruel hand of Beltran Nuño de Guzmán, the most notorious conquistador, to break their spirit of resistance. He was removed by the viceroy, and Bishop Vasco de Quiroga became Primate of the area. Quiroga encouraged the Tarascans to continue their artistic pursuits, ensuring for future generations the richness of the region's crafts. Within easy distance of Morelia are the towns of Uruapan, famed for its lacquerware; Paracho, where handmade guitars are created; Pátzcuaro, known for its pottery; and Erongarícuaro on Lake Pátzcuaro, where the Indian market is ranked as one of the best in Mexico.

The heart of the city is the cathedral with its unusual twin plazas. Begun by Bishop Quiroga in the seventeenth century, it has none of the solid, massiveness of most of Mexico's large churches. It is one of the best examples of Plateresque architecture, so named for its similarity to ornate silver plate. Unlike most Mexican churches where reds and golds dominate, the cathedral has a light-filled interior colored with silvers and blues. It is one of the most beautiful colonial churches in the Americas.

The main square, Plaza de los Mártires, is surrounded by cafés and hotels. Under the arcades, businessmen and students gather each afternoon during siesta. One of the best hotels in Mexico, the Hotel Virrey de Mendoza, is located on the plaza. (See "The Best Little Hotels in Mexico" in the chapter **The Unique and the Random.**) The Mendoza was built in 1744 as a private home. It now features a variety of rooms all furnished in early Victorian fashion. There's also an excellent restaurant in the courtyard, a good place to practice a revered Mexican custom — the long lunch. In the cafés on the square, there's always something to watch, and by mid-afternoon the paperboys come around selling the newspapers. Take your pick. Compare the news in the establishment press, dominated by the government view, with the right-wing papers and the communist paper. Practice your Spanish by reading headlines.

Morelia doesn't thrust itself on the visitor, and you are not duty bound to make the museum rounds or the obligatory visits to this monument or that. Casa de Morelos, home of José María Morelos, the national revolutionary hero for whom the city was named, is one of the sights you should seek out. (The name of the town was changed to Morelia in honor of the native son.) Like the Juárez Museum near the National Palace in Mexico City, the Morelos Museum is a cross between a museum and a shrine. Morelos's personal effects are scattered among his papers, and in the courtyard there are two carriages used by the revolutionary leader. Another small museum worth visiting is the Museo del Estado de Michoacán. Housed in an eighteenth-century palace, the state museum features archaeological artifacts, colonial furnishings and weapons, and several murals.

If you plan to venture into the countryside on a craft hunt, first visit the Casa de las Artesanías, Madero 492. This combination museum and government craft store features some of the best examples of regional art. La Merced Independencia, the local market, has some crafts for sale, also. Morelia has a candy market, two blocks west of the main plaza — Mexicans have a notorious sweet tooth. The suburb of Santa María, in the hills above the city, has several furniture shops where handcarved colonial-style pieces are made.

The climate in Morelia is moderate with summer temperatures in the 70s and 80s, winter temperatures in the 60s. The city is located at 6,000 feet approximately; however, nearby communities are higher and cooler. Watch out for mountain mists as you drive. Dress comfortably, but remember Morelia is a conservative city. In the small towns most Indian women dress modestly, and visitors are expected to dress in a similar fashion.

There's not much to do in Morelia at night, although most people dine late and hotel bars stay open. Twice a week, on Thursdays and Sundays, there are band concerts in the main plaza. The city celebrates all national holidays with the usual fervor.

BOCADITOS

If you are looking for a place to stay for a week or more, try the Hotel Villa Montaña. High in the hills, the luxury hotel overlooks the city and the mountains of Michoacán. No children under 12 are allowed at the hotel; it's peaceful and very genteel. The rooms, both public and private, are filled with antiques.

There are complimentary cocktails before dinner. Meals are included in the price of a room and are served in great style amid beautiful surroundings.

Each room is in its own cottage. Make your reservations several months in advance; the Villa is very popular. Write to Hotel Villa Montaña, Apartdo Postal 233, Morelia, Michoacán, Mexico, or call 2-25-88 in Morelia.

AROUND MORELIA

VITAL STATISTICS

Climate. Pleasant, springlike weather year-round. Summer afternoon rain showers; chilly nights in winter.

Population. 220,000.

Altitude. 6,400 feet.

State. Michoacán.

City phone code. 451.

HOTELS

Posada Vista Bella, Apartado Postal 135 (2-26-24). Next door to the Villa Montaña on Hwy. 15 above the city. A motel decorated in colonial style. Apartments available. B. Cr.

Suites Normandie, Benito Juárez 63 (2-16-70). A superb hotel in a city of superb hotels. A converted monastery with each room individually decorated. Suites available. Some rooms have a view of Morelia's beautiful cathedral. A. Cr.

Villa Montaña, Apartado Postal 233 (2-25-88). This was to be the home of movie actor Tyrone Power, who died before it was completed. Now a luxury retreat set in the Santa María hills overlooking the peaceful town of Morelia. Bungalow suites, fireplaces. All meals included; box lunches available. A. Cr.

Virrey de Mendoza, Portal Matamoros 16 (2-06-33). This magnificent hotel with four-poster beds overlooks Plaza de los Mártires, the main plaza. Victorian decor in a restored eighteenth-century home. A great buy. B. Cr.

RESTAURANTS

Most of the best restaurants in Morelia are located in the hotels, notably Villa Montaña, Suites Normandie, and the Virrey de Mendoza. Reservations are necessary at the Villa Montaña (2-25-88). For snacks, a light lunch, or a quiet drink, try one of the cafés on the plaza.

Carro de la Silla, Calles Pino Suárez and 20 de Noviembre (2-30-95). Specializing in *norteño* food, steaks, grilled meat, and cabrito. Moderate. Cr.

Sandor's, Madero Ote. 422B (2-18-09). Try the local specialties at this popular café: tacos, *bolillos* stuffed with meats and cheeses, enchiladas. Inexpensive. Cr.

NIGHTLIFE

Nightlife in Morelia is practically nonexistent. Late dining is popular and perhaps a stroll after dinner. Hotel bars stay open late.

SHOPPING

Casa de las Artesanías, Madero 492, three blocks from the cathedral.
This government-owned store offers the best crafts of the region. Open
seven days. Fixed prices.

Mercado de Dulces, Gomez Farias, west of the main plaza. Morelia is
the candy capital of Mexico, and the city has one market that sells
nothing but *dulces.*

Santa María, suburb in the hills south of Morelia. This hillside community is famed for its wood-carvers. Good furniture buys.

POINTS OF INTEREST

**Aqueduct, Av. Madero, Cuauhtémoc Park, on the road to Mexico
City.** This seventeenth-century stone aqueduct is an impressive example of colonial architecture.

Cathedral, Plaza de los Mártires. Located in the heart of the city between two tree-lined plazas, the cathedral is unlike any other in Mexico. Begun in 1640 by Don Vasco de Quiroga, a much-loved bishop,
it is a church of extreme delicacy, muted tones of silver and blue, without the reds and golds that dominate most Mexican churches. It is one
of the best examples in Mexico of the Plateresque style.

Church of Santa Rosa de Lima, Calle Santiago Tapia. Famous for its
beautiful baroque *retablo* and the conservatory that adjoins it. The
oldest music school in the New World.

Colegio de San Nicolas, Calle Galeana and Av. Madero Pte. This is
the oldest university in the New World. Moved here in 1580 from Pátzcuaro where it was founded in 1540.

Cuitzeo, 22 miles north of the city on Hwy. 43. This fishing village is
the site of a famous Augustinian convent built in 1551. The church is
decorated in Plateresque fashion. A beautiful drive through the mountains.

Mil Cumbres, 45 miles east on Hwy. 15. *Mil Cumbres* means "thousand mountaintops," and the view from this point is one of the most
beautiful in Mexico. Take a sweater — it's chilly at these altitudes.

San José Purua, 62 miles west on Hwy. 15. Site of a famous mineral
water spa located in a lush canyon. Mud baths and mineral baths are
the order of the day at Hotel Purua (585-4344 in Mexico City for reservations). Expensive.

MUSEUMS

Casa de Morelos, Morelos 323. This was once the home of the patriot-
priest José María Morelos y Pavón, who was executed in 1824. The

museum contains the patriot's personal papers and memorabilia. Morelia, originally called "Valladolid," is named in his honor. Open seven days. Small admission fee.

Museo del Estado de Michoacán, Calle Allende. This eighteenth-century palace near the main plaza is now an archaeological museum and art gallery. Open seven days. Small admission fee.

FIESTAS

The anniversary of the birth of José María Morelos, native son and independence fighter, September 30.

TRANSPORTATION

Buses. First-class bus service from Guadalajara, Mexico City, and other neighboring cities.

Car rental. Agencies include Hertz, Hotel Virrey de Mendoza, Portal Matamoros 16 (2-06-33).

Taxis. Reasonable. Check rate before you get in.

Trains. Morelia is on the main line between Guadalajara and Mexico City. It's worthwhile getting off here for a few days and using Morelia as a base for exploring other towns nearby.

TOURIST SERVICES

Tourist Office (Delegación Federal de Turismo), Palacio Clavijero, Nigromante 79 (2-98-16 or 3-26-54).

TAXCO

Taxco is the quintessential colonial town, an exquisite, small community that tumbles down a precarious hillside in a jumble of red tile, white walls, and pink geraniums. Taxco is everybody's idea of what a Mexican town should look like, and its charm is protected by Mexican law that forbids any construction violating strict standards.

Unfortunately, or fortunately if you happen to be among the *cognoscenti,* too many tourists settle for a day trip to Taxco, leaving Acapulco or Mexico City in a bus and spending the prescribed hour in the silver shops. It is just as easy and much more delightful to spend two or three days in Taxco. Not that there's much to do here, but what makes the town so appealing is that just sitting around and looking at it is worthwhile. A low-slung chair in Paco's or Berta's bar—both have balconies jutting over the zócalo—a jug of wine, and the thou of your choice are all you need. Watching the pigeons land on the magnificent church towers can be effort enough. Nightlife is minimal, bordering on nonexistent, although there's a good, if touristy, floor show at the Hotel de la Borda. And one of the best gourmet restaurants in Mexico is located at La Ventana de Taxco, on the outskirts of town. What little there is to do is interesting without being either intellectually or financially demanding.

Taxco is an intimate town (except for the Holiday Inn that hovers high above the city and boasts a golf course for those who want to play the world's largest colonial sand trap). Once you reach town you will be glad to park your car — the roads into Taxco are murderously picturesque. It's doubtful you would be able to maneuver even the smallest import around the town's cobbled streets even if you wanted to, and don't attempt to drive a motor home or large luxury car into town; check into one of the hotels on the outskirts. This may seem too quaint, but take comfort in the fact that there are no carbon monoxide–belching buses in Taxco, just burros and little VW minibuses called *burritos*. The town is so quiet in the evening you can hear dogs barking high on the hillside or a small band practicing in the valley.

Walking around Taxco can be tiring — the city is located at 5,700 feet above sea level; however, the climate is perfect with daytime temperatures usually in the mid-60s to mid-70s. Rain showers in summer last only a short time. Most of the windows have no glass, just wooden shutters. (Take along mosquito repellent in the summer months.)

Taxco was known as Tlachco before the Spaniards came. The name means "the place where the ball game is played" in Nahuatl. (Now, the only ball game played is soccer in one of the small, cobblestone plazas, the church steps serving as a goal.) This area was under the domination of the Aztecs when the conquistadores came. Cortés, a man with a nose for precious metals, visited Tlachco soon after his arrival, and mining operations followed. The Spaniards soon changed the name of the town to Taxco. By the end of the sixteenth century, the mine appeared to be played out, and Taxco slipped back into tranquillity in the mountains south of the capital. Then, in the mid-seventeenth century, the Frenchman Joseph de la Borde, who would become José de la Borda, found a new, rich vein of silver. During his lifetime, Taxco flourished, and Borda responded to his good fortune by building the beautiful Church of San Sebastián and Santa Prisca, one of the most outstanding examples of the unique Mexican Churrigueresque style.

From the end of the eighteenth century to the 1930s Taxco once again slumbered. Then William Spratling, an architect and teacher at Tulane University, urged by his friend William Faulkner to head south and work on a book, discovered the town. When he arrived in Taxco he found that the artisans were mining small amounts of silver and making primitive pieces in their home workshops. Spratling decided to abandon his academic career and stay in Taxco where he encouraged the artisans to refine their wares. The result, 50 years later, is a variety of silver shops and *tallers,* some of which produce beautiful, original jewelry and silver work. Many of the silver shops allow customers to browse through their workshops and watch the craftsmen at work.

The silver work is not cheap, and prices are similar to those found in Mexico City; however, much of the work is very beautiful. (For a guide to buying precious metals in Mexico, see the chapter **The Enormous Store.**)

Taxco is noted for its celebrations. In late November, early December, a silver festival is held and the smiths compete for a grand prize. Throughout the festival, there are special performances by musicians and dancers who entertain on a stage in the main square, Plaza de la Borda. The major church fiestas, Easter in particular, are celebrated with colorful pageants. On January 18, Santa Prisca is honored.

Although maps of Taxco are available at local hotels, they resemble the random doodles of a neurotic. The town's streets wind around the hillside with abandon, making exploration a necessary pleasure and navigation a frustration. The heart of the city is Plaza de la Borda that, unlike most Mexican squares, isn't square. In the general vicinity of the plaza can be found the restaurants, bars, silver shops, and sights. Visitors usually spend their first day, perhaps their second and even third, in two places—Berta's, a small bar and restaurant in one corner of the plaza (famed for a drink of the same name), and Paco's, an upstairs open-air bar with a magnificent view of Santa Prisca. In fact, a major pastime in the plaza and in Paco's is watching the vendors set up their wares for the afternoon invasion and waiting for the minibuses to spill out their load of tourists, travelers of every shape and shade, notably Japanese, Europeans, and Americans.

Some purists say Taxco is too "touristy," too pleasant, a contrived colonial town, and admittedly the town does lack some of the raw realities of Mexican life to be found in other places. But that doesn't mean the town is false. Taxco is a peaceful retreat in a world of hustle, a town where every window offers a view to inspire the painter or the photographer. It's not manufactured beauty, but beauty nourished by care.

One of the beautiful sights in Taxco is the Church of San Sebastián and Santa Prisca, commonly referred to as Santa Prisca. Lighted at night and surrounded by the feathered paths of a dozen bottle rockets, the church with its pink stone towers and glazed tile roof is a sight unmatched in Mexico. The highly developed rococo style called Churrigueresque is unique to Mexico, and Santa Prisca is one of the best examples. The interior of the church is even more beautiful, with each altar backed by an ornate, gilded *retablo*, more evidence of de la Borda's faith and thankfulness. Inside the doorway sit boxes: one for funds to maintain the church, another for the poor; it is customary to give, no matter how small the offering. Wooden rosaries, similar to those sold at the shrine of Our Lady of Guadalupe in Mexico City, are also sold at the church.

Don José's home is located on Plaza Borda not far from the church he built. A devout man who counted a priest and a nun among his children, Don José built the house in 1759 and, upon his death, left part of it to the church priests who still use it. The front of the house is two stories and the back is five stories, a common architectural device in Taxco. The building is open to the public and also houses a silver shop, Los Castillos.

At the west end of the plaza is Casa Figueroa, which was built in 1767 by a friend of de la Borda's, Count Cadena. Some call it "the House of Tears" because a local magistrate built it using Indian labor. In 1943, the Mexican artist Fidel Figueroa restored the home and turned it into an art gallery and studio, which it has remained. The home is open to the public daily for a small charge.

Two other homes, Casa Humboldt and Casa Grande are open daily to the public. Casa Humboldt is a Moorish-style house built by Juan de Villeneuva in the eighteenth century. He named it in honor of overnight guest Baron Alexander von Humboldt, the scientist and adventurer. The house is north of the zócalo on Calle Pireda. Casa Grande was the mayoral residence in colonial times and the revolutionary hero Morelos slept there. (Like George Washington, Morelos slept in a lot of places.) The house is located on Plazuela de San Juan.

One of the most interesting small museums in Mexico is located behind Santa Prisca. The William Spratling Museum houses the architect's collection of pre-Columbian artifacts. The museum is one of the few in Mexico to follow international custom and label its exhibits in more than one language, a worthy example that should be followed in other Mexican museums.

At the south end of the Plaza de la Borda is the market that serves the community rather than the tourist. It rambles up and down the hillside, through several streets and alleyways. The flower stalls are tucked away under an overhanging building. There are good buys in pottery and candles. If you are staying in the nearby Hotel Meléndez (a bargain), you will be awakened shortly before dawn on market day as the vendors arrive — that is if you have fallen asleep. Taxqueños are notorious for their fiestas; fireworks and brass bands may keep you awake if you happen to arrive on a saint's day. However, on most evenings, the lights go out at nine, and you will be glad to blow out the candle and open the shutters. After all, you probably had a hard day sitting in Paco's watching the pigeons land.

BOCADITOS

There are several day trips worth taking from Taxco. The ones we have listed are all along Hwy. 55 to Toluca where there's a popular Friday market. Buy a good map of the area.

GRUTAS DE CACAHUAMILPA

For a real adventure, explore these caves (grutas), which are thought to be as big if not bigger than Carlsbad Caverns — they haven't been fully explored. A guide takes you to the innermost cavern, but leaves you to follow the path out at your own rate, as lights are extinguished on your heels (that's where the adventure part comes in). You may want to take a flashlight. The rock formations are very beautiful — *Journey to the Center of the Earth* was filmed here. The caves are located approximately 20 miles west of Taxco. There is also a series of neighboring caves called the Grutas de las Estrellas.

CHALMA

Beyond the caves, near the town of Tenancingo is the remote village of Chalma. In 1553, Spanish priests discovered a life-sized crucifix, now called "Our Lord of Chalma," in a cave filled with flowers. Ironically, the cave had been the home of an Indian god represented by a stone idol. The idol had disappeared. The appearance of the crucifix in this holy cave gave rise to mass conversions among the Indians. They still revere the spot and thousands come to worship "El Señor" throughout the year.

TENANCINGO

There are several liqueur factories in Tenancingo. A large variety of fruit-flavored liqueurs are made and sold in the *tiendas* and roadside stands through the area.

MALINALCO

Malinalco is one of several archaeological sites in Mexico that have not been fully investigated. Located eight miles east of Tenancingo, the ruins are on the hillside with some of them in caves, an unusual characteristic more often found in South America.

METEPEC

The last village on Hwy. 55 before you reach Toluca is Metepec, a small community famed for its pottery, notably the colorful Trees of Life. As you drive into town, the children will offer to take you to the *tallers* where you can watch artisans at work before you buy.

AROUND TAXCO

VITAL STATISTICS

Official name. Taxco de Alarcón.
Climate. Springlike weather year-round; cool winter nights.
Population. 60,000, but the town doesn't look this big.
Altitude. 5,500 feet.
State. Guerrero.
City phone code. 732.

HOTELS

Hacienda del Solar, Apartado Postal 97 (2-13-00). An exquisite, small resort covering 80 acres. Horseback riding, tennis, pool, and the restaurant La Ventana de Taxco. Located south of the city, off Hwy. 95. A. Cr.

Holiday Inn, off Hwy. 95, northern edge of city (2-13-00). The view is the selling point at this hotel perched above the city on a hillside. Colonial-style decor. Pool, golf. A. Cr.

Hotel de la Borda, Pedregal 2 (2-00-25). Located on the main highway (Hwy. 95) north of the city. Popular with tour groups. A large but comfortable hotel built around an old mineshaft. A. Cr.

Los Arcos, Juan Ruíz de Alarcón 2 (2-18-36). An attractive new hotel recently opened in a colonial mansion down the hill from the square. The pleasant owner speaks perfect English, and the kitchen is extremely clean and well equipped. C. Cr.

Meléndez, Cuauhtémoc 4 (2-00-06). One of the best bargains in Mexico. In the heart of the city, one block from the main square and overlooking the marketplace. Rooms have great views and aging colonial decor. Good breakfast and lunch served. The water heater sometimes falls down on the job. D. Cr.

Posada de la Misión, on Hwy. 95, northern edge of city (2-00-63). A colonial posada with wooden shutters on the windows and geranium-laden balconies. Get your reservations in writing; guests have been bumped here to make room for tours. The pool is decorated with a mosaic by muralist Juan O'Gorman. Good restaurant with a view. B. Cr.

Santa Prisca, Plazuela San Juan (2-00-80). A perennial favorite, this peaceful spot in the heart of the city has two courtyards with fountains and colonial decor. C. Cr.

RESTAURANTS

Cielito Lindo, Plaza Borda (2-06-03). This small, delightful restaurant on the main square features Mexican and international dishes. Moderate. Cr.

La Ventana de Taxco, off Hwy. 95, south of the city (2-13-00). Gourmet restaurant with a magnificent view of Taxco. Popular with *capitalinos,* who drive here for dinner. Italian and Mexican specialties. Reservations required. Expensive. Cr.

Los Balcones, up from the Plaza Borda (2-06-80). Follow the signs beginning behind Paco's bar at the plaza. Mexican dishes served in a colonial-style dining room. Try for one of the tables near an open window overlooking the town. Moderate. Cr.

NIGHTLIFE

Bar Bacanal, Hotel de la Borda, Hwy. 95, northern entrance to city (2-00-25). This popular spot features cockfights and flamenco dancing (in winter season) in the colonial-style bar. Moderate. Cr.

Berta's, Plaza Borda. Another local favorite and home of the Berta, a rum drink that hits the spot around siesta time. Try for a balcony seat. Located on the main square, practically in the churchyard. Moderate. Cr.

Cantarranas, Hwy. 95, northern entrance to city. A tourist spot. This sixteenth-century hacienda features several rooms, each with its own kind of folkloric entertainment. You move — the entertainers stay put. Moderate. Cr.

Paco's, Plaza Borda. One of those traditional hangouts for gringo and native alike. Spend an afternoon drinking margaritas and watching minibuses unload tourists up from Acapulco for the day-trip specials. Or toast the local cops as they take an afternoon break in the bar. Open-air, overlooking the square. Moderate. Cr.

SHOPPING

Market, off Plaza Borda. Taxco's market is located along a series of winding streets that lead down from the main plaza. Busy, especially in the early morning. Good place to find pots, flowers, leather, and household goods. Don't buy silver here.

Silver shops, throughout the city. The primary tourist attraction in Taxco. Many of the shopkeepers allow visitors to tour their workshops. Be sure to examine each piece for silver markings before you buy.

POINTS OF INTEREST

Casa Figueroa, Plaza Borda. Located at the west side of the zócalo, this colonial mansion was purchased in 1943 for Mexican artist Fidel Figueroa. It is now a gallery and private museum. Constructed in the eighteenth century for the Count of Cadena, it is also called "the House of Tears," in reference to the forced Indian labor that built it.

Church of San Sebastián and Santa Prisca, Plaza Borda. One of the most famous churches in all Mexico. The church, completed in the eighteenth century, is a mixture of Churrigueresque and other baroque styles. Commissioned by José de la Borda, a Frenchman who made millions in the silver mines. The church contains several paintings by Miguel Cabrera.

Walking tours. Practically any walking tour you take in the town will bring you face to face with charming colonial homes, plazas, and churches. Just remember which way you came.

MUSEUMS

Spratling Museum, behind Santa Prisca Church, Plaza Borda. One of the best small museums in Mexico. The excellent collection of Indian art and artifacts assembled by American William Spratling is on display here. Tuesday through Sunday 10–2 and 3–6.

FIESTAS

Holy Week, beginning Palm Sunday. One of the most colorful and religiously significant Holy Week celebrations in the hemisphere. Each day the drama of Holy Week is acted out by a large cast of characters. The drama has its roots both in the Spanish experience and the Indian past.

Silver Festival, late November, early December. This arts festival is a fairly new addition to the Taxco calendar. International artists and performers are invited to participate in plays, concerts, exhibits, and celebrations. Check with your travel agent or the nearest tourist office for actual dates and program.

TRANSPORTATION

Automobiles. Taxco's narrow streets are not navigable by large cars or motor homes.

Buses. First-class bus service from Mexico City, Cuernavaca, and Acapulco.

Taxis. Most residents use the minibuses that operate up and down the steep streets. The buses are called *burros* or *burritos* and the fares are minimal.

TOURIST SERVICES

Tourist Office (Subdelegación Federal de Turismo), Av. John F. Kennedy 28 (2-15-25).

PUEBLA

Just 80 miles from Mexico City, on a plain surrounded by snow-capped volcanoes, lies the city of Puebla de los Angeles. Legend holds that the site was revealed to the Bishop of Tlaxcala in a dream. He saw two angels building a city on a high plain where flowers and trees grew. On the horizon were two volcanoes. When he awoke from his dream, the bishop set off on a journey to find the site.

Nowadays, the city might be called Puebla de los Volkswagens, since the VW plant has brought prosperity and modernization to the colonial settlement. But Puebla still remains a welcome respite from the rush and bustle of the capital. And by staying in nearby Cholula and venturing into Puebla to explore her museums, churches, and back streets, the visitor can savor the unhurried pace of provincial life in Mexico.

There are two roads to Puebla from the capital — one a toll road, a four-lane highway over the mountains; the other slower and toll free. However, both climb to 10,000 feet to cross the circle of mountains surrounding the capital. Once free of the pollution and noise of the city, motorists pull over on the frequent *miradors* ("lookouts") to breathe the cold mountain air and catch glimpses of the snowcapped volcanoes, Mount Popocatépetl and Mount Iztaccihuatl. The toll road leads into Puebla, but if you're headed for Cholula and one of the best hotels in the area, the Club Med Villa Arqueologica, take the San Martin Texmehuacan exit and drive southeast through rich farmland. Along the road are fruit stands where you can buy pears and apples. In the little town of Huejotzingo, pull over and buy some of the local fermented cider; it's sweet and potent. Just a few miles beyond Huejotzingo is Cholula, one of the special towns of Mexico.

Cholula was the most holy city in pre-Columbian times; Cortés reported the city's walls were red with the blood of sacrificial victims. It was to Cholula that Quetzalcoatl fled when he was driven from Tula. To the east lie Mount Popocatépetl and Mount Iztaccihuatl. According to legend the latter is a maiden who grieved for a lover she believed had been killed in battle. She died of her grief. Her lover, however, returned and vowed to stand guard over her until he died. He is symbolized by Mount Popocatépetl.

When Cortés arrived here, the city was flourishing. Fearing he would be attacked by the local population (his mistress, La Malinche, fed his fears), he massacred the Indians before they could attack him. The priests, as if to conquer by symbol, constructed dozens of churches in the area, the largest atop the Tepanapa pyramid. But the Spaniards chose to build their city on the site found by the Bishop of Tlaxcala; some have suggested the spirits of the ancients were too strong in Cholula. One of the most beautiful places to stay in Mexico, the Villa Arqueologica is located in the middle of the village, surrounded by cornfields and immediately facing the Tepanapa pyramid. The plain is dotted with mounds, presumably pyramids and temples buried under the dirt. The city of Puebla is only five miles away on a fast, four-lane highway.

Puebla was founded by the Spaniards shortly after the conquest, and it served as a way station on the road to Veracruz. It was settled by Spanish colonists from Talavera, a town famous for its glazed ceramics, and Puebla soon became equally well known for its Talavera ware. The richly colored, sturdy ceramic tile and dishes can be purchased at several factories in Puebla and shipped to the United States. (The factories are located north of the market. See city listings at the end of the chapter.)

Puebla is well known for *mole poblano*, a national dish usually served at fiesta time. The dish was created, according to legend, by the nuns at the Convent of Santa Rosa. They combined chiles, spices, tortillas, and chocolate to make the rich sauce in honor of a visiting bishop. Most of the restaurants in Puebla serve the local specialty over beef tips or turkey.

Puebla is a modern city where colonial architecture blends with modern drugstores and automobile showrooms. It's an affluent city, founded by Spanish settlers who, like the Puritans of New England, brought with them the work ethic and deep religious beliefs. (Most of the first Spaniards to arrive in Mexico were of aristocratic stock, more concerned with finding vast wealth than in settling the new land.) But behind the modern facade is a colonial city where the market, Mercado Victoria, rambles through a maze of city streets in typical fashion. The market is located east of the zócalo between Avenidas 4 to 10 Poniente and Calle 5 Norte to Cinco de Mayo. The best way to find your way around the market is with a pocket compass. Every turn reveals a new maze of stalls and shops. One area features cooking utensils, including the large clay *mole* pots that are used throughout the city. They are fragile and beautiful and make good mementos of a visit to the city of angels. A large *mole* pot will cost less than fifteen dollars. Baskets, candles (look for the large ecclesiastical kind), kitchenware, and hats are all good buys. You can spend an afternoon wandering around the huge market; if it's late summer, buy a kilo of walnuts from the vendors.

Walnuts are an essential ingredient in another of Puebla's contributions to the Mexican culinary scene—*chiles en nogada*. Mild, green chiles are stuffed, then capped with a sauce made from pomegranate seeds, cheese, and ground walnuts. The dish is supposed to symbolize the red, green, and white Mexican flag.

Puebla has always played a major role in shaping the culture of Mexico. The traditional dress associated with Mexican women is based on a costume created, ironically, by a Chinese girl who lived in Puebla. As a child, she was sold into slavery then freed and adopted by a leading citizen of Puebla who raised her as his daughter. She dressed in a peasant blouse and embroidered skirt and worked among the poor. The costume has become known as the *china poblana* dress.

The city is well known for the role it played in the war against the French who invaded Mexico in 1862. Texas-born soldier General Ignacio Zaragoza beat back the French superior forces at Puebla on May 5, 1862. The French went on to win other battles as part of the campaign to put Emperor Maximilian on the throne, but they were finally defeated and expelled from Mexico in 1867. Cinco de Mayo is celebrated throughout Mexico as one of two independence days. The site of the battle, the Forts of Loreto and Guadalupe, is northeast of the zócalo and is open to the public.

Although many of the city's restaurants, businesses, and bars lie along Avenida Juárez in a new section of the city, the zócalo is still the

225

heart of Puebla. There you will find the Cathedral of the Immaculate Conception, a tile-domed church with a beautiful altar made from the local onyx. (Several blocks south of the zócalo, at Calle 8 Norte and Avenida 2 Oriente, is a so-called artists' barrio where touristy crafts, including onyx ware, are sold.) The zócalo is ringed by government buildings and hotels. One of the best places to try *mole poblano* is the café at the Hotel del Portal on the east side of the zócalo.

Begin your tour of Puebla at the Casa del Alfeñique, the home of Puebla's regional museum. The displays will give you an overview of *poblano* history. The Museo Bello is aptly named; its exhibits include many fine examples of wrought-iron work, furniture, and silver and gold jewelry and plate from colonial times. If you are a librarian or an avid bookworm, visit the Palafox Library. Built in 1646, the library houses 50,000 volumes, numerous colonial maps, and the Nuremburg Chronicle, published in 1493. The reading room is a magnificent example of colonial interior decoration and suggests a library in a Spanish palace. The bookshelves are made from carved cedar, the floor is tiled, and the reading tables are made out of local onyx.

Enthusiasts of sacred art and architecture will enjoy Puebla. There are many examples here of the best and most lavish church styles in Mexico. Puebla, given its Spanish origins, was a deeply religious community and has been loyal to the Church throughout Mexico's stormy ecclesiastical history. The interior of the Church of Santo Domingo is covered with gold leaf, and the church's Virgen del Rosario is adorned with precious gems. The church is located on Cinco de Mayo between Avenidas 4 Poniente and 6 Poniente. The Convent of Santa Rosa, home of the *mole poblano* originators and the largest convent in Puebla, has been restored and is now a museum. The kitchen is a restaurant and bar where you can sample the local specialty. The nuns at the Convent of Santa Mónica went underground in 1857 when Juárez dissolved the monasteries. For 75 years, they continued to operate their convent by hiding in secret rooms and using underground passages. In 1934, they were discovered. Now the convent is a museum. It is located at Av. 18 Pte. 103.

Perhaps one of the most unusual attractions in Puebla, from the point of view of the tourist who expects cobbled streets, burros, and sombreros in Mexico, is the African Preserve, a Mexican Lion Country Safari. The 15,000-acre park has lions, tigers, elephants, rhinos, and all the other exotica found at most zoos. The animals roam the range with the volcanoes as a backdrop. The park is located ten miles from downtown Puebla—there's an admission charge.

Even if you don't take our advice and stay in Cholula, be sure to visit the archaeological site. Tepanapa, the central pyramid, is among the largest in the world. Riddled with a maze of tunnels, the pyramid is not for the claustrophobic. Around the second weekend in July, the villagers celebrate the return of the Virgin to the church atop the pyramid following several months of visits by her to local churches in Cholula.

There are several special fiestas worth attending in the Puebla area. Huejotzingo, the apple cider town near Cholula, celebrates Carnival with a spectacular reenactment of the battles between the Moors and the Spaniards. Of course, Cinco de Mayo merits a big fiesta in Puebla where a mock battle is fought in honor of the Mexican victory.

The climate in Puebla is warm in the summertime, with temperatures in the 80s, and mild in winter, average temperatures in the 60s. It's chilly at night year-round, owing to the altitude.

BOCADITOS

You will need a map to find your way around Puebla. Free maps are available at the Tourist Office, Av. 5 Ote. No. 3, on the west side of the zócalo. Puebla is divided into four sections with the streets numbered and named according to the compass points; however, it's not as simple as it sounds. Streets running north-south are called *calles*; streets running east-west are *avenidas*. Calle Cinco de Mayo is the main north-south street; Avenida de la Reforma is the main east-west street, except after it crosses Calle Cinco de Mayo, its name changes to Avenida General Maximino Avila Comacho.

Take a breath. Everything north of the Reforma is even-numbered — everything south is odd-numbered. And when Calle Cinco de Mayo crosses the Reforma, it becomes Calle 16 de Septiembre.

Take another breath. All streets east of Cinco de Mayo/16 de Septiembre are labeled *Oriente*; all streets west are *Poniente*. All streets south of the Reforma/Avila Comacho are labeled *Sur*; all streets north labelled *Norte*.

Get a map and sit in one of the cafés, have a couple of beers, and figure it out. Always keep your map with you in Puebla.

If you drive into town, park your car in one of the parking garages marked with a large "Estacionmente" or "E" sign downtown. Traffic is congested along the narrow streets, and perhaps because Puebla is a prosperous town, there are a great number of cars on the road.

There's a branch of Sanborn's drugstores at Av. 2 Ote. No. 66 (that's right behind the zócalo), and you can find the usual good selection of drugstore items Sanborn's offers in its other stores. There's also a quiet bar with friendly service. Each afternoon there are free munchies, following the Spanish tradition of serving *tapas* in bars in the late afternoon and early evening.

A good day trip from Puebla is a visit to the spa town of Tehuacán, home of Penafiel mineral water. We've featured a special section on Mexico's spas in the chapter **The Unique and the Random**.

AROUND PUEBLA

VITAL STATISTICS

Official name. Puebla de Zaragoza (in honor of Texan Ignacio Zaragoza, native of Goliad, who was victorious over the French at the Battle of Puebla, May 5, 1862).

Climate. Springlike year-round; chilly nights. Occasional afternoon rain showers.

Population. 900,000.

Altitude. 7,000 feet.

State. Puebla.

City phone code. 22.

HOTELS

El Mesón del Angel, Hermanas Serdan 807 (8-21-00). Luxury hotel set in beautiful grounds on the outskirts of the city. Some rooms have a view of the snowcapped volcanoes. A. Cr.

Hotel del Portal, Maximino Avila Camacho 205 (6-02-11). A colonial-style hotel located in the heart of the city. Parking garage. B. Cr.

Hotel Lastra, Calzada de los Fuertes (2-46-30). Luxury hotel located northeast of the main plaza near the Forts of Loreto and Guadalupe. The hotel's roof garden offers a fine view of the volcanoes. A. Cr.

Hotel Royalty, Av. Portal Hidalgo 8 (2-47-40). An old hotel, bustling with activity. Colonial-style mixed with fifties furniture. B. Cr.

Villa Arqueologica, Cholula (7-19-66 or 1-800-528-3100). One of Club Med's exquisite hacienda-style hotels located at the foot of the Great Pyramid in nearby Cholula. Great views of Cholula's churches and the volcanoes. Excellent French restaurant. Library, small boutique. A. Cr.

RESTAURANTS

Chao Chao, Juárez and Blvd. Atlixo (6-36-24). A cozy Italian restaurant with checkered cloths on the tables and wine bottles on the walls. Moderate. Cr.

Charlie's China Poblano, Juárez 1918 (6-31-84). Another Carlos Anderson production, but you won't find *mole poblano*, the famous local dish, on the menu here. Steak, seafood. Moderate. Cr.

D'Armandos, Juárez 2104 (1-81-61). There's a substantial Italian population in Puebla, hence the proliferation of Italian restaurants. This one serves what has to be the world's largest *osso bucco* on record — delicious. Moderate. Cr.

Hostería de los Angeles, outside the Hotel Royalty on the main plaza.

Good place to try local specialties — *mole poblano, chiles en nogada* (in season). Moderate. Cr.

Villa Arqueologica, 2 Pte. 501, Cholula (7-15-08). Folks come out from the city to sample the French chef's specialties. The waiters are charming and extremely attentive. Expensive. Cr.

NIGHTLIFE

Nightlife is limited to a few student discos near the university, sidewalk cafés, and the mariachis in Plaza de Santa Inés, 11 Pte. and 3 Sur.

SHOPPING

Barrio de las Artistas, Calle 8 Nte., between Avs. 2 and 6 Ote. A mixed bag of handicrafts. Better buys can be found in the market.

Delikatessen, Calle 3 Sur 4118-B at 43 Pte. (0-16-34). A good place to stock up on cheese, sausages, imported foods, and liquors.

Market Victoria, 4–8 Pte. on Calle 3 Nte. Puebla's market stretches for several blocks and offers a multitude of good buys in pottery (huge *cazuelas* and ollas used for cooking *mole*), candles, linens, herbs, toys. Market day is Sunday.

Plazuela de los Sapos, Av. 5 and 7 Ote. Antique shop.

Sanborn's, 2 Ote. 66 (2-94-16). Popular chain drugstore with good selection of books, maps, US magazines. Small, friendly bar that serves *tapas* ("munchies") in Spanish tradition each afternoon.

Tile shops. There are three shops specializing in the famed Talavera tile, and they can be hard to find. (A good map and patience are essential in finding your way around Puebla, which has the world's most complicated street numbering system). La Purísma is located at 4 Pte. 723; La Concepción at 4 Pte. 923; and Cerámica Uriate at 4 Pte. 911.

POINTS OF INTEREST

Africam, Calle Valesquillo. This is Mexico's answer to Lion Country Safari. You can drive through or pick up one of the zebra-striped buses in the zócalo. Open daily. Admission charge.

Cathedral, zócalo. Dedicated to the Immaculate Conception. Begun in 1575 and completed in 1649. The north doorway shows four Spanish Hapsburg kings. The dome is tiled with *azulejos* — brilliant Talavera tiles.

Church of San Francisco, south end of the Paseo de San Francisco. Founded in 1535, completed in 1665. The altar covers the remains of Sebastián de Aparico who was the first road builder in the New World (not counting the Mayan road builders). Sebastián later joined the Order of St. Francis.

Church of Santo Domingo, Cinco de Mayo between Avs. 4 and 6 Pte. One of the best examples of Mexican baroque architecture with its extensive use of tiles and gold leaf.

Cholula, eight miles west of the city. Once one of the most important religious centers in Mesoamerica. Now home to 365 churches, according to legend. Cortés was being entertained here when he was told by La Malinche that the Indians planned to kill him and his men. In turn, he killed 6,000, and the Spaniards embarked on a period of destruction of the great pyramids and temples here. The Church of Nuestra Señora de los Remedios now stands atop what was once the largest (by volume) pyramid in the New World. Many of the surrounding grass-covered mounds are temples that have never been excavated. A beautiful village set on a church-covered plain with the volcanoes Popocatépetl and Iztaccihuatl on the horizon. The pyramid is riddled with tunnels, and visitors may walk through for a small fee. The adjacent ruins have been rebuilt. Unfortunately, the rebuilding is too obvious and the reconstruction lacks beauty. Open daily.

Forts of Loreto and Guadalupe, two miles northeast of the zócalo. The forts stand on the famous battlefield where General Ignacio Zaragoza led his ill-equipped army against the French on May 5, 1862 — one of the great victories in Mexican history. Good view of the city from this vantage point. Small admission fee.

Huejotzingo, ten miles northwest of the city on Hwy. 190. This village is famed for its serapes and apples. There's a popular apple festival from September 23 to October 1 every year.

MUSEUMS

Bello Museum, Av. 3 Pte. 302. An exquisite museum filled with colonial furniture, silverware, and ironwork. Open daily 10-5. Small admission fee.

Biblioteca Palafoxiana (Palafox Library), Av. 5 Ote. 5, south of the cathedral. Founded by Bishop Juan de Palafox y Mendoza in 1646, this library now contains a priceless collection of incunabulae (books printed before 1501). The second floor should be visited — here are cedar shelves, onyx reading tables, and glass flasks filled with water that serve as fire extinguishers. A bibliophile's dream. Open daily.

Convent of Santa Mónica, Av. 18 Pte. 103 at Cinco de Mayo. This was a secret convent during the years that the Church suffered at the hands of the Reformers. The convent is preserved much as it was throughout the centuries. Open Sunday through Friday 10-4, Saturday 10-2. Small admission fee.

Convent of Santa Rosa (museum of folk art), Calle 3 Nte. at Av. 12 Pte. Folk art on exhibit and for sale. The convent kitchen, the legendary home of *mole poblano*, is on view. Open daily.

Museo Regional de Puebla, Av. 4 Ote. and Calle 6 Nte. Known throughout the region as "Casa del Alfeñique" — almond cake house — this old mansion now houses various colonial exhibits. Open daily 10-1, 3-5. Closed Saturday and Sunday.

FIESTAS

Carnival, Huejotzingo, ten miles northwest of Puebla. Famous mock battles are held here every year and Moors fight Spaniards in battles similar to those staged in Spain.

Cinco de Mayo. Naturally a major celebration in the city where the independence battle took place.

Fiestas de Nuestra Señora de los Remedios, September 8, Cholula. A typical village fiesta celebrating the return of the Virgin to the church atop the pyramid after her tour of the neighborhood churches.

TRANSPORTATION

Buses. First-class bus service from the capital.

Car rental. Hertz operates through two agencies in Puebla — Renta Autos de Puebla S.A. at 4 Pte. 2910 (48-43-45) and Viajes H. R., 25 Ote. and 14 Sur (40-31-77) and Av. Juárez 2713 (48-58-88).

Taxis. Reasonable. Check rate before you get in.

Trains. Daily train service from the capital and Veracruz. (For general information about train service in Mexico, see the chapter **There and Back Again** or check at the local tourist office listed below.)

TOURIST SERVICES

Tourist Office (Delegación Federal de Turismo), Av. 5 Ote. 3, Puebla (6-09-28).

Tourist Office (Subdelegación Federal de Turismo), Av. Morelos and 8 Nte., Cholula (7-00-56).

COMMUNICATIONS

Post Office, Calle 16 de Septiembre and Calle 5 Ote.

9

THE ASTONISHING COASTLINES
MEXICO AT LEISURE

Surely, the most hedonistic of modern man's pleasures is sunbathing; like geese flocking south, we follow the sun, determined to toast ourselves in an orgy of sun worship our great-grandmothers would have deplored. In Mexico, the sun rises above the azure waters of the Caribbean in full view of that narrow spit of white sand called Cancún Island and sets in a blaze of orange glory beyond the golden sands of the Pacific beaches. Here it is possible to wallow in sunshine; dive into the warm, clear turquoise waters of the Mexican Caribbean; sunbathe on the cool, fine, white limestone sands of the Yucatán peninsula; and while away the sunset in a hammock on a lonely Pacific beach, the surf roaring as you sip a coco loco. Turn your head and there's a lagoon fringed by palm trees, their yellow-edged leaves standing out against the lush deep green of the Sierra Madre foothills. To the west lies Hawaii; to the east, the Caribbean Islands. Beyond the sunset lies a tomorrow filled with sunlight and cool water, trade winds, and coconut palms — you're in a latitude where indolence is the order of the day.

Mexico has approximately 6,320 miles of shoreline, much of it taken up by magnificent beaches. Her oceans are filled with a variety of wildlife, which attracts sportsmen and nature lovers. And all this belongs to the people. Unlike in the United States, no one may close a beach or forbid access; no one, that is, except the government, and then only for national defense purposes. It is still possible in Mexico to find a cove or stretch of sandbar that is undeveloped, uninhabited, and yours for an hour or a day.

Mexico's Gulf Coast is much like the Texas Gulf Coast, not noted for its beaches. While there are some coastal towns and cities worth visiting, notably Veracruz, there are more beautiful beaches in other parts of the country, particularly along the Yucatán peninsula and the Pacific Coast. The beach lover has a variety to choose from, including well-known tourist spots like Acapulco and Cancún, resorts, game-fishing ports, and retreats where there's nothing to do but swing in a hammock and listen to the surf. Generally, the Mexican Caribbean on the east coast of the Yucatán peninsula, called *La Costa Turquesa* ("the Turquoise Coast") by Mexican promoters, is for water sports enthusiasts. (The Yucatán, owing to its proximity by air to Texas, is a popular weekend getaway spot.) The level of development and human intrusion differs along the peninsula from the plush, highly developed man-made surroundings in Cancún to the remote, back-to-basics facilities on Isla Mujeres. The Pacific coast offers a variety of beach experiences —hideaways, tourist-packed cities, and chic resorts. The Pacific coast is the more developed of the two areas; however, there are still a great number of quiet, remote beaches along the Pacific. If you like nightlife with your sun holiday, the Pacific coast cities and towns have a greater variety to offer.

In order to help you choose the right beach, we have divided this chapter into Hot Spots, Resorts, and Hideaways, and we have included *bocaditos* — tidbits — in each section.

HOT SPOTS

What is a Hot Spot? Acapulco, Puerto Vallarta ("PV" to the initiated), Ixtapa, Cancún . . . in other words, those coastal cities and towns that everyone has heard about, including every travel agent north of the Red River. Some of Mexico's best hotels, restaurants, recreational facilities, and even beaches can be found in the most popular hot spots. In addition, hot spots are convenient for the traveler who doesn't want to rent a car or for someone who plans just a few days in the sun after a week of shopping or pyramid climbing. Also, they are accessible for three- or four-day holidays; many airlines have direct daily flights to the major resorts, and they feature special hotel package deals. Each hot spot has its own ambience, and each attracts a different crowd. The key to having a good time in a hot spot is to pick the right hotel. *Bocaditos* features some favorites; for a more detailed selection see the individual city listings.

VERACRUZ

Known as "Mexico's Sweetheart," Veracruz should probably be re-named "Mexico's Dowager Sweetheart," but that doesn't mean that this charming city is past her prime. Never really a Hot Spot in the same sense as Acapulco or Puerto Vallarta, Veracruz owes her place in this section to her standing as a bustling port city that draws visitors with popular beaches and some of the world's best seafood. Veracruz is at once a charming, colonial city—the oldest city in the Americas—and a city that moves to the marimba beat.

Many of the city's old colonial buildings remain, among them some charming hotels, yet the city is growing fast. Nearby oil fields send their oil through her port, the largest in Mexico. As a port city, Veracruz has a cosmopolitan air, and many nationalities have left their mark here. Pirates roamed the nearby Gulf waters, US Marines landed on her shores, and immigrants settled in the city. The first to arrive was Hernán Cortés who founded the settlement and named it La Villa Rica de la Vera Cruz—the Rich City of the True Cross. (Cortés's first settlement was some 16 miles north of the present city, and visitors can tour the village, now called La Antigua. Mass is held daily in the small church, supposedly the first in America.)

Veracruz served as a vital link to the Old World throughout the years of the viceroyalty. The Black Ships, which brought wealth from the East, landed at Acapulco. From there the treasure was hauled cross-country to Veracruz to be sent on to Spain. This treasure route made Veracruz a target for pirates, and Sir Francis Drake, among others, waylaid a galleon or two in the waters off Veracruz. Today, petroleum products, coffee, sugar, tobacco, cotton, and the rich harvest of fruits and vegetables grown in the nearby lush farmlands find their way to the port. Machinery, chemicals, paper, consumer goods, and drilling equipment are unloaded at the port. The ancient fortress of San Juan de Ulúa, which guards the entrance to the port, is a familiar sight to sailors from all over the world.

Soldiers throughout the centuries have passed through the port under the shadow of the fortress. The US Marines landed in 1847 and in 1914—the second landing was an effort to confiscate an arms shipment that culminated in another one of those unfortunate episodes that have marked the history of the two neighbors, Mexico and the United States. The port was also invaded by the French in 1862 as Napoleon III attempted to foist Maximilian, the Austrian archduke, onto the Mexican people.

Now most of the visitors to Veracruz come more peaceably in search of business deals. Tourists are not a common sight, which for some adds to its charm. But Veracruz is only a day's drive or a short flight from the capital, and the city makes an excellent base for exploring the archaeological sites in the area. It is also a quintessential Mexican city described by its own citizens as "the only beautiful city in Mexico," a false saying but indicative of the pride inhabitants take in their city. It is a private city that strives to maintain its Mexican character in spite of booming business. Although most of the foreign visitors are businessmen and sailors, many Mexicans bring their children to Veracruz to see the historical sights.

There are better beaches in other parts of Mexico, but some of the best sidewalk cafés and seafood can be found around the main plaza. The siesta, which is kept with a religious insistence and no doubt out of necessity in the humid summer afternoons, is marked by the beat of the marimba bands that play in the plaza. Brought into port in the days of the Spanish masters were slaves, and the African influence can be heard in the distinctive music of the marimba bands. The music reaches a crescendo during Carnival, the pre-Lenten festival celebrated with a fervor in Veracruz. Many glasses of the local cocktail, called "Torito" and made from peanut butter, pure cane alcohol, and cream, are raised during Carnival. Reservations are necessary well in advance of the fiesta, which begins one week before Ash Wednesday.

The charm of Veracruz is her indolent, tropical atmosphere, combined with the sense of adventure that being a port city offers. Some of the landmarks have faded and fallen into disrepair, but the city has a charm not found in the new, government-planned resorts.

AROUND VERACRUZ

VITAL STATISTICS

Climate. Hot in the summer; sometimes very humid. Warm winters, except for the occasional *nortes* that bring cold weather from the north. Hurricane zone.

Population. 500,000.

Altitude. Sea level.

State. Veracruz.

City phone code. 293.

HOTELS

Colonial Hotel, Plaza de Armas, Miguel Lerdo 117 (2-01-93). This colonial-style hotel is an old favorite of businessmen and tourists alike. Parking garage. C. Cr.

Gran Hotel Diligencias, Plaza de Armas (2-01-80). A grande dame. Built in the last century on the site of an old inn erected by Cortés's men when they first settled here. Most of the rooms have balconies overlooking the square. C. Cr.

RESTAURANTS

Café Parroquia, Calle Independencia just off the Plaza de Armas, across from La Parroquia, the parish church. This is the business hub of Veracruz. A must stop for every businessman or politician of note if he wants to know what is going on in the city. A great people-watching café.

Prendes, northeast corner of the Plaza de Armas (2-01-53). Some of the freshest seafood in the world is served here. Clients inspect the fish at the table, and Veracruzanos know what fresh seafood is. Very popular with local businessmen. Is there a better way to do business than in a sidewalk café over fresh snapper? Moderate. Cr.

NIGHTLIFE

Nightlife in Veracruz moves to a marimba beat. The bands begin to play in the cafés around the Plaza de Armas at sunset and the beat goes on. . . .

SHOPPING

Market, southwest of Parque Zamora on Av. Hernán Cortés. Veracruz is a large seaport and sailors from around the world come to the market curanderos and brujas (folkhealers, and witches) for cures, potions, and hexes. Of course, there are more mundane things for sale, including kitchenware, vanilla from Papantla, large ollas for cooking fish soups, fruits and vegetables, blankets, and dresses.

POINTS OF INTEREST

Beaches. Two of the most popular beaches are Playa Villa del Mar south of the city, with the nearby villages of Mandingo and Macambo, and Isla de los Sacrificios, named so because the Spaniards supposedly witnessed sacrifices here. Boat trips from the pier to the island are available.

Castillo de San Juan de Ulúa. This fort was built in 1528 and is accessible by boat or by a roundabout northern road.

Church of Santo Cristo del Buen Viaje, seven blocks southeast of the main plaza. Supposedly the oldest Christian church in the New World.

La Antigua, 16 miles north of Veracruz on the coast. Cortés landed here in 1519 and later moved his headquarters to Veracruz. The village is filled with memorials to the conquistador, including one that marks a tree where he was supposed to have tied his horse.

Zempoala, 22 miles north of Veracruz on Hwy. 180. This is the last capital of the Totonacs, the Indians who befriended Cortés when he landed. There's a small museum at the site. One of the more significant remains is the Temple of the Thirteen Steps. Small admission fee.

MUSEUMS

Museo de Arte y Historia Veracruzano, Calle Zaragoza 397. This small museum houses an excellent collection of Olmec, Huastec, and Totonac artifacts. Open daily.

SPORTS

Sailing. The Galveston Bay Cruising Association sponsors the Regatta de los Amigos every two years in June.

Scuba diving. The wrecks of ships, old and new, that cover the harbor bed provide excellent scuba diving opportunities. Check at the pier for scuba rentals and information.

FIESTAS

Carnival, week before Lent. Veracruzanos take to the streets for a week of fireworks and dancing, parades and celebrations.

TRANSPORTATION

Airport. National carriers serve Veracruz.

Buses. First-class bus service from the capital and other neighboring cities.

Car rental. Agencies include Avis — at the international airport (no phone), Collado 241 (2-98-34), and Hotel Veracruz (2-25-16); Hertz (operating as Renta de Carros Veracruz S.A.) — at Simón Bolívar 645 (3-55-54) and at the international airport (2-62-64); National — at Díaz Mirón 1036 (4-41-22) and at the Hotel Exelaris Hyatt in Boca del Río (5-21-00).

Trains. There's daily train service from Mexico City. (For general information about train service in Mexico, see the chapter **There and Back Again** or check at the local tourist office listed below.)

TOURIST SERVICES

Tourist Office (Subdelegación Federal de Turismo), Palacio Municipal (downstairs) (2-16-13).

CANCUN

To some Texans it's known as "Can-coon," while to the writers of promotional copy, it's Can-Cún, which in Mayan, they tell us, means "gold at the end of the rainbow." A gold mine it is; this tourist development project has been a huge success. Begun in the early 1970s by the Mexican government and the Interamerican Development Bank, Cancún now rivals Acapulco in attracting tourist dollars.

Once, a narrow, uninhabited island off the coast of the jungle-covered Yucatán peninsula, now a burgeoning, hotel-studded resort community, Cancún is for those who want to get away from it all and yet not miss their frozen margaritas, golf carts, *hamburguesas*, and afternoon tennis. The hotels are modern and, with few exceptions, expensive by Mexican standards (there are a couple of bargain hotels in nearby Cancún City), and the resort has modern transportation facilities. A new international airport serves the area; most hotels provide minibuses from the airport to the island; and there are free, public buses patrolling the island's main boulevard, which leads into Cancún City. To visit outlying spots, you can rent a car or join a tour. On the island, you can rent a motor scooter for neighborhood jaunts.

Cancún is a popular spot with a variety of people — conventioneers, cosmic cowboys, Houston and Dallas highrollers, preppies, and even world leaders. (Ronald Reagan stayed at the Sheraton during the Cancún summit in 1981.) The main attraction is the beach. The Yucatán peninsula is a limestone ledge that juts out into the Gulf of Mexico on one side and the Caribbean on the other. This limestone, when eroded by the ocean, becomes the fine, white sand of the Caribbean beaches. The sand is cool to the touch; however, don't be deceived. The white sand acts as a natural reflector, and you will sunburn easily here. The water is a magnificent deep blue; the shallow areas turquoise and clear. To the south of Cancún and on nearby islands are coral reefs noted for the richness and variety of their wildlife and their beauty. Tours of the reefs can be arranged at your hotel desk or at the island marina. Cancún is a good spot for first-time divers; the currents in the lagoon are not as strong as those in the ocean. The shallow reefs off the bank surrounding the island are home to a variety of colorful fish. Divers will find tour prices steep — about $30 for two short dives — but the facilities are good. More experienced divers usually head for nearby Cozumel. Other water sports available either through the hotels or at local marinas include deep-sea fishing (marlin runs here and a charter will cost about $300 a day for four), waterskiing, parasailing, cruises along the coast, and windsurfing. Always agree on the price before you rent a boat or gear. (Prices subject to change with devaluations.)

The weather in Cancún is usually glorious with daily temperatures in the 80s and 90s and warm nights. The beaches are cooler than is the interior; however, in the winter, an occasional *norte* will blow through, turning the nights chilly. Of course, the peninsula is in the hurricane zone. Cancún is *not* a good place to be during a major storm. The hotels, although supposedly built to withstand violent weather, are on a very narrow strip of land and surrounded by water, and some fear the island would be inundated by high tides if a hurricane blew over the area. It's wise to postpone your trip if a hurricane is threatening the Caribbean. If you are caught unaware while there, leave the peninsula if possible. The Yucatán is flat and there's nothing to stop a hurricane once it sweeps over the area. Even Mérida, the nearest inland city, has been devastated by storms. Fly anywhere, but leave. During the summer hurricane season, an occasional weather system will stall over the area producing several days of gray skies and drizzle, but this is rare.

Although President Reagan took his own drinking water with him, there's no need for you to take such precautions. Follow the tips in the chapter **There and Back Again**, drink plenty of mineral water, and you should have no problems. The biggest cause of stomach disorders among tourists is overeating and drinking, something you will probably be tempted to do on Cancún, where the restaurants feature a profusion of the local seafood as well as Mexican and gringo specialties. Some of the more authentic Yucatecan restaurants are located in Cancún City (see "Around Cancún" below).

Cancún City is not a typical Mayan community. In fact many of the residents come from faraway regions of Mexico. The Mayans, a petite, friendly people can be easily distinguished from the *mestizos* who work in the hotels. The Mayans have high cheekbones, very straight hair, and almond-shaped eyes. Once you are out in the countryside, you will see a great many "typical" Mayan villages where the people live in *palapas*. These oval-shaped huts have been made in much the same manner for hundreds of years. The walls are made from wooden stakes placed close together that allow the breeze to come through the spaces. There are two entrances facing each other, again to allow the breeze to waft through the hut, and the roof is covered with thick thatch. Inside, hammocks are slung from the main posts. Outside there are pens for turkeys and pigs, and in every Mayan village there are dogs that go on hunting expeditions into the jungle with their masters. Most of the Mayans farm *milpas*, small cornfields, just as their ancestors did, first clearing the land and then burning it off in a method anthropologists call "slash and burn." Throughout the countryside you will see stretches of jungle cut down and burned.

The nearest "real" town to Cancún City is Valladolid, on the road to Mérida. If you are going to Cancún for more than a long weekend, it's worthwhile to rent a car and explore the peninsula. Beyond Valladolid is the archaeological site Chichén Itzá, one of the most beautiful and interesting collections of ruins. (See **Mexico of the Ancients.**) If you stay overnight at the site, you will have a chance to explore them before the tour buses arrive in mid-afternoon. The ruins at Tulum, a two-hour drive south of Cancún, are also popular with tour groups.

Renting your own car will give you a chance to explore some of the sites along the way, including Xel-Ha, a popular snorkeling spot. And about 30 miles northwest of Tulum, which is on the coast, are the inland, jungle-covered ruins at Cobá. Cobá merits an overnight stay, if possible. If you do rent a car, always fill up your tank before you leave Cancún, and fill up again at every opportunity—gas stations are few and far between in the Yucatán. If you are heading south along the coastal road (Hwy. 307), fill your tank at Puerto Morelos, a few miles south of Cancún.

There's one small ruin on Cancún Island, at the Sheraton Hotel. Lighted at night with colored lights, it has to rate as one of the tackiest ruins in Mexico. It's also one of the easiest to climb, thanks to the landscaping.

Shopping in Cancún is limited to several boutiques, many of them with beautiful examples of Mexican crafts expensively priced. Popular artist Sergio Bustamante has a gallery at the Cancún Gran Sheraton. (The prices are still considerably lower than those on his works being sold in the United States.) The market in Cancún City is much like a border town market, but if you sort through the curios long enough you can find some good buys. Several vendors sell good quality Oaxacan dresses at reasonable prices. Be sure to bargain. Cancún is a duty-free port; consequently, many vacationing Mexicans shop here for small appliances. They may be bargains for Mexicans, but they're not for US visitors. Don't leave the Yucatán without buying a bottle or two of the famous *chile habanero* sauce, some local honey, and a bottle of Carabanchal, an anisette-type liqueur found in the market and at the airport. Don't buy any tortoiseshell combs or brooches—they will be confiscated by US Customs. (If you are concerned about the plight of the turtle, don't eat turtle meat, which is sold in some restaurants.) Alongside the tortoiseshell combs, you will usually see items made from black coral that are okay to bring back.

BOCADITOS

It's not widely publicized, but the riptides at Cancún are dangerous. Mexico's beaches are very beautiful and the waters inviting, but in those parts of the country where the waters are not protected by reefs or barrier islands, the tides can be killers. The water off Cancún Island looks deceptively calm; however, there have been several drownings. Heed any warning signs. Don't swim alone, and unless you are a strong swimmer, opt for the pool or the lagoon.

Pack lightly—many of the airlines flying into Cancún have very short turnaround times on the ground, sometimes as little as 20 minutes. It's not an uncommon sight in the Cancún airport to see unhappy tourists filling out lost baggage reports. Chances are your baggage isn't really lost—it just didn't make it off the plane. Since the airport is a 45-minute ride from the beaches, it's sometimes difficult or expensive to make an additional trip to retrieve your bags. You won't need a lot of clothes, so try packing a hanging clothes bag and a shoulder bag; or pack one flight bag with essentials and take the risk of having your other clothes go astray.

There are several rental car agencies at the airport. If you haven't made reservations with a familiar agency, ask around before you rent, because many of the companies are highly competitive. It's possible to make a deal for unlimited mileage if you bargain.

Cancún is an ideal place to spend a long weekend or to finish up a vacation of ruin-hopping in the peninsula. You might consider combining your trip to the beach with a few days in Mérida or at Chichén Itzá.

AROUND CANCUN

VITAL STATISTICS

Climate. Tropical year-round. Summer rain showers, usually in late afternoon. Some cool nights in winter. Subject to hurricanes in late summer and early fall. (Evacuation advised if threatened by hurricane.)

Population. 50,000.

Altitude. Sea level.

State. Quintana Roo.

City phone code. 988.

HOTELS

Cancún Gran Sheraton, Cancún Island (3-01-55). Almost equal to the Camino Real in landscaping, but somehow it doesn't work. The small pyramid at the northern end of the grounds is floodlit at night, probably the tackiest treatment of a ruin in all Mexico. Swim-up bar, huge pool, attentive service. The lobby resembles an airport terminal and is often rife with conventions; you are likely to overhear conversations about baby food manufacturing or bug exterminating. The beach is beautiful but be careful of the strong undertow. Mopeds available. A. Cr.

Cancún Viva, Cancún Island (3-00-19). A brand-new addition on the northern edge of the island overlooking Bahía de Mujeres. The beach is lit at night for midnight swims. Jet-Skis available to guests. Tile floors, attentive service, and immaculate rooms. Our host was especially proud of the TVs in every room, but how many people go to Cancún to watch Mexican TV? B. Cr.

Camino Real, Cancún Island (3-01-00). Positively the most lavishly landscaped of all Cancún's hotels has a swim-up bar in the pool and a saltwater lagoon filled with fish. A. Cr.

Club Med, Cancún Island (1-800-528-3100). The famous French hotel group operates a Club Med on Laguna de Cancún. Excellent facilities, good food, lots of water sports. Call for the Club Med brochure for more details. Not just for "swinging singles." A. Cr.

Dos Playas, Cancún Island (3-05-00). A small but immaculate condominium-motel complex with gardens right out of paradise. The food here is average, but Carlos 'n' Charlie's is nearby. Excellent snorkeling and a nearby dive shop. B. Cr.

El Presidente, Cancún Island (3-02-00). All the comforts of a gracious old villa — escapist, luxury, beautiful gardens, clean beach, attentive staff, and good food. Shops on the first level and quiet sitting areas. Mopeds available. A. Cr.

Hotel Plaza del Sol, Av. Yaxchilan 31 (3-08-88). In Cancún City, this new 87-room luxury hotel is a great place to stay if you plan to explore the region and not limit your activities to the island. B. Cr.

RESTAURANTS

Augustus, Centro de Convenciónes (Convention Center). This is the place to satisfy your craving for pizza, tacos, and hamburgers. Small and funky, with American music. Inexpensive.

Cancún 1900, Centro de Convenciónes, Cancún Island. Good service with an atmosphere that can't be beat. The chicken enchiladas were a disappointment, but the baked Alaska was great — just don't forget to blow it out. Moderate. Cr.

Carlos 'n' Charlie's, Convenciónes Calle. Overlooking a yacht harbor on the lagoon. Linger under the *palapa* at waterside in the afternoon; join the fun inside at night. Good seafood, especially stuffed crab and lobster. Don't bother to dress up, but don't wear a favorite T-shirt either. You may have it ripped from your back by a zealous waiter — that's a C 'n' C tradition. Moderate to expensive. Cr.

Chock and Tere's, across from the Red Cross building in Cancún City. Located on a side street in downtown Cancún, this restaurant is a must stop. The piña coladas and margaritas are sturdy, the lobster and shrimp are cheap, and the waiters dance as they serve. Funk ambience. Try Chocko's chicken enchiladas and Tabasco steak. Good flan and great mariachis. Moderate. Cr.

La Concha, Hyatt Exelaris Hotel. Have lunch in an outdoor setting overlooking the Caribbean. Great grilled seafood served with garlic butter, rice, and vegetables. Tangy seafood cocktails that sometimes include tiny pieces of octopus. Moderate. Cr.

La Confitera, Sheraton Hotel. Tea is served on the terrace amid lush greenery. Finger sandwiches, pastries, Viennese coffee, and classical music. From 3:30–6:30. Inexpensive. Cr.

Perico's, Av. Yaxchilan 71, downtown Cancún. Huge portions of delicious, delightfully presented *norteño* food plus drinks as devastating as a guerrilla raid, all served by waiters dressed as Zapatistas. Definitely a romanticized version of *la revolución*. Emiliano Zapata never ate this well. Moderate. Cr.

Restaurant Mexicano, Camino Real Hotel. This is *the* restaurant where you can get your fill of seafood in an elegant setting. Superb black bean soup spiked with cilantro; flavorful *sopa de lima*. Try the mixed seafood platter that is served in a clay broiler at your table. Moderate. Cr.

Soberanis, Av. Tulum at Cobá, Cancún City. Part of a chain of seafood restaurants dotting the peninsula, but don't let the word *chain* discourage you. Try the squid in its own ink or the house specialty, a seafood cocktail named "Return to the Good Life" — you will understand when you eat one. Also serves good Yucatecan specialties like *pok chuk* ("marinated pork"). Inexpensive. Cr.

NIGHTLIFE

Ballet Folklórico, Centro de Convenciónes, Cancún Island. The center, at the midpoint of the L-shaped Island, features national dances at 9:30 P.M., Tuesday, Wednesday, Friday, and Sunday from October to May. Check at your hotel desk for tickets.

Mariachis and marimba bands, in the lobby bars at the Gran Sheraton, Camino Real, and El Presidente. The groups usually perform at sunset through the early evening hours.

The Mine Company at Club Verano Beat, southern tip of island (3-00-22). Several of the hotels have discos, but this is supposedly the best on the island. Cover charge. Expensive. Cr.

SHOPPING

Delicatessens, various locations. For French pate and Crabtree and Evelyn soups and candies, try La Place Vendome at the Mauna Loa Shopping Center on Cancún Island. In town, you will find various Mexican deli specialties at the liquor shops across from the market on Avenida Tulum.

Bustamante Galleria, Gran Sheraton, Cancún Island. Guadalajara artist Sergio Bustamante has a small gallery at the hotel showing some of his whimsical papier-mâché animals and their hefty prices.

Mauna Loa Shopping Center, Centro de Convenciónes, Cancún Island. Several excellent but expensive boutiques are gathered here. Cancún is a duty-free zone, which benefits mainly Mexican citizens shopping here; however, prices on perfumes and imported china are good for Americans, also. Don't buy electrical appliances here; they are bargains only for Mexican shoppers who normally pay hefty luxury taxes on these items.

Pharmacies, hotel lobbies. There is no pharmacist dispensing drugs on the island; however, most hotel shops stock the usual sunburn and tummy upset medicines.

POINTS OF INTEREST

Archaeological Sites. Various locations. Several tour agencies run daily trips to the Mayan sites; however, with a good map and a rental car or taxi hired for the day, you can enjoy a more leisurely look at some of the superb ruins in the peninsula. You may even want to combine a few days at the beach with a stay at one of the sites; if so, consult the chapter **Mexico of the Ancients.**

Chichén Itzá — well worth an overnight visit; located approximately 130 miles east of Cancún on the road to Mérida. Tulum — this late Mayan site is noted for its beautiful location on the cliffs overlooking the Caribbean; popular with tour groups; located approximately 80 miles south of Cancún on Hwy. 307. Cobá — an extensive site located in the jungle; worth an overnight stay for history buffs; drive south to Tulum and inland 25 miles following signs to the isolated site.

Cozumel, island located off coast, south of Cancún. A popular resort in its own right, Cozumel attracts scuba divers. Air taxis operate from Cancún Airport to Cozumel, as does a car and passenger ferry from Puerto Morelos, 20 miles south of Cancún.

Cruises, various locations. Several companies operate yacht and boat cruises on the lagoons and the bay. Check at your hotel desk.

Isla Mujeres, small island just off Cancún coast. This is one of the untouched areas of the Mexican Caribbean, popular with beach lovers and divers. Accessible from the mainland by ferry from Punta Sam or Puerto Juárez in Cancún City. Buses run from Cancún Island to the ferries, as do taxis. Take along seasickness pills. Scuba gear for rent on the island. Several small cafés.

Xel-Ha, 75 miles south of Cancún on Hwy. 307. This idyllic spot is popular with snorkelers. The Mexican government has created a national park here where the clear waters of the lagoons are filled with tropical fish. Shark nets across the bays keep out larger fish. Snorkel gear for rent. Small restaurant and bar. Some small Mayan ruins dot the park.

SPORTS

Boating. Sailboats, motorboats, and pleasure craft can be rented at Club de Yates, across from the Playa Blanca Hotel, or at Club Pez Vela (3-09-92), across from the Aristos Hotel, on Cancún Island. Check at your hotel desk for more information. Special rates may be available for guests.

Fishing. Deep-sea fishing charters available at above locations. Also check at your hotel desk.

Golf, Pok-ta-Pok Club (3-08-71). This island course was designed by Robert Trent Jones and may be the only golf course with a Mayan pyramid as a hazard.

Scuba diving, snorkeling. The best snorkeling is off the Playa Tortugas dock. Local scuba clubs include Water World, Cancún Yacht Club; Neptuno Sports, Club Verano Beat; and Aqua Tours, located on Kukulcan Blvd. Check with your hotel desk. Best diving is to be found on Isla Mujeres and Cozumel Island.

Swimming. Ocean swimming can be very dangerous on Cancún Island. Swim in the lagoon or in the ocean *only* under lifeguard supervision. Take notice of all warning signs. Children should not be allowed to swim in the ocean.

Tennis. Most of the hotels have courts. Small fee for court lights. The Pok-ta-Pok Golf Club has two Klay Kold courts.

Water sports. Nichupte Lagoon, west of the island, is the best place to enjoy waterskiing. Rentals available at the various piers on the lagoon. The Mauna Loa Marina offers windsurfing lessons on the lagoon.

TRANSPORTATION

Airport. Located approximately 10 miles south of the city. Both international and national carriers serve Cancún. Mexican Customs located at the airport. Most hotels provide limousine service at the airport. Taxis available.

Buses. Cancún is served by first-class buses from Mérida and Chetumal on the border with Belize. There is an excellent local bus system in Cancún—the fare is five pesos regardless of destination. The buses run every 15 minutes from 6 A.M. to midnight and travel the length of the island and into Cancún City. *Ruta 1* or *Hoteles* serves the island.

Car rental. Major rental agencies at the airport. Some discount car rental agencies can be cheaper if you are renting for a week and paying cash. Agencies include Avis—at Hotel Cancún Viva (3-08-28), at Hotel Fiesta American (3-14-00), and at the international airport (3-00-97); Hertz—ask for the Hertz desk at the Aristos Hotel (3-00-11), the Hotel Can-Cún (3-00-44), or the Sheraton (3-09-88), or visit the Hertz desk at the international airport (no phone); National—at Av. Cobá 84 (4-18-51), the international airport (3-01-42), or the Hotel Camino Real (3-03-73, ext. 603).

Mopeds. Most of the hotels rent mopeds to guests by the hour or day. There's a red bicycle path marked on the road into Cancún City, and it's best to stay in this lane.

Taxis. Always settle on the price before getting in. Rates go up after midnight. Prices are not unreasonable; however, the good bus system makes taxi rental unnecessary in most cases.

TOURIST SERVICES

Tourist Office (Delegación Federal de Turismo), Edificio Fonatur, Cancún Island (3-01-23).

COMMUNICATIONS

Newspapers. Few US papers available. Hotels usually provide a free brochure called "Cancún Tips" to guests.

Post Office. Located on Calle Sun Yax Chen in Cancún City.

Telephone service. Avoid long-distance calls. *Always* call collect to the United States. Telephone service is spotty in this remote part of the Yucatán, and most calls go through Mérida to the United States. If the long-distance service is out of order and you must make an emergency call – a real emergency call – you may want to fly or drive to Mérida (210 miles).

COZUMEL

Although Cozumel rates as a hot spot (it has an international airport), there's no chance of it turning into an Acapulco. There's a limit to growth on this island because of the need to import everything from water to soap. A community of some twenty-five thousand people, Cozumel still retains the air of a small island, and it's a popular vacation spot for those who want to enjoy the pleasures of Mexico's Caribbean without all the chic trappings. It's very popular with experienced divers who rate the waters around Cozumel as some of the best in the world.

The island is located just 12 miles off the Yucatán coast. The Spanish landed here in 1518, before Cortés marched on Moctezuma's capital, and they found 40,000 Mayans on the 29-mile long island. The population has since diminished, but foreign interest hasn't. The Yucatán beaches are becoming increasingly popular with Europeans, and you are likely to hear several languages spoken in the cafés. One enterprising young Mayan boy managed to impress us with his mastery of Spanish, English, German, French, Japanese, and his native Mayan tongue.

Most visitors arrive by jet; however, some cross over to the island on the ferry, a long, sometimes rough trip from the mainland. There's really no need to bring your car to Cozumel (it's easy to get around the island), and most tourists rent Vespas, small motor scooters. (The ferry, like most ferries in Mexico, has its own inner clock and sails on a whim, not a schedule, from Playa del Carmen. There's also a small air taxi that runs from the mainland to the island and costs about $20 round trip.)

Cozumel's hotels are located on the western, sheltered shore of the island. The closer they are to the town of San Miguel, the less expensive. Popular hotels, like La Ceiba, the Mayan Plaza, and El Presidente are in the more remote areas of the island—the first two to the north, the last to the south of the town. El Presidente has a reef in the front yard; La Ceiba boasts an unusual dive site, a downed airplane in the water that attracts fish; and the Mayan Plaza has a beautiful beach. The best beaches are north of San Miguel; there you can parasail and windsurf. The best diving and snorkeling is to the south.

Palancar Reef, which some say is one of the world's greatest diving spots, lies on the sheltered, west side of the island; however, scuba diving here is not for amateurs. Take a certified course before you go, and take along your own equipment. Most of the best dives are under 80 feet, and the underwater current is strong. The dives are "drift" dives; the boats unload the divers and watch the bubbles as they drift with the current. Many of the dive shops in San Miguel run tours to the reef daily; check with your local US dive shop before you go for recommendations about who to hire. (Many US dive shops feature package tours to the island.)

There are approximately 15 scuba operations on Cozumel; however, not all of them stay open year-round. Some close down in the summer months. Many rent gear, but experienced divers suggest you take your own gear along. Day rates range from $25 to $40 (subject to devaluations) and sometimes include a lunch of freshly caught fish. Shop around for the best deal.

One of the best spots for snorkeling for first-time divers is Chanca-náb Lagoon, about eight miles south of town. There are entry ladders into the water, and in among the reefs you will see a statue of the Virgin placed there by the fishermen, a traditional gesture among Catholic fishermen. There's a diving concession and a refreshment stand at the lagoon. Another good snorkeling spot is Colombia Lagoon on the south end of the island. Here, fresh spring water flows through underwater caves. There are a few beaches scattered along the west coast, but for the most part, the water laps against coral rock and there's no churning sand to obscure the view. The coral is sharp, and the water, although warm, can feel chilly during a long dive—check with your local dive shop for the appropriate gear to handle these situations. Gloves are recommended.

You don't have to be a diver to enjoy Cozumel. If your idea of a week at the beach is a cuba libre and a good sunset, Cozumel will fill the bill. Or you can go deep-sea fishing; charters are available for several hundred dollars a day. Or you might take a boat tour down the coast to Tulum, the archaeological site; play tennis at one of the luxury hotels; or sign on for a Robinson Crusoe cruise, a boat trip to a remote beach where you will be served a grilled-fish picnic.

Remember to wear stout shoes, a long-sleeved shirt with jeans, and to take along the mosquito repellent when you explore the island's interior. Discover the many interesting species of birds Cozumel harbors (see the chapter **The Unique and the Random**); or investigate the

Mayan ruins that dot the island. Four-wheel drive rental cars are available.

In San Miguel, there are several bargain hotels, including Suites Elizabeth, Bungalows Pepita, Mesón San Miguel, and the Colonial, where you may be able to find a room without a reservation.

The nightlife in Cozumel is not as frantic as Cancún, although there are several bars that remain open until the small hours. Morgan's features dancing, and Carlos 'n' Charlie's has its usual zany fare.

BOCADITOS

If you are looking for a unique diving experience and are willing to pay for it, contact Mary Mykolyk, known locally as María la Bandida. (She was nicknamed for a notorious madam who befriended Pancho Villa.) María operates custom dive tours through Scuba Adventures.

If you want to escape the island for a day, take the 40-cent ferry to Puerto Juárez, near Cancún. (Another, larger ferry plies the waters between Playa del Carmen and Cozumel. This is for those who want to take their car over to the island or those who arrive from the south by bus.) Aerocaribe, an air taxi service, flies between Playa del Carmen and Cancún.

There is air service between Cozumel and Mérida. Tourists can easily combine a trip to Mérida and the nearby ruins with a trip to Cozumel.

AROUND COZUMEL

VITAL STATISTICS

Name of town. San Miguel de Cozumel, the only community on the island of Cozumel.

Climate. Caribbean breezes and sunshine; tropical year-round. Occasional showers in summer. Watch out for hurricanes in season, late summer and early fall. (Evacuation is advisable in a hurricane alert.)

Population. 25,000.

Altitude. Sea level.

State. Quintana Roo.

City phone code. 987.

HOTELS

El Cozumeleño, Apartado Postal 53, Playa Santa Pilar (2-00-50). A posh, modern hotel on the powdery beach north of San Miguel. Lovely. A. Cr.

El Presidente, Playa San Francisco (toll-free 1-800-854-2026). The southernmost hotel on Cozumel and the most luxurious one to specialize in diving. On San Francisco Beach near Palancar Reef. Tennis courts, convention facilities. Best to book through a travel agent and get confirmation in writing. A. Cr.

La Ceiba, Apartado Postal 284, Playa Paraíso (2-03-79). A small, comfortable, congenial hotel with great diving — including a sunken airplane — immediately offshore. The kitchen dishes out some of the best food on the island. Dive packages available. A. Cr.

Mara, Apartado Postal 7, Playa San Juan (2-03-00). Small, friendly, and reasonable. A Mexican-style hotel whose staff is attentive but doesn't speak much English. The rooms are enormous. The beach, just north of town, is better for snorkeling than for sunbathing. B. Cr.

Mayan Plaza, Apartado Postal 9, Playa San Juan (9-00-72). The best beach and prettiest facilities on the island, but it's a long way north of town. Good if you want to be away from it all and don't mind the drive. A. Cr.

Mesón San Miguel, Av. Juárez (2-02-33); Suites Elizabeth (2-03-30); and Bungalows Pepita (2-00-98). All plain, reasonably priced, and close to the pier in town. C. Cr.

RESTAURANTS

Carlos 'n' Charlie's, Malecón. One of the ubiquitous Carlos Anderson restaurants. Manic waiters rip T-shirts from guests' backs and tack them up on the ceiling, offering in exchange a new T-shirt with the restaurant's logo. Seafood, steaks. Noisy, fun. Moderate. Cr.

La Ceiba Dining Room, Hotel La Ceiba (9-00-72). Delicious seafood bisques, heavenly desserts, and some of the best lobster and continental specialties in this part of Mexico. Elegant by local standards, which means you will want to slip into something dry and put on a pair of sandals. Expensive. Cr.

Las Tortugas, five blocks from the pier. A small café under a thatch overhang. Try the *queso fundido, tacos al carbon,* and other *norteño* dishes. The coconut ice cream is great. This is the kind of place where you are likely to run into your hotel manager or the guy who took you diving — a local hangout. Moderate. N.

Pepe's, Av. 5a Sur 2 (2-01-71). Across from the Banco Atlantico, this restaurant has a split personality — checkered tablecloths and hearty enchiladas on the lower level, and white linen, lobster, and chateaubriand above. One of the most expensive places in San Miguel, but you would have to stuff yourself to spend $20 a person. Moderate. Cr.

NIGHTLIFE

Morgan's, about three blocks from the pier. This is the only place in town that approaches a classy nightspot. Live and recorded music for dancing; food and drink. You will recognize it by the lights shining up from the sidewalk in front. Cover charge. Expensive. Cr.

Sidewalk cafés, Malecón. Stroll along the pier at night. Stop for refreshment in one of the sidewalk cafés that line the *malecón,* the quay, along the water's edge.

SHOPPING

Malecón. Several boutiques and arts and crafts shops line the pier. No bargains but some good buys in dresses or resort wear.

Mercado, Av. 25 and Calle A. Rosado Salas. Much of Cozumel's produce and food is shipped in daily. The market is more of a distribution point for the locals than a tourist haven. Some bargains in hammocks and basketry can be found.

POINTS OF INTEREST

Archaeological ruins. There are more than 30 Mayan ruins on the island, none of notable archaeological interest, but certainly worth exploring. Take along insect repellent and wear long pants.

Beaches. The two best are Playa San Francisco on the southwest tip of the island and Playa San Juan on the northwest corner.

Pirates' coves. There are several hidden bays around the island. You could spend a whole day or more digging for doubloons. Unfortunately, Jean Laffitte and Henry Morgan took most of them.

SPORTS

Diving. Diving companies are ubiquitous in Cozumel, and most hotels offer their own packages. Two of the better dive outfits are Discover Cozumel and Scuba Adventures. Discover Cozumel is on the *malecón* near the pier (2-02-80). One of the most reasonably priced excursions now on Cozumel, but too casual for beginners. Two-tank boat dive with lunch $25. Scuba Adventures International, Inc., Apartado Postal 10 (2-07-29). Mary "La Bandida" Mykolyk will arrange custom boat and walking tours, deep-sea fishing, and dive trips. All it takes is money and imagination. If you lack the latter, she'll provide that, too.

FIESTAS

Día de San Miguel, September 20, is celebrated with true fiesta spirit in the island's only town, which bears the archangel's name.

TRANSPORTATION

Airport. There's an international airport on the island served by US and Mexican carriers. Also, local air taxi service from Cancún and Puerto Juárez.

Car rental. Several agencies located at the airport; also jeep and moped rental. Agencies include Avis — at Hotel El Presidente (2-03-22) and the international airport (2-00-99); Hertz (operating as Quintana Roo Rent a Car S.A.) — at Hotel Cozumel Caribe (2-01-00) and at the international airport (no phone); and National — at the international airport (no phone).

Ferries. The passenger/car ferry from Puerto Morelos, 22 miles south of Cancún, and the passenger ferry from Playa del Carmen, 44 miles south of Cancún, serve the island. The ferries invariably do not run according to schedule. Don't miss the last one of the day if you are staying on the mainland.

TOURIST SERVICES

Tourist Office (Subdelegación Federal de Turismo), Biblioteca de Cozumel, San Miguel de Cozumel (2-03-57 or 2-01-81).

COMMUNICATIONS

Post Office, Rafael E. Melgar and Calle 7 Sur, San Miguel de Cozumel.

ACAPULCO

The first glimpse of Acapulco Bay, whether it's from the window of an international jet, a car as you climb over the final mountain range on the road from Mexico City, or the deck of a cruise ship sailing around Isla Roqueta, is always breathtaking. Some cynics say Acapulco is no longer chic, no longer Mexico's premier resort — they are wrong. During the season, from January to April, the city still attracts the so-called Beautiful People who disco and dine the nights away on the beaches and in the hills surrounding the city. Acapulco is one of those hot spots that lives up to its reputation of tropical days and lavish nights.

If it's luxury you're after and you're willing to pay for it, then Acapulco's the place to go. Don't go looking for peace and quiet (although there are a couple of hotels that specialize in it, like the Pierre Marqués); you go to Acapulco to sunbathe and disco, water ski and disco, parasail and disco. The city's discos have become international institutions, engaged in a war to see which can be this season's "in" spot. The best are Armando's, Baby'O, UBQ, Boccacio, Plus 1, and Le Jardin. You must dress to kill to feel at home in an Acapulco disco; otherwise your Mexican cousins will put you to shame. The discos don't open until midnight and sometimes close by dawn. Not all are as crazy as Baby'O where one recent craze was roller-skating. In fact, some are refined and almost genteel. Whether you fancy yourself a

John Travolta or not, you are missing a large part of the Acapulco scene if you don't go to at least one disco during your stay. (Be prepared for high cover charges and expensive drinks.) You don't have to admit you enjoyed it. Just tell everyone back home it was an essential cultural experience.

Discoing until dawn does not make for early morning rising, and Acapulco habitués are not early risers. Get up at noon, have a piña colada for breakfast, sunbathe, take a dip in the pool (don't swim in the bay; it's polluted and the currents can be dangerous), take a walk along the beach, then go to lunch. Late lunches and late dinners are the fashion in Acapulco. The city has a variety of restaurants, some very good, others awful, but you can dine on pasta one night, Mayan food the next, lobster on the beach on another night, and Indian curries the night after that. (We've described our favorites in the Acapulco listings below.)

The key to having a good time in Acapulco is choosing the right hotel. The resort is extremely popular with tourists (there's also been a large influx of Japanese businessmen, and the opening of a Japanese restaurant in the convention center). To avoid the package tour groups, stay at one of the hotels listed below. We've included a couple of hotels where you will bump into tour groups. This can't be helped because some of them know the best places to stay. Acapulco's luxury hotels in season are allowed to charge the maximum rates under the Mexican government's rate schedule. Off season, however, there are bargains to be found, notably the older hotels like El Mirador Hotel on La Quebrada, the rocky promontory on the north edge of the bay.

If you are looking for the Acapulco you saw in those old Esther Williams movies, try the El Mirador. This fifties-style hotel is a bargain in summer. All the rooms have magnificient views of the bay, private balconies, and king-sized bathrooms. The nightclub, La Perla, is a tiered, outdoor affair where you can dance to the Big Band sound and dine under a ceiling covered with movie star autographs. There are cigarette girls and photographers—just like in the movies. From your table you can watch the "famous, death-defying divers" who plunge off the cliffs every night carrying torches so you can watch their fall. Another hotel that has that fifties luxury touch is the Villa Vera Racquet Club on the hill overlooking Condesa Beach.

Of course, Acapulco is still a honeymoon favorite. Acapulco provides the right mix of luxury and activity. The most famous honeymoon haven is Las Brisas, a series of pink bungalows on a cliff south of town, all with a magnificent view of the bay. Packages usually include a pink jeep that, as you drive around town, tells everyone that you are most likely newlyweds. It's best to ask your future helpmate if she or he likes pink before you make reservations at Las Brisas— everything is pink, good but pink.

South of town on Revolcadero Beach, a beautiful, long stretch of uninterrupted sand, is the seven-story Acapulco Princess with its hanging gardens, waterfalls, and swim-up bars. Don't miss it. Shaped like a pyramid, it rises out of a coconut grove like a developer's dream. Next door is the quiet, refined, and expensive Pierre Marqués, also owned by the chain, but preferred by golfers and those who like their hotels classy, not brassy. (The two are located on the road to the airport.)

Revolcadero is a beautiful beach, and beyond the hotel you can drive on the sand or find an isolated area to look for shells. But don't swim in the water. It's sad, but the riptides are extremely dangerous here and there have also been shark attacks (which don't get a lot of publicity in the local press). The same goes for the beaches in town, although they are protected, supposedly, by huge shark nets spanning the mouth of the bay. Each of the beaches in town is open to the public and each has its own atmosphere and flavor, but don't swim off any of them. Use those beautiful hotel pools for you daily dip.

One of the city's newer attractions is the convention center, which features several restaurants and boutiques worth visiting. You will *sometimes* find bargains. A Oaxacan *huipil*, which sold for $100 in Oaxaca, was only $60 in a convention center boutique. Many of the shops are scattered along the Costera, the main street that runs the length of the bay and is named after Acapulco's most prominent citizen, former president Miguel Alemán, now head of Mexico's tourist industry. The market is located at the northern end of the Costera, near the cathedral, a Moorish-looking church. There are some bargains in the market, but mostly it's full of curios and tacky tourist souvenirs.

The convention center features ballet folklórico performances that shouldn't be missed. And there's a golf course nearby and a tennis club. The tennis courts on Condesa Beach are open to hotel guests.

The climate in Acapulco is near perfect year-round, although the rainy season in the summer sometimes brings rain to the resort for a solid day or two. Summer days can be very hot, hence the high prices in the winter season. The climate dictates clothing in Acapulco, and no one expects you to dress for dinner. Take along caftans and long, loose dresses that won't cling to your sunburn. Some restaurants require a jacket for men, but rarely a tie. Men should invest in a couple of cool, cotton *guayaberas* or follow the fashion of the Acapulco gigolos and wear cotton, see-through caftan tops.

BOCADITOS

A rental car is an asset in Acapulco, especially if you don't like to wait for cabs. You can rent a four-wheel drive jeep with unlimited mileage for a reasonable amount at the airport. Make your reservations before you go. Everyone, foreigners included, drives crazy in Acapulco, the worst offenders being the cabbies. Considering that most Mexican drivers are free spirits, Acapulco's drivers are among the freest.

If you cannot summon the courage to rent and drive your own car, rely on cabs. All cab rates are fixed and posted. If you are cheated, report the cabbie's number to the tourist office.

Many of the hotels feature day trips to Taxco, the mountain town some 200 miles north of Acapulco that is famous for its silverwork. It's a beautiful drive through Guerrero to Taxco, and the town itself is one of the prettiest in Mexico (see the chapter **Mexico of the Colonials**). If a day is all you can manage, so be it; but Taxco is worth at least two days. You might consider combining your trip to Acapulco with two days in Taxco. Driving, you can make the trip in four hours.

One place no visitor to Acapulco should miss is La Pie de la Cuesta, the so-called sunset beach. Located north of the city on a narrow spit of beach that faces west, La Pie is a rural enclave near the city of high rises. To the east is a lagoon, fringed with banana and coconut palms; beyond are the foothills of the Sierra Madre. And on the beach are several run-down restaurants, serving grilled fish and coco locos, fresh coconuts filled with tequila. You can rent a hammock on the beach for a few pesos, order a coco loco or two, and watch the sun dip into the Pacific.

AROUND ACAPULCO

VITAL STATISTICS

Climate. Tropical weather year-round; some afternoon rain showers in the summer. Occasionally (very rare) a front will move on shore and bring several days of rain.

Population. 270,000.

Altitude. Sea level.

State. Guerrero.

City phone code. 748.

HOTELS

Acapulco Malibu, Apartado Postal 582, Costera Miguel Alemán (4-23-55). Octagonal rooms (some with wet bars) and marble floors give this hotel a character of its own in a sea of similarity. A. Cr.

Acapulco Princess, Apartado Postal 1351, Hwy. 200 south of the city (4-31-00). A spectacular hotel built in truncated pyramid style. All the rooms have terraces. Set in tropical gardens with a stream running through the lobby bar. Lush, plush, and always full. Reservations must be made through a travel agent. Several excellent restaurants serve everything from burgers to gourmet cuisine. Located south of the city on Playa Revolcadero (watch out for sharks). Regular bus service into town. A. Cr.

El Mirador, Apartado Postal 32, La Quebrada cliffs (3-11-55). This was the chic place to stay before all the new chain hotels hit town. Perched high on the cliffs, the hotel offers its guests spectacular views of the Pacific. Autographs of movie stars decorate the dining room walls and ceiling. Home of La Perla nightclub, where cliff divers perform each night. Great bargain in summer. B. Cr.

Condesa del Mar, Costera Miguel Alemán, Condesa Beach (4-23-55). This luxury hotel has a great view of the bay and is very popular with tour groups. Spectacular swimming pool overlooking the ocean, popular public rooms, beach access. A. Cr.

Hotel Angelita, Quebrada 37 (3-57-34). Located in the Quebrada region of town — the steep cliffs at the north end of the bay. This is where you will find the cheaper hotels. The Angelita has tiled bathrooms, ceiling fans, and advertises its cleanliness. C. Cr.

Motel Kennedy, Costera Miguel Alemán, Playa los Hornos (4-22-83). This motel, one of the few in town, is a bargain. Convenient, quiet. The rooms overlook an interior patio with swimming pool. D. Cr.

Las Brisas, Apartado Postal 281, Carretera Escenica 5255 (4-16-50). If you like to watch "The Love Boat," this honeymoon haven is the place for you. Most of the rooms are contained in bungalows and have their own small pink swimming pools. Those pink and white jeeps you see spinning around town are filled with honeymooners from Las Brisas. Very luxurious and one of the best in town — if you can live with pink. A. Cr.

Los Flamingos, Apartado Postal 70, Av. Lopez and Av. Flamingos (2-06-90). An older hotel that has retained its fifties glamour. A quiet spot with gardens, hammocks on the patio, and a view of Isla Roqueta. On the cliffs at the northern edge of the bay, near Playa Caleta. C. Cr.

Pierre Marqués, Playa Revolcadero (4-20-00). This quiet luxury hotel, popular with golfers, was built by J. Paul Getty. Visitors have dining privileges at the Princess next door. For reservations write P.O. Box 592258, Miami, FL 33159. A. Cr.

Plaza International Regency Hyatt, Costera Miguel Alemán (4-28-88). A brand-new luxury hotel on the beach near the Centro Acapulco, the convention center. All the usual Hyatt appointments. A. Cr.

Villa Vera Racquet Club, Lomas del Mar (4-03-33). Liz Taylor married Mike Todd here, and it's still a popular hangout for the famous and infamous. Just as expensive as some of the town's other top spots but with a lot more character. A. Cr.

RESTAURANTS

Antojitos Mayab, Costera Miguel Alemán at Aviles, Playa los Hornos.
This is one of the best moderately priced restaurants in Acapulco. The
outdoor café features Mayan specialties. Spicy *pok chuk* with dark
Yucatecan beer is best eaten at night, when the sun has gone down and
those cool Pacific breezes waft over the bay. Moderate. N.

Armando's Taj Mahal, Costera Miguel Alemán 2330 (2-42-12). Deca-
dence is very "in" in Acapulco, and this may be the most hedonistic
spot in town. The place looks like a scene out of the Kama Sutra, and
the food is as exotic — Mexican and Indian specialties. Expensive. Cr.

Blackbeard's, Condesa Beach (4-25-49). The pirate motif goes well
with the seafood. Moderate. Cr.

Carlos 'n' Charlie's, Costera Miguel Alemán 999 (4-10-70). Expect a
waiting line at this seafood and Mexican cuisine spot. No reservations
accepted. Closed Tuesday. Moderate. Cr.

Coyuca 22, Coyuca 22 (2-34-68). The name is the address of this classy
restaurant that serves continental food in a Roman Empire–style setting. Reservations necessary. Open only in winter season. Moderate to
expensive. Cr.

Dino's, Costera Miguel Alemán 3645 (4-00-37). Italian food served
with Mexican flair. Some of the best homemade pasta in Mexico is
served here. Try the fettuccine. Moderate. Cr.

Embarcadero, Costera Miguel Alemán, extreme north end (4-27-20).
The jungle atmosphere attracts visitors and monkeys. Run by a successful restaurant team and featuring seafood and steaks. The restaurant has a large salad bar that is a bargain. Don't go to the ladies' mirrored restroom unless you are cold sober. Expensive. Cr.

Longosta Loca, Playa Condesa. One of several on-the-beach restaurants located just north of the Hotel Condesa del Mar. This open-air
spot features seafood of all types, and you can watch the sun go down
as you peel your shrimp.

Normandie, Costera Miguel Alemán at Malespina (2-38-68). This luxury restaurant features French haute cuisine alfresco on a terrace hung
with the stars. Expensive. Cr.

Chain restaurants, various locations. You will find Colonel Sanders,
Big Boy, Tastee Freez, Dona Doni's (a Mexican Dunkin' Donuts), and
Sanborn's dotted along the Costera.

NIGHTLIFE

Calandrias, various locations. These open-air carriages are a relaxing
way to see the city — certainly more relaxing than a taxi cab. Prices are
usually posted, but settle on the score before you get in.

Centro Acapulco, Costera Miguel Alemán, south end of the city (4-70-50). The convention center is a conglomeration of restaurants, boutiques, sidewalk cafés and meeting rooms. Ballet folklórico shows at night, a Japanese restaurant, a mariachi bar, and pleasant grounds decorated with copies of archaeological finds. Check at your hotel desk or call for the day's special events.

Dancing. Try La Perla at El Mirador on La Quebrada (2-11-11); Techo del Mar (2-25-10); or Tiffany's at the Acapulco Princess, south of town on Playa Revolcadero (4-31-00).

Disco. There's a new disco hot spot each season in Acapulco. Right now the fashionable set hangs out at UBQ on Playa Condesa; Boccacio's, Costera Miguel Alemán 5040; Baby'O at the north end of the Costera Miguel Alemán; and Armando's Le Club, Costera Miguel Alemán 2330. The gay crowd likes 9, where straights are welcome also. Most clubs charge a cover; drinks are expensive. Cr.

Moonlight cruises. Check at your hotel desk for phone numbers of various cruise operations. Several boats offer evening excursions on the bay, some with supper or drinks on board.

Nightclub tours, various agencies. Various hotels along the Costera play host to nightclub tour groups, providing either a meal or a cocktail with entertainment, usually ballet folklórico or mariachi bands. Check at your hotel desk.

SHOPPING

Acapulco Joe's, Costera Miguel Alemán 1999. An Acapulco institution where all those T-shirts printed *Acapulco* are sold. Most of the city's boutiques line the Costera on either side of Acapulco Joe's.

Boutiques, throughout the city. Most of the boutiques can be found in hotel lobbies or along the Costera. There are new ones every season. Some of the best include Maria, Maria, Maria, Costera Miguel Alemán and Almendros; Lila Bath, Costera Miguel Alemán 1207; Girasol, Costera Miguel Alemán 999; Bit, Princess Hotel.

El Mercado, streets surrounding the zócalo. Acapulco is not the place to find the best of Mexico's crafts, unless you pay hefty prices in the boutiques and galleries. But the market is fun, if only for the people watching.

El Patio, Costera Miguel Alemán, Diana Circle. This collection of shops is located across from the Hotel Acapulco Continental and features several boutiques and galleries.

El Pueblita, Costera Miguel Alemán and Reyes Católicas. A charming colonial-style square filled with little shops selling clothing, crafts, and artwork by some of the best Mexican artists and craftsmen.

FONART, Costera Miguel Alemán, across from Centro Acapulco. The small government-owned museum and gift shop sells a limited selection of crafts, some at reasonable prices. Good selection of *huipiles*.

House of Eleven Patios, Costera Miguel Alemán and Hidalgo. Several artisans have set up shop here. Their workshops are open to the public.

Supermarkets, various locations. One way to beat the high cost of resort living is to picnic on the beach. You will find all the necessities, including ice and beer, at two large supermarkets located on the Costera — Commercial Mexicana and Super Costera.

Vendors, on the beaches and along the Costera. Vendors in Acapulco are extremely aggressive, particularly the jewelry salesmen. Women work the beaches selling blankets and pareus, those Tahitian all-purpose wraparounds. Stuffed armadillos are another popular item. Always haggle, but remember that once you talk to one vendor you are a marked man.

POINTS OF INTEREST

Beaches. Acapulco's beaches are free and open to everyone. The action varies on each one. The most popular is Playa Condesa in the heart of the city. Unless you are a strong swimmer, take your daily dips in the hotel pool. Playa Revolcadero south of the city is especially demanding. There is a quiet, pleasant beach on Isla Roqueta, the island in the bay, accessible by charter or rental boat.

Centro Acapulco, Costera Miguel Alemán. This impressive convention center was a pet project of one of Mexico's first ladies. Large gardens, dotted with pre-Columbian reproductions. Several restaurants and clubs, varying prices. The El International features Las Vegas–type entertainment; Teatro Nezahualcoyotl is the showplace for ballet folklórico; and in the Centro's plaza there are nightly light and sound shows, Indian flyers, mariachis, and other acts. Catering to Acapulco's growing Japanese fan club is El Chef, a Japanese and continental restaurant. Also, several boutiques and gift shops. Dulces Mexicana sells delicious Mexican candy. Small admission fee to the Centro. Clubs have varying cover charges and admission. Call 4-70-50 for reservations or a schedule of events.

CICI, Costera Miguel Alemán across from Centro Acapulco. This is the place for kids. An aquatic park with exhibits, trained dolphins, and a giant water slide. Small admission fee.

Divers, La Quebrada. Acapulco's famous cliff divers perform four times in the evening and can be seen practicing in the daytime on the cliffs north of downtown. You can watch from the road or sip a drink in La Perla nightclub at El Mirador hotel. Performances at 9:15, 10:15, 11:30, and just after midnight each night.

Fort San Diego, north of the zócalo. This eighteenth-century fort was

259

built by Spaniards for protection against pirate attacks. A visit makes a good change of pace.

Pie de la Cuesta, nine miles north of the city. This is the place to go to watch the sun set into the Pacific Ocean. Hammocks for rent; coco locos — tequila and coconut milk — and fish on a stick for sale. Pounding surf, palm trees, and a sheltered lagoon. Don't swim here; just watch the sun go down. Taxi service is reasonably priced.

Taxco. Day trips to the silver town are popular offerings at the local travel agencies and hotel desks. It's a picturesque ride through the mountains of Guerrero to the town famed for its silver. Several bus companies offer day trips beginning early in the morning, or you can rent a car and drive yourself. Watch out for winding country roads.

SPORTS

Fishing, harbor at the north end of the bay. Deep-sea fishing is popular year-round. Daily rentals vary. Shop around and compare prices. The sailfish season runs from November to May, pompano and snapper year-round.

Golf. The 18-hole course at the Pierre Marqués, called the Princess Country Club, is one of the best anywhere. Lined with palms and tropical bushes, it is cooled by breezes from the Pacific. If you're not staying at the Pierre, check at your hotel desk for details on other courses around town.

Parasailing. It looks fantastic, the view is fabulous, and it's easy. But parachuting behind a motorboat can be dangerous, and your hotel won't be liable for anything that happens if you come down in the bay, crash into a balcony, or land on the Mexican fleet.

Riding, Playa Revolcadero, in front of the Princess hotel. Rent a horse for a wild gallop down the virtually deserted beach.

Tennis. There are several clubs around town, and the Princess and Hyatt Regency hotels boast some of the best. Check at your hotel desk.

Water sports, various locations. Boats can be rented at Hornos and Condesa beaches. (Watch out for the tricky currents.) Some waterskiing operators on these beaches, also. Ask at your hotel desk for scuba information.

FIESTAS

Easter Week (Holy Week). Dates vary. This is a very popular national vacation week. In fact, many of the businesses in the city close so that employees can make their annual trek to the beach.

Día de San Isidro Labrador, May 15. Popular festival with parades and fireworks.

TRANSPORTATION

Airport, 16 miles south of the city. Served by both international and national carriers. Customs located here.

Buses. One of the cheapest ways to reach Acapulco. Daily service on luxury and first-class buses from the capital, Taxco, and Cuernavaca. Local bus service along the Costera very cheap.

Car rental. Major agencies at the airport and in town. Also, popular jeep rentals. Agencies include Avis—at Costera Miguel Alemán 711 (4-20-07) and the international airport (4-16-33); Hertz—at Costera Miguel Alemán 1945 (4-05-65), Hotel Acapulco Continental (4-09-09), the international airport (4-13-53), Condesa del Mar Hotel (4-37-10), and the Holiday Inn (4-04-10); National—at 16 de Septiembre 2 (3-33-65), Costera Miguel Alemán 124 (4-88-39), the international airport (4-40-90), Hotel Acapulco Princess (4-31-00, ext. 429), and the Hotel Exelaris Hyatt Regency (4-28-88).

Taxis. All rates are posted on large signs outside most hotels. Rates are reasonable, although you may want to share a cab to the airport. Acapulco cabbies are renowned free spirits. Close your eyes.

TOURIST SERVICES

Tourist Office (Delegación Federal de Turismo), Costera Miguel Alemán 187 (2-22-70).

Sanborn's, several locations. The familiar oasis. Sells stamps, sunburn lotion, magazines and newspapers from home, postcards, and milk shakes.

COMMUNICATIONS

American Express, Costera Miguel Alemán 709A (4-10-95).

Post Office, Costera Miguel Alemán at the zócalo, north end of town.

Newspapers. *The News,* Mexico's national English language newspaper, is distributed in Acapulco. Several local gossip sheets are distributed in the hotels. US papers available at Sanborn's.

IXTAPA/ZIHUATANEJO

Things worked out so well with Cancún that the Mexican government decided to build another super resort on the Pacific coast near the sleepy fishing town of Zihuatanejo. Ixtapa and Zihuatanejo are sister cities though the two are as different as chalk and cheese. Ixtapa is luxury, high-rise hotels on a near-perfect beach in a setting worthy of the brush of Gauguin; Zihuatanejo is one of those towns that merit the word "quaint." Together they make an ideal couple.

Before the big trucks brought in construction materials for Ixtapa, the loudest noises around here came from the monkeys and the parrots in the jungle. Along the coast, north of Acapulco, are thick jungles and plantations where coconuts and banana palms are raised. Zihuatanejo and Ixtapa are hidden behind this jungle curtain, giving them both that essential vacation ingredient—the aura of exotic distance, of being somewhere different and faraway. A nearby international airport is equally hidden from sight.

Ixtapa is located on a large, curving bay dotted with rocky islands. There are several well-known chain hotels like the Holiday Inn, El Presidente, and the Camino Real, all offering a variety of resort activities from golf to disco. In addition, you can drive into nearby Zihuatanejo to enjoy the ambience or pick up a sailboat charter. The sportfishing is among the best on the Pacific with marlin, pompano, amberjack, sailfish, and other game fish in season. Charters can cost as little as $80 a day for four, a bargain price compared with prices of other resort areas. You can also rent waterskiing equipment or boats at the pier in Zihuatanejo (some call it "Zee Town" for short), and enjoy an afternoon of water sports on the protected bay.

There's even some diving available in Zihuatanejo, hard to find on the West Coast. There's a dive shop on Isla Ixtapa, one of several small islands in the bay, and another on Playa de las Gatas, near the mouth of the bay and only accessible by boat. Both are run by the same family and have dressing rooms and restaurants. The swimming and snorkeling is good around the dive shops, also. And near the pier, there's a third dive shop called El Gato, a nickname for hammerhead sharks.

The hotels in Zihuatanejo, with the exception of one, Posada Caracol, are substantially cheaper than those in Ixtapa and less luxurious. Hotel Catalina and Hotel Sotavento face the ocean on Playa la Ropa, and the rooms have ceiling fans. You can swing in your own hammock on the terrace and watch the sunset. There are several bargain hotels in Zihuatanejo, and you will probably be able to find a room, or at least a place to hang your hammock, without a reservation. This town has an easy, laid-back air.

The juxtaposition of new and old in Ixtapa/Zihuatanejo makes the resort an interesting place to visit. Some cynics suggest this is the way all Mexico's resorts will go in the future, but it's not such a bad combination, and besides it would take centuries to build a brand new luxury resort next to every sleepy Mexican fishing village.

BOCADITOS

It's a three-hour drive from Acapulco to Ixtapa through some very picturesque country. You might want to sample both resorts in one vacation.

Although the hotels are expensive in Ixtapa, it's possible to cut your costs a little by shopping at the resort's supermarket and eating alfresco on your hotel balcony one or two evenings. There's also a liquor store to help you cut down on room service bills, and a bank where you can wire home for more cash.

Other than ventures into Zihuatanejo, which is an adventure in itself, there's not much to see in the surrounding countryside. Ixtapa is located in an isolated area of Mexico — just lie on the beach and relax. Leave the sight-seeing for another trip.

AROUND IXTAPA/ZIHUATANEJO

VITAL STATISTICS

Climate. Tropical year-round. Cool nights in winter as Pacific breezes blow inland. Some summer rain showers. Occasional heavy storm.

Population. 20,000.

Altitude. Sea level.

State. Guerrero.

City phone code. 743.

HOTELS

Camino Real, Ixtapa (1-800-228-3000). Every room in this new luxury hotel has a private balcony and faces the Pacific Ocean. Overlooking Vista Hermosa beach, the hotel has a view at sunset that is remarkable. To the east lie jungles and coconut-fringed lagoons. A. Cr.

Club Med Ixtapa (1-800-528-3100). The latest in the Club Med chain of resorts. All the usual Club Med features — beautifully designed public and private rooms, a variety of sports and activities offered, great food, and G.O.'s, those Club Med guides who are helpful and good-looking ("G.O." stands for *gentils organisateurs*). The currency is in beads, and the pareau (Tahitian wraparound) is de rigueur. A. Cr.

El Presidente de las Palmas, Ixtapa (4-20-13). This rambling, hacienda-style hotel has a huge swimming pool with a *palapa*-covered swim-up bar. Disco. Tennis. Water sports. A. Cr.

Holiday Inn, Ixtapa (4-23-96). Not a bit like those motels you see on the interstate. Luxurious with all the facilities. A. Cr.

Hotel Aristos, Ixtapa (533-0560 in Mexico City). This luxury hotel has 30 self-contained bungalows on the premises. Golf, tennis, and water sports. A. Cr.

Hotel Catalina (4-21-37) and Hotel Sotavento (4-20-32), Playa la Ropa, Zihuatanejo. These two hotels "of a certain age" are up on the cliffs above Playa la Ropa. They offer a sleeping fishing-village ambience, ceiling fans, even hammocks for sleeping on the patio.

Hotel Irma, Playa Madera, Zihuatanejo (4-20-25). One of the best in Zee, high on the cliffs above the beach. The open-air restaurant on the terrace has a great view of the bay. B. Cr.

Las Urracas, Playa la Ropa, Zihuatanejo. If you arrive in town without a reservation, try this small, friendly spot. The bungalows come fully equipped and are set in tropical gardens. C. Cr.

RESTAURANTS

Ixtapa. Most restaurants are in the hotels. They offer a variety of foods in varying settings — some formal, others informal. One of the best for a night on the town is La Esfera in the Camino Real.

Zihuatanejo. Unlike its younger sister, Zee enjoys more relaxed dining, many sidewalk and outdoor restaurants, casual and fun. Some of the best include Coconuts Bar, Pasaje Agustin Ramirez No. 1 (4-25-18) with its self-described "jardín fabuloso"; La Mesa del Capitan, Nicholas Bravo 18 (4-20-27) for steaks, seafood, and Irish coffee; Canaima, Paseo del Pescador (4-20-03) for seafood; and La Tortuga y La Rana at the corner of Cinco de Mayo and Juan N. Alvarez. It's fun to stroll around Zee and find your own special night spot.

NIGHTLIFE

Ixtapa — discos at most of the hotels. La Esfera at the Camino Real stays open until the sunrise.

Zihuatanejo — sidewalk cafés and a walk on the pier. Bed early.

SHOPPING

Ixtapa. There are boutiques in most of the hotels but prices are high. La Puerta, a shopping center across from the Hotel El Presidente, features a liquor store, drugstore, bank, travel agency, and supermarket, all with super prices. If you are staying in a self-contained unit or apartment, shop in Zee. It's cheaper.

Zihuatanejo. There are stores on three main streets, Cinco de Mayo, Cuauhtémoc, and Vincente Guerrero. There is not a great selection of handicrafts in this area.

POINTS OF INTEREST

Countryside tours. Several hotels offer boat trips or bus tours to local fishing villages where visitors can watch nets being made by hand.

Playa de las Gatas, Zihuatanejo. There's a stone wall in the water just off the beach that locals claim was built for Caltzontzin, a Tarascan king, so that he could bathe in private and without being disturbed by the waves.

Tours to Mexico City. Turismo Caleta, the travel agency at La Puerta in Ixtapa (4-24-91), offers day trips by air to the capital or Acapulco.

Wildlife sanctuary. Ixtapa Island, one of several small islands off the coast, has been dedicated as a wildlife sanctuary; however, small tour groups can visit for the day. Usually the price of the tour includes scuba gear, lunch, and a chance to swim in the clear island waters.

SPORTS

Fishing. The deep-sea fishing season runs from December to March, but is good all year. Sailfish, amberjack, and pompano can be found in deep waters; bonito, wahoo, and roosterfish closer to shore. Make arrangements through your hotel or at the pier in Zihuatanejo.

Golf. There are several hotel-connected golf courses in Ixtapa, notably, the Palma Real course, designed by Robert Trent Jones, at the Camino Real. Check at your hotel desk for club privileges at the various courses.

Tennis. Several hotels have tennis courts, some lighted. There is usually a small fee for court lights. Check at your hotel desk.

Water sports. Waterskiing, sailing, and surfing are popular sports. El Embarcadero on the pier in Zihuatanejo can supply information and gear for surfing or scuba diving. The diving here is not as good as that on the Caribbean coast.

TRANSPORTATION

Airport. The airport is just 20 minutes away from Ixtapa and is served by both national and international carriers.

Buses. First-class and luxury buses serve Zihuatanejo from Acapulco and Guadalajara.

Car rental. Agencies include Avis — at the international airport (4-22-48) and Juan N. Alvarez 7 (4-22-75); Hertz — at the international airport (no phone), Cinco de Mayo and Juan N. Alvarez (4-22-55), Posada Caracol on Playa Madera (4-20-95), Paseo de Cocotal (4-30-50), Turismo Caleta at Centro Comercial La Puerta (4-24-91), the Zihuatanejo airport (4-25-90), and the Holiday Inn (4-23-96); National — at the international airport (4-28-88) and Hotel Krystal (4-28-86). Reserve a car in advance especially if you need one on a weekend or during a holiday. Also jeeps, mopeds, and bicycles may be rented in Ixtapa at various hotels.

Taxis. Many hotels run limousine service from the airport; however, a taxi ride is not expensive. Check rates before you get in. Cabs are not metered.

TOURIST SERVICES

Tourist Office (Subdelegación Federal de Turismo), Paseo del Pescador (4-27-16), in Zihuatanejo. No office in Ixtapa.

MANZANILLO

This is a town that means business. As one of the busiest ports in Mexico, the actual city is a hubbub of activity centered around shipping not loafing. Most seaport towns are not noted for their exquisite scenery, and Manzanillo is no exception. Tourists don't come to see Manzanillo, but to visit the beaches around the city. In downtown Manzanillo you will find narrow streets, railroad tracks, and warehouses. It's worth a trip (take a cab) just to look around. Once you've seen enough, head for the Hotel Colonial and gorge yourself on inexpensive lobster and octopus, and wash it down with some Mexican white wine.

Considering Manzanillo is a seaport, the waters around the bay are remarkably clear and clean. Remember, Manzanillo is the home of the famed Las Hadas, where all the "10s" hang out. (For more on Las Hadas, see the description later in this chapter.) Manzanillo has long been a vacation favorite among *tapatíos* (residents of Guadalajara), even before Puerto Vallarta was discovered. One of the best places to stay in the resort area, where you will find hotels, condominiums, and private homes, is La Posada, owned by Bart Varelmann. This pink colonial hotel has 23 rooms, all decorated in an eccentric manner, and there's a large living room featuring Mexican folk art where you can meet the hotel guests. The hotel has a cash bar; serve yourself and pay on the honor system. La Posada typifies Manzanillo where guests prefer to sunbathe, swim, and do little else.

BOCADITOS

Manzanillo makes a good base for exploring the remote beaches of Michoacán to the south and north. Eventually, the highway will connect Manzanillo with Ixtapa, but until then, there are dozens of lonely beaches and fishing villages undisturbed by the tourists.

Fly into Manzanillo and rent a car, but road test it before venturing into the wilds, and top off your tank at every opportunity.

AROUND MANZANILLO

VITAL STATISTICS

Climate. Subtropical year-round. Cool nights in winter; warm, sometimes humid nights in summer. Occasional heavy Pacific storm.
Population. 40,000.
Altitude. Sea level.
State. Colima.
City phone code. 333.

HOTELS

Club Maeva, Bahía de Santiago (1-800-423-2922). A 90-acre resort completely self-contained. Rooms or suites, some villas. Tennis, golf, disco, even a supermarket. A. Cr.

Hotel Mirabella, Playa Azul (Apartado Postal 232). An old favorite in the older part of town. Ceiling fans, a boat dock, and more Mexican flavor than some of the newer hotels.

La Posada, Playa las Brisas (Apartado Postal 135). A home away from home for eccentrics. This delightful hotel has a Bohemian air and is decorated in superb taste. The bar runs on an honor system. B. Cr.

Las Hadas (1-800-423-2922). The resort Bo Derek made famous. The paint may be chipping in a few corners, but the jet set flavor is still there. Luxurious and romantic. A. Cr.

Roca del Mar, Apartado Postal 7 (2-08-05). These condominiums rent for about $500 a week for four (prices subject to inflation and devaluation), but if you like the freedom of a condo with all the luxury, this is for you.

RESTAURANTS

Most hotels have restaurant facilities to match their clientele. For a taste of old Manzanillo, try the dining room at the Hotel Colonial in town, an inexpensive seafood restaurant. For a taste of new Manzanillo, dinner at El Terral at Las Hadas will make for an expensive but luxurious evening.

The road to Bahía de Santiago, the smaller bay north of the city, is dotted with popular restaurants. They include Ostería Bugatti for Italian dishes and seafood, El Vaquero for Mexican Sonoran beef, El Dorado for seafood, and El Gaucho for Argentine grilled meats.

NIGHTLIFE

Nightclubs can be found in most of the hotels and resorts, one of the most notable is La Palapa in Las Hadas. For a taste of Mexican nightlife, try the Bar Social, a café on the main plaza in town.

SHOPPING

Boutiques. Located in most hotel lobbies, usually expensive. Good selection at Las Hadas.

POINTS OF INTEREST

Barra de Navidad, 37 miles north of the city. Get away from the hotels and resorts and back to old Mexico with a trip to the fishing villages along the coast. Fresh seafood at various beach stands.

Cuyutlán, 26 miles southeast of the city. From April to May a 50-foot wave, called "the Green Wave," can be seen off the coast. The color comes from phosphorescent marine organisms.

SPORTS

Fishing. Good deep-sea fishing to be had, especially October through June. Check at your hotel desk for information on charters. In mid-November the International Sailfish Tournament attracts sportfishermen from all over the world.

Golf. Several golf courses at various hotels. Check at your hotel desk for clubhouse privileges.

Tennis. Many of the newer hotels and resorts have tennis facilities. Be ready to pay a small fee for court lights.

TRANSPORTATION

Airport. Located 25 miles north of most of the hotels and the city. International and national carriers serve Manzanillo.

Car rental. Mopeds, jeeps, and bicycles available at some hotels and resorts. Car agencies located in the following places: Avis—at the international airport (3-02-38); Hertz—at the international airport (no phone), the Hotel del Cima, Av. del Mar (1-63-03), and the Holiday Inn (3-22-22); National—at the international airport (no phone) and Balbino Davalos 31 (2-03-02).

Taxis. Cabs are not metered. Check on prices before you get in. Rates reasonable.

Trains. Passenger service from Guadalajara. (For general information about train service in Mexico, see the chapter **There and Back Again** or check at the local tourist office listed below.)

TOURIST SERVICES

Tourist Office (Subdelgación Federal de Turismo) Juárez 111, in the city (2-01-81 or 2-45-60).

PUERTO VALLARTA

It dosen't matter how many new resorts the Mexican government builds, the fact remains, God and Elizabeth Taylor made Puerto Vallarta, and no one can beat that combination. PV has been classy from the start; not with that too-too beautiful air found in Acapulco, but a sort of private, yet humorous class. You know, Mexico a la Tennessee Williams.

To begin with, Puerto Vallarta is in an impossible location, strung out on a series of sheer cliffs and small beaches, squeezed between the ocean and the mountains in a jungle of incomparable beauty. Until they filmed *Night of the Iguana* here, only a few knew about the existence of this paradise; now PV is a popular hot spot. Jets land daily bringing in the sun worshipers, but the town hasn't lost its style. Unlike in Acapulco, here you won't feel left out if you've never made Liz Smith's column or Rex Reed doesn't know you from chopped liver. PV is a town for free spirits. If you happen to have made the cover of Vogue, so much the better.

Most of the hotels are located north and south of what passes for downtown Puerto Vallarta. The heart of the city was once Playa de los Muertos; maybe it was the name, but it's now deader than a doornail, and the action has moved to the *malecón* ("promenade") and the marina near Posada Vallarta. If your hotel is far enough away from the heart of town, you can enjoy swimming in the bay. Unfortunately, the sewage system is somewhat lacking in Puerto Vallarta; avoid drinking the water. In fact, keep your mouth closed in the shower.

There are hotels for every price and taste in Puerto Vallarta, most with spectacular views of the Bahía de Banderas (Bay of Flags). The mountains come right down to the water; don't be tempted to go wandering in them without a guide—ask at your hotel desk for the names of the best. In spite of the terrain, there are several golf courses in Puerto Vallarta. Guests in the local hotels may play at Los Flamingos, located about a 30-minute drive north of town. Tennis is popular and several hotels have their own courts; and water babies can enjoy waterskiing in the bay, but the water is not always clear; turbulence clouds it.

One of the most popular beach activities in Mexico is parasailing. The participant is hooked into a parachute and then towed out to sea behind a boat. As the wind catches the parachute, the person rises in the air. It looks exciting, and it is, but parasailing can be dangerous. In Acapulco, several hotels warn their guests against it and refuse to take any responsibility for accidents. On some occasions, the parachutes have caught the wind and brought the person too close to a high-rise hotel or near a large ship or boat. Be advised before you take a ride.

There are several day trips from Puerto Vallarta. You can visit Playa Mismaloya where *Night of the Iguana* was filmed. This beautiful beach is usually quiet during the week, but on weekends it's a popular spot with the locals. There are changing rooms and a restaurant on the beach. You can reach Mismaloya, south of town, by car, cab, or boat.

Another favorite is Yelapa, which can be reached only by boat. This was once an Indian pueblo, located on an exquisite round bay and surrounded by cliffs and jungle. Party boats leave Puerto Vallarta around 8 A.M. every day and arrive three hours later at Yelapa. At 3 P.M., it's time to head back, but you won't want to. You will want to lie on the beach and watch the sunset, to eat another of those lemon and coconut pies the children sell, or swim just one more time in the blue water. There is one hotel, Lagunita, at Yelpa, but it's usually full; or you could rent a *palapa* on the hillside. Some are primitive; others have plumbing; the best rent for about $300 a month.

Puerto Vallarta is a good place to rent a home, also, although many are quite expensive. It's the kind of town you won't want to leave, and one you will certainly come back to.

BOCADITOS

The marina in Puerto Vallarta is where you can catch the car ferry to Cabo San Lucas on the Baja peninsula. The ferry leaves on Tuesday and Saturday, and returns on Wednesday and Sunday. The trip takes 17 hours and a a cabin costs about $40. Add another $40 if you are taking your car. (Prices may vary owing to fluctuation of the peso. Check with the nearest Mexican tourist office.) The cars are locked during the voyage, so remove everything you will need. Be sure to take motion sickness medicine. Ferries are notoriously flat bottomed and even good sailors find them uncomfortable. No reservations are accepted; however, you can buy your ticket in advance.

AROUND PUERTO VALLARTA

VITAL STATISTICS

Climate. Tropical weather year-round. Cool nights in the winter. Occasional rain showers.

Population. 60,000.

Altitude. Sea level.

State. Jalisco.

City phone code. 322.

HOTELS

Camino Real, Playa de las Estacas, Apartado Postal 95 (2-00-02). Part of a chain. Luxurious. Disco and supper club. A. Cr.

Fiesta Americana at Los Tules (2-20-10). Luxury hotel with tennis club, seafood bar, island in the pool. A. Cr.

Hotel Playa de Oro, Airport Road (Hwy. 200) (2-03-48). Luxury hotel on beautiful grounds. Private boat dock. Mexican decor. A. Cr.

Lagunita, Yelapa, an island near Puerto Vallarta. This is a back-to-basics vacation—hammocks hanging under the trees, saltwater showers, and no need to dress for dinner. For reservations write 31 de Mayo 62, Puerto Vallarta. C. N.

Playa Bucerias, north of town, Apartado Postal 522. A jungle hideaway, luxurious but hard to find. A. Cr.

Posada Vallarta, Airport Road (Hwy. 200) (2-14-59). An old favorite with PV habitués. Colonial atmosphere, Mexican decor. Noted for its French chef. A. Cr.

Quinta María Cortez, Apartado Postal 356. A guest house run by an ex-showgirl from Texas. One of the best places to stay if you want to meet all the characters in town. A. Cr.

Río, Morelos 17 (2-03-66). A good bargain for this luxury resort town. Owner Manuel Sierra will knock himself out for you and knows everyone and everything to do in PV. C. Cr.

RESTAURANTS

Carlos O'Brian's, Av. Díaz Ordaz 116 (2-14-44). Is there anywhere Carlos Anderson has not opened a restaurant? Typical Anderson funky decor, zany menu. Tell the waiter it's your birthday, and the joint goes crazy. Good food. Moderate. Cr.

Casablanca, Av. Díaz Ordaz 570 (2-17-23). On the *malecón* next to the Hotel Océano. Decorated with giant exotic animals made from papier-mâché. The daily dinner specials, fresh seafood, and wild game are among the best dishes in PV. Favorite haunt of celebrities. Dinner only. The bar has a generous happy hour. Moderate to expensive. Cr.

Chico's Paradise, south of town seven miles past Playa Mismaloya (2-07-35). A hideaway built on terraces in the mountainous jungle among waterfalls, orchids, and tropical birds. Excellent food in this open-air setting includes ribs, steaks, and Mexican specialties. Open noon till dark. Also a boutique. Moderate to expensive. Cr.

Chino's Paraiso, just past Playa Mismaloya. Aptly named. Paradise. Great food. Grilled steaks and seafood in a jungle setting. Moderate. Cr.

El Set, one and a half miles south of town on road to Manzanillo (2-03-02). Perched on a cliff overhanging the ocean. Ask to sit near the rail, and watch the waves crash on the rocks below. Patrons may use the freshwater swimming pool on one of the lower terraces. Attentive service, excellent seafood, exotic drinks. Open for lunch and dinner.

Las Margaritas, Juárez 592 (2-12-15). International menu plus regional foods of Mexico. Features some of the best mariachi music in Puerto Vallarta. Service is slow, but the food is worth the wait. Expensive. Cr.

Posada Vallarta, Airport Road (Hwy. 200) (2-14-59). French cuisine in a tropical setting. The hotel's French chef draws good reviews, and his food is served with flair in the hotel's outdoor restaurant. Moderate to expensive. Cr.

NIGHTLIFE

City Dump Discotheque, Ignacio Vallarta 257. The most popular disco in Vallarta. Young, single crowd. Music too loud for conversation. Open 10 P.M.–4 A.M. Expensive. Cr.

El Nido, Hotel los Cuatro Vientos, Matamoros 520 (2-01-61). The name means "the nest," and you will feel as though you are in an eagle's nest high in the sky under the stars in this rooftop bar. Great view of PV. Moderate. Cr.

Fiesta nights. Several of the larger chain hotels offer Mexican fiesta nights. If you are lonely, it might be a good way to meet someone. Check at your hotel desk for more information.

SHOPPING

Av. Juárez. This boutique row has some of the best shops and galleries in Mexico. The high prices reflect Vallarta's status as a jet-set hangout.

Galeria Lepe, Lazaro Cardenas 97. The most famous artist in town, Manuel Lepe, sells his paintings here. His naive pictures of little angels and children playing in Mexican villages are as renowned as Liz Taylor's house in these parts.

Malecón, the pier. Some of the cheaper boutiques are located along the pier. Also vendors prowl the sidewalks.

Playa de los Muertos. Act dead and the vendors won't bother you.

POINTS OF INTEREST

Playa de los Muertos. Not the most beautiful but by far the most popular beach in town, in spite of the name — Beach of the Dead. Equally popular with locals and visitors. Rent deck chairs or mats, sailboats, waterscooters, or take a parasail ride. The waterfront is lined with thatched roof restaurants serving breakfast, lunch, and exotic drinks. Restaurant food is OK, but only the brave should buy from the street vendors. Boutiques and strolling vendors sell clothing, artwork, souvenirs.

Playa Mismaloya. The movie Night of the Iguana was filmed on this beach south of town. There's a small hotel and bar. You can drive here or take a launch from PV.

Yelapa. This small getaway island is a favorite place for visitors eager to leave civilization behind. There's one small hotel on the island (see above), but otherwise it's just sand and palm trees. Check at the city pier or your hotel desk for trip information. Make reservations for day trips two or three days in advance. Several cheap restaurants on the island serve fresh seafood.

SPORTS

Donkey polo. Popular pastime on Playa de los Muertos. You don't have to be Prince Charles to play.

Fishing. Deep-sea charters available at the malecón. Also check at your hotel desk.

Hunting. Quail and deer hunting in the nearby mountains. Also iguana hunting for those with a desire to hunt reptiles. Ask at your hotel desk or at the tourist office for information about guides and licenses.

Water sports. Everything from swimming to waterskiing, scuba diving to snorkeling.

FIESTAS

The first 12 days of December are dedicated to fiestas connected with the Virgin Mary, culminating in the Fiesta of the Virgin of Guadalupe on December 12.

TRANSPORTATION

Airport. International and national carriers serve Puerto Vallarta.

Buses. First-class bus service from Guadalajara and other cities.

Car rental. Agencies include Avis—at the international airport (2-11-12) and at kilometer 2.5 on the highway to Tepic (2-14-12); Hertz —at the international airport (2-04-73) and in the Hotel Océano, Hotel Delfín, Posada Vallarta, Holiday Inn, and Posada del Angel; National— at the international airport (no phone) and at kilometer 1 on the highway to the airport (2-11-07).

Taxis. Reasonable. Not metered. Settle on a fare before you get in. Available by the day.

TOURIST SERVICES

Tourist Office (Subdelegación Federal de Turismo), Libertad and Morelos (2-42-43).

COMMUNICATIONS

Post Office, Morelos, one block north of the zócalo.

MAZATLAN

Mazatlán is a hot spot in more ways than one; located west of Durango, it's one of the warmest resort towns in Mexico. But that doesn't deter the fishermen who come here in droves every year to enjoy some of the best game fishing in the world. But there's more to Mazatlán than fishing stories—this is one of the best beach bargains in Mexico, in a time of diminishing bargains. Not the most glamorous or the most chic of Mexico's hot spots, Mazatlán is wholesome fun. It is a place where you can take the whole family, even pack 'em up in the motor home if you like. There are several campsites near town.

There's no sleeping until noon here; most people get up at dawn to ready their tackle for the day's battle of wills. Sailfish, marlin, blue marlin, shark, black marlin, and tuna all run nearby, and there are several respectable fishing guides and charter operations, many of them along the *malecón*. Also, hunting is good in the nearby mountains. (For tips on hunting and fishing in Mexico, see the chapter **The Unique and the Random**.) Don't try to operate without a fishing or hunting license. The penalties can be high.

The charter prices in Mazatlán are also bargains. As many as ten fishermen can hire a boat and tackle for $220 a day (subject to peso fluctuations), considerably less than at other large resort towns in Mexico.

Mazatlán has attracted many California retirees who have given the town a North American flavor, which is why it's a good place for a family vacation. The nightlife is not as sophisticated as Acapulco or Cancún, and you can take the kids along to places like Señor Frog's and the Shrimp Bucket (owned by the Carlos 'n' Charlie's folks) where the whole family will enjoy good food and wacky waiters.

Most of the hotels are located along the beachfront; however, several are across the road from the beach. If you are taking small children, inquire about the hotel's specific location before you make your reservations. The Camino Real, the Holiday Inn, the Playa Mazatlán, and the Hotel Suites las Flores are on the beach.

Downtown Mazatlán has resisted Americanization and is *muy Mexicano* with its zócalo and bandstand. The market is a good place to begin your shopping. You will find some good bargains in Mazatlán, unlike many of the other Mexican hot spots.

BOCADITOS

The ferry to La Paz lands at Mazatlán and costs about the same as the ferry from Puerto Vallarta to Cabo San Lucas, approximately $40 for a cabin, $40 for a car. You cannot make reservations in advance, but you can buy your ticket a couple of days ahead of time. You might consider taking the ferry across to Baja; then, after a few days of exploring that region, cross back over to Puerto Vallarta.

AROUND MAZATLAN

VITAL STATISTICS

Climate. Hot summers; warm winters. Subtropical with occasional northers blowing in cold days in the winter. Can be very humid midsummer. Infrequent Pacific storms.

Population. 170,000.

Altitude. Sea level.

State. Sinaloa.

City phone code. 578.

HOTELS

Mazatlán abounds in good, family-style hotels. We have listed just a few. Check with your travel agent for special bargains and rates. The newer resorts attract more visitors, but Mazatlán is bargain country.

Camino Real, Playa Sábalo (2-33-22). Standing on a rocky point, this modern hotel has all the ameniti s—pool, tennis, putting green, disco. A. Cr.

Hacienda Mazatlán, Playa Norte (1-70-80). Popular hotel with families. Although the hotel is not on the beach, which may be a problem with younger children because they have to cross the road to reach the sand, there's a children's pool. Some rooms have refrigerators. Nightly dancing in the lounge. A. Cr.

Holiday Inn, Playa de las Gaviotas (2-11-88). One of the prettiest locations in town and on a rocky beachhead. Some rooms have kitchens. Two swimming pools; sailboat dock. A. Cr.

Hotel La Siesta, Olas Altas 11 (1-26-40). This remodeled old hotel is a downtown landmark and a bargain. C. Cr.

Plaza Gaviotas, Playa de las Gaviotas (2-02-66). This motel-style hotel set in a tropical garden is a great bargain, and its location facing the beach (all the hotels on Playa de las Gaviotas are separated from the beach by a road) is not a disadvantage at these prices. C. Cr.

RESTAURANTS

Chuy's Chew Choo, Océano Hotel, Camarón Sábalo (2-31-11). Only Carlos Anderson would name a restaurant this way. You can dine on steak and seafood on the terrace or in the "chew choo," an old dining car. Anderson's restaurants are always fun, lively, and the food is reasonably good. Moderate. Cr.

Doney's Restaurant, Canizales and Cinco de Mayo, downtown (1-26-51). This landmark café specializes in *carne asada* and other northern Mexican specialties.

Lafitte, Camino Real Hotel, Camarón Sábalo (2-33-22). Continental cuisine in a luxurious setting. Classy for Mazatlán. Expensive. Cr.

Mamucas, Simón Bolívar Pte. 73 (1-34-90). Mexican-style seafood and lots of it. Squid, oysters, lobster, shrimp—all fresh. Moderate. Cr.

Pekin, Benito Juárez Nte. 4 (1-33-30). Cantonese specialties served with Mexican hot sauce. Moderate. Cr.

Rolf's, Av. del Mar 225 (1-20-43). In this restored old mansion you will find an eclectic mix of fresh seafood, German specialties, and continental cuisine. Expensive. Cr.

Tony's, Plaza de las Gaviotas (2-03-77). Mexican specialties are served in this 100-year-old mansion. Live music. Moderate. Cr.

NIGHTLIFE

Discos. Most of the larger hotels have discos. Two popular hangouts for the "deesco" crowd are La Jirafa, Av. Camerón Sábalo 200, where there is usually a line, and Life in Español, Olas Altas 33 Sur, a Carlos Anderson enterprise.

Mexican Fiesta nights. Several hotels hold these fiesta nights on Saturdays when the cruise ships come into harbor. Two of the most popular are held at the Sábalo Nightclub in the Camino Real and at the Hotel Playa Mazatlán on Las Gaviotas Beach. The programs include dinner, folkloric dances, mariachis, and dancing. Check at your hotel desk for more information.

SHOPPING

Arts and Crafts Center, in front of Los Flores Hotel, Playa de las Gaviotas. Local craftsmen and artisans gather to work and sell their wares.

Market, Cinco de Mayo and Zaragoza, downtown. A large, bustling market with bargains in cookware, fresh vegetables, herbs, kitchen linens, and some handicrafts.

Plaza Gaviotas, Hotel Playa Mazatlán, Playa de las Gaviotas. This shopping mall features a variety of boutiques selling resort wear, crafts, jewelry, and leather goods.

POINTS OF INTEREST

Arañas. Various locations. The name means "spiders," which does not invoke romantic images; however, a ride in one of these horse-drawn carriages can be a charming way to see the city.

Beaches. The beaches are more intimate in Mazatlán than those in Acapulco. Not quite as glamorous, but just as much fun. The best are Las Gaviotas and Sábalo at the north end of the bay. Playa Norte is more the people's beach and has sidewalk restaurants, mariachis, and vendors on hand. Surfers like Olas Altas, but weak swimmers should watch out for currents. Boat trips are available to Isla de Piedra, a primitive island, unfortunately popular with weekend vacationers.

Cruises. Mazatlán has a busy harbor and the largest shrimp fleet in the country. Several travel agencies offer harbor cruises that begin at the harbor lighthouse.

SPORTS

Fishing. Mazatlán is famous for its big-game fishing. January through May is the top season. Check at your hotel for charter rates.

Golf. If you are a member of a club in the United States, you can play at the El Cid Country Club on Sábalo Beach Road north of town. Check at your hotel desk for information on other golf courses in the area; there are several nine-hole courses at some of the larger hotels.

Horseback riding. A popular pastime on Sábalo Beach. Inexpensive.

Hunting. Mazatlán is a popular base for hunters. There's good duck, quail, wild pig, deer, wildcat, and rabbit hunting in the mountains. Check with your hotel for charters or with the nearest US-based tourist office for information about hunting and fishing in the area.

Water sports. Sailboats, water skis, and surfboards for rent at hotels and on various beaches. Limited scuba diving.

FIESTAS

Carnival, week before Lent. Rio on a small scale. Street dancing, parades, costume competitions, fireworks — the best place to celebrate Carnival in Mexico. Mexicans also indulge in seafood-eating binges during Carnival, and Mazatlán with its huge shrimp fleet is not a bad place to indulge.

Feast of the Immaculate Conception, December 8, one of the most important religious festivals of the year.

TRANSPORTATION

Airport. The international airport is served by national and international carriers.

Buses. Luxury and first-class bus service from Guadalajara, Durango, and points north. Local bus service is good, but ask for advice from your hotel bell captain.

Car rental. Agencies located at the airport include Avis — at Camaron Sábalo 1000 (3-62-00) and the international airport (2-14-87); Hertz (operating as Autos Rentas del Pacífico S.A. de C.V.) — on Camarón Sábalo (2-12-12) and at the international airport (no phone); and National — at the international airport (2-40-00) and on Camarón Sábalo (3-40-77).

Taxis. Cabs are not metered, but fares are reasonable. Check rate before you get in.

TOURIST SERVICES

Tourist office (Delegación Federal de Turismo), Paseo Claussen and Zaragoza, downtown (1-49-66).

RESORTS

We've chosen four very special resorts that we think are the top of the line in Mexico. These are places you won't want to leave, hotels that offer you a small world of self-contained pleasure.

An explanation of official hotel rates appears at the front of the book.

LAS HADAS

Thanks to movies like *10*, Las Hadas is undoubtedly one of the most famous resorts in Mexico. The name means "the fairies" and the resort's creator, Bolivian tin magnate Atenor Patino, produced a fantasy creation of white stucco that looks remarkably like a dream castle out of *Arabian Nights*. The Las Hadas signature, the mixture of Moorish, Spanish, Greek, and Mexican architecture is now widely copied.

In 1976, Patino sold out to Casolar, a Latin American company that gave the place a much-needed face-lifting. Now Las Hadas attracts a mixed bag of visitors, including affluent Europeans, rich Mexicans, and honeymooning Americans. There are 163 rooms and 37 suites at the resort, which sits above Manzanillo Bay surrounded by bougainvilleas and palm trees. The suites have terraces; some have living rooms and private pools.

Four restaurants are located within the hotel compound. The menus are as eclectic as the architecture. Lagazpi serves gourmet continental cuisine, and diners can look at the murals of Spanish artist Fernando Calderón and listen to piano music. Mexican food is on the menu in Las Piñas, where you will find a huge breakfast buffet daily. The Oasis, on the beach, serves seafood and grilled steaks for lunch; and El Terral is an open-air terrace restaurant where you can dine to the sounds of a waterfall. After dinner, if you are so inclined, there's the La Palapa disco where you can "deesco" until the wee hours.

The beach at Las Hadas is small, but ideal. White umbrellas and tents provide shade, and you order drinks by raising a flag to summon a waiter. There's also a large pool with a swim-up bar, waterfall, an island, and a bridge. The hotel marina is where you will find scuba and snorkeling gear, waterski boats, catamarans, parasailing, and the Las Hadas cruisers that take guests deep-sea fishing (some of the world's largest sailfish have been caught in local waters). There's also a trimaran for trips to Manzanillo. Las Hadas also contains the usual collection of boutiques and small shops, a drugstore, and a doctor's office.

The guest at Las Hadas can jog on the beach every day, join in the backgammon tournaments, go fishing, play golf, work up a thirst playing tennis, join the underwater scavenger hunts organized by hotel personnel. But because this is a total resort, all he or she has to do is fly into Manzanillo, take a cab to the hotel, check in and do absolutely nothing for a week.

(For reservations at Las Hadas, write to Las Hadas Hotel, Postal 158, Manzanillo, Colima, Mexico, or call toll free 1-800-423-2922. A. Luxury.

CLUB MED

Of course, the French know they have it, and they flaunt it, but in such a delightful way that it's hard to feel miffed. It is *savoir faire*, that ability to put things together just right. The Swiss might make the most precise hoteliers; the British, at their best, provide the best service; but the French know just how to spice a vacation to make it a perfect experience.

Ahead of the game, several Frenchmen decided after World War II that people wanted to get away from it all, so they invented Club Med, a place where the guests threw away their business suits, donned pareus like native Tahitians, lived in rooms where there were no keys, and used beads for currency. The idea caught on and now there are Club Meds all over the world, including Africa and the Far East.

There are three Club Meds in Mexico — one at Cancún, another on the Pacific coast between Puerto Vallarta and Manzanillo called Playa Blanca, and the latest edition at Ixtapa/Zihuatanejo on the Pacific coast. Guests usually stay for a week; pay a lump sum that includes everything except alcoholic drinks and special activities; and, in return, are given classical music at sunset, rivers of red and white wine with meals, and a chance to meet a variety of people from around the world.

A standard feature at all Club Meds is the *gentils organisateurs*, a French world that translates as "nice organizers" but means much more. The "G.O.'s" are camp counselors for grown-ups, and they come in male and female types. Most are tanned, talented, and gorgeous, which makes looking at them easy on the guests. The "G.O.'s" teach you how to snorkel or dive, how to ride a horse on the beach or sail a windsurfer, perhaps how to disco or play backgammon — in other words, how to do whatever your heart desires within reason and the law. Many of them also entertain at night in floor shows and nightclub acts. And some serve as guides on trips to nearby sites and cities.

French, Spanish, and English are spoken at the Mexican clubs, and the food is a mixture of Mexican and Continental. No one is expected to dress for dinner, and bikinis and Tahitian pareus are standard wear. Most meals are served buffet style.

Although the clubs have a reputation for attracting young professionals and college kids, older couples and families can enjoy a vacation at one of Mexico's Club Meds. There are special activities for children at some of the clubs (check with Club Med reservations about age restrictions and facilities), leaving parents free to enjoy themselves.

Club Med also operates five Villas Arqueologicas at some of the important sites in Mexico, and these are open to the general public. The Club Meds are open only to members; however the membership fee is quite small and is included in the price of your package. Airline charters run from many US airports to the Clubs, or you can arrange your own transportation. Rental cars are usually available at the Clubs for ventures into the countryside.

For a complete package of information on Club Med's Mexican facilities call toll free in the United States 1-800-528-3100.

PLAZA CAREYES

Located about 60 miles north of Manzanillo and 90 miles south of Puerto Vallarta, Hotel Plaza Careyes ranks as one of Mexico's best beach hotels. The hotel is on the south end of a remote bay shared only by the Club Med facility at Playa Blanca on the far north end of the bay. Part of a 3,700-acre resort development by an Italian-Mexican business group, Plaza Careyes is in no danger of losing its charm. The resort has eight miles of perfect beach, and only four percent of the property is scheduled to be developed.

There are just 28 rooms at this remote, luxury spot, all housed in a beige, Mediterranean-style building. The red tile roofs and the profusion of tropical flowers stand out against the blue sky over the Pacific. Every room is decorated with handwoven textiles and Mexican folk art, and each has its own balcony or terrace.

There are tennis courts nearby, no golf, but facilities for sailing and diving, and a stable of horses for riding on the beach. The food is good, and there's a paperback library near the swimming pool.

The resort also features several large homes that accommodate up to six persons; rates are about $350 a day. The homes are fully staffed. A double room at the hotel costs about $130 with meals (rates subject to inflation and devaluation).

To reach Plaza Careyes, most guests fly into Manzanillo and then rent a car or cab for the 40-mile drive (the airport in Manzanillo is located some distance from the city) along Hwy. 200 to the resort.

For information or reservations, write Harry Jarvinen and Associates, 1717 Highland Avenue, Los Angeles, CA 90028, or call toll free 1-800-421-0767.

CLUB AKUMAL-CARIBE

This retreat along the Caribbean coast on the Yucatán peninsula, south of Cancún, used to be a private club where millionaires came to go sportfishing or diving.

The bungalows that are shaded by coconut palms look out on a blue lagoon, separated from the ocean by a small, coral barrier reef. In these sheltered turquoise waters, the freshwater fish of the springs mingle with their saltwater cousins.

The hotel is very popular with Mexican businessmen and Europeans. Just 60 miles from Cancún, Club Akumal-Caribe is easy to reach either by cab or rental car. All along the highway from Cancún are a variety of hidden beaches and lagoons that can be found by asking local guides. Beyond Akumul, on Hwy. 307, are the ruins at Tulum and Cobá.

Club Akumal-Caribe is an ideal spot to enjoy excellent snorkeling in luxury surroundings.

For reservations, write to Club Akumal-Caribe, Schiller 410, Mexico 5, DF, or call toll free 1-800-828-7447. A. Luxury.

HIDEAWAYS

In a country with over six thousand miles of shoreline, it's not difficult to find a hideaway that most gringos and many Mexicans know nothing about. We've picked a few of our favorites; some are well known, others are not so famous. The best way to find your own beach hideaway is either to drive your own car to Mexico, rent a car, or take the second-class buses that stop at every hamlet. To make it easy for you to locate the hideaways, we've divided the country's beaches into sections. Except for portions of the Pacific coast and a few miles on the Yucatán coast, it's possible to drive along Mexico's coastline and find your own favorite, private spots. We've included a guide to beach camping in the chapter **The Unique and the Random.** Read those guidelines before you decide to camp out, and avoid camping in Guerrero, where there are several groups of bandits and insurgents. Many of the hotels in the small fishing towns are so inexpensive that it's hardly worth camping out.

ISLA MUJERES

This tiny island off the coast of Yucatán is no secret, but its size and the fact it is served only by two small ferries make it a hideaway in our book. There's one luxury hotel on the five-mile island (see Isla Mujeres hotel listings that follow), and several inexpensive hotels where you usually won't need reservations. If the hotels, by chance, are full, head for Hank's Hammock Haven, more formally known as Las Hamacas, on the north end of the island. For under two dollars a day, guests get a couple of hooks for their hammocks and a lock-up for their valuables.

There are two ferries to the island, which is located less than two miles from Cancún. The car ferry runs irregularly from Punta Sam near Cancún; the passenger ferry is more reliable and leaves from Puerto Juárez, just north of Cancún. You can rent scooters or cars on the island.

Some of the hotels in Cancún run day trips to Isla Mujeres, usually to El Garrafón, a seafood restaurant and snorkeling outfit on the south end of the island.

There's a small town at the north end of the island where you will find several hotels and restaurants — try Ciro's Lobster Pot and Boca del Rio in town, María's and Kim-Ha, south of town on the beach. The seafood — lobster, conch, and rock shrimp — is caught in the nearby waters. The beach restaurants have changing rooms so guests can go from table to ocean or vice versa.

A company called "Mexico Divers" runs trips to nearby Isla Contoy, a bird sanctuary. While you snorkel, the guides cook on the beach. The trips cost about $20. (Prices subject to change with devaluation.) And that's about all there is to do on Isla Mujeres — swim, snorkel, eat, and swing in a hammock.

AROUND ISLA MUJERES

VITAL STATISTICS

Climate. Tropical year-round. Occasional summer storms; some cool nights in winter. Located in a hurricane zone, evacuation recommended if hurricane threatens.

Population. 6,000.

Altitude. Sea level.

State. Quintana Roo.

City phone code. 988.

HOTELS

Berny. A small and basic hostelry two blocks from the pier and one block from the water. All the rooms have baths and balconies, a few are air-conditioned. The much-touted swimming pool is the size of a footbath, but who needs it with the Caribbean almost at the door? B. Cr.

Las Hamacas (Hank's Hammock Haven), north end of island. For under $2 a night you can meet a lot of footloose and suntanned Europeans who have all learned to sleep in a piece of fishnet suspended from two hooks with a lightbulb burning overhead. Separate baths and showers for men and women, but otherwise it's all together under one big, tin-roofed barracks. Beyond cheap.

Zazil-Ha. The only thing approaching a luxury hotel on this delightfully laid back island. Off by itself on a small, crystal clear lagoon on the northern tip of the island, yet only a ten-minute walk from the pier. For reservations write Calle 60 No. 49, Mérida, Yucatán. A. Cr.

RESTAURANTS

Boca del Rio, in town. Great and inexpensive seafood — especially the *brocheta mixta* (lobster, shrimp, turtle, steak, and vegetables on a skewer). Eat outside and watch the passing scene. Inexpensive.

Ciro's Lobster Pot, in town. Tasty, reasonably priced lobster dinners and shrimp. Hearty breakfasts. Moderate. Cr.

Kim-Ha, on the south end of the island, near María's (see below). Adds international flair to local seafood in a beach setting. It may not be in the same class as María's, but it still earns its share of kudos. Moderate. Cr.

María's. Some claim this is one of the top five or ten restaurants in Mexico. It is the top eatery on the island and serves some of the country's most succulent seafood. In spite of its continental aspirations, María's is a relaxed place where you can snorkel before or after lunch, provided you bring something to put on over your swimsuit. Expensive. Cr.

NIGHTLIFE

Romance and moonlight are the two standards by which Isla Mujeres is judged. The island provides plenty of both.

POINTS OF INTEREST

Archaeological ruins. The Spaniards found dozens of small female terra-cotta figures on the island when they landed — hence the name. The Mayans worshipped Ixchel, the goddess of fertility here, and there are traces of Mayan temples to be found at the south end of the island.

Hacienda Mundaca. This nineteenth-century mansion was once home to the smuggler and pirate Antonio de Mundaca.

Isla Contoy. This small island is a wildlife sanctuary to the north of Isla Mujeres. "Robinson Crusoe" cruises are offered by various dive shops on the pier. The cruises combine a day's diving with an outdoor fresh fish barbecue.

SPORTS

El Garrafón. This may be the best snorkeling spot on Mexico's east coast. It has an attractive concession area with restaurant, bar, and changing rooms. Snorkeling equipment for rent.

Mexico Divers, near the pier. No padded seats on the dive boats, but a fun and safety-conscious operation that manages to please snorkelers and divers, experienced and novice alike. The fresh fish lunch included in the day trip is out of this world.

FIESTAS

National holidays are celebrated in a low-key manner. A local favorite fiesta is Día de la Virgen de Guadalupe, December 12.

TRANSPORTATION

Air taxi. Service from Cancún, Cozumel, and Mérida. The most expensive way to get to the island but one of the more reliable. Fares begin at about $20 a person; however, rates fluctuate with peso devaluations and inflation.

Car rental. There are three ways to get around on the island—rent a VW bug, a scooter, or walk. The island is five miles long and just over one mile wide.

Ferries. The island is served by two ferries from the mainland. The passenger and car ferry leaves from Punta Sam, just outside Cancún; the passenger ferry leaves from Puerto Júarez in Cancún daily. Schedules are posted. There are several journeys a day; however, the ferries rarely run on time. Be patient while you wait. Those susceptible to seasickness might opt for the air taxi or take medicine. Fares are inexpensive.

TOURIST SERVICES

Tourist Office (**Subdelegación Federal de Turismo**), Guerrero 7 (2-01-80 or 2-01-73).

CABO SAN LUCAS

For years, the Baja peninsula was an isolated finger of desert and mountains that pointed south to the equator. Now, roads have been completed all the way to the tip of the finger, Cabo San Lucas, and slowly tourists are discovering a new playground.

Here at the joining of the Sea of Cortés and the Pacific, whales and dolphins have frolicked for centuries. Game fish like marlin and sailfish elude fishermen in the blue waters, and pelicans roost by the hundreds in the rocky cliffs that line the shore. The beaches here are small and isolated, and some have long been the winter home of seals and migratory birds.

There are several luxury hotels in Cabo San Lucas and a couple of trailer parks that rent spaces for as little as $5 a night. Campers can find isolated camping spots along the coast. (See Cabo San Lucas listings below.)

The easiest way to get to Cabo San Lucas is to fly; several airlines serve the new airport in Cabo. Or you can drive down Hwy. 1 from California. There are also four car ferries serving the peninsula—one

from Mazatlán, another from Puerto Vallarta, a third from Topolobampo, and a fourth from Guaymas.

BOCADITOS

For a spectacular look at Mexico, take the Copper Canyon train from
Chihuahua to Los Mochis, near Topolobampo, and then the ferry to
La Paz and on to Cabo San Lucas. (For information on the Copper
Canyon train, see the last chapter.)

AROUND CABO SAN LUCAS

VITAL STATISTICS

Climate. Sunny California year-round. Occasional heavy rainstorms
come in from the Pacific. Infrequent hurricanes.

Population. 10,000.

Altitude. Sea level.

State. Baja California.

City phone code. 684.

HOTELS

Hotel Hyatt Baja, Cabo Bello and Cabo San Lucas (1-800-228-9000).
Typical Hyatt luxury but in an isolated location. Tennis courts and
water sports facilities. A. Cr.

Hotel Twin Dolphin, Bahía Santa Marta (1-800-421-8925). This beautiful hotel is located in a secluded bay where hotel guests can sit poolside and watch the dolphins frolic in the nearby ocean. Tranquil.
A. Cr.

RESTAURANTS

El Regional, Morelos and 16 de Septiembre. Popular with both visitors
and locals. Serves Mexican specialties and delicious seafood, notably
ceviche. Inexpensive. Cr.

Hotel restaurants. In this small town of only 10,000, the hotel restaurants are the only "luxury" dining available. However, there are several small sidewalk cafés and stands for the adventurous.

NIGHTLIFE

Watch the sunsets, dine late, go to bed early. There is one disco at the
Hyatt, but somehow Cabo doesn't attract the disco crowd. Alfonso's,
a bar located at the harbor, is a local hangout for those who like to
drink a cold beer with their sunset.

POINTS OF INTEREST

Los Arcos. These famous rock formations are located at the point where the Sea of Cortez meets the Pacific Ocean. Boat trips available from the harbor. You will see pelicans, seals, perhaps a whale or two, on your way.

La Playa de Amor. Hyped as a lover's beach, this isolated bay can be reached only by boat. Sailors will charge a small fee to drop you off and pick you up. Isolated, peaceful—great for lovers.

San Jose del Cabo. This old mission town located about ten miles northeast of Cabo San Lucas is where you will find leatherwork by the Pericue Indians.

SPORTS

Fishing. Some of the best sailfish and marlin fishing in the world is available in the Sea of Cortez. Charters at the harbor.

Scuba diving. The clear waters around Cabo are popular with divers. Check at the harbor or your hotel desk for information.

FIESTAS

Día de San José, March 19. The usual fireworks, fun, and parades.

TRANSPORTATION

Airport. International service to Cabo San Lucas and La Paz. Also national airline service from other parts of Mexico.

Buses. First-class bus service from Tijuana, Ensenada, and La Paz.

Car rental. Agencies include Avis at San José del Cabo International Airport (no phone)—and Hertz at Hotel Hacienda del Cabo (3-02-11) and Hotel Hyatt (3-00-06). Reservations may be made through La Paz car rental agencies at the international airport.

Ferry. The car ferry from Puerto Vallarta serves Cabo San Lucas twice a week. A cabin costs approximately $40, and there's a $40 charge for your car. (Prices may change owing to peso fluctuations.) The ferry leaves Puerto Vallarta on Tuesday and Saturday and returns on Wednesday and Sunday. The trip takes 17 hours. Take seasickness medicine. No reservations.

TOURIST SERVICES

Tourist Office (Delegación Federal de Turismo), Plaza de la Constitución, La Paz, Baja California (9-16-82). This is the nearest tourist office.

BEYOND CANCUN

Some of the most accessible and interesting hideaways are located along Hwy. 307, from Cancún to Chetumal, on the border with Belize. Each year, new hotels and resorts claim a little more of the jungle, but there are still several remote hotels along this stretch of highway.

About 30 minutes south of Cancún at Puerto Morelos, where the ferry departs for Cozumel, are the Cabañas de Ojo de Agua, a small dive lodge that caters to small groups.

Punta Bete, about 60 minutes from Cancún, is the home of Captain LaFitte's *cabañas* and Cabañas Marlin Azul (A. Luxury), two isolated hotels where you can rent a bungalow for two. Both have restaurants and offer diving and sportfishing tours. Punta Bete is also the home of one of our favorite hideaways, Kailuum, home of luxury camping. (See "Luxury Camping" in the chapter **The Unique and the Random.**)

South of Punta Bete is Xel-Ha, the popular snorkeling spot, and Chemuyil, a lagoon surrounded by gardens. Several hotels are planned for this area. Farther down the coast is Tulum, the archaeological site, where you won't find a hotel, but where you will find several coves suitable for camping. There's also a good camping spot between Xel-Ha and Chemuyil called X-Cacel. The beach has dressing rooms and showers.

Bocaditos: Many of the hotels along the road to Chetumal don't require reservations. If one is full, ask the manager to recommend another; you can always sling your hammock on the beach for the night or head into Cancún City.

BEYOND ACAPULCO

For a long time, Hwy. 200 along the Pacific coast dwindled into a dead stop south of Acapulco. Now the road leads to Puerto Escondido and Puerto Angel in Oaxaca. It takes a day to reach the farthest point, Puerto Angel, from Acapulco, perhaps longer if the potholes in the road haven't been repaired. There is a road over the mountains from Oaxaca, but it's only recommended if you have a four-wheel drive vehicle—the road is not paved all the way. There's also air taxi service (stress on the word *taxi*) from Oaxaca to the two coastal towns.

What awaits the hardy traveler at the end of the day are two virtually unspoiled beach communities. Puerto Angel is on a hidden bay, circled by steep cliffs. A small naval base, several seafood restaurants, and a couple of inexpensive hotels are here—try the Hotel/Restaraunt Sonaya. You can hire a local fisherman to take you fishing, or go to a nearby beach for the day. There's one first-class hotel in town, the Villas Angel del Mar.

Puerto Escondido is well named; this "hidden port" is a little larger than Puerto Angel. The restaurants and hotels line the beach and everything is cheap here. Surfing is a popular pastime, but you will have to bring your own board. You can buy hammocks at a store owned by Leo Mendoza Cortés. He also sells *licuados,* fruit and milk drinks, and rents diving gear. Diving is recommended only for those who have a great deal of experience.

For accommodations, try the Hotel Paradiso Escondido, on a hill above the beach, or Las Palmas on the beach. Three miles north of town is Hotel Viva, a new resort.

Bocaditos: Take along quinine medicine if you plan a trip to the southern beaches; malaria has been found among some residents and visitors to the area.

You won't find much English spoken here. Practice your Spanish before you go.

BEYOND IXTAPA

Approximately 90 miles north of Ixtapa/Zihuatanejo, Hwy. 200 ends temporarily and the road heads inland towards Uruapan. At the junction is Playa Azul, a quiet haven on the Pacific. Some say this will be the next Cancún or Ixtapa, but for now, it's a sleepy little town set among a million coconut palms. There are inexpensive hotels on the beach. Try the Hotel Playa Azul, the Hotel Delfín, or Bungalows de la Curva (all C. Inexpensive).

The beach is the main attraction in town and there are several small cantinas and *refresco* stands. The surf here is very powerful; watch out for riptides.

BEYOND PUERTO VALLARTA

The Bahía de Navidad ("the Bay of the Nativity") is approximately 30 miles north of Manzanillo, but light years away in time. Two small villages, Barra de Navidad and Melaque, both popular with visitors from Guadalajara, are peaceful, quiet havens after the noise of some of the large beach towns.

The hotels are cheap. Try the Hotel Tropical in Barra de Navidad (B. Moderate). The Hotel Melaque and Posada las Gaviotas (D. Bargain) are plain, functional, and blessed with beautiful locations in the small village of Melaque, sometimes called San Patricio/Melaque. At Pueblo Nuevo, on the road between the two, there's a new resort with a marina, tennis courts, and a swimming pool (A. Luxury).

Hwy. 200 hugs the coast until a point just beyond Chamela, when it cuts across the mountains to Puerto Vallarta. There are several hotels and fishing villages along the way. Eight miles north of Melaque is Bahía de Tenacatita, known for its bodysurfing. There's a hotel on the beach and a trailer park (B. Moderate).

Another eight miles north is Hotel Tecuan, a country-style hacienda on a hill overlooking a remote beach. And the next turnoff is the road to the Hotel Plaza Careyes (see above) where, if you've made your reservations, you can spend a week in idyllic surroundings. The Club Med Playa Blanca is at the north end of the same bay.

Bocaditos: Watch out for rock and mud slides on Hwy. 200.

ON THE ROAD TO SAN BLAS

To reach the fabled beach town of San Blas, you will have to drive north from Puerto Vallarta, cutting inland by way of Tepic (a good place to find crafts made by the Nayarit Indians), or drive south from Mazatlán.

Just beyond Puerto Vallarta is the border between Jalisco and Nayarit. Pay the 11-peso bridge toll and drive into one of Mexico's most agriculturally rich states, Nayarit, and into mountain time. To the left is Punta de Mita, a rocky promontory where you will find a restaurant, and Playa des Tiladeras, one of the few beaches in this area with no sharks offshore.

It's a long, tough drive from Puerto Vallarta to San Blas, even though it's only 100 miles. Consider breaking your journey at Rincón de Guayabitos, a small resort community on the coast. Try the Motel Estancia San Carlos (C. Inexpensive). The next day, drive inland to Tepic, stopping to buy the local crafts, and then head west to Santa Cruz, a beautiful town of cobbled streets, flowers, and vaqueros. There are several houses for rent in Santa Cruz, but no hotels.

A few miles to the north is a turnoff to Las Isletas, a favorite surfing spot where the waves often break for a mile. There are several *refresco* stands under *palapas* on the beach if you would rather watch.

They say pirates once lived in the crumbling mansions that line the streets of San Blas. It's one of those delightful legends that has its origins in fact and fancy. San Blas was once a major port where the Spaniards unloaded their Black Ships from the Orient at the Andalusian-style customs house. Now the customs house is a ruin, and the large mansions owned by merchants have been turned into impossibly cheap hotels. Try the Los Flamingoes and El Bucanero (D. Bargain).

San Blas is located at the mouth of a river, and the ocean is beyond a large palmetto-dotted sandbar. A thick jungle, where banyan trees hung with Spanish moss hide all manner of flora and fauna, surrounds the town. The main attraction in San Blas is taking a cruise of the jungle lagoons. Boats leave from the marina next door to the Posada Casa Morales (B. Moderate). Boats also leave Las Isletas on similar tours. The cruises cost about $30 a person for a day of exploring jungle waterways where you'll see fish and colorful birds. (Prices may be lower owing to devaluation.)

Bocaditos: Don't forget the mosquito repellent.

10

THE BEST
OF THE BORDER

HOT SPOTS
AND BARGAINS

A border is a modern reality rooted in the dark ages, a line drawn by statesmen and soldiers that dictates differences. The Rio Grande, that meager excuse for a border, meanders through some of the most desolate country in North America. It serves as an arbitrary line between two very different countries, and yet on both sides of the river the scrubland is as rugged, the mesquite trees are just as gnarled and ornery, the cactus blooms with the same incongruous beauty, the sky is as big, and the road as lonely. But to the north is Texas; to the south Mexico. And although there are subtle shadings of both lands on both sides of the river, the immutable fact remains—they are different.

For some twelve hundred miles, in an irony of geography, two countries, one among the largest in the Third World, the other one of the richest of the industrial nations, share a common border. Third World meets status quo in a fury of neon signs, bargain-basement stores, traffic jams, and gasoline fumes. These are not the most picturesque towns in North America. They have none of the colonial charm of towns to the south. No magnificent glass and steel skyscrapers reminiscent of Dallas and Houston dominate the skyline. These are frontier towns, dusty and hot, waiting on the edge of the future. To the Mexican villager who heads north looking for work, the border town is a mecca, a boom town with jobs to be had—if he's lucky.

Unemployment is astronomical and poverty plagues both sides of the river.

First-time visitors to the border towns are apt to be overwhelmed. In Mexico, life is lived in the streets; a Mexican may eat, drink, make a living, celebrate, mourn, even die on the street. All this is exaggerated in the border town, where competition for work is stiff, where what industrial development brings can be seen in the thick wallets and big cars of the tourists, and where enterprising Mexicans, surely among the world's most innovative and ingenious salesmen, compete for those same tourist dollars.

Like the frontier towns of the Old West, the border towns along the Rio Grande are bawdy and brash. Those separated by only a short, concrete bridge, like Laredo and Nuevo Laredo, Ciudad Juárez and El Paso, are brassy twins who share a symbiotic relationship. Mexicans cross over to buy groceries, to shop in the discount stores, to look for work, and to buy cars, washing machines, color televisions, and blenders. (Recent peso devaluations have affected trade on the northern side of the border; however, many Mexicans still work on the US side.) Gringos cross over to wallow in back-to-basics fun, to eat, to drink, to laugh, and to shop for peppers and gasoline, for plant pots and tequila. Farther down the river, McAllen keeps a respectful distance from her sister city Reynosa, the two separated by the old flood plain of the Rio Grande; and Brownsville, like her neighbor Matamoros, has none of that crowded frenzy found along the upper Rio Grande. Here, the two cities loll about the river delta in an unhurried, lazy way.

Each of the towns is unique; each has its own special haunts, longtime favorites of Texans—we've included them at each city's listings in this chapter. But before you plan a border sortie, there are a few things to keep in mind.

Most US insurance companies issue policies that cover drivers within the 12-mile frontier zone south of the border. Texas policies usually have this provision; check with your agent if you are not sure. It's only necessary to buy special insurance if you go beyond the 12-mile limit. You won't need any special visa or tourist cards to visit the border towns. Mexican customs agents usually recognize a short-timer on the loose, and they will wave you through—don't even pull into Customs. Just cross the bridge and drive to the main street. Border police are stationed at the bridge exit and will stop you if they have a question.

In most border towns there is adequate parking, although it can be hard to find in crowded cities like Nuevo Laredo. It's worth paying a young boy a few quarters to look after your car.

The Mexican peso and the US dollar are interchangeable on both sides of the border; unless there's a crisis over the peso you will see pesos being accepted at McDonald's in Laredo and dollars at the Cadillac Bar in Nuevo Laredo. (For advice about what to do during a devaluation, see the chapter **There and Back Again**.)

Those Texans born along the border pass back and forth with an envied ease. They are at home in both cultures, and many speak a border Tex-Mex, a combination of English and Spanish. The same is true for those born on the south side of the river; many of them have business interests, in-laws, and kids in school in the United States. Consequently, the wandering tourist has few problems making himself understood—English may be better understood than broken Spanish.

Unless you are suspected of smuggling something into Mexico, notably guns, automobiles, or television sets, Mexican Customs won't stop you; unfortunately, US Customs doesn't have this same laissez-faire attitude. You will be asked to state your citizenship, place of birth, where you have been, and what you have bought. Sometimes you will be asked to pull over and undergo either a thorough search or a token one. Don't argue. Just do as the man says. (See **There and Back Again** for what you may and may not bring back into the country.) In addition, along the Texas border, you will be asked how much liquor you have purchased. You may bring one quart a month into the United States, and you must pay Texas liquor tax on that— approximately 45 cents. Usually, the liquor agent will allow you to bring in a case of Mexican beer in addition. (The larger border towns have their own breweries where beer can be a bargain.) Tax is also due on the beer.

Many border aficionados opt to stay in hotels across the river. This cuts down on border hassles and can be less expensive. The service in most of the hotels is superb and includes opening the bar before noon on Sunday to prepare Bloody Marys for beleaguered guests. However, since most hotels on both sides of the border employ Mexican personnel, the same gracious service is available north of the Rio Grande, *sans* Sunday morning hangover cures.

Occasionally, in the smaller towns, there are bullfights, but the rings do not attract the better fighters. Juárez does have a first-class Plaza de Toros, and some of Mexico's top bullfighters appear there. Don't go to a bullfight unless you are familiar with the art or prepared for the spectacle. (For an overview of this quintessential Latin event, see the chapter **In the Heart of the Country.**)

Bocaditos: There are two sides to every border. For a complete guide to Texas cities and towns along the border see *Texas*, a Texas Monthly guidebook by Patricia Sharpe and Robert S. Weddle.

BORDER TOWN SHOPPING

Border shopping is a Texas tradition; a once- or twice-a-year ritual for border aficionados who are almost out of dried chiles and desperately low on Mexican coffee. Those fortunate enough to live near the border may have some of the lowest grocery bills in the nation; however, those who venture across the Rio Grande often don't see the bargains for the red plaster bulls. There's more to shopping in Nuevo Laredo or

Cuidad Juárez than black velvet paintings and fluorescent plant pots. (Recent devaluations have made the bargains even more attractive. Unfortunately, many Mexicans and US merchants are suffering as the peso's value vis-à-vis the dollar falls. In the past, there were just as many Mexicans seeking bargains in US stores as there were US citizens shopping south of the border.)

KITCHENWARE

Cooking utensils of every description are sold in Mexican markets and household stores. Essential tools for Mexican cooks, such as *molcajetes* and *metates*, make unusual and inexpensive gifts for American gourmets. The *molcajete* is a round mortar and pestle; the *metate* is a saddle-shaped utensil used to grind corn for tortillas. The smaller *molcajete* is used to grind chiles. Both are made from volcanic rock, and Mexican folk tradition says that a man should eat one *molcajete* in his lifetime — a feat possible because of the grinding down of the utensil along with the corn and chiles.

Wooden spoons and spatulas are also cheap in the market. A good Christmas stocking stuffer for a cooking buff is a *molinillo*, a wooden rattle-shaped whisk used to whip chocolate.

Glass jars with screw-top lids are much cheaper in Mexico than in the United States. And glassware, like the large glass barrels used by street vendors selling fruit juices, is ideal for serving sangría or punches at picnics.

Clay cooking utensils (*casuelas*) make excellent bean pots or casserole dishes. However, don't use them on top of the stove without a heat deflector. Clay nesting bowls are great for dips and chips.

Baskets, shopping bags, and straw mats are also bargains. Brooms are quite inexpensive, and lidded tortilla baskets are a steal.

Tablecloths, aprons, napkins, and printed scarves (which can be used as napkins) are good buys. Look for specially designed tortilla towels in the haberdashery stalls — two round pieces of heavy material sewn together two-thirds of the way along the edge, leaving an opening for warmed tortillas. And, speaking of tortillas, the flat iron (or curved clay) *comal* used to heat them is another essential border town purchase.

One of the noteworthy purchases to be made along the border is spatter enamelware. This same ware sells for outrageous prices in chic US shops and catalogs, especially when it's combined with four red and white bandannas, plus a can of chili, and touted as a Texas chili kit.

DECORATIVE ITEMS

Perhaps the most visible bargains south of the Rio Grande are the plant pots and lawn statuary. Mexican ingenuity blossoms on border town pot rows. During the King Tut rage, plaster images of the boy-king filled the stalls. However, one of the best examples of border "camp" is the colorful three-foot ceramic model of Pancho Villa, a burrito in one hand and a beer in the other — the very item to brighten an expanse of River Oaks greenery. But look behind the plant stands shimmering with mirror chips for the real buys: simple clay pots in every size and shape. Always bargain with the pot vendors until you feel guilty about the bargain you've struck.

With the exception of pots and practical household items, most border markets are not noteworthy for good folk art or crafts. Onyx chess and backgammon sets, leather jackets and belts, paper flowers, and tile trays are standard market fare; however, it is possible for the discerning shopper to find small treasures among the mountains of tourist souvenirs.

Antique shops and stalls are in business in several of the border towns. Don't buy "antiques" in the market, unless the price is low and you are not concerned with authenticity.

STOCKING THE PANTRY AND THE BAR

The Mexican border market offers food bargains galore as well as some of those rare but essential ingredients for Latin American dishes. Rice, pinto beans, flour, and sugar may be bought at bargain prices; however, the Mexican government has issued limitations on exporting edible goods in order to discourage Americans from taking undue advantage of low prices. Restricted items are posted at Mexican exit points.

Coffee is the real bargain for American shoppers. Coffee shops are usually located near the central market, and you can buy the beans or have them ground. A kilo (approximately 2.2 pounds) sells for about five dollars. (Prices may be lower owing to devaluation.) Freeze the beans or the ground coffee and it will last for months.

Check out the grocery shops for garlic (also sold in long strands by street vendors), dried chiles, *achiote* (a spice), and *limones*, the small limes essential for good margaritas or tequila sipping. There are several varieties of dried chiles — the small, thin red ones can be used in Chinese cooking, and the wrinkled and brown smoked jalapeños (*chipotles*) make an unforgettable barbecue sauce.

Don't ever leave a border market without buying some Mexican chocolate. Although this is sold in most Texas supermarkets, it's cheaper in Mexico. For the uninitiated, Mexican chocolate is a mixture of cocoa beans, cinnamon, and sometimes ground almonds. Melted in warm milk, whipped, and served with fresh *buñuelos* on a cold winter morning, it's the closest thing to Mexican heaven.

The border bakeries (*panaderías*) are also worth a visit. Unfortunately, the rolls and cookies won't last longer than a day, but they do make the long drive back into the Texas interior more memorable.

FURNITURE

Custom-made furniture is a standard border business. It's best to deal with a well-known furniture maker; some of the less expensive pieces are not treated against rot. Most dealers will arrange for shipping, at least as far as the US side of the border; others will ship to your home.

CIUDAD JUAREZ/EL PASO

Juárez is the largest, oldest, and most sophisticated of the border towns. Three Spanish missions — one of which is still in use — were established here in 1680, before the border officially existed. Originally, Juárez was named in honor of the mission Nuestra Señora de Guadalupe del Paso del Norte — hence the origin of the name El Paso, Juárez's city sister. In 1888 the name was changed to honor Benito Juárez who led a government in exile from the city during the occupation by Emperor Maximilian and the French. You can visit Juárez's headquarters on Avenida 16 de Septiembre.

In the 100 years since Juárez set up his headquarters there, Juárez has grown to over half a million people, making it Mexico's fifth largest city. Juárez is a mecca for rural Mexicans who come looking for work. There's a large industrial park on the edge of the city where several US firms employ Mexican labor to assemble television parts or put together jeans for sale in the United States. Like most border towns, Juárez has assimilated some gringo institutions — fried chicken restaurants are cropping up at the same rate as Mexican restaurants are appearing in Chicago. But Juárez is still one of the best places to find great Mexican food, and owing to the city's cosmopolitan air, there are several very good Chinese restaurants. Most of the bars, restaurants, and hotels are located in three areas — the traditional tourist drag along Avenida Juárez across from the Santa Fe International Bridge; a tourist area near the Bridge of the Americas called ProNaF, the acronym of the government agency charged with frontier promotion, Programa Nacional Fronterizo; and the Avenida 16 de Septiembre.

If you don't have your own car or rent one, getting around Juárez can be expensive. Cabs are pricey, but Juárez is really too big to explore on foot, and the summer heat can make walking unenjoyable. Remember, the city is in the middle of the Chihuahua desert.

A good place to begin your shopping tour is the Centro Artesanal in the ProNaF shopping center. This is one of the government craft stores that can be found throughout Mexico. There are only two good ones along the border — the one here and the store in Matamoros — perhaps because the local merchants don't like the competition. The border is free enterprise in action. However, the good government craft stores serve a vital function for tourists who may not be aware of what to look for in Mexican crafts or who are reluctant to barter in the markets. The center features an excellent selection of crafts made by the Jalisco Indians — yarn paintings, beadwork, and baskets are good buys. There are few bargains, but the prices are good when compared with the prices in some of the more exclusive boutiques. The center accepts credit cards and Texas checks. (Many border shops accept Texas checks with identification. Remember the penalty is severe for bouncing a check in Mexico.)

The border shops and markets often receive crafts from artisans working in the interior. A discriminating buyer can find lacquerware from Michoacán, copper from Santa Clara del Cobre, and pottery from Oaxaca. Often, these crafts seem to arrive in waves from the interior, especially at Christmas time. One year, tin ornaments from San Miguel de Allende will find their way north; another year, straw ornaments from around Pátzcuaro will be in vogue. It's especially important when buying clothes in the market to have a good understanding of Mexican crafts. You don't have to visit the source in Mexico to find good crafts if you know what you are looking for, although chances are you will find better prices at the village where an item is made. (For a guide to shopping, see the chapter **The Enormous Store.**)

Surrounding the Centro Artesanal are several boutiques where you will find samplings from some of Mexico's top dress designers.

From ProNaF drive west along Avenida 16 de Septiembre. There are stores and malls along the avenue, many of them modeled after American stores. Mixed in between the Mexican K-Marts are several tourist-oriented boutiques. A few blocks before Avenida 16 de Septiembre joins Avenida Juárez you will find the hub of the city, the Mercado Juárez. This is where you see bargains mixed in with the schlock. Haggling is a respected tradition in the border markets where the vendors are usually much more agressive than their cousins to the south. The standard border fare — leather coats, embroidered dresses, macrame, ceramic pots, baskets, and blankets — are alongside the produce and meats.

Heading north along Avenida Juárez toward the Santa Fe Bridge you will see the usual collection of shops selling leather, ceramics, and jewelry. Look for Cerrada de Teatro, a small street leading off the main street, where you will find several good buys in shops like Casa Mendoza, Armando's, and Mueblos Coloniales Mexicanos.

Border shopping should always be punctuated with several cool, salty margaritas. There is no shortage of places to eat and drink in Juárez; try Chinese food one night, Boquilla black bass from a nearby lake the next, and menudo for breakfast to help cure your hangover. (See the restaurant listings.)

Juárez has several added attractions that make the city a good place to spend more than a weekend. You can bet on the greyhounds Wednesday through Sunday at the Juárez Race Track, located just past the Plaza de Toros on Avenida Juárez. The best seats are in the Jockey Club, where you can eat and lose money at the same time. Call 778-6322 for reservations.

There are two bullrings in Juárez, one on Avenida de Juárez and another on Avenida de 16 de Septiembre called the Plaza Monumental de Toros. The season runs from Easter to September and, according to tradition, *corridas* are held on Sunday usually at 5 P.M. Most hotels either sell tickets to the *corridas* or will be able to tell you where to buy them.

AROUND CIUDAD JUAREZ

VITAL STATISTICS

Climate. Hot, dry summers, cold winters, occasional snow storms. Strong winds whip through El Paso del Norte in both winter and summer.

Population. At last count 500,000, but growing every day.

Altitude. 3,702 feet.

State. Chihuahua.

City phone code. 32. From El Paso dial 1-32 and the local number; you do not need the international dialing code.

HOTELS

Hotel El Presidente, ProNaF Circle (3-00-47). Formerly the Camino Real. Located in the heart of the ProNaF (government) tourist district. A luxury hotel with all the comforts. A. Cr.

Sylvia's, Av. 16 de Septiembre 1587 Ote. (2-24-00). One of those border institutions to which Americans flock to enjoy the service, the atmosphere, and the cool, dark bar. Colonial-style, of course. B. Cr.

RESTAURANTS

Balmoral Room, Hotel El Presidente, ProNaF Circle (3-00-47). Excellent continental cuisine served in a romantic atmosphere. Moderate. Cr.

Casa del Sol, ProNaF Circle (3-65-09). A continental café with a knack for turning local specialties into delicious fare. Try the Boquilla black bass. Moderate. Cr.

Julio's Café Corona, Av. 16 de Septiembre 2220 (3-33-97). One of several Julio's located on both sides of the border. Features good Mexican food of the south-of-the-border variety as opposed to Tex-Mex. Inexpensive. Cr.

La Fogata, Av. 16 de Septiembre 2323 (3-00-40). In every border town there is a restaurant called La Fogata. This is one of the best. Specializes in grilled meats and *norteño*-style dishes. Inexpensive. Cr.

Martino's, Av. Juárez 412 (2-33-70). Continental cuisine with a few local specialties, like Boquilla black bass. Try the stuffed mushrooms. Moderate. Cr.

Shangri-La, Av. de los Américas 113 (3-00-33). Some of the best Chiinese food south of the Rio Grande. An El Paso–Juárez institution. Elegant atmosphere but reasonable prices. Moderate. Cr.

NIGHTLIFE

Disco, Av. Juárez 600 through 800 blocks. Dance until the sun comes up on Juárez's disco row. The ambience varies, the cover charges are anywhere from $2 to $5, and the drinks are expensive. J&W's plays honky-tonk and cowboy-chic; Alive is snooty and swank; Copacabana has a Carmen Miranda beat; and Sarawak is posh and chic.

Kentucky Club, Av. Juárez 629 (2-06-47). Classic Old Mexico bar with good service and relaxed atmosphere. Open till the wee hours of the morning on weekends. Moderate. N.

Mariachi Bar, Av. Juárez and Tlaxcala (4-19-03). They are playing your song—for a price. This traditional mariachi gathering stays open till four on weekdays and six on weekends. Moderate. Cr.

SHOPPING

Avenida Juárez, main street running from International Bridge in downtown El Paso. A popular rule of thumb is that the stores get better the farther they are from the border. Avenida Juárez has a mixture of tourist traps and good craft shops. Some of the best include Cerrada del Teatro, Casa Mendoza, Armando's, and Mueblos Coloniales Mexicanos.

Avenida 16 de Septiembre. This road runs west from the ProNaF center to join Avenida Juárez. Most shops cater to locals, including the modern shopping center Rio Grande Mall. Cookware and housewares can be bargains. Stay away from appliances.

Centro Artesanal, ProNaF Circle. Owned and operated by the government, this craft shop and exhibition hall features a variety of Mexican crafts from throughout the country at fixed prices.

Market, located just west of the junction of Av. Juárez and Av. 16 de Septiembre. The local market is teeming with people every day. Great buys in vegetables, cookware, herbs, spices. Look for the white cheese made by Mennonites in southern Chihuahua and chile wreaths and cinnamon sticks at Christmas time.

SPORTS

Juárez Race Track, east of Av. 16 de Septiembre (8-63-22). Follow the signs past the bullring to the greyhound track. Call for reservations at the Jockey Club, and you can dine while your dogs run away with all the money. Greyhound racing Wednesday through Saturday at 9 P.M. Horse racing every Sunday at 2:30 during the summer.

Turf Club, Av. Juárez, one block from International Bridge (2-21-79).

Off-track betting. Monday and Tuesday 9:30–7:00, Wednesday through Sunday 9:30–midnight.

FIESTAS

All national fiestas are celebrated with spirit in Juárez. Of particular note are Cinco de Mayo, May 5; Independence Day, September 16; Fiesta of Our Lady of Guadalupe, December 12; Día de los Muertos (Day of the Dead), November 2.

TRANSPORTATION

Airports. International airport located in El Paso; national airport in Juárez.

Buses. Luxury and first-class bus service in Juárez to points south.

Car rental. If you rent on the US side you will need to buy Mexican insurance, available at the El Paso airport. Agencies include Avis at Av. 16 de Septiembre Ote. 999 (4-00-19) and Hertz at the international airport (4-05-11).

Taxis. Taxis on both sides of the border are reasonable. US cabs are metered. Taxis ply their trade back and forth across the river.

Trains. Juárez is a major railroad center, particularly for freight. Passenger trains here head south for Chihuahua. (For general information about train service in Mexico, see the chapter **There and Back Again** or check at the Mexican consulate listed below.)

TOURIST SERVICES

Customs. Both US and Mexican customs offices are open 24 hours. There is no tourist office in Ciudad Juárez. The Mexican consulate is at 601 N. Mesa St. in El Paso.

OJINAGA/PRESIDIO

This frontier town suffered when the passenger service between Ojinaga and Chihuahua was discontinued. Hard times have come, but the town is an authentic reflection of northern Mexico and an outpost in the midst of glorious scenery. The action is all along the main street, directly across from the bridge. Prices are cheap.

AROUND OJINAGA

VITAL STATISTICS

Climate. Harper's Hardware Store on Main Street in neighboring Presidio used to be an official weather station for the US Weather Bureau, and up until 1968 Presidio was reported time and again as the hottest spot in the nation on many summer days. In 1968, the bureau made Marfa the official observation point, but that hasn't changed the weather in Presidio and Ojinaga—the mercury still passes the 100-degree mark on many days during the summer. In winter, expect balmy, pleasant weather.

Population. 20,000.

Altitude. 2,594 feet.

State. Chihuahua.

City phone code. No direct dialing; operator-assisted calls only.

HOTELS

Hotel y Motel Rohana, Calles Juárez and Trasviña y Retes (9-01). A border institution. Tiled floors, high ceilings; heated and air conditioned. Considering the Rohana has no competition, the prices are a remarkable bargain. D. Cr.

RESTAURANTS

Hotel y Motel Rohana, Calles Juárez and Trasviña y Retes (9-01). The only hotel in town also serves the best food in town. The Tex-Mex cuisine is renowned, and the restaurant is a mecca for borderphiles. Try the quail dinners. Inexpensive. Cr.

TRANSPORTATION

Buses. US lines serve the area, and travelers can transfer to Mexican carriers for travel into the interior.

Trains. There used to be passenger train service between Ojinaga and Chihuahua, the starting point for the famous Copper Canyon train ride to Los Mochis (see the chapter **The Unique and the Random**). Although passenger train service is now suspended, several travel agencies run buses from Presidio to Chihuahua. One of the best agencies with experience booking the train tour is Big Bend Travel Service, Box B, Presidio 79845 (915-229-3466).

TOURIST SERVICES

Tourist office. There is no Mexican tourist office in Ojinaga; however, there is a Mexican consulate in Presidio at 730 O'Rily St.

CIUDAD ACUÑA/DEL RIO

This is a small town and a favorite with border aficionados. There's no market in Acuña but lots of wholesale shops where you can find some bargains.

AROUND CIUDAD ACUÑA

VITAL STATISTICS

Climate. Hot summers, mild winters. Heavy thunderstorms in summertime.
Population. 40,000.
Altitude. 948 feet.
State. Coahuila.
City phone code. 877.

HOTELS

Crosby's Hotel, Calles Hidalgo and Matamoros (2-10-58). The heart and, some say, soul of the city. The hotel is built around a patio, and for over 50 years Texans have been making the pilgrimage to Mrs. Crosby's place to refresh themselves after a day in the city's dusty streets searching for bargains. D. N.

RESTAURANTS

Crosby's Restaurant, Calles Hidalgo and Matamoros (2-10-58). Mrs. Crosby offers not only rest for the weary but also nourishment. Try the quail or the *biftec tampiqueño* along with a cold Tecate from the popular bar. Inexpensive. N.

NIGHTLIFE

Crosby's Bar, Calles Hidalgo and Matamoros (2-10-58). There is no doubt that Mrs. Crosby holds a monopoly on tourist trade in this border town. The bar at Crosby's is another one of those gringo institutions that dot the border. Inexpensive. N.

SHOPPING

Calle Hidalgo. The city's main street is where you will find an array of border bargains. Visit Jesse's Wholesale Curios for glass, blankets, and pottery; La Paloma for Mexican designer clothes; Casa Uxmal for blankets; and Casa Quetzal for copper and pottery.

POINTS OF INTEREST

Lake Amistad Reservoir, 12 miles northwest of the city, accessible from both sides of the border. The artificial lake, created by treaty, covers over 105 square miles and is 74 miles long. On the Mexican side there are a restaurant and a hotel, the El Mirador, which is also headquarters for a hunting guide service. The countryside north and south of the border abounds in wild game.

TRANSPORTATION
Buses. First-class bus service to and from the city by US and Mexican lines.

TOURIST SERVICES
Tourist office. There is no Mexican tourist office in Ciudad Acuña; however, there is a Mexican consulate at 1010 Main St. in Del Rio.

PIEDRAS NEGRAS/EAGLE PASS
Piedras Negras used to have a rough-tough image, though that's hard to believe when you view the cathedral surrounded by palm trees in the middle of town. Not one of the best border towns for shopping, Piedras Negras does have a few gift shops on the main street and a small Centro Artesanal, which is run by the government and offers a variety of crafts. Many people head to Piedras to eat.

AROUND PIEDRAS NEGRAS

VITAL STATISTICS
Climate. Hot summers; mild winters. Dry and dusty in the summertime with occasional thunderstorms.
Population. 28,000.
Altitude. 722 feet.
State. Coahuila.
City phone code. 878.

HOTELS
Most visitors to Piedras Negras stay in Del Rio at one of the several chain hotels in the city.

RESTAURANTS
Club Moderno, Calles Allende and Zaragoza (2-00-98). Five blocks west and south of the International Bridge, this restaurant is the city's raison d'être in the minds of many gringos. The food is a mixture of Continental and Mexican and the portions are huge. Moderate. Cr.

Don Cruz, Calles Allende and Zaragoza (2-10-92). Located just behind Club Moderno, its competitor, this restaurant offers some excellent Mexican specialties, including *huachinango veracruzano*. Moderate. Cr.

SHOPPING
Calle Zaragoza. One block west of the International Bridge, this street

is home to the local market, several gift shops, and a government-run Centro Artesanal that offers a small but good selection of crafts.

POINTS OF INTEREST

A Mexican visa will enable you to travel beyond the 12-mile federal border zone and visit several interesting sights.

Guerrero, 35 miles south of the city. Take Hwy. 57 out of the city for approximately three miles; turn left onto Hwy. 2. Guerrero is the site of the Spanish mission settlement San Juan Bautista, the springboard for the founding of missions in Texas. Santa Anna's armies slept here on their way to the Alamo.

Múzquiz, 100 miles southwest of Piedras Negras. Take Hwy. 57 south for 75 miles, turn right at Nueva Rosita, and head west for 25 miles. Múzquiz, a typical Mexican town, is visited at certain times of the year by the nomadic Kickapoo Indians. (You may see their huts under the International Bridge in Piedras Negras.) The Kickapoo, originally a Wisconsin tribe, were driven south. Some settled on a reservation in Oklahoma; others eager to maintain their religion and way of life split from the tribe. Now they follow a nomadic existence between Mexico and southern Texas, many times working in the migrant stream.

TRANSPORTATION

Buses. First-class bus service on US and Mexican lines to and from the city.

TOURIST SERVICES

Tourist office. There is no Mexican tourist office in Piedras Negras; however, there is a Mexican consulate in Del Rio at 140 Adams St.

NUEVO LAREDO/LAREDO

Nuevo Laredo, pronounced New-wave-o La-ray-doh by most Texans, is the ultimate Mexican border town, a small oasis of brassy, sometimes classy joints where you eat and drink the days and nights away. To get to Nuevo Laredo, you must first drive 55 mph through some of the loneliest country and on some of the straightest roads in the United States. By the time you reach the river, it's time to unwind. In summer, Nuevo Laredo is hot and dusty; in winter the wind can cut through you, but that doesn't matter — there are dark bars with warm tequila. The noise, the smells, the garish signs all give Laredo the look of a painted lady, an aging but gutsy madam. No one comes back from Nuevo Laredo relaxed, just purged.

Two blocks beyond the old International Bridge, still the most popular crossing, is the market, temporarily located in a plaza since the old one burned down when someone tossed a cigarette butt into a fireworks stand. Across the street on Avenida Guerrero, the main street that leads up from the bridge, is the incomparable Marti's, perhaps the best import shop on the border where the best of Mexico's crafts and arts are sold. The shop also features an extensive collection of jewelry and exotica from around the world. Don't be taken aback by the multizeroed price tags on some items. There are good buys on linens and glassware upstairs.

The best way to get around Nuevo Laredo is by car, although parking can be a headache. (Ignore the parking meters. They don't work.) But it is possible to stay in one of the US hotels near the International Bridge and walk over to the market and shops. About a mile from the bridge is "pottery row," where you can find incredible bargains on flower pots, as well as some of the tackiest statues and garden fountains on the border.

AROUND NUEVO LAREDO

VITAL STATISTICS

Climate. Can be torrid in summer, cold in winter. Usually tolerable in the spring and fall.

Population. 200,000 officially, but no doubt larger because it is a border town.

Altitude. 438 feet.

State. Tamaulipas.

City phone code. 871.

HOTELS

El Río Motel, Av. Reforma (4-36-66). Tourist headquarters south of the river. Once a bargain, this pleasant motel has upped its rates (like everyone else), but it's still a good place to stay if you have a car or don't mind taking cabs to the town's hot spots. B. Cr.

La Posada, Convent St., Laredo (512-722-1701). There are several chain hotels on the north side of the border, including the nearby Hilton Inn, but La Posada is a Laredo tradition. Built in the manner of a Mexican hacienda, this motor hotel sits on the northern bank of the river, virtually next door to the US Customs House. A favorite. A. Cr.

RESTAURANTS

Cadillac Bar, Belden and Ocampo (2-00-15). Sit in the Cadillac long enough and you will meet someone you know. This is a gringo shrine, a must stop for either a Ramos gin fizz or a meal. The seafood is the best bet. The lighting is fluorescent, the white tablecloths are stained, and the waiters are less than gracious; but everyone goes here. Moderate. Cr.

Café Ernesto, Hwy. 85, just south of the last monument in town dedicated to Simón Bolívar. A hole-in-the-wall café with good food. Breakfast for two costs less than an Egg McMuffin and coffee. Ernesto is famous for having found a Stradivarius in an old piano — the newspaper clippings are on the wall. Inexpensive. N.

El Rancho, 2114 Guerrero (2-59-87). The sign says "Su majestad el taco" and the taco does reign here. Oil cloth–covered tables, beer hall atmosphere. Inexpensive. N.

El Rincón del Viejo, 4834 González (2-25-23). The paint is peeling and the garden is overgrown, but this is one of the best places in town to eat the local *norteño* specialties like *cabrito* and *fajitas.* West of the city's main drag, El Rincón is a little hard to find but persist — it's worth it. Moderate. Cr.

LaFitte's, 2925 Victoria (2-22-08). The decor is de Toulous-Lautrec meets New Orleans and sees green. Good Gulf seafood. Try the Aphrodisiac cocktail, a seafood melange with a Mexican touch. Expensive. Cr.

LaFuente, El Río Motor Hotel, Reforma (2-36-00). The restaurant poses as a colonial garden complete with trickling fountain. Good food. Mexican wine list. Popular Sunday morning breakfast spot. Moderate. Cr.

La Palapa, 3301 Reforma (2-99-95). You order your meat by the kilo here. It's grilled over mesquite, then served up with *frijoles borrachos* and corn tortillas. Sit outdoors or inside under the thatched roof. Moderate. Cr.

Nuevo León, 508 Guerrero (2-16-60). Meat-eaters only. The *cabrito* in the window is the menu. Baby goat and the fixin's. Inexpensive. N.

Mexico Tipico, Av. Guerrero 934 (2-15-25). Grilled meat cooked *norteño* style, *bolillos* stuffed with a variety of fillings, *cabrito,* tacos, and enchiladas. Try the *brocheta* (skewered meats and peppers). Mariachis haunt the place on weekends. Moderate. Cr.

The Winery, Av. Matamoros 332 (2-08-95). Located one block south of the *mercado,* this relatively new face on the Nuevo Laredo scene is a product of the Longoria clan, the business family that owns large chunks of real estate along the border. The continental and Mexican food is good; the decor mixes Victorian, Early American, border camp, and pseudo-Versailles. Try the baked potato stuffed with caviar. Moderate to expensive. Cr.

NIGHTLIFE

El Río Motel, Av. Reforma (4-36-66). The nightclub here is one of the hot spots in town. It's always packed for the consistently good floor show. In Spanish. Usually groups with a Brazilian beat. Loud. Good bar. Moderate. Cr.

Mariachis, Mexico Tipico, Av. Guerrero 934. Popular restaurant with outdoor patio where you can drink or eat while the mariachis play.

Remember, you make a request, you pay. Inexpensive. Cr.

LaFitte's Piano Bar, 2925 Victoria (2-22-08). Whether it's hot and dusty or cold and wet outside, inside it's dark and cozy. Closed Monday. Moderate. Cr.

The Pub, Av. Matamoros 332 (2-08-95). Downstairs from and affiliated with The Winery restaurant. The trompe l'oeil paintings are interesting, the drinks good (one of the best margaritas in town), and the beer cold. Try a *botana* tray, an assortment of munchies. Football games on Sunday; live music on Friday and Saturday. Moderate. Cr.

SHOPPING

Avenida Guerrero and Avenida Matamoros. Guerrero is the main drag, and most of the tourist shops are in the first three blocks near the old International Bridge. Farther south there are shops selling ceramics and housewares. Matamoros runs parallel to Guerrero and in the fourth and fifth blocks from the bridge you will find greengrocery stalls and a coffee bean shop.

Centro Artesanal, Guerrero at Monclavio Herrera. This government-owned craft store is not one of the best, but under the dust you may find good buys at fixed prices. Opens irregularly.

Deutch's, Guerrero 310. Next door to Marti's (see below), this well-known jewelry store does custom work for many Texans. Good prices on French perfumes, also. Cr.

Market. Border markets seem to suffer from fires more frequently than those in the interior. (The market in Matamoros burned down several years ago.) The market has moved to Plaza Juárez, one block south of its original location in the 400 block of Guerrero, since a 1982 fire. Mostly tourist gewgaws, but some good buys on dresses.

Marti's, Av. Guerrero. Just three blocks from the old International Bridge, Marti's is a border sanctuary packed with the best Mexican crafts and an eclectic variety of items from around the world. The prices for Mexican crafts are higher than in the interior but still reasonable. You can spend $5 here or $50,000. Furniture, creations by Sergio Bustamante, jewelry, French perfume, designer clothes, Indian silks, *molas* from Panama, and more. Accepts Texas checks. Cr.

Rafael's, Av. Reforma. Across the street from El Río Motel, this custom furniture store has a new upstairs showroom and is growing each month. Rafael will build any piece of furniture for you in Spanish colonial or modern style. Reasonable prices. Also stocks other craft items. Cr.

SPORTS

Turf Club, two blocks north of the bridge on Plaza Juárez at Bravo and Ocampo. Nuevo Laredo now has a horse and greyhound track, and you can make bets on the horses at this betting club (next door to the Church of Santo Niño de Atoche). The club monitors by wire races in the United States and Mexico City. You can pick up a copy of the house rules and bet limits at the counter. Small bar and restaurant. Open Wednesday through Sunday 10–8; Monday and Tuesday 10–4. (The new track was opened late spring 1983.)

FIESTAS

George Washington is a big hero in these parts on both sides of the border. Washington's birthday is celebrated for a week around February 22. Call Laredo Chamber of Commerce (512-722-9895) for exact dates.

TRANSPORTATION

Car rental. Agencies include Hertz (operating as Auto Arrendadora Laredo S.A., Ocampo and Baja California (4-04-64).

TOURIST SERVICES

Customs. Both US and Mexican Customs are open 24 hours a day. There is no tourist office in Nuevo Laredo. The Mexican consulate's office is at 1612 Farragut St. in Laredo.

REYNOSA/McALLEN

Reynosa is something of an aberration among border towns because there's no US town immediately across the river; McAllen is several miles north across the flood plain. The home of a large Pemex plant, Reynosa isn't dependent on tourism for much of its income; therefore, the nightlife here is not as frantic as the nightlife in Nuevo Laredo. Most of the shops, restaurants, and bars are clustered around Boulevard Miguel Alemán and Calle Zaragoza near the bridge. Many of the shops are also nightclubs, a convenience since most visitors stay in McAllen, which has several gracious hotels.

AROUND REYNOSA

VITAL STATISTICS

Climate. Generally warm year-round. Hot and humid in summertime. Occasionally cold in winter owing to northers.

Population. 150,000, but may be larger since this is a border town.

Altitude. 112 feet.

State. Tamaulipas.

City phone code. 892. From McAllen dial 1-96 and the local number; you do not need an international dialing code.

HOTELS

La Posada, 100 N. Main, McAllen (512-686-5411). Most tourists visiting Reynosa stay in McAllen at one of the chain hotels near the interstate or at the airport. But the best in town is La Posada, a colonial-style hotel with lots of tile, old furniture, good service, and a peaceful atmosphere. A. Cr.

Motel Virrey, Hidalgo and Balboa Pte. two and a half miles south of the International Bridge on Hwy. 40 (3-10-50). Moderately priced motel has air-conditioned rooms and is convenient for travelers either returning from the interior or setting out. Adjacent restaurant, El Virrey, serves excellent food. C. Cr.

RESTAURANTS

La Cucaracha, Aldama and Ocampo 1000 (2-01-74). Continental and Mexican cuisines are served in style at this watering hole, a longtime favorite on the border. Try the quail or game dinners. Moderate to expensive. Cr.

Sam's Place, Allende Ote. 990 (2-00-34). Another border hangout favored by visitors for decades. Mexican dishes and game specialties. Moderate. Cr.

US Bar and Grill, Puente Internacional (2-76-23). Located in the tourist district just across the bridge. Features excellent Mexican specialties. Moderate. Cr.

El Virrey, Hidalgo and Balboa Pte., on Hwy. 40 two and a half miles south of the International Bridge (3-10-50). Excellent regional specialties such as *carne asada, cabrito,* and Gulf shrimp. Moderate. Cr.

NIGHTLIFE

Treviño's Bar and Gift Shop, Puente Internacional (2-14-44). A dark, popular bar with great margaritas and mariachis. You must walk through the gift shop to get to the bar. Moderate. Cr.

The Imperial, Puente Internacional (2-13-09). High camp. The waterfall rises and falls with the organ music while colored lights revolve. Moderate. Cr.

Dutch's, Ocampo Nte. 1020. A favorite hideaway. The windmill outside signifies that the Dutch owner has brought a little Dutch hospitality to the neighborhood. (He married a local girl.) Quiet with a saloon singer. Moderate. N.

SHOPPING

Astra Supermercado, Hidalgo and Balboa Pte., two and a half miles south of the International Bridge on Hwy. 40 (3-06-59). In search of ingredients for Mexican dishes? Search no more. This supermarket features spices, cheeses, vegetables, and fruits that are essential to any Mexican kitchen.

Fruit and Vegetable Market, Hidalgo, ten blocks south of the main plaza. Hundreds of chiles, vegetables, fruits, and herbs for sale at the stalls. Unbeatable prices.

Zaragoza Market, Hidalgo and Porfirio Díaz, one block south of the main plaza. This is the tourists' market where you will find good buys in blankets, dresses, belts, and onyx bookends and backgammon sets.

Zona Rosa, one block from the International Bridge. A mix of bars and boutiques. Bargains and good buys in glassware and baskets among the usual tourist gewgaws.

TOURIST SERVICES

Customs. Both US Customs and Mexican Customs are open 24 hours a day. There is no tourist office in Reynosa. The Mexican consulate's office is at 1418 Beech St. in McAllen.

MATAMOROS/BROWNSVILLE

Perhaps it's the tropical Gulf coast heat, but Matamoros doesn't have that brash, often bawdy air shared by many of the border towns. The first sight to greet the visitor is a boulevard lined with large homes and elegant boutiques—stop at Myrta's and Barbara's for Mexican designer dresses. Farther down, beyond the El Presidente, is the Centro Artesanal, where you will find a good selection of unfinished, colonial-style furniture and ceramics. One of the best places to sip a cold margarita is Los Dos Repúblicas, a large shop with a dark, cold bar across from Mercado Juárez on Calle 9A. The market is located in the heart of the city and has a large number of curio stalls displaying the usual tourist trinkets. There are some good buys in dresses and onyx ashtrays mixed in with the leather whips and velvet sombreros.

AROUND MATAMOROS

VITAL STATISTICS

Climate. Warm winters; hot and humid summers. Occasional northers blow in during the winter. Hurricane season from late summer to early fall.

Population. 200,000. (Like population statistics for most border cities, this figure is probably an underestimate.)

Altitude. Sea level.

State. Tamaulipas.

City phone code. 891. To dial Matamoros from Brownsville, dial 132 plus the local number; you do not need an international dialing code.

HOTELS

Fort Brown Motor Hotel, 1900 E. Elizabeth St., Brownsville (512-546-2201). Just a short stroll from the International Bridge and convenient for border hops or preparations for forays into the interior. Set in beautiful gardens. A. Cr.

El Presidente, Av. Obregón 249 and Constituentes (3-94-40). Because the hotel is next door to the Centro Artesanal, this is a good location for shoppers. Spanish decor. Good service. B. Cr.

Hotel Regis, Calle 10A No. 109 (2-15-89). A small, comfortable colonial-style hotel in downtown Matamoros. Predominantly Mexican clientele. C. Cr.

RESTAURANTS

Drive-In, Calle 6A and Hidalgo (2-00-23). Another border watering hole with good food but overdone decor. Waterfalls, violins, and more catering to the Marie Antoinette in us all. Moderate to expensive. Cr.

Santa Fe Restaurant, Gonzales 6A (2-07-46). A Chinese restaurant set in a border town and named after a city in New Mexico? Ponder these mysteries as you enjoy the great food, quiet atmosphere, and impeccable service. Moderate. Cr.

Texas Bar, Calle 5A No. 138 (2-03-25). Guaranteed to draw a crowd with a name like that, and it does. Next door to the US Bar on the square. Good food, especially the game dinners. Moderate. Cr.

US Bar, Calle 5A No. 73 (2-14-75). Located on the square. Decor is Las Vegas tacky, but the food is good. Seafood, Mexican, and continental specialties. Moderate. Cr.

NIGHTLIFE

Los Dos Repúblicas, Matamoros and Calle 9A (2-47-50). A quiet, dark, and cold bar near the market. Excellent margaritas. Moderate. Cr.

SHOPPING

Avenida Obregón. This broad avenue runs from the International Bridge south. It's home to several boutiques selling clothing and crafts, including Myrta's Dress Shop, Av. Obregón 23; Bertha's (for agate), Av. Obregón 22; Barbara's (for clothes), Av. Obregón 40; and Garcia's, Av. Obregón 80.

Centro Artesanal, Iturbide and Av. Obregón. Located next door to the El Presidente in an adobe-style building. This is one of the best government-owned craft centers on the border. Large, with exhibits of custom-made furniture, weavings, pottery, and jewelry.

El Mercado, Calle 9A. One of the best markets on the border, rebuilt after a fire some years ago. Good buys include clothing, housewares, glass, and plant pots.

TRANSPORTATION

Car rental. Agencies include Avis at the international airport (3-84-16).

TOURIST SERVICES

Customs. Both Mexican and US Customs are open 24 hours. There is no tourist office in Matamoros. In Brownsville, the Mexican consulate's office is in Rooms 214–215 of the Pasol Building at 940 E. Washington.

NUEVO PROGRESO/PROGRESO

There's only one reason to come to Nuevo Progreso — Arturo's Restaurant, a gringo institution par excellence that is known for its game dinners. A couple of liquor stores and curio shops make up the rest of the town.

11

SUNSETS AND TEQUILA

ENJOYING THE GOOD LIFE

Once upon a time there was a food critic who had the misfortune to get lost in the deep, dark forest of French haute cuisine, and as he stumbled about in a bog of sauces and a haze of clarified butter, he made the unforgivable error of writing that Mexican cookery was one of the world's poorest. This fable should have ended with the food critic being dragged atop an Aztec pyramid and simmered gently in a pot of *mole poblano*; instead, he was allowed to escape Texas under the misapprehension that a Mexican Dinner No. 3 (with guacamole salad and obligatory praline) is the apex of Mexican cooking.

Don't misunderstand the moral of this story. It is not a potshot at Tex-Mex cooking. Tex-Mex is a basic part of the Texas diet, the burger-and-fries branch of Mexican cooking. Even the immortals—Claiborne, Bocuse, and Child—must get a hankerin' for a burrito once in a while. There is no sin in having taco juice on your chin, but if you make the same unfortunate mistake as the food critic in our tale, you are depriving yourself of some of the world's greatest culinary delights. Mexico has given the world tomatoes, the cocoa bean, vanilla, chiles, pumpkins, squash, maize, avocados, papayas, and mangoes. Without these Mexican products there would be no chocolate, no ketchup, no pasta *bolognese*, no vanilla fudge, no guacamole.

There is a relationship, of course, between Tex-Mex cooking and Mexican cuisine. Tex-Mex has its roots in the cooking of northern Mexico, where many of the dishes were created by vaqueros on cattle drives or in ranch kitchens. Texans share with their northern Mexican neighbors a taste for barbecue and hot chile sauces, spicy stews and flour tortillas. But such tastes reflect only one regional aspect of Mexican cooking. Mexican cuisine is a mélange of influences — Indian, Spanish (itself a mixture of Roman, Celtic, and Arabic), a dash of French, Oriental (Mexican dishes can be traced to the noodle shops and rice paddies of the East), and African — all flavored with the spices brought across the Pacific Ocean by the Spanish Black Ships. Some dishes are complex, others simple, veritable examples of the now chic *cuisine minceur*, which lauds the use of fresh ingredients. The grinding stones of the Indians, however, have long precluded the Cuisinarts of the modern chef. *Salsa cruda*, a relish made from tomatoes, onions, fresh chiles, and *cilantro*, is ground in a *molcajete* and served uncooked. On the other hand, all the complexity of a great French sauce can be found in *mole poblano*, a rich chocolate-chile sauce made from spices, tortillas, nuts, chocolate, and chiles.

Mole poblano may sound like a strange juxtaposition of foods — chocolate and chiles — but then Americans consume thousands of peanut butter–and–chocolate candy bars. Tourists often miss the best dishes because they are discouraged by the ingredients; if you think you might prefer not to know what you are eating, taste first and ask questions later. Raised on steak and hamburger, Americans eat few of the so-called variety meats found in other ethnic cuisines. *Menudo* may taste terrific until you find out it's made with a cow's stomach. And don't be afraid that Mexican food will be too hot for you; many of the chiles used in Mexican cuisine are found in the *salsas*, the sauces and relishes added to dishes. If you do taste a chile-spiced dish that is too hot, try a spoonful of sugar to abate the burning. Most chiles are not too hot for Texans who are familiar with the fiery jalapeño. But beware if you travel in Yucatán; that innocent-looking bottle of hot sauce probably contains the juice of the *chile habanero*, which will leave you begging for water like a legionnaire lost in the desert.

If you want to read up on Mexican cooking before you go, try the books of Diana Kennedy, a longtime Mexico resident who has won international acclaim for her adventures into the mystery of Mexican food. Her books are filled with everything from recipes by master bakers to the secret concoctions of bus drivers. Follow Kennedy's example and don't be afraid to ask the waiter or the woman cooking in the marketplace for the recipe of a favorite dish.

While many restaurants in Mexico specialize in international cuisine, you won't have any difficulty finding classic Mexican cooking. From Mexico City's fine ethnic restaurants to sidewalk stands and neighborhood cafés, authentic Mexican dishes reflect various regional tastes found throughout the country.

Here's a rundown of the essentials of Mexican cooking, followed by a selection of some of the more popular regional dishes. We've also included a guide to Mexican drinks and a special look at Mexican munchies. *Bocaditos*, at the end of the chapter, lists some of the best places to find authentic Mexican cuisine.

TORTILLAS

Maize was one of the first plants domesticated in Mexico and has remained a staple of the country's millions. The word *tortilla* comes from the Spanish word for pancake, although the tortilla was part of the pre-Columbian diet.

Tortillas are made from *masa*, a flour made from corn kernels. Traditionally the corn is soaked in lime and water, then ground on a *metate*. Today much of the *masa* is ground commercially or in the local miller's shop, and many Mexican housewives buy their tortillas ready-made from the local *tortillería*.

The tortilla is used to make a variety of dishes in Mexico, and the names of these dishes vary throughout the country — enchiladas, *flautas, chalupas, gorditos,* and tacos. Most of the dishes consist of a folded or rolled tortilla that has been lightly fried or heated on a *comal*. The tortilla is then filled and either dipped in or garnished with *salsa*. In the north, tortillas are made from wheat flour, but corn tortillas are used for enchiladas and *flautas*.

Masa is also used to make tamales, an ancient Indian dish in which the *masa* is mixed with lard and broth, spread on a corn husk or banana leaf, filled with beef, poultry, or chiles, and folded and steamed. (In Mexico, the singular is *tamal*, not *tamale* as it is in the Southwest.) Tamales sweet with sugar and spices are often made at fiesta time.

Some *antojitos* ("snacks") are also made from *masa*. These small, often boat-shaped mounds are filled with meat or chiles and fried or steamed.

Another ancient dish, still found among the Indians and served in the marketplaces, is *atole*, a gruel made with masa that is served in colorful gourds.

FRIJOLES

Beans — kidney, pinto, pink, and black — are also a fundamental staple of the Mexican diet. Pinto beans are cooked with salt pork, water, onion, *cilantro*, and garlic to make *frijoles borrachos* ("drunken beans"), a popular side dish for barbecue in the north. In the south and Yucatán, black beans are used to make soups or refried. *Frijoles refritos* are a popular side dish from breakfast to dinner. Translated as "refried beans," *refritos* really means "well-cooked beans" — cooked beans are mashed and fried in lard. Good refried beans should be lumpy and steaming, not too dry or pureed. Fresh farm cheese is sometimes sprinkled on top for variety.

Garbanzos and lentils are also popular in some areas of Mexico. In Querétaro, a soup made from lentils, tomatoes, and *nopales* ("cactus pads") is served.

CHILES

The chile is the most obvious symbol of Mexican cooking. There are hundreds of varieties, some hot, some mild. They vary from the long, waxy Anaheim pepper used for *chiles rellenos* to the fiery *habanero*, which is said to burn the hands of pepper harvesters. High in vitamins and iron, chiles play a pivotal role in many Mexican dishes. *Chiles anchos* are soaked and ground to make enchilada sauce; jalapeños are smoked to produce the wrinkled, brown *chipotle* peppers; and *serranos* are chopped and eaten raw in *salsa cruda*. Peppers may have different names in various parts of the country, but they can be seen in every marketplace, piled high in fresh green, red, and yellow stacks or spread out on a white cloth, drying in the sun.

Every restaurant has a bowl of the house *salsa* on the table next to the salt and pepper, and it is liberally spread on everything. *Salsas* vary; some are cooked, others chopped or ground in the *molcajete*. Most are made with tomatoes and chiles. *Salsa verde* is made from *tomatillos*, the Mexican green, paper-husked tomatoes. And there is no substitute for freshly made *salsas*.

Chiles are also used to make *moles*, the sauces that are used on everything from tamales to turkey. *Mole poblano* is named after the city of Puebla in honor of the local legend about a group of nuns who, caught unawares by a visiting bishop, created the sauce from the contents of their larder. In truth *mole* has its origins in Indian food — chocolate is ground with chiles, spices, nuts, herbs, and tortillas to make a rich, dark aromatic sauce.

Another notable *mole* is the *mole negro* of Oaxaca, a black, spicy sauce usually mixed with pork and served in tamales. *Mole verde* is a piquant sauce, which is used in chicken dishes.

Chiles are not just a spicing agent; they can also be found in main dishes, stuffed and sauced — try *chiles nogada*, chiles stuffed with pork and served with a walnut sauce.

While chiles are essential to Mexican cooking, other herbs and spices also play important roles. Cumin and oregano are vital in dishes like *menudo* (tripe soup) and *pozole*, a rich hominy stew native to Chihuahua. *Cilantro*, sometimes called Chinese parsley in the United States, is an important ingredient in *salsa cruda* and guacamole. Cinnamon and vanilla are two favorite spices, and garlic is used in many soups and *salsas*. In Yucatán, the spice *achiote* (the seeds of the annatto tree) is used to make a paste that is spread on meat before it is barbecued. The juice of sour oranges is used to marinate the meat.

ANTOJITOS

Antojitos are Mexican hors d'oeuvres. The Spanish custom of munching on something more than peanuts while you drink has been successfully transplanted to Mexico. *Botanas*, the snacks most often served with drinks, vary from *carnitas*, little bites of meat served with *salsa*, to *queso asado*, a sort of Mexican fondue. *Chicharrones* are the deep-fried skins of pork, salted and perhaps dusted with chili powder. Chiles, particularly jalapeños, are served stuffed with cheese or tuna, and that familiar Texas snack nachos appears in various forms throughout Mexico. Tortilla chips topped with beans, guacamole, and chorizo are called *panchos*.

BEBIDAS

There is a variety of drinks—both familiar and new—available in Mexican restaurants and bars. Of course, the most famous is the margarita. Of all life's liquid delights, the margarita ranks high in the pantheon of revered and honored pleasures. It is a recognized ritual in Texas that the first drink south of the border should be an ice cold, salty-sour drink, named incongruously after the daisy. Whether that first sip is taken atop the Latin American Tower while watching the sun set over Mexico City, or in the frigid, air-conditioned darkness of a bar in the middle of a steaming Nuevo Laredo, the first margarita is anticipated and relished.

Something happens to a margarita when it crosses the border into the United States. It grows fat and sugary, and only the most discriminating bartenders hold fast and true to tequila dogma and make a margarita as God intended one to be made—with freshly squeezed lime juice, Triple Sec, and tequila. North of the Rio Grande, we are served disco margaritas, frozen, sweet concoctions that glow in the dark. (Unfortunately, this heresy is creeping south, and in several of the large resort hotels, especially in the new beach resorts, these abominations are being served in place of the real thing. Tequila manufacturers should rise up and take a leaf out of the French Champagne producers' notebook. A noisy cry of disapproval should echo around the world everytime a pseudo margarita is found posing as the real thing.)

The best Mexican tequila is aged, has a golden color, and is made *only* from *Agave weber*—try the Sauza, Cuervo, or Herradura brand. With a wedge of lime and a lick of coarse salt, tequila will warm your innards and, in sufficient quantities, give you the courage of Pancho Villa. If you are not a gulper, try a sip or two of the best tequila in a brandy snifter after dinner. Mexican bartenders have a field day with their native liquor, serving it in everything from Bloody Marys to coconut shells. The ever-popular Tequila sunrise—orange juice, grenadine, and tequila—makes a good eye-opener.

Mescal is the initial produce of the pressing of the agave plant. (Pulque, the popular drink among the working classes, is made from fermented agave.) Mescal is popular among crazed gringos. If tequila makes you brave, mescal makes you ferocious. Usually served with lime and salt, mescal has a warmer, rougher taste than tequila, and whoever gets the last shot in the bottle gets to eat the *gusano*, the maguey worm—a real treat. Agave worms are a delicacy and are served with guacamole salad in some parts of the country. In one area of Chihuahua, rattlesnakes are substituted for worms in the mescal barrels; after all, if a worm helps the flavor, a rattlesnake is a gourmet's delight.

The most popular drink among Mexicans is not tequila but brandy, usually a light brandy similar to that produced in California. Some of the best is bottled under the Presidente label. Try a Campeche cocktail —Coke, mineral water, lime juice, and brandy.

Most of Mexico's domestic grape harvest is used to make brandy; however, a few vineyards produce wines of variable quality. The vines were brought from Spain by priests and have continued to grow free from the phylloxera (plant lice) that devastated vines in Europe in the last century. The principal wine-growing regions are the Bajío, the rich farming valley in Central Mexico, and in Baja California. Quality varies, although Pedro Domecq, a brandy distiller, bottles several palatable, reasonably priced wines under his label. The reds are usually dry, heavy and not very good; whites are dry but better; and the rosés are sweet and light enough to enjoy with fruits and fresh bread.

If the wines of Mexico are lacking, its beers are not. Some of the best beers in the world are produced south of the border, and they are excellent accompaniments to rich, spicy Mexican dishes. Among the best —Negro Modelo, a dark beer; Dos Equis, a rich, medium-dark beer with a taste of hops; Corona, light with a limey taste; Tres Equis, a light, American-style beer; Modelo, also light; Superior, an excellent beer, both dark and light; Tecate, the familiar beer served in a red can with lime and salt; Bohemia, a popular German-style beer; and Leon Negro, a heavy, dark beer from Yucatán. And it might be worthwhile to check out any popular local beers.

Most soft drinks are called *refrescos* in Mexico. There is the ubiquitous Coca-Cola, as well as orange drinks, grapefruit sodas, and a popular apple drink, Sidral. *Líquados* or *aguas frescas*, fruit-based drinks that are for refreshment or use as a digestive, are available everywhere from the finest restaurants to street corner stands. They are made from any fruit and served with water and ice.

A cold beer, a *líquado*, or a Campeche cocktail may hit the spot before an hour or two of shopping, but nothing can replace a glass of water for really quenching the thirst. Mexico had the Perrier habit long before it took root here. Mineral water has been popular since ancient times, and the most popular brand is Tehuacan—Cortés supposedly had some hand-delivered to him from the source. Drier than Perrier, a little gassier but without the aftertaste of Vichy water, Tehuacan and a wedge of lime will satisfy the thirst of even the thirstiest tourist. Another popular brand is Penafiel. Just ask for *agua mineral con gas.*

No Mexican meal would be complete without a cup of Mexican *café de olla*—coffee simmered with sugar and cinnamon in a clay jug. And for breakfast try the drink of the gods, Mexican chocolate—a mixture of cocoa beans, almonds, cinnamon, and sugar, whipped with warm milk until the drink is frothy.

Another popular mealtime drink in Mexico is *sangrita*, not to be confused with sangría, fruited wine. *Sangrita* is a mixture of orange juice, grenadine, and ground chiles, a sweet-hot drink that is good with Mexican dishes.

Next to tequila, Kahlúa, the so-called national liqueur, is one of the most popular tourist buys in Mexico's liquor stores, but there are other liqueurs worth sampling. Almendrado is a sweet liqueur made from tequila and almonds. From Yucatán, try Ixtabentun or Carabanchal, both anisette-flavored drinks made with honey; and in Oaxaca try the local mescal-honey liqueur, a warm after-dinner drink.

SOPAS

Soups can be a meal by themselves in Mexico. The popular tortilla soup is usually made from chicken broth, tomatoes, and *chiles anchos* and topped with crumbled cheese and pieces of shredded tortillas. Some soups, like *pozole* and *menudo,* are almost stews. (*Menudo* is served in the cantinas because it is thought to prevent or cure hangovers.) In Pátzcuaro, homeland of the Tarascan Indians, a rich chile-cheese soup is served with fresh *bolillos* and *mantequilla* ("butter"). Two famous soups are *sopa azteca,* made from brains, and *sopa de flor de calabaza,* made from squash blossoms. Garlic soup, fish stews made with tomatoes and chiles, onion soups, and bean soups are served throughout the country.

Sopa seca ("dry soup") is also served as a soup course in Mexico. In one version, *fideo* (a vermicelli-like noodle) or rice is simmered with tomatoes and peppers. (So-called Spanish rice is often called *sopa* by Mexican-American cooks in the Southwest.)

HUEVOS

Eggs may taste different to you in Mexico. The yolks are more yellow, probably because they are ranch eggs, laid by chickens not raised in feedlots. Texans should feel at home with egg dishes in Mexico, particularly at breakfast. *Huevos con papas* ("eggs with potatoes") and *huevos con chorizo* ("eggs with sausage") are familiar to any Texan who has breakfasted at the local Mexican-American bakery; however, in most restaurants you will have to order a side dish of tortillas if you want taco-style eggs—*bolillos* ("bread rolls") are usually served with breakfast. *Bolillos* spread with refried beans, sprinkled with cheese, and toasted are very popular for breakfast.

In northern and Central Mexico, a regional specialty at breakfast is *huevos rancheros*—fried eggs served on lightly fried corn tortillas, which are spread with refried beans and topped with *salsa cruda*. Another northern specialty and rarity is eggs scrambled with yucca blossoms. The traditional breakfast dish in Yucatán is *huevos motuleños*, fried eggs on corn tortillas, which are spread with refried black beans and topped with diced ham, peas, and cheese and spiked with *chile habanero* sauce.

PESCADOS

Mexico has a rich harvest of seafood, and many Mexicans go on a seafood-eating binge during the spring to celebrate that fact. Even in the capital, far away from any rivers or seashore, fresh seafood is available daily. *Ostiones* ("oysters"), *camarones* ("shrimp"), and *huachinango* ("red snapper") are all served with a Mexican flair, perhaps with chiles or in garlic sauce. Conch, abalone, squid, octopus, and, unfortunately, turtle meat can be found on most famous seafood restaurant menus.

Two of the most famous Mexican seafood dishes are *ceviche* and *huachinango veracruzano*. The first can be a mixture of seafood or a single catch like shrimp, abalone, conch, or firm white-fleshed fish, marinated in lime juice, served with fresh chopped peppers, onions, and tomatoes, and sprinkled with *cilantro*. (Variations on *ceviche* abound.) The second is red snapper in the Veracruz style, grilled and topped with diced tomatoes, onions, and chiles.

For the most part, seafood is served as it should be in Mexico, freshly caught and simply prepared. Seafood cocktails, usually called *coctels* on Mexican menus, can be sufficient for lunch. For example, the popular chain of seafood restaurants in Yucatán, Soberanis, serves a seafood cocktail called "Return to the Good Life," which is a variety of seafood served in a tall soda-fountain glass and topped with tomato-horseradish sauce, onions, and *cilantro*. Squid in its own ink and octopus are also available in Yucatán, and along the country's beaches small stands offer freshly grilled fish on skewers.

But perhaps the best fish delicacy is the *pescado blanco*, the small whitefish found in Lake Pátzcuaro in the highest lands of Michoacán. These small, sweet fish are sautéed in butter and served with wedges of small limes at every meal in the lakeside towns. Recently, there has been a shortage of this delicate fish. The government is attempting to restock the lake.

CARNES

Before the Spanish Conquest, the Indians ate turkey, wild game, and a certain kind of small, edible dog. You won't find dogs on the menu anymore, but Mexican cooks still create magnificent dishes with turkey and wild game, notably quail. Methods of cooking meat vary throughout the country. In the northern vaquero country, meat is often grilled over charcoal or barbecued. Monterrey is justly famous for *cabrito*, milk-fed goat. *Carne asada* is another northern specialty — large cuts of beef or goat grilled over charcoal on a rotating spit. And in the border towns, sidewalk vendors sell *barbacoa*, the head of a cow grilled over coals in a can resembling a garbage can with holes in the bottom.

A popular dish, especially with tourists, is *carne à la Tampiqueña*. Usually a flank or a strip steak grilled over coals, this dish is served with corn tortillas, refried beans, strips of peppers, and guacamole salad. Mexican beef is range fed (although some restaurants, particularly along the border, import US beef) as opposed to most US beef, which is grain fed in feedlots. Consequently, Mexican beef may taste different. The meat is a little tough, but the flavor is similar to game and can become an acquired taste.

Pork does taste better in Mexico; it is richer and not as dry as US pork. Poultry also has a better flavor, perhaps because chickens in Mexico peck about under the stars, in fresh air, eating grasses and herbs, and are not confined to skyless chicken factories.

The art of sausage making, which came along with goats, cattle, and pigs, was introduced to Mexico by the Spanish. Sometimes called "chorizo," or *longaniza*, good Mexican sausage is a far cry from the greasy pork snout- and pigs' feet–filled chorizo sold in many Texas meat markets. Each region of Mexico makes its sausage in a different manner with various spices and perhaps tequila or brandy. Some types are smoked, others dried.

Beef jerky (*machacado*) is another of the butcher's arts, particularly in northern and Central Mexico. Try *machacado con huevos* for breakfast in place of chorizo or *tocino*, the thick bacon usually cooked to a crisp by Mexican cooks.

Meat is generally served grilled or poached in a sauce, sometimes marinated, then baked in a herbed crust or wrapped in banana or avocado leaves. Chiles, *salsas*, and grilled peppers aside, few vegetables are served as side dishes in Mexico. Squash, cactus, corn, potatoes, and hominy are usually served in a soup or stew flavored with a rich meat broth. In Mexico there is little waste of any part of the animal — intestines are washed and filled with sausage, brains are added to soup, the head is saved for tamales or *barbacoa*, the stomach for *menudo*, the feet for pickling (chicken feet serve as a thickening agent in soups), and the skin or hide for tanning or deep-frying *chicharrones*.

POSTRES

Mexican desserts are rich, sweet, and varied. Many have their origins in Spanish delicacies, which were originally influenced by the sweet tooth of Arab chefs. The list includes flans served with caramel or walnut sauce; *chongos*, a rich rennet dessert; fruit and nut pastes; *arroz con leche*, a creamy rice pudding; or guavas with fresh cheese. The spicy, complex tastes of Mexican *mole* dishes are best complemented by a small, sweet dessert or a bite or two of fresh fruit and cheese. Mexican pastries are not usually served after a meal but reserved for mid-morning and late-evening snacks.

Mexican cooking can please everyone from the meat-and-potatoes man to the more adventurous. (Vegetarians can enjoy meals in Mexico but should be aware that many dishes are fried in lard rendered from pork fat.) If you are hungry for meat, order *carne a la tampiqueña* or a side dish of *cabrito*; if it's simplicity you want, try a mango, cut like a flower and served on a stick, or a plate of *pescado blanco* with butter; and if you are in search of the exotic, try guacamole with maguey worms, sopa azteca with brains, *tunas* (the fruit of the cactus) with cheese, or crepes stuffed with *huitlacoche*, the much-prized corn fungus. Remember, there's more to Mexican cooking than that Mexican Plate Dinner No. 3.

MEXICAN MUNCHIES

The sun is dipping into the Pacific Ocean with an orange fury, turning the whitewashed buildings of Puerto Vallarta a delicate shell pink. It's raining, one of those afternoon drizzles in Oaxaca that leave a sheen on the palm fronds and mimosa leaves. High on the mountainside, a dog is barking; somewhere a brass band is playing; and the lights of Taxco are glittering in the clear night air. Suddenly, wherever you are, it happens — sick of room service, tired of waiters, weary of signing your name, you long to relax on your patio with an uncomplicated glass of wine or a generous homemade drink and a nibble or two of some exotic treat. Don't waste the sunset; create your own movable feast.

All of our Mexican munchies can be found in the markets and *tiendas*, or small grocery stores, of even the smallest towns. If you are in one of the larger cities, search out the local delicatessen or stock your basket at one of the large supermarkets. Conasuper is the government-owned chain. Liquor and wine are sold at *tiendas*; beer and ice are available at the local *cervecerías* ("breweries"). If you drive to Mexico, take along a small ice chest. If the hotel's desk clerk asks any questions, tell him it's for your film, which must be kept cold. Most of the larger hotels serve buckets or small bags of ice; however, some of the smaller hotels don't have this service. Pack a heating coil and a pocketknife, preferably one equipped with a corkscrew, and throw in a small plastic juicer for making margaritas. If your room has only one glass, buy a cup or glass at the local market. Dishes and glassware are incredibly cheap in Mexico. Add something for the soul to your shopping list; flowers and candles from the local market can do wonders for a room gone stale.

WINE

Mexican wines vary in quality. Brandy distiller Pedro Domecq (see "Bebidas" above) sells a number of drinkable, reasonably priced domestic wines. Hidalgo, grown and bottled north of Mexico City, is a passable heavy red. There are some excellent wines bottled in the Baja, but you won't find these at the local *tiendas*. The larger liquor stores also stock wine from South America and eastern Europe. The Common Market wines, particularly French ones, and the California wines are expensive.

BREAD AND PASTRIES

The tortilla may be the staff of life in Mexico, but it is the *bolillo*, a type of French roll, that is served in most restaurants. The French brought their bread-making techniques with them in the last century when Napoleon III's troops invaded Mexico. *Bolillos*, served with coffee or wine, fresh butter, and strawberry jam (*mermelada de fresas*) from the state of Guanajuato, can be the best way either to start or to end your day. Most *panaderías* ("bakeries") are open from early morning to late at night; some stay open 24 hours a day. Try *pan dulce*, Mexican sweet rolls, or sugar-dusted crisps and cookies. Gingerbread pigs are wonderful with a hot cup of tea. Most *panaderías* are self-serve affairs; just pick up a tray and a pair of tongs and help yourself. But don't be tempted to buy more than you can eat in one day; Mexican bakers use no preservatives.

FRUIT

It's best to buy only fruit you can peel — avocados, mangoes, bananas, papaya, pineapple, or the strawberry-flavored fruit of the prickly pear cactus (*tuna*).

CHEESE

Unless you buy it at a large supermarket or deli, cheese is only for the adventurous. The cakes of goat cheese in the market look appetizing, but you should resist the temptation; market cheese is most likely made from nonpasteurized milk.

CANDIES

The Mexican has a sweet tooth to match that of any Englishman. Candies, like *cajeta* (made from goat's milk in Celaya), are regional specialties. In Guanajuato, a rock candy shaped like corpses (*charamuscas*), is sold in the market. Every market has a candy stall. Try a variety, but remember, Mexican candy can be cloyingly sweet.

ANYTHING GOES ON A RITZ

Sardines, olives, squid, smoked clams, onions, peppers stuffed with tuna — all these and more come in bottles and cans at the *tienda*. Be sure to try pickled cactus (*nopalitos*) and sweet onions (*cebollas*).

HAPPY HOUR

Stocking a bar in a hotel room in Mexico is an exercise in frugality and convenience. Most types of liquor are inexpensive, with the exception of Scotch, imported European wines — especially French — liqueurs, and bourbon. Go native: tequila, Mexican brandy (light, like California brandy), and Puerto Rican rum are all bargains. First, stock up on those indispensable small sweet limes (*limónes*) sold in every Mexican market. Limes can be squeezed for margaritas (three parts tequila, two parts lime juice, one part triple sec) or added to rum and Coke for a tart cuba libre. Try a Campeche cocktail — Mexican brandy, mineral water, Coke, and lime juice. Liquor is sold at most *tiendas* (don't forget the salt), and most of the stores stay open late. Ask the shopkeeper if there is a local liqueur; for example, in Oaxaca, mescal is mixed with honey (a guaranteed sedative), and in Valladolid, Yucatán, an anisette type of liqueur called "Carabanchal" is available.

NIGHTCAPS

You are exhausted, your feet are killing you, and your knees ache from climbing pyramids all day. What you need is a cup of *manzanilla* ("chamomile") tea. Renowned throughout the world for its soothing properties, *manzanilla* will help unwind your muscles and relax your knees. Served with a spoonful of Mexican honey, it is the best nightcap south of the border. *Manzanilla* tea bags are sold at the local *tienda*. *Miel* ("honey") can be found throughout the country. In Cuernavaca, a brand named after the Empress Carlota is sold; and in Yucatán, honey from the agave blossoms is available in old Presidente brandy bottles.

BOCADITOS

We have picked some of Mexico's finest restaurants in which you will find regional and national specialties served at their best. These are not necessarily expensive restaurants or posh establishments, but simply a potpourri of favorites. The listings describing what to see and do around each city and town also give local restaurants, their addresses, and their specialties.

ACAPULCO

Antojitos Mayab, Costera Miguel Aleman and Aviles, across from Playa de Hornos. Miles away from the Yucatán, this small outdoor café serves some of the best Yucatecan food in the Republic. Inexpensive. N.

CIUDAD JUAREZ

La Fogata, Av. 16 de Septiembre 2323 (3-00-40). In every town in

Mexico, there is a *La Fogata*, a word used much as we use "grill," as in Harry's Bar and Grill. These unrelated restaurants serve *norteño*-style food, which has its roots in the range cooking of the vaqueros. La Fogata serves grilled meats with chiles or oregano and fresh bass from Lake Boquilla in Chihuahua. Inexpensive. Cr.

CUERNAVACA

Las Mañanitas, Ricardo Linares 107 (2-46-46). A landmark restaurant of the first class. Mexican specialties served in a lush garden where peacocks roam. Dress code. Reservations. Expensive. Cr.

GUADALAJARA

The restaurant with no name, Madero 80, Tlaquepaque (35-45-20). Recognized as one of the best restaurants in Mexico, this hard-to-find restaurant in the popular shopping suburb of Tlaquepaque serves Mexican specialties in an old mansion filled with antiques and artwork. Expensive. Cr.

Hacienda de la Flor, Zapopan. Another jewel hidden behind high stone walls in the tiny suburb of Zapopan (take Avenida de las Americas north out of the city and follow the signs). Taxi drivers know where the restaurant is. Expensive. Cr.

MERIDA

Alberto's Continental Patio, Calles 64 and 57 (1-22-98). There's a feeling of tropical luxury in Mérida that is exemplified at Alberto's. Yucatecan specialties are served along with Arab delicacies. Expensive. Cr.

NUEVO LAREDO

Nuevo León, 508 Guerrero (2-16-60). This border town is brash and brassy, a quintessential frontier town. The local specialty is *cabrito*, grilled sucking goat. If you can't eat it on the ranch under the stars, then sit down at one of Nuevo León's metal tables and order cold beer and *cabrito*. Pluck some of that juicy hot meat, dress it with spicy salsa, and roll it in a tortilla. With the taco in one hand and a beer in the other, settle down for a two-fisted feast. Inexpensive. N.

MEXICO CITY

In a city of 15 million, odds are that a great number of restaurants rank among the best. The following restaurants rate very high on a culinary scale, and they all serve regional specialties with flair in gracious Mexican settings. Reservations are recommended, especially on weekends, and some have dress codes.

Circulo del Sureste, Lucerna 12 (535-2704). Yucatecan specialties like chicken cooked with saffron and spices and baked in banana leaves, pancakes made with coconut milk, barbecued pig flavored with *achiote*. A popular Mexican custom is to serve a "digestive" following the meal. Try Ixtabentun, an anise-flavored liqueur made in the Yucatán. Moderate to expensive. Cr.

Fonda del Recuerdo, Bahía de las Palmas 39-A (545-7260). Among the regional offerings are specialties from Veracruz and Puebla. Try the crab soup or the ranch-style appetizers — deep-fried pork skins, guacamole, tripe, and *salsas*. *Agua fresca de chia*, made from chia seeds, will help you digest the tripe. Moderate to expensive. Cr.

Fonda del Refugio, Liverpool 166 (528-5823). Here the chef creates dishes from Mexico's diverse culinary resources. For dessert try *quince paste* from Pátzcuaro or walnut custard and Chiapas coffee served with sugar, cinnamon, and cloves. Reading the menu can be an exercise in gourmet poetry. Try the romantic tones of *manchamanteles*, Puebla pork cooked with apples, sweet potatoes, bananas, and pineapple. Expensive. Cr.

Hacienda de los Morales, Av. Vazquez de Mella 525 (540-3225). Like all the great restaurants in the capital, the atmosphere here is as important as the food. Gracious dining is the norm in these bastions of Mexican *haute cuisine*, but the setting of this particular restaurant is superb. An old hacienda filled with antiques, aged Saltillo tile, Talavera tiles highlighting the cornices, and everywhere a multitude of tuxedoed waiters. On the menu, a Mexican feast — tiny oysters from Veracruz; mango mousse; and that great Mexican delicacy, crepes filled with *huitlacoche* (corn fungus). Reservations required. Expensive. Cr.

La Marinera, Liverpool 183 (511-2466). Seafood is a passion with many Mexicans, and at La Marinera you can sample some of the best from both coasts and Mexico's lakes. Eel omelets for the adventurous, grilled lake perch for the more conservative. Wash it down with beer served in earthenware mugs. Moderate to expensive. Cr.

Loredo, Hamburgo 29 (566-3433). This Zona Rosa restaurant offers a tempting array of regional specialties. Haddock from the state of Tabasco is stuffed with oysters, shrimp, and abalone and served in a hot sauce; avocados are stuffed with eels; and you will be stuffed after you finish the chocolate cake or a custard flamed in cognac. Expensive. Cr.

Mesón del Caballo Bayo, Av. de Conscripto 360 (589-3000). Picture yourself in *charro* costume, a gentleman cowboy, riding over your estate. At this popular restaurant you can live out your fantasies as the owner of a beautiful, restored hacienda. Dine on lamb wrapped in cactus leaves and cooked over a pit barbecue, beans and tortillas with *cabrito*, and an ice-cold Tecate with salt and a wedges of *limónes*. To whet your appetite, try a house specialty, a "Bull" — lime juice, sugar, rum, beer, and vodka — guaranteed to make you serenade your companion. Moderate to expensive. Cr.

Prendes, 16 de Septiembre 10 (585-4199). This popular restaurant is where you will see Mexico's politicians hard at work on *ceviche* and other specialties. After all, man does not live by politics alone. A house specialty is *gusanos de maguey* (deep-fried cactus worms). Like the beer commercial says, you only go round once in life. Moderate. Cr.

San Angel Inn, Palmas 50, San Angel (548-6746). This famous restaurant is in the quiet suburb of San Angel south of the city. The ambience is magnificent and the food equal to it. The old hacienda is a popular luncheon spot on Saturdays when tourists and locals visit the nearby Bazar Sábado, an arts and crafts fair. One of the house specialties is roast duckling with blackberry sauce. The restaurant has a good selection of wines, including some Mexican wines, which are moderately good, and some Chilean wines, which are excellent. For dessert try a selection of regional cheeses. Expensive. Cr.

12

THE ENORMOUS STORE

A Shopper's Paradise

Shopping in Mexico — these three little words can turn the most vehement mall-hater into an ardent consumer south of the border. The man who regards Christmas shopping as a sort of penitential pilgrimage will spend hours wandering around Mexican craft shops, and the woman who prides herself on being an efficient, budget-minded shopper will return with suitcases bulging.

Mexico is the ultimate store. The whole country is a marketplace. The variety of crafts sold in the streets and plazas, in the *mercados*, and on the sidewalks is matched only by the abundance of Mexican bargains, the stuff that Texas cocktail party chatter is made of.

" . . . and after we left Pátzcuaro — that's where we found the copper plates for two dollars each and I found that white serape for only twelve dollars — well, then we drove to Uruapan to check out the lacquerware. Just as we turned off the highway into town, John spotted this roadside stand where this man was selling animals carved out of the local rock. His fish were just fantastic, and he wanted only sixty pesos each for them. John got two for one hundred pesos — he's such a good bargainer. We put them in the rock garden with that adorable bird bath we found in Guadalajara — the one that looks like Saint Francis of Assisi. You know Marcy said she saw the same thing in Macy's catalog for fifty dollars. Can you imagine that?"

If shopping for bargains and finding them is inevitable in Mexico, the activity is also essential. Show up at the border without a single purchase and the US Customs agent will cast a Buddha-like gaze on you, scrutinize every wrinkle of your face, and examine every centimeter of your luggage. Shopping is expected of you on both sides of the border. But you don't need an excuse to shop in Mexico. Shopping is a part of everyone's daily routine. For every hour you spend in a Mexican market, you are dipping into the social whirlpool, experiencing the real Mexico, getting to know its people, and picking up the lanuage — not to mention improving relations between Mexico and the United States.

The ingenuity of the Mexican salesman is matched only by the susceptibility of the US shopper. The Mexican vendor cajoles; he teases, tantalizes, and flirts. He flourishes his blankets like a matador and presents his paper flowers like a courtier. He urges you to touch, to feel, to fall in love. The wrong color? The wrong size? *Momentito.* He appears with another and another, pulled from some nearby magician's bottomless hat. He knows your Achilles' heel: you really want to buy something. And, as they say in Mexico, *¿Por qué no?* ("Why not?"). Who wouldn't want to take back a little piece of Mexico, a *recuerdo* of mountain villages, white beaches, and sidewalk cafés?

When conquistador Bernal Díaz del Castillo first saw the Aztec market at Tenochtitlán, he ran out of words to decribe its pleasures. Shopping and trading were an integral part of pre-Columbian life. Aztec merchants had a special status in society; they served as spies, and trade was a convenient overture to conquest. But Aztec avarice was no match for the gold fever that fired the conquistadores. Soon Mexico's wealth was being exported, its mines exhausted, its treasures sent to Spain. After the Spanish came the French, then the British and the Americans, who acquired huge haciendas, built railroads, drilled for oil, and sent the profits home out of Mexico. Today the huarache is on the other foot, as millions of gringos are conquered each year by the work of Indian and mestizo craftsmen.

In the *Popol Vuh*, the Mayan book of legend, pots and baskets are given souls; perhaps it is this reverence, this raising of the mundane to an equality with man, that gives life and charm to Mexican crafts. A ten-cent pot, carried carefully north and placed on a bookshelf, takes on a life of its own. A familiar serape grows more beloved with age. There's a fragility, a mortality, about Mexican crafts that adds to their attraction. Look for the life of the piece and for the hand (mark) of the maker when you buy.

There is no distinct line between art and craft in Mexico; the everyday *olla* ("pot"), praised for its simplicity of line and purity of design by the collector, serves a household function in many Mexican kitchens. There are, however, two distinct categories of crafts — those native Indian crafts that were established in pre-Columbian times and those influenced by the Spanish and by later innovations. For example, the bowls and pots used for cooking by most villagers are made in much the same manner as the Mesoamerican Indians made them hundreds of years ago. The *huipil*, the blouse worn by many Indian women, is a precolonial garment that has survived with little change; however, the serape is an essentially postconquest style of clothing that evolved when the wool industry was introduced to the New World. Other assimilated crafts and techniques include the glazing of pottery, metalworking, and furniture making. The craftsman in Mexico is always adopting new materials and designs, and Mexican artists have an uncanny ability to incorporate new concepts and develop new forms in their work. For example, the women of Tehuantepec wear gold US dollars mounted in their necklaces. The coins were spent by American adventurers who crossed the Mexican isthmus on their way to the California Gold Rush. And in the village of Ameyaltepec in Guerrero, craftsmen have taken the designs they once painted on their pottery and reproduced them on *amatl* paper. These "bark paintings," named after the paper they are produced on, show village life in brilliant colors. Naive and notable for their lack of perspective, they are excellent examples of Mexican folk art.

You don't have to visit Guerrero to find bark paintings or Mérida to find a Yucatecan hammock. Many of Mexico's best crafts find their way to the markets of the larger cities or into the arts and crafts shops in the tourist areas. However, there is no substitute for the actual experience of bumping your rented Volkswagen down a dirt road and into the dusty square of a village renowned for its pottery or weaving. Prices are better; the craftsman is on hand to show you his techniques, to take special orders, and to create a unique work to your specifications.

Arts and crafts abound throughout the country, but there are two areas especially noteworthy for their rich variety of crafts. Pátzcuaro, a colonial town about two hundred miles from Guadalajara, is a good base from which to explore the village crafts of the Tarascan Indians. Farther south, Oaxaca is the center of Zapotec and Mixtec Indian cultures, which produce some of the best folk art in Mexico. In both Pátzcuaro and Oaxaca, and in any one of the small nearby villages that surround them, a ritual as old as the pyramids is acted out each week as the Indians gather on market day.

In the early morning hours, long before sunrise, when the mountains are as black as Oaxacan pots, the stars guide small, often barefoot, Indian women as they work their way down the mountainside. They carry large bundles on their heads and, more likely than not, carry a sleeping baby as well. At their heels follow older children carrying their share of the family's burdens. The men, bowed by the weight of the load balanced on their backs and anchored to their forehead with an ancient head sling, follow the women down to the valley. There, by first light, the family can be seen waiting at the side of the dirt road for a bus to appear, rolling through the dusty early morning light like an elephant walking through a sandstorm. The bus is crowded. Baskets, bundles, old cardboard boxes, and crates are lashed to the roof; and, inside, old women gossip, men smoke, chickens squawk, and children laugh at the antics of a piglet wrapped in a burlap sack.

It is market day, comprising a series of events common to every part of Mexico, no matter how large the city or small the village. The Indians call it *tianguis,* and little has changed since the days of the great Aztec market at Tlatilco. The buses, trucks, and burros are postconquest additions, but the head slings, the weekly treks to town, and even the physical arrangement of the marketplace are rooted in Indian tradition.

If the town is large or wealthy, the local government may have erected a new marketplace with a tin roof and running water: and after a few years, if the local government is patient, the Indians may indeed decide to move to the new market. Tradition plays a major role in market-day rituals. (After a long public relations effort, the city of Oaxaca has persuaded some of the vendors to move to the new market by the railroad station, but most of them still flock to the old marketplace.) In the smaller towns and villages, the main plaza or an adjacent network of streets serves as the marketplace. Some are a maze of stalls and dark passageways—the market in Taxco is built on a series of winding staircases. Others, like the market in Guanajuato, are sheltered under iron and glass roofs, vaguely reminiscent of Victorian railway stations. And in small towns like Tlacolula in the Valley of Oaxaca, famed for its Sunday Indian market, the stalls line the church walls and the vendors are protected from the sun by large white canvas sheets. But no matter where the market is housed or sheltered, it is laid out in a pattern handed down from ancient times.

Herb vendors line one row, their mountain flowers, grasses, seeds, and bark stacked in neat mounds. In another section the hat sellers offer everything from felt, western-styled hats to the campesino's tasseled straw hats. Household stalls with plastic tablecloths and aprons, tortilla cozies and dish towels, also sell dishes and bowls of every shape.

Another row of vendors offers traditional kitchenware—*cazuelas* and ollas, *comales* and tortilla presses, mountains of small brown bowls. And there is a rope stall where sisal bags, hammocks, baskets, and mats are for sale. At each stall hangs a mane of rope, of varying widths and lengths to be used to tie this package or make a sling for that bundle.

The *carnicerías* ("meat markets") form a long, stinking row of stalls. The chorizos—sausages made from sweet head and cheek pork with hot red chiles and sometimes flavored with tequila—hang in heavy strands like garlands. On the counter are bowls of purple strips of overripe meat. Thin yellow chicken wings and legs, the goosepimpled expanse of their skins interrupted here and there by an unplucked feather or two, are piled high in buckets.

If there is horror in the *carnicerías*, there is joy in the carefully built pyramids of shining green peppers and fat green onions. The small, yellow-green *limónes* conjure up visions of giant margaritas, while the mangoes and papayas look lush enough to have been delivered from the Garden of Eden.

There's no hawking, no advertising of wares, except around the clothing and blanket stalls, where customers are urged to touch, to examine. And there is a constant hum, a steady drone made up of gossip and chicken squawks, piglet squeaks, and children's screams; the rhythmic thump of watermelons landing on upturned palms as young men unload a truck; and the quiet, mournful prayers of old women on their knees before the Virgin of the marketplace.

She sits in the center of the market, candles burning around her and wilting flowers stuck into old cans and broken glasses at her feet. It is mostly old women who come to her and vendors who leave their stalls to pray to her for a good business day. The shrine is an island of quiet solitude within a cacophony of humanity.

Outside, the streets are filled with diesel fumes of old buses; but the fumes do battle with the smell of tortillas, fried meat, and steamed corn and garlic that already fills the air, competing with the aroma of fresh bread from the *panadería* across the street. Those who don't want to indulge in street vendor fare can explore the lunch stalls inside the market. They offer complete meals, meat and tamales with beans and rice, a beer or fruit juice—these are the Mexican equivalent of our diners, where truck and bus drivers can gather to discuss the day's events.

The *tianguis* is Mexico in microcosm. Order exists beside disorder; beauty is flanked by horror; and quiet, singular moments occur in an atmosphere of general hubbub. The best time to visit a marketplace is in the morning, to watch as the trucks unload and as the burros, sad-eyed and all-suffering, are herded to a nearby alley to spend their day with fellow beasts of burden. Early in the morning, when the flowers are fresh and the peppers shiny, the market is alive and new. By nightfall there's disorder and sadness; widows pick through the rotted fruit piled in the gutters, and dogs sniff around the meat stalls. There's an unchivalrous hurry about the place as vendors, like guilty lovers, pack up and leave. The men rush to the nearby cantinas; the women to mass or home to prepare dinner; the villagers to the old buses that brought them; and the businessmen, whose shops line the market square, to the café on the plaza to talk politics and drink brandy.

The ritual is over for another day. The stalls are shrouded in sheets; the tiled meat counters have been washed down and the soapy water tossed in the gutter; an old man has bargained with a bread vendor for a bag of stale rolls to feed himself and his dogs; and a young mother, carrying a large basket filled with the day's purchases, is trying to steer her sticky-fingered children away from a vendor selling puppets. And in the heart of the marketplace, among the shrouded stalls, the candles flicker at the Virgin's shrine.

Wherever you go in Mexico, the marketplace should be your starting point. A tour of the *mercado* on market day will give you an idea of the crafts available in the region. Always ask questions about the piece — how it was made and where it came from. It's a good idea to ask prices in the market before you visit local arts and crafts shops. The Mexican government operates special stores, FONART shops, which stock crafts from throughout the country. In some areas, Mexico City for example, the FONART shops are excellent with large and varied stock; however, in other areas, particularly the border towns, the FONART shops can be disappointing. Always haggle in the marketplace or with street vendors; the FONART shops and private stores have fixed prices. Throughout this guide, each city's listing includes descriptions of local markets and shops.

BOCADITOS: THE ART OF BARTERING

We may pride ourselves on our great ingenuity and democratic tradition, but when was the last time you haggled with the grocery store manager? Whether you buy a dozen cartons of this or ten boxes of that, a price tag is a price tag is a price tag.

In Mexico, the art of haggling is alive and well, at least in the marketplace where fundamental capitalism hasn't been replaced by a more sophisticated brand. Americans, especially those who never look for mismarked packages of steak in the meat cooler, are often reluctant to haggle; but, by your refusal, you are denying both yourself and the merchant one of the great joys of shopping in Mexico. In the Mexican marketplace, haggling is SOP. Once you get into the rhythm of it, you will love every minute.

Follow these haggling rules and practice on the grocery store manager before you go.

Rule 1: Practice looking nonchalant. Watch Cary Grant's old movies. As you stroll through the market, look mildly interested, as though you had (yawn) so many serapes at home that you couldn't possibly buy another. This doesn't mean you should look disgusted.

Rule 2: Bone up on Mexican arts and crafts. Know a good buy from a bad one. Ask meaningful questions about dyes, looms, and weaves. Pick up and examine the item carefully, nodding once or twice, perhaps murmuring a compliment or two.

Rule 3: Never rush up to an item in the market and say, "Oh! Look! Just what I've been looking for all over Mexico!" A sucker deserves to pay through the nose — an old Mexican market saying.

Rule 4: If you are interested, ask the price. Say, "*Gracias,*" and look around at other items. It helps to shop in mixed couples. Two women look like easy marks; two men will usually be ignored. Your partner can direct your attention to something else or say, "You don't need another dress." Ask the prices of several items, keeping in mind the price of the piece you want. Come back to it and ask the price again. "It's too much," you say. "How about two hundred pesos?" "No? Well, I am going to look around. Thank you." Walk away. Or, if the merchant has come down on his price, dicker back and forth until you reach a mutually agreeable amount.

Rule 5: Always be polite; this includes trying to master a few words of Spanish about how beautiful, cheap, or expensive something is. Think of haggling as a high school dance where everyone knows who wants to dance with whom, but certain rituals precede a couple's getting together. Even if the item is pitifully cheap, always pause. This is a ceremonial dance, remember.

POTTERY

Although a multitude of designs and styles of pottery is available in Mexico, there are basically two types: the fragile, unglazed ware made in the pre-Columbian manner and the sturdier, glazed and ornately decorated pottery influenced by the Spanish. Indian craftsmen have worked in clay for hundreds of years and continue to make beautiful symmetrical pieces by using the inverted saucer method without the aid of the potter's wheel. One saucer is placed upside down on the ground; a second is placed right side up on top of it. The potter throws the clay into this saucer, which he rotates with one hand while he shapes the piece with his other hand. In pre-Columbian times, the pots were decorated by dipping them in a slip (a mixture of water, clay, and pigment) before they were fired. Designs were either etched on the surface before firing or features made from clay were attached to the surface. Glazes were introduced by the Spanish, and this technique is seen at its most magnificent in the Talavera ware. Produced in Puebla, this brilliantly colored, ornately designed pottery is considered by many tourists to be representative of traditional Mexican pottery. It is in fact a reproduction of a time-honored Spanish ware. Another Spanish technique that has been revived in Guanajuato is majolica — this glazing technique calls for the earthenware to be covered in an opaque glaze and then decorated before firing.

Much of the Indian-style pottery is extremely fragile, but breaking a pot is considered good luck in Mexico. In pre-Columbian times, all the pots in the household were broken every 52 years when the two wheels of the Indian calendar, the *tonalpohualli*, meshed, marking the end of one life cycle and perhaps the end of the world. The pots were broken so that evil spirits could not invade them. When the world didn't end, everybody uttered a big sigh of relief and went about making new pots.

Before you buy pottery in the marketplace, always ask if the glaze contains lead (*plomo*). To make sure, after you return home, pour white vinegar into the bowl and leave it overnight — if the vinegar has turned gray or black by morning, don't use the pot to cook or serve food in. To temper fragile pieces, fill them with salt and bake in a very slow oven overnight.

The most common pottery pieces include *cazuelas* ("lidded casseroles"); *ollas* and *ollitas* ("pots"); *cántaras* ("large water jugs"); and *comales* ("clay platters") used for heating tortillas over a charcoal fire. Indian craftsmen have also adapted their art to tourist tastes and produce cups, saucers, serving platters, and punch bowls.

Some of the best places to find good examples of Mexican pottery include the following:

Tlaquepaque, a suburb of Guadalajara, offers a variety of pottery shops, some selling excellent examples of native ware, others catering to the tourist trade.

Tonalá, another suburb of Guadalajara, is famous for animal-shaped pieces glazed with dull reds, browns, and blues on a cream background, and appropriately called Tonalá ware. The most famous Tonalá potter is Jorge Wilmot, whose work is sold at better arts and crafts shops throughout the country.

Puebla, an hour's drive from Mexico City, is noted for its Talavera ware. The pottery shops and factories are downtown. Attractive tiles, dinner services, bowls, and vases are produced there. Some of the factories ship.

Oaxaca, particularly the village of San Bártolo Coyotepec, produces famous black pottery. (If you drive to San Bártolo, take the road to the airport and you will drive through one village named San Bártolo before you arrive at the second San Bártolo—San Bártolo Coyotepec.) For years there has been some controversy over the origin of the "blackness" of this pottery. Some say it comes from the Coyotepec clay; others, from the smoke that fills the closed kilns as the pieces are fired. Whatever the reason, the pottery, particularly the work of a woman named Doña Rosa, is among the most beautiful in Mexico. Since her death in 1980, Doña Rosa's *taller* ("workshop"), in the village of San Bártolo, is run by her son and his family; many of her pieces are still available there. Doña Rosa was one of the few native potters to sign her work, such was her fame.

The Oaxacan market has a good selection of greenware, simple pieces decorated with a green glaze. Oddly, however, the blackware is not readily found in the market.

Dolores Hidalgo, a small town near San Miguel de Allende in the state of Guanajuato, is a must for those interested in tiles and brown cookware.

Guanajuato, capital of the state of Guanajuato, is an old, very Spanish town, best known for its majolica ware. You won't find it in the market, but the FONART and several studios in town offer small selections. The best selection of majolica can be found in the FONART shops in Mexico City, particularly the shop on Avenida Juárez. Glazed an opaque greenish cream color, then decorated with pastels and a vivid cobalt blue, this ware is very beautiful.

Tzintzuntzán, near Pátzcuaro in Michoacán, is a small village on the shores of Lake Pátzcuaro. The local Tarascan Indian potters produce some of the most charming native pottery in the country. Encouraged by Helen O'Gorman, an artist and wife of the muralist Juan O'Gorman, the Indians decorate their pottery with naive, Picasso-like drawings — fishermen, swans, fish. Some designs are executed in brown on a cream background; others are green on brown. This same ware can be found in nearby Pátzcuaro.

Patamba, near Guadalajara, is renowned for its pineapple ware, green-glazed pineapple-shaped pots and jars, which are sold throughout the Guadalajara area.

BASKETS

The basket is as ubiquitous as the pot in Mexico. Some of the best are made from reeds; beware of those made from split bamboo, because they are susceptible to infestation and may be slowly eaten away. Tiny piles of dust on the ground beneath such baskets are a telltale sign of insect problems.

The Yucatán peninsula is famed throughout the world for the henequen industry. Vast areas of the flat coastal plain have been cleared so that the slow-growing agave can be cultivated. The leaves of the agave are squeezed by large mechanical crushers, and the raw stringlike fibers are dried to make sisal. The rope made from the sisal fibers is incredibly strong. Yucatecans use the rope to make hammocks, carpets, and wall hangings, which are sold in the markets and at the sisal plantations that dot the highways in the peninsula.

Shopping bags made from straw or sisal are good buys in Mexico — a good shopping bag should be at the top of your list.

For baskets, hammocks, and straw goods visit the cities listed below:

Mérida, capital of Yucatán, produces world-famous hammocks in a variety of sizes, the most popular size being the *hamaca matrimonial*, a large, family-sized hammock. Prices are reasonable. Carpets, hats, and wall hangings are sold at the sisal plantation shops; carpets can be boxed for you at the factories.

Tzintzuntzán, the village near Pátzcuaro, in addition to its pottery, has bargains in straw mats, mobiles, and decorative wall hangings.

Oaxaca and surrounding villages feature local markets with vast selections of baskets, mats, and *bolsas* ("expanding string bags"), which hold everything from wine bottles to Christmas packages. Basket connoisseurs should visit the Sunday market in Tlacolula, a few miles southeast of Oaxaca on the Pan American Highway, for crushable straw baskets with brightly woven designs.

San Juan del Río and Tequisquiapán, north of Mexico City, off the

Pan American Highway near Querétaro, are best known for their willow basketry.

Toluca, west of Mexico City, offers one of the best Friday markets in the country.

GOLD AND SILVER

At one time, Mexico produced much of the world's silver, and in cities such as Guanajuato the king's mines fed the coffers of Spain. The beautiful colonial town of Taxco is undoubtedly the most famous of the silver cities, although silversmiths there actually use materials from mines all over the country. Excellent silver craft is also sold for comparable prices in Guadalajara and Mexico City. When buying silver, always check the item for the Sterling or .925 silver mark. Never buy silver from a street vendor; when looking for quality, shop at a reputable jewelry store or *taller*. The same principle applies to buying gold jewelry—shop at stores with good reputations.

Several banks in Mexico sell Mexican gold peso pieces, which are extremely beautiful and, as gold prices fluctuate, often a worthwhile purchase for both the investor and the collector. Buy from a bank, not a vendor.

One item made by silversmiths but not sold in jewelry stores is the *milagro*. These small, delicate pieces represent the heart, the head, a leg, or kidney—whatever the afflicted part of the body is—and they are pinned on the skirts of a saint in an appeal for intercession. Many of the crafts shops collect *milagros* and use them to decorate bookends or boxes.

Opals are sold in and around Querétaro and can be a good buy. Beware of bargains, and never buy from a street vendor.

The Mesoamerican Indians worked in jade, which, according to legend, was found in Mexico; however, no jade deposits have been found in modern times. Beware of anyone trying to sell you "Mexican" jade.

Don't buy jewelry or combs made from tortoiseshell; it's illegal to import them into the United States because they are made from the sea turtle, an endangered species. Tortoiseshell items are sold in Veracruz and Yucatán.

CLOTHING

Clothing represents some of the best and worst examples of Mexican folk art found in the *mercado*. The best clothes are made from natural fabrics and dyes; the worst are woven from acrylics in fluorescent colors.

A postconquest garment, the rebozo is the scarf or shawl that Spanish priests insisted Mexican women wear to cover their heads in church. Today, in the southern Highlands, some Indian women use the rebozo as a winding cloth or a turban, rather than as a shawl. The colors and patterns of the garment indicate the village of the wearer. A tight weave with smooth threads indicates quality.

A garment that has its origin in ancient times is the *huipil*. Like the rebozo, this simple blouse has designs that vary with each region or village. Basically, the *huipil* is two rectangular pieces of material, usually cotton, sewn together leaving holes for the arms and neck. Some are long; others are short and worn over a skirt. The most beautifully embroidered are those from the Yucatán Peninsula, the southern Highlands, and the Pacific Coast of Mexico.

One of the better known clothing buys in Mexico is the *quechquemetl*—the poncho to tourist and salesman alike. This triangular-shaped garment is the feminine equivalent of the serape; although, unlike the serape, the *quechquemetl* is a precolonial garment. The serape is worn only by men in Mexico; it may be acceptable for foreign women to wear serapes in the larger cities, but in the smaller villages such unisex dress may be regarded as inappropriate. Always ask if a poncho or serape is made from wool (*lana*) and whether the dyes are natural or chemical. Mexican weavers are returning to the use of natural fibers and dyes, and many of the methods used to produce dye hundreds of years ago are in use today. The *caracol* ("snail") produces a deep purple color, and materials dyed with this color have a distinct fishy odor.

Don't feel compelled to buy only items made from natural fibers and dyes; although handmade items are the most beautiful, some of the mass-produced blankets make ideal picnic rugs or children's bedspreads. However, if a salesman says it's wool, examine the blanket and burn it to prove it's wool—don't be fooled—sometimes the horizontal threads are cotton or acrylic.

There are several popular, modern clothing styles sold in the markets and shops. The *guayabera*, the popular tropical shirt worn throughout Latin America and southern Texas, is sold everywhere, but the best are made in Yucatán. Oaxacan embroidered dresses are popular party and beach wear in Mexico and Texas; consequently, there are many imitations. Always look for handsewn, closely stitched embroidery. Handmade items are usually recognizable by irregularities in weave or design. If you are worried about colors running, wet a handkerchief or Kleenex and squeeze the material. If the color bleeds, dry clean the item several times before washing to avoid fading.

Those bulky white and brown sweaters you see on chilly nights in Mexico City are made in Toluca but can be found in markets throughout the country.

In addition to native handmade clothes, several fashion designers inspired by Mexican folk art produce beautiful resort wear. Look for the following labels and expect to pay anywhere from $50 for a blouse to two or three hundred dollars for a caftan: Gonzalo Baner, Josefa, Georgia, Tachi Castillo, Mama Carlotta, Vercellino, and Bustamante.

Next to T-shirts, hats are the biggest seller among tourists. Avoid wearing a hat that makes you look as if you are making fun of Mexican customs—leave the velvet sombrero in your room. Women should not wear men's hats.

Some villages and towns where you can find exceptionally beautiful items of clothing are the following:

Santa María del Río, near San Luis Potosí, on the Pan American Highway, is famous for its beautiful rebozos.

Jocotepec, near Guadalajara, is the home of the white serape, a high-quality soft woolen garment with simple designs.

Tlaxcala, a small town and state near Mexico City, boasts wonderful woolen rugs.

Mérida, in Yucatán, overflows with *guayabera* factories. Mérida is also the place to buy genuine Panama hats. Also look for the beautifully embroidered white cotton blouses (*huipiles*) in the market.

Pátzcuaro, near Morelia, overlooking Lake Pátzcuaro, is a must for shoppers interested in woven goods. Visit the House of the Eleven Patios, a government crafts area where Tarascan women use the saddleback loom to weave beautiful serapes and blankets.

Teotitlán del Valle, near Oaxaca, is a few miles down a dirt road off the Pan American Highway. Some of the best serapes, blankets, rugs, and wall hangings are made in this village. A visit to the local *taller* is worthwhile, and craftsmen will make blankets to order. Designs vary from reproductions of ancient Mixtec patterns and Picasso paintings to pictures of Ché Guevara.

Santa Tomás, another small village near Oaxaca, is famous for its beautifully woven belts (*fajas*). You don't even have to get out of your car to make a purchase; dozens of children will be waiting to descend on you from the moment they spot the dust rising from your wheels.

Tenancingo, about thirty miles south of Toluca, is an excellent place to find beautifully woven rebozos.

METALWORK

With the exception of precious metals and copper, most metalwork has its origins in colonial times. Wrought iron, for example, is a Spanish art. Look for strongly welded seams and no rust spots.

Decorative tinwork, such as masks and candlesticks, can be found all over Mexico. The town of San Miguel de Allende is especially noted for its tinsmiths.

Machetes, those vicious-looking knives carried by farmers in the fields, are sold in most markets; however, those from Oaxaca are highly prized, particularly those with bloodthirsty mottoes etched on the blade.

The most famous metalwork is done in Villa Escalante, a small town in Michoacán, which everyone still calls by the old name of Santa

Clara del Cobre. Copper here is recycled into beautiful platters and bowls, candlesticks and lamps, and burnished with burro dung. The platters are embossed by hammering by hand; a popular design is a ring of small fish, the *pescado blanco* found in nearby Lake Pátzcuaro. Santa Clara is a short drive from Pátzcuaro.

FLEETING ARTS

The fiesta is an art form in Mexico, a mixture of theater, dance, music, and mummery. Perhaps most important to the spirit of such celebrations are the craftsmen; some of their works linger, others are fleeting — fireworks and candies consumed during the height of the fiesta.

The master craftsman of each village and town is responsible for the community's fireworks, elaborate displays of magic, light, and noise that are essential to any fiesta and often to the weekly religious celebrations as well. Fireworks making is an intricate art passed down from father to son; if you visit the plaza before a fiesta begins, you may be lucky enough to see a craftsman tediously at work, assembling great towers of powder-filled bamboo stakes and paper-wrapped fuses called *castillos*. His craft is impermanent, but the best fireworks maker can transform a passing vision into art.

While the fireworks craftsman and his sons create grand illusions, the local baker works on a smaller, though no less creative, scale. Candies and cakes, elaborate anytime, are unbelievably embellished at fiesta. The Day of the Dead, November 2, especially challenges the baker's art. Cakes shaped like small graves, crucifix cookies, and spun-sugar corpses appear on the *panadería* shelves. In Guanajuato, a dour city that boasts mummies in catacombs, the *dulcerías* sell spun-sugar skeletons that have a cigarette stuck between the teeth and a small bottle of tequila gripped in a bony hand.

Saints' days and political celebrations are the usual excuses for a fiesta; however, in some remote areas, fiestas revolve around a cult figure, perhaps a famed folk healer (*curandero*). The *curandero* is a familiar figure to anyone living in Mexico or the barrios of Texas. Shops and stalls selling herbs, potions, and spells are found in the markets of Mexico and in the Chicano neighborhoods of Dallas and Houston. A rough bark paper, *amatl* paper, is sometimes used by *curanderos* to cure illnesses, take away the evil eye, or invoke a spell. Geometric, primitive figures of Indians are cut from the bark paper and set afire, sometimes burned over the victim, to cast a spell. These paper images are mounted on dark brown *amatl* paper and sold in tourist shops throughout Mexico; the more superstitious avoid them.

Wooden toys are another of Mexico's charming but impermanent creations. Toy airplanes with propellers that spin, dogs that wag their tails as they drink from a small bowl, mice on a string, striking snakes in matchbox-size boxes, spinning tops, and dancing puppets are just a few of the toys sold on every street corner in Mexico.

Finally, the piñata is the fantasy creation without which any Mexican family gathering would be incomplete. These crepe-paper creations are said to represent the Devil; the blindfolded child who wields the stick is Faith, and the goodies inside are Faith's reward for beating the Devil. Piñatas come in a variety of traditional shapes and sizes.

DECORATIVE ARTS

Mexico is a country rich with folk art, both the utilitarian and the purely decorative. And, in addition to the native artists working in the primitive tradition of their small villages and towns, Mexico has a wealth of artists working in classical mediums. Mexican muralists are among the best in the world. If you are interested in buying Mexican art work, visit the Zona Rosa galleries in Mexico City.

A popular artist, Sergio Bustamante, is the creator of whimsical animals made from papier-mâché or metal. Bustamante's works fill a small store one block from the Reforma on Calle Hamburgo and are featured in many boutiques and galleries throughout the country.

More serious art collectors search long and hard for *retablo* paintings. These religious motifs, often executed on tin, celebrate a victory over illness or misfortune. Primitive in execution, these paintings are left in village churches as small offerings of thanksgiving; they fetch high prices in galleries and antique shops.

The photographer's backdrop is another rare find for the collector. At every fiesta, on market day, and in the plazas, photographers — sometimes using antique cameras — have their subjects stand in front of a backdrop usually painted with a scene of a famous Mexican historical site.

At many of the archaeological sites, vendors will try to sell you artifacts of questionable authenticity. It is illegal to export genuine pre-Columbian art from Mexico, with only a few exceptions. However, good reproductions are available at better crafts shops and galleries. Ask for a certificate describing the item and keep your sales slip.

There are several decorative art forms that are much cheaper to buy than Bustamante animals, *retablo* paintings, or rare collectibles. Bark paintings from Guerrero can be found throughout the country. Look for those with the best detail, and check for a penciled signature; avoid the bird and flower paintings executed in fluorescent colors. Mounted and framed, bark paintings can be beautiful gifts.

The Huichol Indians have long made *ojos de Dios* ("God's eyes") to ward off the evil eye. Made from brightly colored yarns, God's eyes can be found in crafts shops, although, like *amatl* figures, superstitious tourists avoid them. The Huichols also produce yarn paintings, mounted on wood covered with beeswax. These feature fantasy figures and animals.

And perhaps the most decorative and familiar art form found in Mexico is the "tree of life," which tells the story of Adam and Eve. The trees are made in the village of Metepec, near Toluca.

FURNITURE

Buying furniture in the *mercado* can be a mistake; what seems to be a high-quality piece a few months later may be reduced by insects within the wood to a pile of wood dust in your living room. If a cherished piece begins to leave telltale dust tracks, check with your local furniture restorer; he may be able to dip it for you. Custom-made colonial-style furniture is available at shops in the larger cities and in workshops at the border; many will ship. One of the most popular styles is leather and wood patio sets (*equipales*) made in Jalisco. Tlaquepaque, a suburb of Guadalajara, is a good place to find these barrel-shaped chairs.

Shopping for antique furniture, often overlooked by tourists, can be worthwhile in Mexico. If you drive to Mexico City, check out La Lagunilla Market—it's an Art Deco paradise with brass bedposts, chandeliers, and old family portraits. Shipping can be a hassle, but if you fall in love with an old wardrobe, check with the tourist office about shipping requirements.

WOODWORK

Mexico exports many hardwoods, and craftsmen throughout the country are experts at working with wood, producing birdcages, fiesta masks, musical instruments, walking sticks, boxes, and cutting boards.

Many villagers have a woodcarver who makes the figures of the saints (*santos*) for the churches and fiestas. The antique *santos* found in galleries can be expensive.

Fiesta masks, particularly from Guerrero and Mexico City, are another unusual collector's item. These colorful, sometimes grotesque, animal-like masks have their origins in Mexico's Indian heritage.

There is excellent lacquerware, especially hardwood chests and gourds, made in Mexico, some of it vaguely reminiscent of Chinese work. Several painstaking methods are used to create the effect. Look for carefully incised lines, and place a drop of water on the surface—it should bead up as though on a waxed surface.

Centers for the art of woodwork include:

Apizaco, near Mexico City, is famous for its carved walking sticks.

Puebla, Uruapan, and **Pátzcuaro** are all centers of the lacquerware trade.

Paracho, north of Uruapan, is noted for musical instruments, particularly guitars.

LEATHERWORK

Tanning was introduced in Mexico by the Spanish and quickly mastered by village craftsmen. Huaraches, leather jackets, bags, belts, and boots are all found in profusion, particularly in the border markets. Always try on both huaraches before you buy, and beware of metal studs, which may cause blisters. Many stores in Mexico City and Guadalajara make leather coats to order; check with the tourist bureau before making a major purchase to ensure that the store you're dealing with is a reputable one. Several Mexican fashion designers work in leather. Look for the Aries, Pandora, and Bustamante labels.

Leather made from the skins of endangered species is not allowed to be imported to the United States. Check with the local American authorities if you have any questions. US Customs publishes a brochure, "Know Before You Go," which lists forbidden items.

GLASSWARE

Mexican glassware is particularly fragile, and pieces often vary in size. If you need a half dozen wine glasses, it's best to buy eight in case of breakages. Ask to see all the glasses before they are wrapped, because one may be smaller or larger than the rest.

The best glassware comes from Guadalajara and Monterrey, where large glass factories create everything from delicate crystal to hand-blown primitive-looking pieces.

13

THE UNIQUE
AND THE RANDOM

SIDETRIPS
FOR THE SPIRIT

Wander through this chapter. Roam the pages looking for a
new experience. Browse and search for the unique and the
random. Here is a potpourri of side trips for the spirit and challenges to the flesh — a literary tour for those eager to improve as
they indulge, a sampling of Mexican spas from the ascetic to the
sensual, luxury camping for those with a hankering to get away from
it all in style, and the inside story on hacienda havens and the best little
hotels in Mexico.

Experience the unique Mexican expression the fiesta, and plan your
vacation by a calendar of fiesta dates from around the country. Take
a spectacular train ride through the Copper Canyon, a trip for railroad
buffs and novices alike through some of the world's most inspiring
canyons and mountains. Learn from bird-watcher Suzanne Winckler,
who has contributed a comprehensive essay on bird-watching in the
country that the experts agree is a bird-watcher's paradise. For outdoor adventurers are some tips on camping, hiking, and mountain
climbing and a list of national parks in Mexico; for hunters and
fishermen, a rundown on how to handle the red tape south of the
border.

LITERARY TOUR

"I never travel without my diary. One should always have something
sensational to read in the train."

—Oscar Wilde
The Importance of Being Earnest

J. R. Ewing and John Connally aside, few people can claim their
diaries would make good vacation reading. Most of us fall back on
more mundane material, usually chosen by either of two tried, but not
always true, methods. The first might be called the "I'm-going-to-
finish-this-damn-book-once-and-for-all" method of selection. Members of this school of thought embark on a vacation with an almost
masochistic desire for self-improvement. They can be seen clutching
heavy copies of *The Fountainhead* or *The Gulag Archipelago* as they
head for the airport gate. Good intentions soon wither, however, and
within five minutes of takeoff they are asking the flight attendant for
this week's *People* or scanning the in-flight magazine.

The second approach to vacation reading is common among the
absentminded—those who leave an interesting best-seller on the bed
table only to find themselves frantically scanning the airport news-
stand for a gothic romance or murder mystery worth reading. It's no
wonder books taken on vacation become poolside props—portable
symbols of noble intentions left to curl in the heat.

Select your vacation reading as carefully as you choose a hotel.
Match your book to the mood of your trip. If your tastes run to the
eclectic, try a morning in Mérida with Jane Austen or an afternoon in
Chapultepec Park with Proust; but if you want to heighten your
appreciation of the country, read something rooted in the Mexican
experience. The works of Mexico's best writers are available in English
translation—you might also take along the Spanish edition—and several major authors have written about the Mexican scene, notably
D. H. Lawrence and Graham Greene.

Both Lawrence and Greene wrote travel essays on Mexico—a genre
British writers mastered before World War I and continued to favor during the unsettled years between the wars. Lawrence's *Mornings in Mexico* usually appears together with his *Etruscan Places*,
a series of essays on his travels in Italy. The former paints sensual
and evocative portraits of life in Mexico's rural areas. Greene, whose
poison pen is familiar to devotees of his fiction, writes with pene-
trating wit about his Mexican travels. Both men also wrote important novels set in Mexico—*The Power and the Glory* by Greene and
The Plumed Serpent by Lawrence. Both writers capture the ever-
present duality of Mexican life. Reading Greene's novel, you sweat
in the heat of the Veracruzano jungle; reading Lawrence you feel
Mexico's past.

Lawrence also wrote poetry during his stay in Mexico; many of these poems about the ancient gods make good reading atop a ruin or on a hillside overlooking an archaeological site. Another poet attracted by the Mexican experience was Wallace Stevens, whose juxtaposition of images triggers the imagination.

Mandatory for any enlightened traveler south of the border are the works of the modern Mexican poet Octavio Paz, a stern, passionate, and yet sympathetic critic of modern man. Paz's two best-known works of criticism are *The Labyrinth of Solitude: Life and Thought in Mexico* and *The Other Mexico: Critique of the Pyramid.* Paz writes about his fellow writers north of the border: "Almost all of the North Americans who have written about Latin America, not excepting so distinguished a poet as Wallace Stevens, have been exalted by our indigenous past or by our landscapes but, just as invariably, have considered the contemporary Latin America to be insignificant." They have written about Latin America, Paz continues, as "ruins and scenery, with here and there a dim, bungling human being—the waiter or manager at the hotel."

Paz doesn't mince words, and *The Labyrinth of Solitude* is recognized as a critical masterpiece. The notion of Mexicans wearing masks, a device Paz uses to illuminate his theme, has become an accepted metaphor for the Mexican character.

On October 2, 1968, in the Plaza of Tlatelolco, the heart of the old Aztec market and often called the Plaza of the Three Cultures by modern-day Mexicans, several hundred students protesting government policy were shot down by troops. At that time Paz was ambassador to India, a post he resigned in protest following the massacre. A lecture he delivered at the University of Texas in Austin in response to that event was later published under the title *The Other Mexico: Critique of the Pyramid.* In this short work many of the themes found in his earlier works are revised. He sharply criticizes both the developed countries and the Mexican political system and offers insights into the Mexican Revolution.

In *Labyrinth,* Paz reviews Mexico's artistic past and examines briefly the work of Sor Juana Inés de la Cruz, a Roman Catholic nun whose poetical and philosophical works were written in the seventeenth century during the height of colonial power. The works of Sor Juana reveal the mind of a deeply religious woman whose romantic nature and colonial background make her significant for Mexico's literary heritage.

Though you may not be a history buff, don't ignore the works of Sor Juana or other good books about Mexico's past. The following five books tell you a lot without getting bogged down in historical detail or political discussion.

One of the best books about the Spanish Conquest was written by a man who went to great lengths to ask his readers' forgiveness for his literary shortcomings, the conquistador Bernal Díaz del Castillo. John

M. Cohen has translated and edited a new Penguin edition of *The Conquest of New Spain*, eliminating some of Díaz's rambling passages and brightening the prose style.

Another book worth reading is Fanny Calderón's reminiscences of Mexico City in the 1840s. *Life in Mexico*, by Madame Frances Erskine Inglis Calderón de la Barca, is a look at life in the capital city through the eyes of an engaging Scottish New Englander.

Long treatises on archaeology are not everyone's favorite bedtime reading, but few of us can resist a fairy story. The *Popol Vuh* is a collection of Mayan legends written after the conquest and based on stories handed down from one generation to the next. Corn grows into boys, and pots talk in this small book, perfect for reading as you sit on the veranda at the Hotel Mayaland at Chichén Itzá watching the hummingbirds gather nectar in the mimosa trees.

If you are an incurable romantic, find a copy of *The Cactus Throne* by Richard O'Connor (it is out of print — try the library), and cry your way through this heart-wrenching biography of Maximilian and Carlota. This book is recommended for quiet reading in the gardens of Chapultepec Castle, where once they walked.

Finally, in the history department, no one should contemplate a trip to Yucatán and the ruins in particular without John L. Stephens's *Incidents of Travel in Central America, Chiapas, and Yucatán*. This nineteenth-century travelogue is one of the genre's best; looking out on the Yucatecan jungle, you can imagine the adventure this Yankee traveler felt as he was carried through the jungle by Mayan bearers.

For a look at modern-day Mexico, try the works of Oscar Lewis — *The Children of Sánchez*, *A Death in the Sánchez Family*, and *Five Families: Mexican Case Studies in the Culture of Poverty*. Lewis takes a studied, compassionate look at the life of a working man and his family.

Further insight into modern Mexico can be found in the works of the much-lauded novelist Carlos Fuentes, whose books are available in translation. His surrealistic style captures the Mexican spirit. Another Spanish language novelist who was born in Colombia but lives in Mexico is Gabriel García Márquez, renowned for his stories of the mythical village of Macondo, a village where men live together and yet alone. García Márquez won the Nobel prize for literature in 1982.

One of the most famous novels about Mexico and the pervasive solitude of life in Latin America is *Under the Volcano* by the Englishman Malcolm Lowry. Critics call Lowry's novel a modern classic and find it reminiscent of works by James Joyce and Joseph Conrad. Concerned with the disintegration of a British consul living in the small town of Quahnahuac, the tale is told through the eyes of Monsieur Laruelle, a French movie producer and childhood friend of Geoffrey Firmin, the doomed consul. Lowry lived in Cuernavaca, and it was there that the seeds of this great novel took root. Like Greene's *The Power and the*

Glory, Lowry's novel is a superb work detailing the European experience in Mexico.

Another Anglo who wandered south was Jack Kerouac, whose beat ramblings can be found in *On the Road* and *Desolation Angels*. Perhaps the most mysterious expatriate of them all was B. Traven, author of the short story that became the movie *Treasure of the Sierra Madre*. Two new biographies purport to have unraveled the mystery of his origins. One of these is *The Secret of the Sierra Madre: The Man Who Was B. Traven* by Will Wyatt. B. Traven, most likely of Germanic or Scandinavian origin, lived and wrote in Mexico throughout the thirties. His short stories are enjoying a renewed popularity.

A recent bestseller, compared by the critics with James Clavell's *Shōgun*, was *Aztec* by Gary Jennings. This popular novel is an absorbing account of Mexico around the time of the conquest.

For a familiar voice, Texans can turn to the works of J. Frank Dobie, among them *Apache Gold and Yaqui Silver*, tales of adventure in the mountains of Chihuahua.

If our list of offerings seems a little on the heavy side, too much philosophy and not enough laughs, we suggest you cheat a little. Look south to Brazil for the works of Jorge Amado, whose novels are set in the Bahia region of Brazil, where Portuguese, African, and Indian mix in a potpourri of mischief. These are among the funniest books being written in South America. Settle down in your deck chair or hammock with a copy of *Doña Flor and Her Two Husbands* (perhaps you saw the movie?) and chuckle your way through the afternoon.

Bocaditos: There are, of course, many excellent bookstores in Mexico, particularly in Mexico City, but books are expensive south of the border. You may be able to find some of our suggestions there, but you will pay more for them, particularly in the tourist areas. Check the bibliography at the back of the book for more suggestions.

SPAS

Legend holds that the Mayan Indians, who were the first to confront European man on the shores of the Yucatán peninsula, were frightened by the intruders' beards, their horses, and the sticks that shot fire. Although it went unrecorded, the Mayans may have also been offended by the smell of the Spanish sailors and adventurers. These men seldom bathed, and in contrast, the Mayans were meticulously clean—even the smallest Mayan village had its steam bath. The Aztec emperors routinely sent to the spa at Tehuacán for a supply of mineral waters.

Many of the spas first used by the Indians still exist, and modern Mexicans, like their European cousins who eventually acquired the bathing habit, enjoy weekends in these pastoral resorts. Today Mexicans continue to drink the same mineral waters that the Aztecs enjoyed. Soaking in steamy, mineral-rich water can be the best way to shed those city blues or revive a sagging tourist spirit. Maybe if Cortés had taken time out to soak, his blood might not have been so fiery.

There are two kinds of baths in Mexico, spas with hotel accommodations and public baths, *balnearios,* popular among Mexico's working classes. The *balnearios* often have picnic facilities, changing rooms, children's parks, and sometimes camping facilities. Throughout the country, the universal symbol of a diver is used on signs to denote a nearby bath. Spas usually have hotel facilities ranging from expensive to reasonable. The waters are often thermal, heated deep within the earth, and they are usually enriched with minerals. Although "taking the waters" has been a popular habit regarded as health giving for hundreds of years, doctors have found no firm evidence that bathing in hot water makes you healthier – but it does make you feel better. Some of the spas offer exercise facilities, massage rooms, tennis, golf, and beauty routines; others stress vegetarian diets and yoga classes. Some are mini-resorts where the emphasis is on cure through luxury. Both spas and *balnearios* dot the country, and many are in Central Mexico. We've listed the major spas that usually require reservations; however, don't be afraid to investigate some of the lesser known spas. Ask to see a room and inquire about the rates and special facilities before you check in.

Owing to recent devaluations of the peso, some hotel room rates have plummeted, while others have been adjusted to reflect the peso's value *vis-à-vis* the dollar. Since the 1982 devaluations the Mexican government has instituted a range of maximum rates to regulate charges. The *A–D* rating system used in this guidebook is based on those ranges. (See "How to Use This Guide" for an explanation of the rate categories.)

HOTEL SPA SAN JOSE PURUA

This is one the most popular spas and has a 1950s glamour about it. The thermal water is bicarbonate rich, and hotel guests sit around the pool soaking in it and wearing yellow mud masques collected from the nearby Tuxpan River. The hotel, which opened in 1942, is set in a jungle canyon in Michoacán. The furnishings are a la fifties, but the service lavish. Massages, personal mineral baths in secluded rooms, facials, horseback riding, and tennis are all available. Hotel Spa San José Purúa is in southeast Michoacán near Zitácuaro. (Take the Zitácuaro turnoff on the Mexico City–Guadalajara road, Hwy. 15.) For reservations write to Hotel Purúa Hidalgo, Reforma y Colón 27, Mexico 1, DF, or call 585-4344 in Mexico City. (Meals included.) A. Expensive.

COMANJILLA

The Hotel Balneario at Comanjilla, near León, is known for its sulphur-rich waters. The hotel is quiet and decorated in a rustic colonial style. Each room has its own huge tiled tub that you can fill up with thermal waters. There are two large swimming pools surrounded by flower-filled gardens and fed by the springs. For reservations write to Hotel Balneario Comanjilla, Apartado Postal 111, León, Guanajuato, or call 2-09-42 or 2-90-91 in Comanjilla. (Meals included.) B. Moderate.

IXTAPAN DE LA SAL

Just a 90-minute drive from Mexico City, Ixtapan de la Sal is a town dedicated to taking the waters. Located west of Cuernavaca and south of Toluca, the town is centered around a five-story luxury hotel, the Hotel Ixtapan. The spa has all the facilities — massage rooms, carriage rides, movies, a health club, large swimming pools, even boating. One of the most luxurious experiences to be had in Ixtapan is at the Roman baths. The baths are a 1930s Hollywood version of the real thing. Located in the public *balneario,* the baths have an entrance decorated in Art Deco fashion. Each room is named after a great French mistress, like Madame DuBarry, and each has two lounging couches and a private pool. After the attendant closes the door, the pool fills and you soak in the thermal water in private. Before he leaves, he recommends that you rest on the couch after your soak. (This is good advice to follow after any thermal soaking.) Hotel guests are admitted free to the baths.

Behind the large indoor pool at the spa is the Parque de los 13 Lagos. The lakes are tiered on the hillside and a mini-train winds through the park. For reservations write to Hotel Ixtapan, Paseo de la Reforma 132, Mexico 6, DF, or call 535-7622 in Mexico City. (Meals included.) A. Luxury.

HACIENDA SPA PENAFIEL

The hotel in the hometown of one of Mexico's most popular mineral waters is a grande dame circa the 1930s, aging gracefully but with a few visible wrinkles. Penafiel is bottled in Tehuacán, and you can visit the source near the hotel. If you are driving to Oaxaca or staying in Puebla, the hacienda is a good place to break your journey or spend a day. And you can fill up your water bottle at the Penafiel tasting room.

For reservations write Hotel Hacienda Spa Penafiel, Puebla, Puebla, or you can call 2-01-90 in Tehuacán. In Mexico City, write Central Reservaciónes, Hoteles, Dubin, Hotel Reforma, Reforma y Paris, Mexico 4, DF, or call 546-9680. (Two meals included.) C. Inexpensive.

OAXTEPEC

Oaxtepec is really a total resort and it attracts large crowds from Mexico City every weekend. Not many tourists venture into the large park, which was once a spa frequented by Moctezuma. There are 24 sulfur pools in the park, as well as picnic and camping facilities. The Instituto

Mexican Seguro Social (IMSS), the Mexican social security and health care system, operates the complex, and foreigners are allowed to rent lodgings whenever there are vacancies—usually during the week. Some of the rooms have kitchens, and there's a supermarket in the park. For information, write Departamento de Promoción y Reservaciónes, Paseo de la Reforma 506, Piso 19, Mexico 16, DF, or call 553-6011 in Mexico City. To reach the park, take the Mexico City–Cuernavaca toll road and look for the Oaxtepec turnoff. (No meals included.) C. Inexpensive.

HOTEL FUENTES DE TABOADA

Five miles west of San Miguel de Allende on Hwy. 51, the resort features thermal waters, swimming pools, and horseback riding. You can visit for the day or stay at the hotel. For reservations, write Hotel Fuentes de Taboada, Apartado Postal 100, San Miguel de Allende, Guanajuato. B. Moderate.

VEGETARIAN SPAS

Rancho Rio Caliente, home of Dr. Lytton Bernard's papaya diet, is just 20 miles from downtown Guadalajara on Hwy. 15. Located in La Primavera forest, it attracts a mixed clientele who enjoy communal dining, yoga, hiking, lectures, and Jacuzzis. For reservations, write Rancho Rio Caliente, Apartado Postal 1187, Guadalajara, Jalisco. B. Moderate.

One of the most famous Mexican vegetarian health resorts is Villa Vegetariana near Cuernavaca. Not a true "spa"—there are no spring waters—but equipped with all the facilities to make you feel better. Write to Villa Vegetariana, Apartado Postal 1228, Cuernavaca, Morelos. B. Moderate.

LUXURY CAMPING

You must belong to a special breed to be a successful and happy camper. If you were a Green Beret, an Eagle Scout, or graduated from Texas A&M or one of those modern prep schools out in Colorado that mix mountain climbing with Latin, then you can probably roll your sleeping bag (ever notice how it never fits back into the stuff bag?) and head south. But for most of us, camping is all freeze-dried foods and dirty socks.

One man in Mexico doesn't see it that way. Arnold Bilgore, a onetime CBS correspondent and a longtime habitué of Isla Mujeres, figured out that the key to camping was to do what the Victorians did —put the Man Friday back into it. And he volunteered for the role.

The result is catered camping—tents with maid service and gourmet food. All the camper does is lie back in a hammock and listen to the surf while Bilgore and his collection of Mayan helpers sweep out the tents, make the beds, stock the bar, and light the candles at dinner time. No aristocratic Englishman on a tiger hunt ever had it this good.

Kailuum, as Bilgore's camping paradise is called, is south of Cancún at Punta Bete, a long stretch of perfect beach shared only by a rustic group of *cabañas* named Captain LaFitte's. There's absolutely nothing to do here — just swim, walk on the beach, count the stars, pick up the shells. There's no electricity, just candles everywhere at night. In the afternoon, everyone retires to his hammock for an hour or two of peaceful contemplation.

The large tents are covered by a *palapa*, a thatched roof that extends out to form a natural patio where two hammocks are slung. Each tent sleeps two, and fresh towels are provided each morning. The tents face the ocean and are shaded by palm trees. Just a few steps away is the large *palapa* that serves as a communal bathroom with private shower stalls. And at the south end of the site is a large palapa where meals are served.

In a small kitchen, equipped with kerosene stoves, Bilgore creates miracles with the help of two Mayan women. Friday night is lobster night. At Christmas and Thanksgiving there's turkey with all the trimmings, and on other nights shrimp in coconut shells, eggplant creole, black bean soup, fresh bread, bananas Foster a la Bilgore, and Mexican wine. The infantry was never like this.

Most visitors to Kailuum stay at the campsite, rarely venturing into the countryside, although Bilgore will give visitors a lift to the Cozumel ferry if he's heading that way. Some pick up a rental car at the Cancún airport and make excursions to nearby Xel-Ha to snorkel or to Tulum to see the ruins, but most just lie around and unwind. (Kailuum attracts a mix of visitors — college students, young professionals, businessmen, and businesswomen who want to relax without phones, schedules, and alarm clocks. Some get up early to jog on the beach; others rise at noon and head for the bar, which is run on an honor system.)

Reservations are recommended. However, some guests stumble across the campsite and find room to stay. It's located about a 60-minute drive south of the Cancún airport on Hwy. 307 — look for the sign advertising Captain LaFitte's cabins; there's no sign for Kailuum. Rates in early 1983 were as follows: single (one person to a tent) $28.50; double (two persons to a tent) $20.75 each; triples (three persons to a tent) $16.50 each. Rates include breakfast and dinner. Arrangements can be made for lunch, also. For reservations call Camptel Ventures (408-262-5460) in California.

HACIENDA HAVENS

It is an architectural trait inherited from the Moors, the habit of building small, personal paradises behind high walls. Here among wonderful, secret gardens, cool waters trickle from stone fountains, exotic flowers bloom, and ferns trail in loose abandon. Here you find low-slung leather chairs, rough-hewn wooden tables, richly glazed tiles, and silent servants ready to obey any whim. Only the occasional cry of a flamingo or the sound of the chapel bell disturbs the reverie.

These islands of peace and tranquility still exist in Mexico, dotting the landscape like oases in the desert. There is no substitute for the luxury of a hacienda. The mood is pure, innocent indolence. The order of the day is yours to write — to rise late, to dine late, to dance under the stars until morning.

We have selected some of Mexico's hacienda havens. Some are expensive, others reasonable, but few will cost what one night at the Paris Ritz will. In fact, some are outright steals. (See "How to Use This Guide" for an explanation of the rate categories.) If you can't stay, stop by for a drink or lunch.

HACIENDA DE CORTES

Six miles south of Cuernavaca, in the village of Atlacomulco, is the hacienda Cortés gave to his son. This is a hideaway of the first class. There are 21 guest rooms, and the dining room is constructed around a sixteenth-century sugar mill. Emiliano Zapata, foe of the *hacendados*, used the home as a headquarters. For reservations write Hacienda de Cortés, Atlacomulco, Apartado Postal N 273-D, Cuernavaca, Morelos, or call 5-00-35 in Cuernavaca. A. Luxury.

HACIENDA VISTA HERMOSA

The name means "beautiful view," and it is. This hacienda also built by Cortés is located 40 miles south of Cuernavaca near Lake Tequesquitengo. The hacienda is now a total resort with tennis courts, horseback riding, a theater, and even a disco. The swimming pool was constructed under the arches of an old aqueduct. There's also a bullring and a cockpit on the property. There are several large suites, one a bridal suite with its own swimming pool. A double room includes breakfast. For reservations write to Hotel Vista Hermosa, Tequesquitengo, Morelos, or call 2-03-00 in Tequesquitengo or 546-4540 in Mexico City. B. Moderate.

HACIENDA COCOYOC

This was once an Aztec spa that the Spaniards turned into a sugar plantation; now it's a resort with a hotel, villas, and condominiums. Located just 20 miles east of Cuernavaca, near Cuautla (Zapata's home), it's popular with *capitalinos*. The roots of the trees that shaded the Aztecs are imbedded in the hacienda's walls. A convenient location for those who want to explore Xochicalco, the nearby archaeological site, and Tepoztlán, a colorful village. (See "Around Cuernavaca" in the chapter **Mexico of the Colonials.**) Some suites have private pools. For reservations, write Hotel Hacienda Cocoyoc, Río Amazones 85, Mexico 5, DF, or call 511-4460 or 514-1428 in Mexico City. B. Moderate.

MANSION DEL CUPATITZIO

In the heart of the beautiful state of Michoacán, in a volcanic valley rich with wildflowers and eucalyptus trees, lies the city of Uruapan. Adjacent to the city is the national park Junta a la Rodilla del Diablo Parque, known for its volcanic formations and flora. On the edge of the park is the Mansión del Cupatítzio, an old, white stucco hacienda that attracts visitors from as far away as Mexico City and Guadalajara. For reservations write to Hotel Mansión del Cupatítzio, Apartado Postal 63, Uruapan, Michoacán, or call 3-21-00 in Uruapan. B. Moderate.

HOTEL EL PRESIDENTE GUANAJUATO

Most of the hotels in the El Presidente chain are modern high rises; however, in an old suburb of Guanajuato called Marfil, where many of the silver barons built huge haciendas and mansions, El Presidente has restored an old hacienda. The Hacienda de San Gabriel Barrera was one of the grandest, and the hotel chain has restored it to some of its former splendor. For reservations, call the El Presidente toll-free number in the United States (1-800-854-2026). B. Moderate.

THE BEST LITTLE HOTELS IN MEXICO

In addition to those luxury hotels located in old haciendas, there are many Mexican hotels housed in restored convents, mansions, and old mill buildings. These hotels capture the spirit of Mexico. We've picked a few of our favorites.

THE EL PRESIDENTE, OAXACA

Like its sister hotel in Guanajuato, the Hotel El Presidente in Oaxaca is not the usual tower of steel and glass favored by this chain. The hotel is in the old convent of Santa Catalina, founded in 1576 and closed in 1862. The Mexican government has declared the convent a national monument, and only minor alterations have been permitted. The rooms are the original, high-ceilinged cells. Located just a few blocks from the zócalo, the hotel is an excellent place to stay as you explore the area. Call Hoteles El Presidente, Mexico, toll free in the United States (1-800-854-2026). A. Luxury.

POSADA DE XOCHIQUETZAL, CUERNAVACA

This small hotel located in the heart of Cuernavaca was once, again according to one of those ubiquitous legends, the home of Cortés's paramours. Behind the high walls you find a delightful garden filled with fuchsia bougainvillea and a fountain decorated with small statues of frogs. There's an excellent restaurant in the hotel serving many Mexican specialties. For reservations write Posada Xochiquetzal, Leyva 200, Cuernavaca, Morelos, or call 2-02-20 in Cuernavaca. C. Inexpensive.

LAS MAÑANITAS, CUERNAVACA

This world-famous hotel was created amid the ruins of an old house. The garden is filled with exotic flora and fauna. Peacocks and flamingos stroll the grounds. The restaurant has a famous French and Mexican menu. For reservations write Las Mañanitas, Ricardo Linares 107, Cuernavaca, Morelos, or call 2-46-46 in Cuernavaca. A. Luxury.

HOTEL VIRREY DE MENDOZA, MORELIA

This quiet, stately hotel on the main square was originally built as a home in 1744. The rooms, all large, are decorated in nineteenth-century fashion, many with large four-poster beds. The hotel surrounds a picturesque patio where meals are served. For reservations write Hotel Virrey de Mendoza, Portal de Matamoros 16, Morelia, Michoacán, or call 2-06-33 in Morelia. B. Moderate.

CASA DE SIERRA NEVADA, SAN MIGUEL DE ALLENDE

This small hotel, near the main plaza, was built as an orphanage in 1735. There are only five rooms and five suites in the American-owned hotel. The guests feel as though they are in a private home rather than a hotel. The restaurant is well known for its continental specialties, including homemade pasta. For reservations write Casa de Sierra Nevada, Apartado Postal 226, San Miguel de Allende, Guanajuato, or call 2-04-15 in San Miguel. B. Moderate.

POSADA DE DON VASCO, PATZCUARO

This colonial-style inn is just a few steps from Lake Pátzcuaro, high in the Michoacán highlands. The thick blankets on the colonial antique beds are welcome when the night mists come up from the lake. Each night before dinner, guests gather around the patio to watch folk dances and listen to music. For breakfast, try freshly caught *pescado blanco* sautéed in butter and served with fresh rolls and Mexican coffee. For reservations write Posada de Don Vasco, Apartado Postal 15, Pátzcuaro, Michoacán, or call 525-9081 in Mexico City. B. Moderate.

CASA DE LOS TESOROS, ALAMOS

The name means "House of Treasures," and this small hotel in the once-abandoned, now chic town of Alamos in the Sonoran desert is a treasure. Each of the 15 rooms has a fireplace to help you feel warm on cool desert nights and thick walls to keep out the sun. Alamos is located halfway between Guaymas and Mazatlán and was once the home of Spanish silver barons. Many homes have been restored, but residents say the ghosts of the silver barons still haunt the town. Alamos is a hideaway in the true sense of the word — you will have to fly to Ciudad Obregon and rent a car and drive to the town or hire a driver. For reservations write Casa de los Tesoros, Apartado Postal

12, Alamos, Sonora, or call 8-00-10 in Alamos. (Meals included.) B. Moderate.

QUINTA MARIA CORTES, PUERTO VALLARTA

If you are looking for a romantic place to take someone special, try this small, eclectic hotel. It's really a house with several suites suspended on a cliff above Conchas China Beach. For reservations write Quinta Maria Cortés, Apartado Postal 356, Puerto Vallarta, Jalisco, or call 2-13-17 in Puerto Vallarta. A. Luxury.

VILLA VERA RACQUET CLUB, ACAPULCO

Remember the fifties? You will at the Villa Vera Racquet Club, but it won't remind you of Chubby Checker—this is strictly Gary Grant. This Mediterranean-style hotel is on the hill above Condesa Beach. If you don't want to walk to the fun below, settle back into a lounge chair around one of the hotel's 20 (yes, 20) swimming pools and have Acapulco at your feet. For reservations write Villa Vera Racquet Club, Lomas del Mar, Acapulco, Guerrero, or call 4-03-33 in Acapulco. A. Luxury.

BOCADITOS

The best little chain hotel in Mexico: Club Med's Villas Arqueologicas are not only proof that a chain hotel can be as memorable as any small, privately owned hotel, but they are also a good buy. Located practically next door to the ruins at Cholula, Teotihuacán, Cobá, Chichén Itzá, and Uxmal, they are quiet, reasonably priced, and serve excellent meals. Each hotel is built around a courtyard and swimming pool. Some have tennis courts, and the hotel at Cobá even has its own ruin. Although owned by the Club Med corporation, the hotels are open to anyone.

The hotel at Uxmal is located approximately 50 minutes from the Mérida airport, and there's a sound and light show in the evenings. Excursions to the nearby sites at Kabah, Labná, and Sayil are offered. Cobá is a 90-minute drive from Cancún, 30 minutes inland from the site at Tulum on the coast. The visitor to Cobá can be an adventurer by day in the jungle and dine in luxury at night. The hotel at Chichén Itzá is a 90-minute drive from Mérida; and there's a small airport at Chichén Itzá, also. Cholula is one of Mexico's most interesting towns (see "Puebla" in the chapter **Mexico of the Colonials**), and the Villa is an excellent getaway from the capital. Anyone who wants to fully explore Teotihuacán (most people try to see it all in a day) should stay at the Villa there.

All the Villas have libraries with books on archaeology in several languages. They are run by Frenchmen, usually, and the kitchen is often under the command of a French chef. The restaurant at Cholula features many French specialties and attracts *poblanos*, residents of nearby Puebla.

For reservations call 1-800-223-7820 toll free in the United States. B. Moderate (meals included); C. Inexpensive (no meals included).

FIESTAS: THE PERENNIAL PARTY

The Mexican author and critic Octavio Paz has written in *The Labyrinth of Solitude:* "Fiestas are our only luxury . . . the Mexican does not seek amusement; he seeks to escape from himself, to leap over the wall of solitude that confines him during the rest of the year . . . when he discharges his pistol into the air, he discharges his soul."

Fiestas, on the surface, appear to be large street parties, but they are much, much more and they vary in style and flavor, purpose and resolution. The insights of Mexicans like Octavio Paz are helpful to an outsider trying to understand the fiesta, but the best way is to experience one.

We were worn out. It had been a long, beautiful but exhausting drive up from the Pacific coast, through the mountains of Guerrero, high into misty pine-covered alpine meadows. We left the tropical lowlands early in the day after eating a hurried breakfast in Zihuatanejo; by noon we were deep in the mountains, wending our way past almost vertical cornfields. It was dark when we checked into the old posada in the lakeside colonial town of Pátzcuaro. Our room was decorated with antique furniture, the high bed smothered in soft woolen blankets used to ward off the cold (the mountain air gets trapped in the thick plaster walls). After a quick, almost mercurial shower (because the chill in the air made standing still in the tiled bathroom impossible), we were feeling somewhat renewed and decided to walk to the main plaza for dinner.

It was September 15, the eve of Diez y Seis, the anniversary of Padre Hidalgo's cry for Mexico's independence from Spain. At midnight the local mayor was going to cry the *grito* in the square, calling on all Mexicans to be free.

It was not yet the traditional Mexican dinner hour, and the restaurant overlooking the plaza was empty except for one other couple enjoying a quiet, early dinner. We ordered our meals and settled down with a drink and fresh rolls, when suddenly an entire Mexican family, bent on celebration, entered the dining room. The quiet hours of early evening were forgotten. A fiesta was about to begin.

The children raced around the dining room and ran screaming to the balconies as the first fireworks erupted. One of the young men in the family went downstairs and came back with a mariachi band and a couple of bottles of tequila. Soon various members of the family were joining in the music, passing the bottles back and forth; and as the celebration began in earnest we were buried in an assault of children's giggles, fireworks, and mariachi music.

Suddenly the manager of the restaurant appeared. Using our kind of logic, we assumed he would call a halt to this madness. With a swig from the tequila bottle, his arms around the mariachi players, he launched into a magnificent solo. It was too much. He was wonderful. We applauded and toasted him.

The spirit of fiesta is infectious. After dinner, we found ourselves joining the *paseo*, the traditional circling of the plaza. We bought confetti and curled rings of paper, which we threw into the air, unraveling them like flying snakes. We were only slightly alarmed when a group of vaqueros pointed their pistols heavenward and discharged their guns with a Mexican whoop. And we watched in awe as the local fireworks artist and his sons, holding great rockets in their hands, reached down nonchalantly with a cigarette and set fire to the fuses.

After dazzling fireworks lit the sky and sent echoes down to the lake, the crowd gathered around a tower that had been erected in the middle of the plaza. It was scaffolding of bamboo and paper fuses filled with gunpowder, looking something like a fragile bird cage; but suddenly it became one of Cervantes' windmills, roaring and spitting, casting wheels of colored light into the sky. Young boys ran under the flaming tower to show their bravery, and everyone else dodged and ducked as the wheel of fireworks spun off, hit a tree branch, and fell into the square. The show was an artist's masterpiece, not one of those Fourth of July displays all red, white, blue, and loud. This was like a domino construction — one fuse set off a liquid pattern of light against the night sky.

Fiesta is not mere celebration; it is more than street theater; it is closer to communion. The political and religious feasts have some similarities to celebrations in other countries, but many of Mexico's fiestas are rooted in the pre-Columbian past. Perhaps the most notable is the Day of the Dead, November 2, when Mexican families visit the graves of their ancestors and village elders. Cookies and cakes are baked in the shape of skulls and caskets, and a feast is taken to the cemetery, where the children play games on the graves. It is a celebration of triumph over death, as though it did not exist.

Paz also believes that wealthy countries have few fiestas and that the art of celebration has been debased almost everywhere but in Mexico. A slightly xenophobic view maybe, but among the developed nations, celebrations have little in common with fiesta. In Scandinavia, the people celebrate the beginning of spring with a bacchanalian fury; in Japan, the populace communes with nature during yearly cherry-blossom viewings and kite-flying ceremonies; in England, medieval rituals are still performed; and in France, whole cities shut down for the month of August and the people head for the beach.

In Mexico, fiesta is an individual rite, although politics and the Church have sometimes built a ritual around it. Fiesta is a carnival, a word that has its root in the Latin *carne vale* ("flesh farewell").

In the village of Teotitlán del Valle, in the hills of the Valley of Oaxaca, we witnessed a true fiesta. We had driven down a long dirt road in an effort to visit the *tallers* of the local weavers whose blankets and serapes are well known throughout Mexico. As we parked the rented VW in the small marketplace, we heard a brass band playing what sounded like a mournful German march. The music seemed to come from the plaza in front of the church on the north end of the marketplace. Out of curiosity we climbed the steps into the plaza and there, under a large tree, surrounded by a brass band, was a group of young men dressed in fantastical costumes made from large scarves, feathers, and pieces of fringed cloth, and wearing white campesino trousers and shirts. They were leaping slowly to the mournful music. Under a cloister, along the church wall, a large group of older men sat on wooden benches. We were drawn to the scene as were a handful of other spectators, both villagers and tourists.

The young men formed two rows while one dancer weaved his way between them, his giant Aztec-style feathered headdress dipping with each leap. The rattles in his hand kept time to the music. The band played on one side of the plaza, and the old men sat across from them. On the far side a group of small, uniformed boys sat on a wooden bench and squirmed restlessly. Most of the boys wore peaked caps, but one wore a plumed Napoleonic hat and carried a small sword. A large number of gold coins hung from his jacket. At the end of the bench, sitting in a wooden chair, was an old man, dressed in a similar uniform with various gold coins hanging from his doublet and a large gold earring hanging from a drooping earlobe. He was asleep.

A makeshift throne at the head of the dancers was empty. Two small chairs beside the throne were occupied. Two small girls, one dressed as an Indian, the other wearing a blue and pink Spanish costume, sat in the chairs.

Moving randomly among the dancers were two men in pig masks, their wooden mouths rounded as though the characters were whistling. Tusks protruded from the wooden cheeks, and the men wore floppy hats, giving them the appearance of scarecrows. Occasionally, they would run into the crowd and shake their rattles at the children, scaring them.

As the music droned on, one of the old men carried a tray among the others who emptied their cigarette packages onto it. The tray and a bottle of mescal were passed from man to man, some taking a cigarette, all taking a sip of mescal and then spitting a little into the dirt.

This was an incredible scene. The dancers with their Aztec headdresses wore tennis shoes; a young man from the village was dressed in bell-bottoms and platform shoes, and he carried a large radio; electric lights shone around the saints inside the church, and yet on the outer wall was a piece of ancient Mixtec frieze. Someone was taping the band music; the "pigmen" were shaking their rattles; and a woman and her daughter, sprays of gladioli in hand, were kneeling at the church door. A vendor was selling *helados* ("popsicles"), and the dozen or more splotches of mescal and mud formed a pattern on the ground. All around the plaza the smell of tortillas cooking hung in the air.

As we watched the dance, the old man in the uniform awoke and in a tumble of Spanish ordered his "men" to come to order, to sit straight. As the main dancer sat on the throne, the old man drilled his troops. Then he turned and walked toward the throne and, in a flowery speech, bid farewell to the young man and embraced him. As the old man returned to his seat, we could see the tears streaming down his wrinkled cheeks.

The dance began again. Sitting with the old men was a gringo, dressed in a work shirt and a leather cap, and as an honored guest he had been given many shots of mescal. He was Cayuqui Estage Noel, his title *jefe de taller de investigación de teatro indigena de la escuela de bellas artes* Universidad Autónoma Benito Juárez de Oaxaca — head of the indigenous theater workshop at the School of Fine Arts, the University of Benito Juárez in Oaxaca. Noel is an expatriate American who has become absorbed in Mexico. He explained that we were enjoying a rare privilege. Once every four years the young men of the village dance for 24 hours to mark their graduation from the dancing brotherhood. Representing Aztec warriors, they dance to mourn the defeat of Moctezuma. The lead dancer represents Moctezuma; one girl represents the emperor's mythical daughter; and the girl in the Spanish costume is the infamous La Malinche, Cortés's mistress. The tearful scene we had just witnessed was Cortés's farewell to Moctezuma; the conquistador had to return to Veracruz to consolidate his power.

This was not theater. This dance was real to all the participants. By nightfall the young men would be weary, but they would dance on. The men in masks were the old idols; Cortés and his troops represented the new gods. This dance symbolizes a death, and a birth, an emergence of both the young men and Mexico into a new period of life. That is the spirit of fiesta — the synthesizing of life and history.

FIESTA CALENDAR

Every day in any Mexican village or town, a fiesta is beginning or ending. These are some of the best and the brightest, the biggest and the smallest.

January 1: New Year's Day is celebrated throughout the country, but all of Oaxaca is particularly festive.

January 6: Santos Reyes, a national holiday celebrating the three magi; many Mexican children receive their Christmas presents on this day.

January 15: Fiesta in Jocotepec, near Guadalajara, on the shores of Lake Chapala — includes dancing, bullfights, and cockfights.

January 17: Feast Day of San Antonio Abad. Children throughout Mexico take their animals to church to be blessed.

January 18: Taxco's fiesta honors Santa Prisca, the town's patroness.

January 20: San Sebastián's Day is celebrated in Chiapa de Corzo in the state of Chiapas and in León and Guanajuato in the state of Guanajuato.

February–March: *Carnaval* is a celebration tied to the Lenten season; fiestas are held in Acapulco, Huejotzingo in the state of Puebla, Mazatlán, Mérida, Veracruz, and Tepoztlán in the state of Morelos.

February 2: Día de la Candelaria, a fiesta surrounding the blessing of seeds and candles, is held throughout Mexico.

March–April: Easter week celebrations take place throughout the country, notably in Taxco and Pátzcuaro.

March 10–21: A strawberry fair is held in Irapuato in the state of Guanajuato.

March 21: The birth date of President Benito Juárez is celebrated at his hometown, Guelatao, in the state of Oaxaca, about 30 miles from the capital, Oaxaca City.

April 2: Fiesta de San Idelfonso is celebrated in Izamal, Yucatán, near Mérida.

April 15–May 5: A fair in the city of Aguascalientes honors St. Mark.

April 15–17: Fiesta of the Flowers is held in Fortín de las Flores, on the road from Mexico City to Veracruz.

May–June: Corpus Christi Day is a religious holiday whose date varies; children are blessed in the main cathedral of each town; a large ceremony is held at the National Cathedral, Mexico City; and in Papantla, Veracruz, a pre-Hispanic ritual, the Dance of the Flying Birdmen, is performed.

May 1: Labor Day parades are held throughout Mexico.

May 3: Feast of the Holy Cross (La Santa Cruz) is celebrated at Milpa Alta in the Federal District and at Valle de Bravo in the state of Mexico.

May 5: Cinco de Mayo, a celebration of Mexican independence that marks the 1862 defeat of Napoleon III's troops at Puebla.

May 15: San Isidro's Day, honoring the patron saint of livestock, is celebrated throughout the country; animals are decked out in flowers.

May 20–28: Fiesta of the Hammocks is held in Tecoh, Yucatán.

May 31: Regional fair begins in Tehuantepec in the state of Oaxaca and continues through June.

June 24: Feast Day of San Juan is observed throughout Mexico and is popular because so many Mexicans bear the name of the saint.

July: Lunes del Cerro, the Fiesta of the Guelaguetza, is usually held the last two Mondays; folk dances are performed in a large, open-air arena, overlooking the city of Oaxaca.

July 22: Fiesta honoring St. Mary Magdalen is celebrated in Uruapan in the state of Michoacán.

August 15: Assumption Day is celebrated throughout the country, notably in Tlaxcala, the small state near Mexico City; carpets of flowers decorate the churches on this day.

August 27–31: Fiesta de la Morisma, pageants that reenact battles between Moors and Christians in Spain, is held in the city of Zacatecas, northwest of Querétaro.

September 1–30: The entire month is devoted to national celebration.

September 7–8: The Nativity of the Virgin is observed in Tepoztlán in the state of Morelos.

September 15: The eve of Diez y Seis, the anniversary of Mexican Independence from Spain, begins at 11 P.M.; throughout Mexico, the local *jefe* (in Mexico City it's the president) stands in the zócalo and shouts *el grito*, the cry of Father Hidalgo for freedom from Spain. The Mexico City celebration can be dangerous because the large crowds squeeze into the main square; try a celebration in one of the smaller towns.

September 29: Feast Day of San Miguel is a big celebration in San Miguel de Allende, including the running of the bulls through city streets.

October 12: Día de la Raza, Columbus Day, is celebrated throughout Mexico, particularly in Guadalajara, in the midst of its Octoberfest.

October 12: The return of the Virgin of Zapopan — the revered image of the Virgin tours the city churches in Guadalajara throughout the year and returns to her church in the suburb of Zapopan amid great celebration.

November 1–2: All Souls' Day and Day of the Dead, the most important Indian festivals in Mexico, are celebrated with enthusiasm in the island town of Janitzio near Pátzcuaro, Michoacán; at Mixquic in the Federal District; and at El Romerillo in the state of Chiapas.

December 8: Our Lady of Health fiesta in Pátzcuaro honors the town's patroness, Nuestra Señora de la Salud.

December 12: The Feast Day of Our Lady of Guadalupe, Mexico's revered patron saint, is celebrated throughout the country but particularly at the Basílica of Our Lady of Guadalupe in the nation's capital, the site of a vision of Our Lady to a poor Indian.

December (Christmas week): Pageants and *posadas*, reenactments of the Holy Family's search for a place to stay in Bethlehem, are staged throughout the country — Oaxaca, San Miguel de Allende, and the capital celebrations are notable.

December 23: Noche de los Rábanos (Night of the Radishes) is held in the city of Oaxaca. Local farmers bring large, intricately carved radishes to the main square for a lively competition.

COPPER CANYON

One of the saddest chapters in the history of transportation has been the decline of the passenger train in the United States. The formerly essential railway carriage seems to be going the way of the dinosaur. Not so in Mexico. Trains are still the lifeline of the nation, with many serving remote areas beyond the reach of concrete and asphalt. It's possible to climb aboard a train in El Paso and get off 2,000 miles later in Mérida, richer for the experience and not much poorer in the pocketbook. Mexico's trains are bargains—bargains often ignored by the tourists.

One train tourists do know about is the so-called Copper Canyon train, the one that crosses the Chihuahuan desert, climbs the Sierra Madre, then descends to the Pacific coast. For one hour the train passes through the Barranca del Cobre, the Copper Canyon, a pink and gold geological wonder that rivals the Grand Canyon. Copper Canyon and Urique Canyon together extend for 900 miles across northern Mexico. At one point, called El Divisadero de Barrancas, the two meet in a spectacular union of rock formations. The train stops here to allow visitors to look 6,000 feet down to the canyon floor where tropical flowers bloom and temperatures hover year-round in the 90s, while above, on the canyon rim, the air is cold in summer and bright with the reflection of sun on snow in the wintertime.

The track runs a dramatic route from isolated Chihuahua in the northern desert to Los Mochis on the Pacific coast. An idea conceived in 1877 by an inspired American, Albert K. Owen, who wanted to ship midwestern grain to the deep Pacific ports, the task was completed in 1961. There are no roads paralleling the track, and the vehicles that do serve the villages and logging camps in the sierra were brought in on railroad cars. The track is 400 miles long and sometimes climbs to a mile and a half high in the mountains. It takes 12 to 20 hours to make the journey, depending on track conditions and the class of train you travel on, and the train travels through 86 tunnels, over 39 bridges, and up and down mountains. At one point in the journey the track falls 6,000 feet in 90 miles, and at another it doubles back on itself, hugging a cliff.

The train, properly known as Ferrocarril de Chihuahua al Pacífico, leaves Chihuahua around 8 A.M. and arrives at Divisadero by mid-afternoon—if the schedule holds up. With the scheduled stop of 20 minutes, there's just enough time to look at the canyon and examine the handwoven sashes, belts and baskets being sold by the Tarahumara Indians. Some travelers leave the train here to stay in one of four hotels located along the route.

The Tarahumara Indians, many of whom serve as guides at the hotels, have long resisted modernization. Known for their ability to run long distances, many of the Tarahumara still leave the canyon's caves in winter to migrate to the canyon floor.

There are no towns along the route, only small villages and hotels at El Divisadero. Those travelers who get off the train usually stay a couple of days in the canyon, then go on to Los Mochis. There's no air service from Los Mochis, so the only way back to Chihuahua is on the train. The small town of Topolobampo on the coast near Los Mochis is the home port of a car ferry that crosses to La Paz on the

Baja, and it's possible to fly from La Paz back home. Experienced back-packers and hikers also get off the train along the route and hike through the canyon; however, the hiking is rough and dangerous in bad weather and should not be undertaken without the advice of a guide.

In Los Mochis, the entertainment is to go deep-sea fishing or take a boat trip to watch the seals on Farillon Rock in Topolobampo Bay. You'll find excellent bass fishing at Río Fuerte along the southern part of the route.

BOCADITOS

For information about the Copper Canyon train, write to the nearest Mexican Tourism Office or to Ferrocarril de Chihuahua al Pacífico, Apartado Postal 46, Chihuahua, Chihuahua, or call 2-22-84 in Chihuahua. A first-class one-way reserved seat is approximately $12. (Price subject to change according to the fluctuating value of the peso.) There are several classes of trains in Mexico, and several kinds serve the Copper Canyon route. The best is the Vista train, which features special viewing platforms. The Vista train departs around 8 A.M. on Monday, Thursday, Saturday, and Sunday. A first-class train leaves a little earlier on Monday, Tuesday, Thursday, Friday, and Saturday. The Vista train is supposed to have a dining car and the first-class train a snack bar; however, when traveling by train in Mexico, always take a back-up supply of snacks. Soft drinks and beer are sold by vendors along the way.

There are several hotels along the route, including the Hotel Cabañas Divisadero de Barrancas, located at the lookout point where the canyons join. The hotel specializes in hiking, horseback riding, and jeep tours to nearby Indian settlements. Rooms have fireplaces and rates include meals (B. Moderate). The hotel provides transportation to the train. For reservations write the Hotel Divisadero de Barrancas, Aldama 407-C, Apartado Postal 661, Chihuahua, Chihuahua.

Four of the five hotels located along the canyon route are owned by the Balderama family. The popular Copper Canyon Lodge, located at the highest point of the railroad, near the logging town of Creel, is a 30-minute journey from the train station. A double room with meals includes transportation from the train. B. Moderate.

The Hotel Misión is another possibility for lodging along the train route. It takes an hour on the hotel bus to reach the village. The hotel features horseback riding. Beyond the canyon, on the Río Fuerte is the Posada del Hidalgo, a popular spot for bass fishermen. The Balderamas also own the Hotel Santa Anita in Los Mochis where they keep the kitchen open for the arrival of guests on the train.

For reservations at any of the four Balderama hotels write Viajes Flamingo, S.A., Hotel Santa Anita, Apartado Postal 159, Los Mochis, Sinaloa.

To reach Chihuahua, fly from Juárez or take the first-class train. To make reservations between Juárez and Chihuahua, write National Railways of Mexico, P.O. Box 2200, El Paso, TX, or call 2-25-57 in Juárez.

BIRDS OF PARADISE

Mexico has about a thousand species of birds — twice as many as Texas has. Over the last 50 years a handful of bird-watchers and ornithologists have explored Mexico, and their pioneer spirit has in a way legitimized the country as a birding paradise. There are now several professional bird tour agencies that specialize in Mexico, and numerous excellent field guides (see the list at the end of this section). You can travel to Mexico in grand style, a birding expert at your elbow, or go on your own with the confidence that you will be able to identify the many exotic birds you will see. Vast areas of Mexico are still unexplored, but trips to the following places are tried and true and will guarantee your seeing birds.

RANCHO DEL CIELO
Location: Northeastern Mexico (Tamaulipas)
Habitat: Cloud forest in the eastern Sierra Madre

Ranch of the Heavens, as Rancho del Cielo roughly translates, is the northernmost cloud forest in the Western Hemisphere, and when the misty clouds (*neblina*) roll in off the Gulf of Mexico, it does seem that you are in heaven. It is a biological station operated by Southmost College in Brownsville and is closed to the general public. But several times a year, in summer and sometimes in December, you can go there on special week-long tours. June is the best month to go — many of the orchids and bromeliads bloom, and the birds sing at their loudest, longest, and best. Rustic cabins provide lodging, and there is a lovely central meeting hall with a huge fireplace.

A few of the birds in this area are the rufescent tinamou, collared forest-falcon, chachalaca, singing quail, military macaw, bumblebee hummingbird, blue-crowned motmot, blue mockingbird, black-headed nightingale thrush, crimson-collared grosbeak, and rufous-capped brush finch.

Tour reservations: Tours are limited to a maximum of 22 people. For current dates and prices, write Fred Webster, Jr., 4926 Strass Dr., Austin, TX 78731.

RANCHO CIELITO
Location: Northeastern Mexico (Tamaulipas)
Habitat: River woods in tropical lowlands

Rancho Cielito is on the banks of the Río Sabinas. It is a privately owned retreat located very near El Encino, a small village on Hwy. 85 about 50 miles south of Ciudad Victoria. Large Montezuma bald cypress line the sparkling river, which has several fine swimming holes. It is one of the last large areas of river woods left in northeastern Mexico. There is plenty of room to roam on the 150 acres. A trip to Cielito can be as relaxed or as rugged as you want to make it.

Some of the birds you will see are the chachalaca, blue ground-dove, green parakeet, red-crowned parrot, green-breasted mango, barred antshrike, kiskadee, clay-colored robin, and fan-tailed warbler.

Accommodations: The quarters are simple but comfortable. You must bring your own food; if you wish, a cook will help you prepare your meals. For current prices and reservations, write or phone Jack Berryman, 856 W. Price Rd., Brownsville, TX 78520, or call 1-512-546-5131.

CIUDAD MANTE – CIUDAD DEL MAIZ
Location: Northeastern Mexico (Tamaulipas and San Luis Potosí)
Habitat: Tropical lowland farmland to remnant cloud forest and arid plateau

Many of the birds at Rancho del Cielo and Rancho Cielito can be seen by taking day trips from the town of Ciudad Mante, which is 70 miles south of Ciudad Victoria on Hwy. 85.

El Abra: About 15 miles from Mante on Hwy. 85 you will pass out of flat farmland and start rising to the village of El Abra. Shortly past the town, you will pass a huge cleft in the cliff on the west (right) side of the highway. It is easy to miss when driving in this direction, so one passenger should keep an eye on the cliff. This cave is an excellent place to be an hour or so before sundown. Pull well off the road (there's considerable traffic on this highway), and set up a telescope to watch the changing of the guard. At dusk the bats fly out of the cave as the green parakeets go in to roost. Both species are greatly reduced in number these days, but you will see a few. Keep your eyes on the sky above the cliff, where you should see at least one bat falcon soaring in preparation for catching its evening meal. Kestrels and peregrines are a possibility here, too, so look for larger falcons. Barn owls also sometimes come to feed on the bats.

El Salto–El Naranjo area: The 35-mile trip to the valley of the Río Naranjo passes over three impressive mountain ranges. Leave Mante early (by 6 A.M. at least) so you will have plenty of morning time to bird. (Gauge the time it takes you to drive to El Naranjo so you can allow enough time to drive back to Mante before dark.) As you approach the town of El Naranjo, note the turnoff on your right to El Salto; you can spot the road by the power lines that bring electricity from the hydroelectric plant at El Salto. About six miles up the El Salto road you can pull off on your left for the small waterfall. This is a great place to see white-collared swifts at close range (they are usually just silhouettes high up in the sky). They like to fly into the spray of the waterfall. Two more miles up the road you will come to El Salto – the giant hulk of a waterfall that seldom cascades with water since the river was diverted for a hydroelectric plant. Some of the birds you should see are the ferruginous pygmy-owl, blue-crowned motmot, social flycatcher, masked tityra, and black-headed saltator.

The stretch of road outside El Naranjo is the richest birding area of the trip. It passes through moist oak woodlands to drier oaks and on to an arid plateau. To bird-watch on this highway, find a convenient place to pull off, park, lock the car, and walk along the road. Look for chachalaca, military macaw, singing quail, blue-crowned motmot, brown-backed solitaire, blue mockingbird, rose-throated becard, and crimson-collared grosbeak. You will not be able to bird the entire stretch of this road in one day. It is best to return at least two or three days.

Accommodations: Los Arcos, a pleasant, quiet motel on the south edge of Mante, has been catering to bird-watchers for years. For reservations write or call Los Arcos, Ciudad Mante, Tamaulipas (2-08-70).

RANCHO LIEBRE BARRANCA
Location: Western Mexico (Sinaloa)
Habitat: Oak, pine, and fir forest on the Pacific slope of the western Sierra Madre

This hidden canyon off Hwy. 40 is the best birding spot in western Mexico and home of the beautiful and rare tufted jay. You can reach the area by flying to Mazatlán, then renting a car and making the two- to three-hour drive up the mountain to Rancho Liebre. Or you can travel overland on Hwy. 40. Although arduous—it will take at least three days from the border—the driving trip is worth the time. The scenery is remarkable. This is not the trip, however, for people who hate to drive in mountains.

The forest on Hwy. 40 gets especially lush once you pass the lumber town of El Salto. Two exceptional places to pull off are Buenos Aires, 35.5 miles west of El Salto, and Espina del Diablo (Devil's Backbone), 8.5 miles past Buenos Aires. From here the road gets more and more winding, and you don't want to get caught on it at night. The only hotel in the area, the Villa Blanca (see "Accommodations" below), is still 43 miles ahead.

Rancho Liebre Barranca is a deep canyon about a one-mile hike from the forest station (*estación forestal*) that is 1.2 miles west of the village of El Palmito (El Palmito is on Hwy. 40 about 130 miles west of the city of Durango). There is a place to park by the station; also, just behind the station is a dirt road, which is the trail up to the barranca. You can drive part way up this road if you have a four-wheel drive or high-clearance vehicle (check first to see if the road is muddy). This well-trod path leads to a breathtaking overlook into the barranca.

The tufted jays can be difficult to see. They usually roam the barranca in small flocks, and some people with only a day to spend at Rancho Liebre have missed them. To guarantee a sighting, plan to spend two or three days in the area. Usually you hear the jays first; listen for loud, persistent, fussy calls; follow the sound; and keep an eye out for flashes of white and blue-black—their plumage is so distinctive that the birds can be seen even at great distance across the barranca. Other birds found here are the crested green thick-billed parrot, whip-poor-will, white-naped swift, Rivoli's hummingbird, blue-throated hummingbird, eared trogon (rare), mountain trogon, coppery-tailed trogon, white-striped woodcreeper, Steller's jay, blue mockingbird, gray-silky flycatcher, streak-backed oriole, red-headed tanager, and Mexican junco.

Finding Birds in Western Mexico, by Peter Alden, is an excellent guide to Rancho Liebre Barranca and other birding spots in western Mexico (see the bibliography).

If you decide to drive overland to Rancho Liebre, check your car's brakes and water system before you depart. If you go between November and February, take warm clothes.

Accommodations: If you wish to stay in the area rather than commute from Mazatlán, the Villa Blanca is your only choice (fortunately, it is lovely). It is a 12-room Bavarian-style inn, 22 miles west of the Rancho Liebre Forest Station. The food is good; you can get Wiener schnitzel as well as *chiles rellenos*. Write at least eight weeks in advance for reservations to Hotel Villa Blanca, La Capilla del Taxte, Postal Santa Lucia, Sinaloa.

PALENQUE
Location: Southeastern Mexico (Chiapas)
Habitat: Lowland rain forest

Palenque, the most elegant of the Mayan ruins in Mexico, looks like the city of Oz. The ruins sit amid a relatively undisturbed forest — virtually the last stand remaining in an area that was once covered with huge trees. This pocket gives some idea of the extent of habitat destruction in the southern rain forests of Mexico. One of the most relaxing ways to bird at Palenque is to climb the steps of the Temple of the Inscriptions, sit down facing the forest, and watch for birds flitting among the trees. A major trail that leads off behind the left side of the Temple of the Inscriptions is the standard birders' hike. If you are lucky, you may hear (and see) howler monkeys. Look for the slaty-breasted tinamou, stripe-tailed hummingbird, purple-crowned fairy, keel-billed toucan, short-billed pigeon, hermit hummingbird, black-faced antthrush, royal flycatcher, blue honeycreeper, bananaquit, and crimson-collared tanager.

If you have the time, money, and nerve you should consider taking a flight into the Mayan ruins of Bonampak or Yaxchilán from Palenque. These are about the last places in Mexico you can count on seeing scarlet macaws, and harpy eagles have been seen in recent years. These flights are in small craft (four to six passengers, including pilot), and they can be risky. The flight gives you a spectacular overview of the last extensive rain forest in Mexico; it is rapidly being cut down and will be largely destroyed in a decade or so. To make arrangements inquire at the Palenque airport.

Accommodations: The Hotel Chan Kah is the birders' choice in Palenque. It is not in the town of Palenque (which is about five miles away), but near the ruins. It is quiet and has a nice open-air restaurant. The owner, Roberto Romano, takes a great interest in archaeology and natural history. For reservations, write him at Chan Kah, KM 31, Carretera a las Ruinas, Palenque, Chiapas.

CATEMACO
Location: Southeastern Mexico (Veracruz)
Habitat: Lowland rain forest

Southeastern Mexico near Veracruz is a very rich birding area, especially for tropical hawks and eagles. The town of Catemaco, built on the banks of a deep blue volcanic lake, is a popular resort for Mexicans. Bird in town around the lake, then take the road northeast of town that heads toward the fishing village of Sontecomapán (about ten miles from town) and the Gulf of Mexico. The road also branches to the right, this fork going around the lake to the village of Coyame. Spend at least a day on each fork. Stop anywhere along the roads to bird in the remnant woods and scrubby fields, and keep an eye on the sky for hawks. In Sontecomapán it is possible to pay a fisherman to take you out in his launch for a few hours. In the mangrove-lined lagoon you can see numerous birds, possibly even the elusive sungrebe or the gray-necked wood-rail. (This trip is only for people who speak enough Spanish to negotiate clearly with the fisherman.) Past Sontecomapán is a tropical research station (*Estacion Biologica de los Tuxtlas*), which preserves all that is left of the undisturbed rain forest in this area. This forest is *strictly off limits* unless you have written permission from the university in Mexico City. Write to the following address, allowing five weeks at least for a reply: Carlos Marquez Mayandon, Director del Instituto de Biologia Tropical, Apartado Postal 70-153, Mexico 20, DF. You will, however, see plenty of birds without going into the research station, including the magnificent frigatebird, snail kite, white hawk, black hawk, great black hawk, black hawk-eagle, collared forest-falcon, bat falcon, aplomado falcon, limpkin (lagoon), ruddy crake (lagoon), collared plover (beach), sungrebe (lagoon), gray-necked wood-rail (lagoon), short-billed pigeon, brown-hooded parrot, red-lored parrot, violet sabrewing, slaty-tailed trogon, citreoline trogon, collared trogon, keel-billed toucan, red-capped manakin, lovely cotinga, chestnut-headed oropendola, Montezuma oropendola, and crimson-collared tanager. It would be easy to spend a week comfortably birding and exploring the Catemaco area. The road to Sontecomapán is not paved and could be difficult going in the rainy season.

Accommodations: There are two excellent hotels in Catemaco. Hotel Berthangel is on the town square by the bright yellow cathedral and about two blocks from the lake. For reservations write Hotel Berthangel, Catemaco, Veracruz. Motel Playa Azul is on the edge of town on the banks of the lake. It is more secluded, with beautiful, birdy gardens. For reservations write or phone Playa Azul, Catemaco, Veracruz (3-00-01 or 3-00-42).

CERRO SAN FELIPE
Location: Southern Mexico (Oaxaca)
Habitat: Humid oak, pine, and fir forest on the southern rim of the Central Highlands

There are five endemic jays in Mexico, all of them splendid birds in splendid settings. One of them — the dwarf jay — can be found in Cerro San Felipe, a national park 20 miles from the city of Oaxaca. At 10,000 feet, the forest has a grandeur very similar to that of the Colorado Rockies. To get there, leave Oaxaca heading southeast on Hwy. 190; three miles from town turn left (north) on Hwy. 175 toward Guelatao. Go 17 miles until you get to La Cumbre and turn left onto a dirt road instead of following the main highway. Two or three miles down this road you will encounter thick forest — prime dwarf jay habitat. You will also see band-tailed pigeon, Steller's jay, gray-barred wren, russet nightingale-thrush, ruddy-capped nightingale-thrush, cinnamon flower-er piercer, and Mexican junco.

On the outskirts of Oaxaca is Monte Albán, the Zapotec ruins, which is a good birding spot for arid-land species, such as the lesser road-runner, Oaxaca sparrow, and rusty sparrow. Go early to see the birds and to avoid the crowds.

A nice (but relatively birdless) side trip is to El Tule, about five miles southeast of Oaxaca City on Hwy. 190. There you can see the largest tree in the world in circumference, a Montezuma bald cypress with a girth of 42 meters that is estimated to be about 2,000 years old.

Accommodations: Hotel Misión de los Angeles is an old inn in downtown Oaxaca. Write or phone for reservations to Calzado Porfirio Díaz 102, Oaxaca, Oaxaca (6-15-00). Oaxaca is a bustling city with one of the best markets in Mexico, but it can be unnerving to drive around in; don't leave the hotel without a map.

MAYAN RUINS OF THE YUCATAN PENINSULA
Location: Yucatán Peninsula
Habitat: Arid lowland thorny woods

The extent to which you will want to bird on the Yucatán peninsula will depend in large part on your interest in archaeology, an avocation that tends to sneak up on bird-watchers. Because of the arid terrain, the birds are rather scarce, especially compared with the numbers in neighboring Chiapas, but several species can be seen nowhere else in Mexico. Unless you are planning a long car trip through Mexico, the quickest way to bird-watch in Yucatán is to fly to Mérida or Cancún and rent a car. Chichén Itzá, the best known of the Mayan ruins, is 75 miles from Mérida and has many hotels; Uxmal is 50 miles from Mérida and has few accommodations. You might consider going instead, or in addition, to the smaller, often less-touristed ruins—Nabah, Sayil, Xlapak, Muna, Labah, and Tulum to name a few. Birds you can expect to see in Yucatán include rufescent tinamou, collared forest-falcon, black-throated bobwhite, red-billed pigeon, Aztec parakeet, citreoline trogon, turquoise-browed motmot, blue-crowned motmot, collared acaçari, Yucatán jay, black catbird, tropical mockingbird, rufous-browed peppershrike, and yellow-billed cacique.

Accommodations: The Yucatán peninsula is a very popular tourist area. It is best to make all airline, hotel, and car rental reservations through a travel agent at least six months before your trip.

COZUMEL
Location: Off the coast of Quintana Roo
Habitat: Small island of coconut groves, sandy beaches, and offshore coral reefs; the interior is chiefly woodlands and overgrown fields.

This island is a favorite with bird-watchers who also like coral reefs and tropical fish. The birding is easy and in a morning's outing you can usually see all the specialties of the island. The regimen for birders on Cozumel is to be out birding by dawn. Rent a car or motor scooter and drive north or south from the town of San Miguel to the woods on the island. By 9 A.M. or so the birds have quieted down and are hard to see. It is time to return to your hotel for breakfast and to spend the rest of the day snorkeling or scuba diving. Some of the birds you will see are the magnificent frigatebird (seaside), white-crowned pigeon, Caribbean dove, Yucatán woodpecker, Yucatán flycatcher, tropical pewee, Caribbean elaenia, Cozumel wren, Cozumel thrasher, black catbird, Cozumel vireo, Yucatán vireo, stripe-headed tanager, and rose-throated tanager. Spring and fall are interesting times to go to Cozumel; migration is in progress and you can see many species of warblers and other North American migrants.

Accommodations: Make your airline and hotel reservations through a travel agent at least six months before your trip.

BIRDING GUIDES

The following guides are listed in order of decreasing usefulness in the field:

Peterson, Roger Tory, and Chalif, Edward L. *A Field Guide to Mexican Birds.* Boston: Houghton Mifflin, 1973. If you can take only one field guide to Mexico, this is the one.

Edwards, Ernest P. *A Field Guide to the Birds of Mexico.* Sweet Briar, Virginia: Ernest P. Edwards, 1972. An adequate species-by-species guide. Also by the same author: *Finding Birds in Mexico* (1968) and *1976 Supplement to Finding Birds in Mexico.* Both are excellent site guides to birding spots.

Alden, Peter. *Finding Birds in Western Mexico.* Tucson: University of Arizona Press, 1969. An invaluable book for traveling in western Mexico.

Davis, Irby L. *A Field Guide to the Birds of Mexico and Central America*. Austin: University of Texas Press, 1972. This is a quirky and hard-to-use guide, but it contains good supplemental information.

Sutton, George M. *Mexican Birds: First Impressions*. Norman: University of Oklahoma Press, 1951. Long out of print, this book is worth tracking down in a library for its fine narrative introduction to birding in northern Mexico.

CAMPING AND HIKING

In a country of unrestricted beauty, it's difficult to resist the temptation to head into the hills in search of a hermit's existence or lay claim to an uninhabited stretch of beach and pretend to be Robinson Crusoe. But unless you are an experienced camper and hiker or a born adventurer, don't attempt to conquer the unknown without a great deal of preparation.

Camping is not a national pastime in Mexico, perhaps because a vast majority of the rural population lives less than comfortably. Those eager to embrace Mother Nature usually don't live with her every day. Many Mexicans cook on kerosene stoves, carry water from communal wells, and sleep on the ground or on wooden bunks. Consequently, there is no great demand for camping facilities; those that do exist are privately owned and cater to tourists. However, there are several national parks that allow camping. You won't find organized campsites or park rangers with helpful hints on pitching a tent. What you will find in the parks is natural, unspoiled scenery.

Along the Pacific coast, around Mazatlán, there are several campsites for recreational vehicles, but in the interior there are few places where motor homes can successfully maneuver. One of the best guides to campsites in Mexico is *Rand McNally's Campgrounds and Trailer Parks in Mexico*. The American Automobile Association also offers a guide to major campsites for its members. And the Mexican National Park Service provides free information about hiking and camping in the country's protected parks. Write Mexican Parks, Aquiles Serdan 28, Piso No. 4, Mexico, DF, or call 521-1122 in Mexico City.

Experienced campers can find a place to pitch a tent anywhere in the countryside, but you should follow two basic rules — never camp alone and avoid camping in the state of Guerrero, where there are pockets of insurgents and drug-dealing bandits. Always ask permission if there's a home or farm nearby, and don't camp in the immediate vicinity of a village water supply.

Camping on the beach can be the ultimate experience in Mexico: sling your hammock from a couple of palms near a freshwater lagoon; build a *palapa* from dried palm fronds, and let the sun be your alarm clock. If you venture south to the beaches along the coast of Oaxaca and Chiapas, take along a supply of quinine; there have been some reports of malaria in this area. It's always better to camp with a group on the beach, and don't take new equipment or a brand new car into remote areas. Although Mexico's beaches are supposed to be public property, you will be chased off in some places—don't argue, just move on. Popular beach camping spots include the Pacific coast around Puerto Vallarta and Manzanillo, the east coast of the Yucatán peninsula, and Isla Mujeres.

Backpacking around Mexico has become increasingly popular among young Europeans, who have discovered what a lot of Americans knew for a long time—that Mexico is a beautiful country to conquer on foot. There are no youth hostels in Mexico, but there is a profusion of third-class hotels. Practically every Mexican town or village has a cheap, clean hotel. The variety of buses and the cheap train transportation make backpacking popular, also. Besides, it's one of the best ways to learn the language. However, there is little regard in Mexico for what are called "jippies," and if you hike down to the border, you may have difficulty crossing if you've clung to your sixties hairstyle. In addition, some communities do not take to wandering free spirits; many have purged their plaza of "jippies." Oaxaca is one of the few places where they are tolerated. In fact, the square sometimes reminds a visitor of the pre-preppie days. If you plan to backpack through Mexico, try to travel with company and avoid the remote areas in the mountains.

Here's a sampling of trails and campsites in some of Mexico's national parks.

LAGUNAS DE ZEMPOALA

This series of lakes southwest of Mexico City is surrounded by mountain meadows covered with pines. The trails are exhilarating, but give yourself time to become accustomed to the high altitude. The lakes are the heart of an 11,000-acre park that also attracts fishermen. There's a small entrance fee and camping is permitted. Take the old, toll-free road from Mexico City to Cuernavaca, and look for the Tres Cumbres exit. Follow the road through the town of Huitzilac to the park.

EL CHICO NATIONAL PARK

Rural *ejidatarios*, communal farmers, operate this park, which is located northeast of the capital near Pachuca. There's a shelter, and camping is permitted on the lakeshore. Take Hwy. 85 from Mexico City to Pachuca and follow the signs to Los Venados.

CUMBRES DE AJUSCO PARK

This is a few miles from the center of Mexico City and is a great favorite with *capitalinos* who enjoy picnicking on the mountainside and hiking through the pine forests. The high altitude, 12,000 feet, offers a series of beautiful vistas across the Valley of Mexico. The park is near the 1968 Olympic Village in the southwest portion of the city district.

MIGUEL HIDALGO Y COSTILLA NATIONAL PARK

Here you will find Valle de Silencio, Valle de los Conejos, and Valle de las Monjas — the valleys of silence, rabbits, and nuns — quiet mountain meadows where you can camp, picnic, go horseback riding, or just lie in the grass and watch the stars come out. The park is located on the Mexico City–Toluca Highway (Hwy. 15), just a few miles from the capital.

DESIERTO DE LOS LEONES

The name means "desert of the lions," but the park is no desert and there are no lions. Located southwest of the capital, beyond the suburb of San Angel, the park is filled with pine trees. Here you will find the ruins of the Convent of Santa Desierto (hence the name) and a variety of trails and picnic sites. Take the Periferico beltline highway to the southwest and look for the park exit. The park is open daily from 10:00 A.M. to 5:30 P.M. No camping permitted.

BOSENCHAVE NATIONAL PARK

This wilderness park spans the border of Michoacán and the state of Mexico. Many think Michoacán the most beautiful state in Mexico. The high mountain meadows are covered in wildflowers in the spring, and the climate is invigorating year-round. There's good fishing during the summer rainy season in Laguna del Carmen. Take Hwy. 15 from Mexico City to Toluca. Approximately ten miles west of Toluca, turn onto the Valle de Bravo road and look for the signs to Bosenchave. Camping permitted.

MONTEBELLO NATIONAL PARK

This is a 13,000-square-mile park near the city of Comitán in southern Chiapas. Strictly for the adventurous. The park runs to the Guatemalan border and there are deep woods and lakes within its boundaries. The Chincuiltic archaeological zone, which has not been fully excavated, is within the park's boundaries. Hiking and camping allowed.

CONSTITUCION DE 1857 NATIONAL PARK

One of two national parks on the Baja peninsula, this beautiful area in the Sierra de Juárez is 90 miles from Mexicali. Take Hwy. 2 toward Tijuana, take the La Rumurosa exit, and drive 45 miles south to the park entrance. Ponderosa trees, granite formations, and a lagoon make this a popular camping and hiking spot.

SAN PEDRO MARTIR NATIONAL PARK

Closed in winter when the snows blanket the sierra, this magnificent park, about 140 miles south of Ensenada, is one of Mexico's most beautiful. The Mexican national observatory, Observatorio San

Pedro, is on the park's highest peak. Nearby is Picacho del Diablo with a height of 10,156 feet. To the east lies the desert. The park is located near San Talmo, south of Ensenda. Camping, hiking, and horseback riding permitted.

MOUNTAIN CLIMBING

Mexico is a land of mountains; two-thirds of her surface is covered by rugged peaks, volcanic ranges, and canyons. Many of the most spectacular peaks surround the capital: Mount Popocatépetl (17,872 feet); Mount Iztaccihuatl (17,454 feet); and to the east, Mount Orizaba (18,851 feet). With peaks like these, it's easy to be tempted to emulate Sir Edmund Hillary. Don't try it. Unless you are an experienced climber and are familiar with each geological quirk of the mountain, attempting to climb one can be extremely dangerous. The Mexican government frowns on amateur attempts.

The volcanoes can be particularly dangerous to climb because the ash makes footing slippery, and the mountains whip up their own blizzards in the rainy season. Mount Popo, as it is commonly referred to, does have a shelter halfway to the summit, before the ash line, where climbers pause. The climb takes about eight hours.

If you want to join a climbing expedition, write to the Asociación Alpina de Mexico, A.C. Las Huertas 93-C, Mexico, DF, or contact the nearest Mexican tourist office for information.

HUNTING AND FISHING

Mexico has a reputation among sportsmen as the home of some of the finest wild game in the world — whether it be marlin or deer, sailfish or javelina. Gone are the days, though, when ranchers could ride south across the river for a day or two of hunting. The regulations for hunting and fishing in Mexico are complex, and the paperwork is absolutely *necessary*. Importing firearms into Mexico is a serious offense, so don't attempt to bypass the rule book.

The government provides detailed information on guides, seasons, regulations, and tournaments. For fishing information, write Dirección General de Pesca, Av. Alvaro Obregon 269, Mexico 7, DF. For hunting information, write Dirección General de Caza, Serdan 27, Mexico, DF.

Fishing rules and regulations are not as complicated as those governing hunting. The best way to expedite the paperwork is to hire one of the guides recommended by the government tourism officials. Plan your trip well in advance. A good place to begin is at the nearest Mexican tourist office or consulate (see the lists at the back of the book for addresses). Although fishing tackle and boats may be taken into Mexico with the proper permits and with little hassle, guns are a different proposition. If you fly into the country with a gun, it will be confiscated and, perhaps, returned a few days later. There is a limit to the number of guns you may take into Mexico, and certain guns are strictly prohibited. The tourist office will provide all the proper instructions.

In addition, hunters must have a special permit designating which species they are hunting, as well as a letter of reference from their local sheriff or chief of police, five signed passport photographs, and a letter describing the gun in detail with serial numbers. All this costs about $15. Once you are inside Mexico, you will have to pay an average of $40 for licenses from the state government and register your weapons with the army. You can avoid some of this by signing with a guide who understands the bureaucracy.

The red tape isn't over. The United States has strict regulations governing importation of game, and most border states, including Texas, have their own standards and requirements. For a guide to US rules, request a copy of "Pets and Wildlife" from the nearest US Customs office—check the government pages.

Fishing is an easier proposition, although it's still wise to hire a guide.

In Mexico you may hunt (with the appropriate paperwork) wild turkeys, wolves, bighorn sheep, quail, ducks, foxes, lynx, deer, bears, sometimes jaguars (depending on their ecological status), grouse, armadillos, boars, and ocelots—the cost of licenses varies with each species. For some (for example, the bighorn sheep), the license is very expensive.

Mexico's waters are rich with game fish, marlin and sailfish being two popular catches. Bass fishing in northern Mexico and in the central lakes is very popular, also. Spearfishing is illegal in most places; however, there are certain areas where it is not prohibited. Check with the local tourist office (see the list at the back of the book).

BOCADITOS

Standard camping and backpacking gear is appropriate in Mexico. Heavy sleeping bags are not necessary because temperatures rarely drop below 40 degrees at night, except in the high mountains around Mexico City. Camping equipment is better made and less expensive in the United States, but you can purchase gear at the following stores in Mexico City: Campicentro, Av. Revolución 1328; Productos Deportivos, Campestres, 2ª Privada, Callejón; General Anaya II, Churubusco (544-8848); La Casa de Excursionista, Félix Cuevas 832-A (559-2598).

Geological survey maps and regional maps are available at Detenal, San Antonio de Abad 124, in Mexico City (578-6200). Some areas of the country have not been surveyed.

Supermarkets in the large cities stock many of the food items you may need. Hardware stores (*tlapalerías*) or local grocery stores (*tiendas*) also stock items essential to campers. There is no freeze-dried food available in Mexico. White gasoline can be bought at paint stores and camping equipment stores.

APPENDIX

Gathered together below for your convenience are the addresses and phone numbers of the US and Canadian embassies in Mexico, the Mexican embassies in the United States and Canada, Mexican National Tourist Offices and Mexican Consulates in the United States and Canada, US Consulates in Mexico, and Mexican state tourist offices.

EMBASSIES

The United States and Canada maintain embassies in Mexico City. If you encounter any difficult legal, medical, or personal problems, contact your embassy. The US Embassy also issues advisory bulletins to tourists about local political and economic affairs and will advise any US tourist on the advisability and feasibility of travel in remote areas of Mexico.

US Embassy, Paseo de la Reforma, Mexico City, DF, (905) 553-3333

Canadian Embassy, Calle Schiller 529, Colonia Polanco, Mexico City, DF, (905) 254-3288

The Mexican government is represented by its ambassadors in Washington, DC, and Ottawa. Embassy personnel will be glad to answer any questions that you may have about travel in Mexico and will direct you according to your needs to other agencies. Services offered at consular offices in other cities are available at the embassies, also.

Mexico Embassy, 2829 16th St. NW, Washington, DC 20009, (202) 234-6000

Mexico Embassy, 130 Albert St., Suite 206, Ottawa, Ontario K1P 5G4, (613) 233-8988

MEXICAN TOURIST OFFICES

For information about travel in Mexico, including tourist facilities and attractions or transportation (particularly railroad schedules), write the nearest Mexican National Tourist Office.

Mexican National Tourist Offices in the United States:

Atlanta: Peachtree Center, Cain Tower, Suite 1201, Atlanta, GA 30303, (404) 659-2409

Beverly Hills: 9701 Wilshire Blvd., Suite 1201, Beverly Hills, CA 90212, (213) 274-6315

Chicago: 233 N. Michigan Ave., Illinois Center, Room 1413, Chicago, IL 60601, (312) 565-2785

Dallas: 1535 W. Mockingbird, Dallas, TX 75219, (214) 263-4672

Denver: 425 S. Cherry, Suite 640, Denver, CO 80222, (303) 355-0517

Houston: C. E. Lummus Tower, Suite 1370, 3000 Post Oak Road, Houston, TX 77056, (713) 840-8332

Miami: 100 Biscayne Blvd., Suite 2804, Miami, FL 33132, (305) 371-8037

New Orleans: One Shell Square Bldg., Suite 1515, New Orleans, LA 70139, (504) 525-2783

New York: 405 Park Ave., Suite 1203, New York, NY 10022, (212) 755-7212 or 755-7261

San Antonio: GPM South Tower, Suite 240, 800 NW Loop 410, San Antonio, TX 78216, (512) 341-6212

San Diego: San Diego Federal Bldg., 600 B St., Suite 1220, San Diego, CA 92101, (619) 236-9314

San Francisco: 50 California St., Suite 2465, San Francisco, CA 94111, (415) 986-0992

Tucson: 5151 E. Broadway, Suite 1535, Tucson, AZ 85711, (602) 745-5055

Washington, DC: 1156 15th St. NW, Suite 329, Washington, DC 20005, (202) 296-2594

Mexican National Tourist Offices in Canada:

Montreal: 1 Place Ville Marie, Suite 2409, Montreal, P.Q. H3B 3M9, (514) 871-1052

Toronto: 101 Richmond St. West, Suite 1212, Toronto, Ont. M5K 2E1, (416) 364-2455

Vancouver: 700 W. Georgia St., Vancouver, B.C. V7Y 1B6, (604) 682-0551

MEXICAN CONSULATES

For information about tourist permits, passports, and visas and guidelines for businessmen, hunters, fishermen, sailors, and pilots, contact the nearest Mexican consulate.

Mexican consular offices in the United States:

Albuquerque: 505 Marquette NW, Western Bank Bldg., 17th Floor, Albuquerque, NM 87102, (505) 247-2139

Atlanta: 410 S. Omni International Bldg., Atlanta, GA 30303, (404) 688-3258

Austin: Perry Brooks Bldg., 716 Brazos St., Austin, TX 78701, (512) 478-2866

Boston: One Post Office Square, Suite 1550, Boston, MA 02109, (617) 426-4942

Brownsville: 724 E. Elizabeth, Brownsville, TX 78520, (512) 542-4431

Calexico: Imperial Avenue and 7th Street, Calexico, CA 92231, (619) 357-3863

Chicago: 141 W. Ohio, Chicago IL 60610, (312) 670-0240

Corpus Christi: 160 Guaranty Bank Plaza Bldg., Corpus Christi, TX 78475, (512) 882-3375

Dallas: 4229 N. Central Expressway, Dallas, TX 75205, (214) 522-9740

Del Rio: 1010 S. Main St., Del Rio, TX 78840, (512) 775-2352

Denver: 1050 17th St., Suite 2500, Prudential Plaza Bldg., Denver, CO 80202, (303) 832-2621

Detroit: 1249 Washington Blvd., Room 1515, Detroit, MI 48226, (313) 965-1868

Douglas: 515 10th St., Douglas, AZ 85607, (602) 364-2275

Eagle Pass: 140 Adams St., Eagle Pass, TX 78852, (512) 773-9255

El Paso: 910 E. San Antonio, El Paso, TX 79901, (915) 533-3644

Fresno: 2839 Maritosa, Fresno CA 93721, (209) 233-3065

Houston: 2105 Fannin, Suite 200, Houston, TX 77002, (713) 654-8880

Kansas City: 823 Walnut, Kansas City, MO 64106, (816) 421-5956

Laredo: 1612 Farragut St., Laredo, TX 78040, (512) 723-0990

Los Angeles: 125 Paseo de la Plaza, Edificio Biscailuz, Los Angeles, CA 90012, (213) 624-3261

Lubbock: First National Bank Bldg., Suite 1242, 1500 Broadway, Lubbock, TX 79401, (806) 765-8816

McAllen: 1418 Beech St., P.O. Box 603, McAllen, TX 78501, (512) 686-0244

Miami: 1444 Biscayne Blvd., Suite 308, Miami FL 33132, (305) 371-5444

New Orleans: 1140 International Trade Mart, 2 Canal St., New Orleans, LA 70130, (504) 522-3596

New York: 8 E. 41st St., New York, NY 10017, (212) 689-0456

Nogales: 135 Terrace Ave., Nogales, AZ 85621, (602) 287-2521

Philadelphia: 21 S. 5th St., Philadelphia, PA 19106, (215) 922-4262

Phoenix: Western Savings Bldg., Phoenix, AZ 85015, (602) 242-7398

Presidio: 730 O'Rily St., Presidio, TX 79845, (915) 229-3745

Sacramento: 2100 Capital Ave., Sacramento, CA 95816, (916) 446-4696

St. Louis: 1015 Locust St., Locust Bldg., Suite 922, St. Louis, MO 63101, (314) 436-3233

San Antonio: 127 Navarro St., San Antonio, TX 78205, (512) 227-9145

San Bernardino: 588 W. 6th, San Bernardino, CA 92410, (714) 889-9836

San Diego: 225 Broadway, San Diego CA 92101, (619) 231-8414

San Francisco: 870 Market St., Suite 516, San Francisco, CA 94102, (415) 392-5554

San Jose: Bank of America Bldg., 12 S. 1st St., Suite 1014, San Jose, CA 95113, (408) 294-3414

Seattle: 1425 4th, Seattle, WA 98101, (206) 682-3634

Mexican consular offices in Canada:

Montreal: 1000 Sherbrooke West, Suite 2110, Montreal, P.Q., (514) 288-2502

Toronto: 2701 Commerce Court West, Toronto 105, (416) 922-2718 (in Ontario)

Vancouver: Suite 1402 Royal Centre, 1055 W. Georgia St., Vancouver 5, B.C., (604) 684-3547

US CONSULATES IN MEXICO

The US government maintains several consular offices throughout Mexico that provide information services to Mexican citizens but also assist tourists with information about traveling conditions or offer assistance or advice should a problem arise.

Ciudad Juárez: Av. López Mateos 294 (3-40-48)

Guadalajara: Progreso 175 (25-29-98 or 25-27-00)

Hermosillo: Third Floor, Issteseon Bldg., Miguel Hidalgo and Costilla 15 (3-89-22)

Matamoros: Av. Primera 232 (2-52-50)

Mazatlán: Circunvalcion 6 and Venustiano Carranza (1-29-05)

Monterrey: Av. Constitucion Pte. 411 (43-06-50 or 43-06-59)

Nuevo Laredo: Av. Allende 3330, Colonia Jardín (4-05-12 or 4-06-18)

Tijuana: Tapachla 96 (6-10-01)

STATE TOURIST OFFICES

Mexican tourist offices are listed under "Tourist Services" for each town. In addition, a complete listing by state of tourist offices follows that includes several towns with tourist offices not listed elsewhere. The federal district is also included.

Aguascalientes: Aguascalientes—Av. López Mateos Ote. 1500, Mezzanine (6-35-05)

Campeche: Campeche—Av. Ruiz Cortinas 61 (6-55-93) and Plaza Moch-Couch (6-38-47); Ciudad del Carmen—Calle 22 No. 102 (2-04-10)

Coahuila: Monclova—Madero and Carr 57 (3-25-06); Saltillo—Blvd. Francisco Coss and Acuña (3-75-44 or 3-91-43); Torreón—Av. Morelos and Treviño (2-40-60 or 2-61-71)

Colima: Colima—Palacio de Gobierno (2-43-60); Manzanillo—Juárez 111 (2-01-81)

Chiapas: Tuxtla Gutiérrez—Av. 14 de Septiembre Pte. 1824, Edificio de Tourismo (2-07-32)

Chihuahua: Chihuahua—Av. V. Cattanza 505 (2-63-63 or 2-78-85); Ciudad Juárez—Av. Malecón and Francisco Villa (4-01-23)

Durango: Durango—Palacio de Gobierno (1-21-39, 1-11-07, or 1-56-00) and Gómez Palacio, Blvd. Alemán Ote. 250 (4-44-34)

Guanajuato: Guanajuato—Av. Juárez and 5 de Mayo (2-15-74, 2-22-32, or 2-31-49); San Miguel de Allende—Artega 98 (3-00-61)

Guerrero: Acapulco—Costera Miguel Alemán 1253 (2-21-70, 2-22-46, 2-60-16, or 2-60-09); Taxco—Av. John F. Kennedy 28-9 (2-05-79 or 2-15-25); Zihuatanejo—Centro Comercial Ixtapa (4-22-07 or 4-21-23)

Hidalgo: Pachuca — Palacio de Gobierno (2-24-17)

Jalisco: Guadalajara — Av. Juárez 638 (14-01-23); Puerto Vallarta — Libertad and Morelos (2-02-42 or 2-02-43)

Mexico: Toluca — Palacio de Gobierno (5-21-87 or 5-01-31)

Mexico City, Distrito Federal: Mexico City — Paseo de la Reforma (512-1529 or 512-0062)

Michoacán: Morelia — El Nigromante 79 (2-37-10) and Palacio Clavijero (2-98-16); Pátzcuaro — Casa de los Once Patios (2-14)

Morelos: Cuautla — Reforma (2-09-27); Cuernavaca — Av. Morelos 205-A (2-34-95 or 2-18-15)

Nayarit: Tepic — Emiliano Zapata Pte. 27 (2-02-74)

Nuevo Leon: Monterrey — Emilio Carranza Sur 730 (42-34-88 or 40-10-80)

Oaxaca: Oaxaca — Av. Independencia and Garcia Vigil, Palacio Municipal (6-38-10)

Puebla: Cholula — Av. Morelos Nte. 68 (47-00-56); Puebla — Av. 5 Ote. 3 (46-09-28 or 46-12-85)

Querétaro: Querétaro — Madero 105, Bajos (2-27-02, 2-28-02, or 2-00-36); Tequisquiapan — Independencio 1 (3-04-30)

Quintana Roo: Cancún — Av. Tulum (3-01-23 or 3-00-84) and Palacio Municipal (3-00-94); Chetumal — Av. Alvaro Obregón 241 (2-09-42); Cozumel — Fidelcomiso Cozumel and del Caribe Xel-Ha (2-03-57 or 2-05-40); and Isla Mujeres — Av. Guerrero 7 (2-00-68)

San Luis Potosí: San Luis Potosí — Av. Jardín Hidalgo 12-A (2-31-43) and Valles Negrete 724 (2-04-71)

Sinaola: Culiacán — Blvd. Francisco I. Madero and Obregón (3-34-49); Mazatlán — Paseo Clanssen and Zaragoza (1-49-66)

GLOSSARY

Here are three simple rules to adopt, followed by a glossary of helpful words and phrases:

1. Don't tack an *el* or *la* on the front of an English word and expect to be understood. A few words are equivalent in Spanish, but they are the exception.

2. At every opportunity, interject *por favor* and *gracias* into your speech.

3. Beware of street Spanish. Slang should not be used in polite conversation.

GREETINGS AND COURTESIES

Welcome.	*¡Bienvenidos!*
Hello.	*¡Hola!* or *¡Bueno!*
Good day. Good afternoon.	*Buenos dís. Buenas tardes.*
Good night.	*Buenas noches.*
Goodbye.	*Adios* or *Hasta la vista;* often just *Hasta.*
Pardon me.	*Perdon* or *Dispénseme;* say *¿Con permiso?* if passing in front of someone.
Please.	*Por favor* or *Sírvase; Hago el favor de* ("Do it as a favor.")
Thank you.	*Muchas gracias.*
You're welcome.	*De nada.* ("It is nothing.")
Pleased to meet you.	*Mucho gusto.*
Greeting a man.	*Señor.*
Greeting a married woman.	*Señora.*
Greeting a young woman.	*Señorita.*

The words *hombre* ("man") and *mujer* ("woman") should never be used in addressing people.

MAKING CONVERSATION

What's going on?	*¿Qué pasa?*
What time is it?	*¿Qué hora son?* Or more correctly: *¿Qué hora es?*
It is hot. (. . . cold.) (. . . sunny.)	*Hace calor.* (. . . *frio.)* (. . . *mucho sol.)*
Do you speak English?	*¿Habla inglés?*
I don't understand.	*No entiendo.*
I don't know.	*No sé.*
What? Please repeat yourself	*¿Cómo? ¿Mande?*
How do you say . . . in Spanish?	*¿Como se dice . . . en éspañol?*

Really, is that so?	¿Verdad?
Why?	¿Porqué?
Could you help me?	¿Puede usted ayudarme?
I need . . .	Necesito . . .
I want . . .	Quiero . . .
No.	No.

GETTING AROUND TOWN

Driver.	El manajero.
Address.	La dirección.
Take me to . . .	Lléveme a . . .
Where is the . . .	¿Dónde está . . .
. . . post office?	. . . el correo?
. . . bank?	. . . el banco?
. . . airline office?	. . . la oficina de aviones?
. . . taxi stand?	. . . el sitio?
. . . bus stop?	. . . la parada?
. . . beach?	. . . la playa? (This also means "parking lot.")
. . . airport?	. . . el aeropuerto?
. . . church?	. . . la iglesia?
. . . drug store?	. . . la botica? Or . . . la farmácia?
. . . station?	. . . la estación?
. . . marketplace?	. . . el mercado?
. . . supermarket?	. . . supermercado?
When does one (or it) leave? (. . . arrive?)	¿Cuándo sale? (. . . llega?)
Which way?	¿Por dónde?
How far?	¿Hasta dónde?
Near; far.	Cerca; lejos.
To the right; to the left.	A la derecha; a la izquierda.
Straight ahead.	Derecho.
Open; closed.	Abierto; cerrado.

SHOPPING

Show me . . .	Enséñeme . . .
What color?	¿Qué color?
What size?	¿Qué tamaño?
What kind?	¿Qué clase?
May I try it on?	¿Me puedo probarlo?
This doesn't work.	No sirve.
It doesn't fit.	No cabe.
I like this one.	Este me gusta.
How much does it cost?	¿Cuánto cuesta?
It's very expensive.	Es bastante caro.

DRINKING AND DINING

Waiter.	*El mesero.* Waiters are usually addressed as *joven* ("young person").
To get a waiter's attention.	*¡Oiga!*
A table for . . .	*Una mesa para . . .*
Menu.	*La lista* or *la carta.*
Food.	*La comida.*
Beverages.	*Las bebidas.*
Bring me . . .	*Traígame . . .*
. . . drinking water.	*. . . un vaso de agua purificada.*
. . . beer.	*. . . una cerveza.*
. . . soft drink.	*. . . un refresco.*
Where is the ladies' rest room? (men's rest room?)	*¿Dónde está el lavabo de damas? (. . . de señores?)*
The check.	*La cuenta.*
Breakfast.	*El desayuno.*
Lunch.	*La comida.*
Dinner.	*La sena.*

MOTORING

I would like to rent a car.	*Quisiera alquilar un automóvil.*
Follow this street. (. . . highway.)	*Siga esta calle. (. . . carretera.)*
Gas station.	*Una estacion de gasolina.*
Fill the tank.	*Llene el tangue.*
Oil.	*El aciete.*
Road.	*El camino.*
Map.	*El mapa.*
Brakes.	*Los frenos.*
Tires.	*Las llantas.*

HIGHWAY SIGNS

Inspection.	*Aduana.*
Yield right of way.	*Ceda el paso.*
Dangerous curve.	*Curva peligrosa.*
Keep to the right.	*Conserve su derecha.*
Crossing.	*Cruce.*
Landslide.	*Derrumbe.*
Slow.	*Despacio.*
Road closed.	*No hay paso.*
No passing.	*No rebase.*

No parking.	*No estacionarse.*
Bridge.	*Puente.*
Dip.	*Vado.*
Speed bump.	*Tope.*

EMERGENCIES

I need . . .	*Necesito . . .*
. . . a doctor.	*. . . un medico.*
. . . the police.	*. . . la policía.*
. . . the hospital.	*. . . el hospital.*
. . . an ambulance.	*. . . una ambulancí.*
I have an ache in my . . .	*Tengo dolor de . . .*
. . . stomach.	*. . . estomago.*
. . . head.	*. . . cabeza.*
. . . tooth.	*. . . muelas.*
It hurts here.	*Me duele aca.*
I am ill.	*Estoy enferma.*

BIBLIOGRAPHY: MEXICO BY THE BOOK

The following bibliography contains an eclectic sampling of books of both fiction and nonfiction to heighten your Mexico experience. Book prices are lower in the United States, so buy before you go.

Calderon de la Barca, Frances. *Life in Mexico during a Residence of Two Years in That Country.* New York: AMS Press, 1913. A witty memoir of life in the capital during the mid-nineteenth century written by a Scottish Yankee married to a Mexican man who moved in powerful circles.

Coe, Michael D. *The Maya.* New York: Thames and Hudson, 1980. A fascinating, easy-to-read thin volume on the Maya with abundant illustrations and photographs.

Davies, Nigel. *The Aztecs.* Norman: University of Oklahoma Press, 1980. Davies, a graduate of London University and the Escuela Nacional de Antropologica is well known for his works on Mexico's pre-Hispanic roots. This book is a detailed history of the sudden rise of the Aztecs and their subsequent downfall.

de Benitez, Ana M. *Pre-Hispanic Cooking.* Mexico City: Ediciónes Euroamericanas, 1974. This small bilingual cookbook is more than a collection of recipes—it is an insightful look at everyday pre-Hispanic life. Available in Mexico and by special order in the United States and Canada.

Diaz del Castillo, Bernal. *The Conquest of New Spain.* New York: Penguin Books, 1963. A weighty volume of reminiscences by the conquistador presents history through an adventurer's eyes. The latest Penguin edition, translated by J. M. Cohen, has been trimmed to a handy and readable size.

Fehrenbach, T. R. *Fire and Blood: A History of Mexico.* New York: Collier Books, 1973. The author, a native Texan, documents in bold and gripping style 3,500 years of Mexico's history. A broad, sweeping look at Mexico's past.

Ferguson, William M. *Maya Ruins of Mexico in Color.* Norman: University of Oklahoma Press, 1977. An excellent guide to Maya ruins published by the University of Oklahoma, which has been responsible for several excellent texts in this subject area. An oversized book with detailed drawings and photographs. Excellent source for research before you go, but a little cumbersome to be carried along.

Fernandez, Justino. *A Guide to Mexican Art.* Chicago: University of Chicago Press, 1969. A survey of 20 centuries of Mexican art and architecture. A good comprehensive pocket guide.

Fuentes, Carlos. *The Death of Artemio Cruz.* New York: Farrar, Straus & Giroux, 1964. One of several excellent novels by this contemporary Mexican writer available in translation. Fuentes, like Octavio Paz, examines the Mexican psyche and soul.

Greene, Graham. *The Power and the Glory.* New York: Penguin Books, 1977. A novel about a priest hunted during the anticlerical movement of the twenties.

Hunter, C. Bruce. *A Guide to Ancient Maya Ruins.* Norman: University of Oklahoma Press, 1974. Well-illustrated, readable, yet scholarly guide to the great Mayan sites. Maps included. Convenient pocketbook size.

Kennedy, Diana. *Recipes from the Regional Cooks of Mexico.* New York: Harper & Row, 1978. An eclectic collection of recipes gathered over the years in Mexico from the author's old friends. Diana Kennedy is a renowned expert on Mexican cuisine. Her other books include *The Cuisines of Mexico* and *The Tortilla Book.* All three are essential texts for the visitor who wants to try the local specialties during vacation or to recreate them at home.

Lawrence, D. H. *The Plumed Serpent.* New York: Random House, 1955. A sensual novel centered on the legend of Quetzalcoatl.

Lewis, Oscar. *The Children of Sanchez.* New York: Random House, 1961.

Nelson, Ralph. *Popol Vuh: The Great Mythological Book of the Ancient Maya.* Boston: Houghton Mifflin, 1974. This new translation of the sacred book of the Quiche Maya makes delightful reading. The myths were originally passed on orally and then written down shortly after the conquest.

Norman, James, and Schmidt, Margaret Fox. *A Shopper's Guide to Mexico: What, Where, and How to Buy.* Garden City, New York: Doubleday, 1973. One of the best paperbacks available on shopping for crafts in Mexico. Detailed and accurate.

Paz, Octavio. *The Labyrinth of Solitude: Life and Thought in Mexico.* New York: Grove Press, 1962. A thought-provoking examination of the Mexican psyche. Should be required reading for any American headed south.

Paz, Octavio. *The Other Mexico: Critique of the Pyramid.* New York: Grove Press, 1972. Developed from a series of lectures delivered at the University of Texas at Austin in 1969, these collected essays are, in the author's words, "a critical and self-critical continuation" of his work in *The Labyrinth of Solitude.*

Peterson, Frederick. *Ancient Mexico: An Introduction to Pre-Hispanic Cultures.* New York: Paragon Books, 1979. A complete, comprehensive, one-volume text noted for its excellent scholarship, yet readable style. Good background text for the visitor eager to understand many of the ancient ruins in Mexico.

Simpson, Lesley Byrd. *Many Mexicos.* Berkeley: University of California Press, 1960. A classic text on the history of Mexico, noted for its wit. Originally published over forty years ago, it has been updated by the author. Excellent glossary.

Sten, Maria. *The Codices of Mexico.* Mexico City: Panaroma Editorial,

S. A., 1979. This English translation of a Mexican work examines the codices of the Indians, the so-called painted books, and their fate. Available in Mexico and on order in Canada and the United States.

Stephens, John L. *Incidents of Travel in Central America, Chiapas, and Yucatán.* 2 vols. New York: Dover Publications, 1969. Adventures of the nineteenth-century traveler who rediscovered many ancient Mayan sites. A must for the serious traveler.

Thompson, J. Eric. *Maya Archaeologist.* Norman: University of Oklahoma, 1963. The author, one of the world's noted Maya scholars, relates his adventures as an archaeologist in the 1930s. The book complements the adventures of an earlier explorer, John L. Stephens.

INDEX

Acapulco, 2, 12, 32–33, 35–36, 38–39, 252–261; hotels, 255–56; restaurants, 257
Agricultural products, 7
Air travel, 36–37. *See also names of individual cities*
Ajijic, 123
American Plan, 33
Angling. *See* Fishing and deep-sea fishing
Archaeological ruins: Bonampak, 141, 145, 152–53; Chiapas, 139–41; Chichen Itzá, 139, 158; Chincultic, 153; Cholula, 137–38, 148–49; Cobá, 141, 158–59; Dainzu, 173; Dzibilchaltun, 159–60; Edzna, 160; El Tajin, 139, 149; Great Temple excavations, 104, 135; Ixtepete, 123; Izamal, 160–61; Kabah, 161; Kohunlich, 142, 161–62; La Venta, 153–54; Labiteyeco, 138, 173; Labna, 162; Manlinalco, 149–50, 220; Mitla, 138, 156, 173; Monte Albán, 138, 156–57, 173; Palenque, 141–42, 154–55; Sayil, 162; Teotihuacán, 81, 136–38, 150–51; Tula, 63, 142, 151–52; Tulum, 139, 141, 163; Tzintzuntzán, 142; Uxmal, 139–40, 163; Xochicalco, 138–39, 152, 206, 210; Yagul, 138, 157–58, 173; Yaxchilan, 155; Zaachila, 138, 173; Zempoala, 238
Architecture: baroque, 100, 102, 230; Churrigueresque, 65, 100, 104, 202, 217–18; colonial, 72, 198, 235; La Belle Epoque, 73, 181; Moorish, 196, 219; Neoclassical, 105; Plateresque, 212, 215; pseudo-Gothic, 202
Automobile, rental. *See names of individual cities*
Automobile, travel by, 39, 53–65
Aztec calendar, 2–3, 104, 144
Aztec Indians, 2–3, 25, 50, 70, 72, 136–37, 330

Baja peninsula, 284
Barre de Navidad, 267
Bartering, 334–35
Baskets, 337–38
Beaches, 237, 239, 248, 251, 254–55, 259, 272, 276, 280, 286–89
Bird-watching, 190, 248, 366–73

Boating, 245
Bonaparte, Napoleon, 12, 18
Border towns, 291–311
Bourbons, 12
Breweries, 61, 293
Brownsville, TX, 37
Bullfighting, 77–79, 99–100, 117–18, 128, 293, 297
Bus, travel by, 38–39. *See also names of individual cities*
Business, travel for, 33–34

Cabo San Lucas, 285–86; hotels, 285; restaurants, 285
Calderón, battle of, 13
Camping, 373–78; luxury, 352–53
Canadian Embassy, 108, 379
Cancún, 33, 36, 39, 239–47; hotels, 242–43; restaurants, 243–44
Cancún City, 240
Carranza, Venustiano, 22
Carranzistas, 9
Castillo, Bernal Díaz del, 10, 67–68
Caves, 209, 219–20
Central Plateau, 31
Ceramic tile factories, 224, 228
Cerro Gordo, 16
Chalma, 220
Chapala, 122–23
Charreadas, 116, 129
Chiapas, 2, 30
Chiconcuac, 80
Chihuahua, 29, 63–64, 364–66
Children, traveling with, 35
Chilpancingo, 13
Cholula, 81, 137, 148, 224
Chula Vista, 122
Churches of interest, 35, 72, 81, 100–102, 115, 128, 167, 173–74, 176–77, 180–81, 184, 191, 194–95, 201–2, 204, 209, 215, 217–18, 222, 226, 229–30, 237
Cinco de Mayo, 31
Ciudad Acuña, 301–3
Ciudad Juárez, 2, 21, 37, 296–300; hotels, 296; restaurants, 298–99
Cliff divers, 253, 259
Climate, 32
Clothing, 338–40
Club Med, 279–80; Cancún, 243, 279; Ixtapa, 263, 279; Playa Blanca, 279–80